Looking Back

S. LEIGH MATTHEWS

Looking Back

Canadian Women's Prairie Memoirs and
Intersections of Culture, History, and Identity

THE WEST SERIES
ISSN 1922-6519

UNIVERSITY OF
CALGARY
PRESS

University of Calgary Press
2500 University Drive NW
Calgary, Alberta
Canada T2N 1N4
www.uofcpress.com

LIBRARY AND ARCHIVES CANADA CATALOGUING IN PUBLICATION

Matthews, S. Leigh (Sandra Leigh), 1967-
          Looking back : Canadian women's prairie memoirs and intersections of
culture, history, and identity / S. Leigh Matthews.

(The West series, ISSN 1922-6519 ; 1)
Includes bibliographical references and index.
ISBN 978-1-55238-096-3

1. Women pioneers—Prairie Provinces—Biography. 2. Women pioneers—Prairie
Provinces—Social conditions. 3. Women pioneers in literature. I. Title. II. Series: West
series (Calgary, Alta.) ; 1

FC3238.M38 2010   971.2'020922   C2010-904483-5

The University of Calgary Press acknowledges the support of the Alberta Foundation for the Arts for our publications. We acknowledge the financial support of the Government of Canada through the Canada Book Fund for our publishing activities. We acknowledge the financial support of the Canada Council for the Arts for our publishing program.

This book has been published with the help of a grant from the Alberta Historical Resources Foundation.

This book has been published with the aid of a grant from Thompson Rivers University.

Printed and bound in Canada by Marquis Book Printing Inc.
∞ This book is printed on FSC Silva paper

Cover image: Prairie Homstead by Andrew Penner (www.istockphoto.com)
Cover design by Melina Cusano
Page design and typesetting by Melina Cusano

For Grandma Matthews and Nana West.

Sadie Victoria Landry Matthews,
Bankend, Saskatchewan, circa 1940.

CONTENTS

ACKNOWLEDGMENTS

This study has been a long journey, and could not have been completed without the aid and encouragement of many individuals and institutions over the last decade. I would like to thank the Calgary Institute for the Humanities and the Calgary Women's Writing Project for receipt of the Winnie Tomm Memorial Scholarship, as well as the Izaak Walton Killam Memorial Fund for Advanced Studies and the Social Sciences and Humanities Research Council of Canada, whose research fellowships originally enabled me, in the form of a doctoral dissertation, to explore the memoirs gathered here as a means to share the authors' voices and experiences with a larger audience.

The financial support noted above allowed me to work full-time on this project while living with my family in Kamloops, British Columbia, but the project itself would never have been conceived in the first place were it not for the supportive and inspirational atmosphere of the English Department at the University of Calgary. I would like to thank the Department for considerable financial contributions to my research and writing activities. Most especially, I am deeply indebted to Dr. Helen Buss, whose presence at the University of Calgary drew me to Alberta, and whose encouragement, advice, criticism, and patience illustrates her knowledge of the subject and her dedication to the project of advancing education.

I would also like to acknowledge that I have previously published some of the materials that make up this study. Portions of Chapter One and Chapter Two have been published as "(Nearly) Sacred Achievements: Culinary Place in Women's Prairie Memoirs," in a Special Issue of *Essays on Canadian Writing* titled "Food, Cooking, and Eating in Canadian Literature," with Guest Editor Kathleen Batstone, 78 (2003): 16–41. Portions of Chapter One and Chapter Four have been published as "The 'precarious perch' of the 'decent woman': The Spatial (De)Construction of Gender in Canadian Women's

Prairie Memoirs," in *History, Literature, and the Writing of the Canadian Prairies*, edited by Alison Calder and Robert Wardhaugh (University of Manitoba Press, 2005), 141–74.

I would like to thank everyone at University of Calgary Press for the attention to fine detail that occurs when assembling such a book, and especially to Donna Livingstone, whose persistence and vision has ultimately enabled these womens' voices to be heard. Finally, to Dania Sheldon, whose careful and efficient gaze graced the manuscript in its final stages in order to create a comprehensive index.

❊ 1 ❊

Introduction:
"Untilled Fields"

Funny, how the stories you read when you are young take such a
hold on you. They are like friends that mold and often seem to be a
part of your own life, as if you had helped live them.
    – Edna Jacques, *Uphill All the Way* (1977)

For the woman artist is not privileged or mandated to find her self-
in-world except by facing (affronting?) and mounting an enormous
struggle with the cultural fictions – myths, narratives, iconograph-
ies, languages – which heretofore have delimited the representation
of women. And which are culturally and psychically saturating.
    – Rachel Blau DuPlessis, "For the Etruscans" (1985)

Their sharing is a gift of themselves, and a gift to themselves also;
a restoration of themselves into our history.
    – Eliane Leslau Silverman, *The Last Best West: Women
on the Alberta Frontier, 1880–1930* (1984)

Looking back now, I realize that the white, English-speaking image of the "Prairie Woman"[1] existed as a fairly dominant force in my early life and imagination. Indeed, I remember (still with a tremor of excitement) sitting down in front of the television in the fall of 1974 to watch the premiere of the series *Little House on the Prairie*, adapted from the autobiographical-inspired fiction by Laura Ingalls Wilder. Although I did eventually read the whole collection of books by Wilder, it was the visual images provided by the television series that became the stimulus to a considerable portion of my childhood imaginative life. Indeed, both myself and my younger sister once owned bonnets in the style of those worn by the women in Walnut Grove (the town of Wilder's childhood reminiscences), and those bonnets, when worn with our ankle-length Christmas skirts, became the vehicle by which we imagined ourselves living on the Canadian prairies. In actual fact, we spent the majority of our childhood in Kamloops, British Columbia, a region of Canada more commonly known for its mountains, pine trees and sagebrush than for flat land and prairie grass. Despite this geographic difference, we imaginatively translated the half-acre gully that composed the backyard of our family home into our own *Little House* setting – complete with the child-size log home we used as a playhouse – and took special pleasure in recreating the television series' opening scene, which depicted the Ingalls children, pure joy written across their faces, running down a grassy incline and headed towards a wagon sitting stationary and occupied by beaming parents Charles and Caroline Ingalls.

However, despite my immediate pleasure in such recreations, a problem ensued that seemed always to intervene in my psychological commitment to the project – a problem that would eventually direct the course of my professional literary studies. You see, as much as I loved the ritual of sitting down to watch *Little House* for an hour once a week, even as a young girl I already sensed a fairly glaring difference between the images presented to me on the screen and my own private (though limited) knowledge of prairie life. More specifically, I found myself confused by the apparent gap that existed between

---

1   I have chosen to capitalize the term "Prairie Woman" here because I agree with critics such as Terry Goldie who suggest that we should be careful to distinguish between a cultural image and "the people the image claims to represent" (6).

the always cheerful, fair-skinned television image of Caroline Ingalls and the endlessly mystifying reality of my own paternal grandmother's dark-skinned, deeply furrowed, and often unsmiling face. Unlike Caroline, whose dominion was primarily domestic, whose body was perfectly proportioned, and whose demure personality expressed itself with a slight smile accompanied by the words, "Oh, Charles," Sadie Victoria Landry Matthews inhabited her body, face weather-worn and back slightly curved, as a symbol of her life of labour. Indeed, as I instinctively recognized, she wore that body as an outright contradiction of the more sanitized television image.

Years later, when my academic exposure to both prairie history and prairie literature renewed my old interest in settler women, I was again intrigued by what I perceived to be the dominance of cultural images and the apparent poverty of sources representing the reality of prairie women's lives. The major problem with cultural images is that they so often deny complexity in favour of a stereotyped norm of experience. So it is with the white, English-speaking Prairie Woman image, which assumes a precise correspondence between the label itself and some culturally understood meaning that does not often allow for differences in experience, whether those differences are accounted for by personality, cultural background, class, geography, marital status, etc. Whether dealing with fictional texts, settlement propaganda literature (such as CPR or Dominion Government pamphlets), or even early historians' interpretations of the western settlement process, cultural representations of the Prairie Woman have provided a rather static either/or (Prairie Woman as "cheerful helpmate"/Prairie Woman as "reluctant emigrant/drudge") image. Both sides of the Prairie Woman coin are abundantly present in contemporary accounts of western settlement life. For example, in *Janey Canuck in the West* (1910), Emily Ferguson creates the image of the heroic farming couple when she writes about her travels across the prairies and her discovery of the process of nation-building at the level of the individual farm:

> In one blessed spot, a ginger-headed Icelandic giant was turning over his first furrow.... Behind, in the furrow, walked the mother and three little children. They were partners in this undertaking. It was a supreme moment for them. The turning of the civic sod

was never half so vital. They had crossed a hemisphere to turn this
furrow. The steading was holy ground, and, metaphorically, I took
off my shoes. These folk are of the few elect. (17)

On the other hand, in 1915, feminist and social reformer Nellie McClung
recounts the stereotypical belief that farm women lived a life of unending
drudgery:

> "Poor girl!" say the kind friends. "She went West and married a
> farmer" – and forthwith a picture of the farmer's wife rises up be-
> fore their eyes; the poor, faded woman, in a rusty black luster skirt
> sagging in the back and puckering in the seams; coat that belonged
> to a suit in other days; a black sailor hat, gray with years and dust,
> with a sad cluster of faded violets, and torn tulle trimming, sitting
> crooked on her head; hair the color of last year's grass, and teeth
> gone in front. (*In Times* 109)

Over time, such cultural images have tended to take on mythic proportions.
In fact, one of the major motivations of Canadian women's historiography has
been to illustrate that the reality of prairie women's lives rested somewhere on
a continuum of experience encompassing both of the either/or extremes, and a
great deal more in between. As anthropologists John W. Bennett and Seena B.
Kohl note regarding the use of first-person sources when seeking to more fully
understand western settlement, "in the older literature, westering women were
often portrayed as either sunbonneted helpmates or reluctant pioneers, though
our source material tells us that there was a considerable range of experience
between these two extremes" (50–51).

In seeking to get a little bit closer to the "range of experience" of those
white, English-speaking women who actually participated in western
settlement, I longed to find a way to hear their voices. However, my initial
foray (in the mid- to late 1990s) into the study of prairie women's lives
suggested that there were no first-hand accounts, readily available at least,
that could be used for comparison to the cultural images as a means to
complicate the traditional dichotomy. At first glance, it appeared that real

life prairie women had been silent partners in the project of western settlement. However, my understanding of the situation changed when I read a
novel titled *The Curlew Cried: A Love Story of the Canadian Prairie* (1947),
written by Nell Wilson Parsons. I was so enticed by Parsons's fictional representation of settlement life on the Canadian prairies – and especially by
her dedication page, stating, "To my Mother, Ann Wilson, and my favorite
Aunt, Rachel Jessop. Both knew the early days of the Canadian prairie"
(5) – that I went back to the library catalogue and resubmitted her name.
One other item appeared on the screen: something called *Upon a Sagebrush
Harp* (1969), which sounded suspiciously like another romanticized vision
of prairie life, but from the call letters I knew I would not be entering the
fiction section of the library. I entered, rather, the Canadian history section,
and found the text. *Upon a Sagebrush Harp* was the first Canadian prairie
memoir I had ever read, and from it began an academic journey during
which I discovered that there exists a body of prairie memoirs (in libraries,
on used-bookstore shelves, in private collections, and usually under years
of accumulated dust), most of which had been written and published after
1950 by women who had themselves experienced prairie life in the late
nineteenth and early twentieth centuries. This unique and "virtually untilled field" (Siddall 923) of prairie memoirs suggested to me that, not only
did these women have something they felt it necessary to write down – to
enunciate and thereby preserve for posterity – but also that, through publication, they very deliberately sought to share that something with a public
audience.

Despite their obvious attempts to be heard, however, these women's
memoir voices have been all but lost to the Canadian cultural record,
even within academic circles. While my own private collection of these
texts derives almost completely from the bibliographic trails provided by
historians,[2] nevertheless, as of yet, there has been no full-length study by a

---

2   In particular, the following were invaluable sources of information: Carol Fairbanks
     and Sara Brooks Sundberg's *Farm Women on the Prairie Frontier: A Sourcebook for
     Canada and the United States* (Metuchen, N.J. and London: Scarecrow Press, 1983)
     and Linda Rasmussen et al.'s *A Harvest Yet to Reap: A History of Prairie Women*
     (Toronto: The Women's Press, 1976).

Canadian scholar of any disciplinary background on these published memoirs.[3] However, the existence of autobiographical texts, including memoirs (sometimes called "reminiscences" or "personal accounts") has often been noted, especially in the field of history, where acknowledgments of such texts and lamentations over their general dismissal have been fairly frequent. As early as 1980, in her article designating "Saskatchewan Women, 1880–1920" as a viable "Field for Study," Ann Leger Anderson asserted that "little has yet been done to investigate thoroughly such items as newspapers, travel accounts, reminiscences, manuscript collections, local histories, or official records to rediscover the women of late-nineteenth century Saskatchewan and reconstruct their lives and its social context

---

3   This lack of concerted attention by Canadian scholars to personalized accounts of
     prairie settlement contrasts with the situation in American scholarship. For ex-
     ample, in the context of the American west, historian Sandra L. Myres noted the
     lack of attention to a "treasure trove of material" written by "frontierswomen" and
     published her own study, *Westering Women and the Frontier Experience 1800–1915*
     (1982), based "on the many diaries, journals, letters, and reminiscences" which had,
     until that point, been left "ignored or overlooked" in previous historical studies
     (xvii). In her study, Myres sought to combat cultural images of "westering women"
     that "did not conform to the reality of most women's lives" (7). More recently, lit-
     erary critic Brigitte Georgi-Findlay has explored *The Frontiers of Women's Writing*
     (1996) in an effort to recover the "female voices that seemed to be missing from
     the story of westward expansion as told in the literature of frontier heroes, west-
     ern discovery, exploration, and travel, and in the stories, novels, and movies that
     comprise the genre of the Western" (ix). See also John Mack Faragher, *Women and
     Men on the Overland Trail* (New Haven, CT: Yale University Press, 1979), Lillian
     Schlissel, *Women's Diaries of the Westward Journey* (New York: Schocken Books,
     1982), Susan Armitage and Elizabeth Jameson, eds., *The Women's West* (Norman
     and London: University of Oklahoma Press, 1987), Glenda Riley, *The Female
     Frontier: A Comparative View of Women on the Prairie and the Plains* (Lawrence,
     KS: University Press of Kansas, 1988), and Susan Armitage, *Women in the West: A
     Guide to Manuscript Sources* (New York: Garland Publishers, 1991). It should also be
     noted that American scholars have quite often included consideration of Canadian
     settlement texts of varying types, as well as images of the "pioneer" or "prairie"
     woman in Canadian writing, in studies with a transnational perspective, such as:
     Fairbanks and Sundberg's *Farm Women on the Prairie Frontier* (noted above), Carol
     Fairbanks's *Prairie Women: Images in American and Canadian Fiction* (New Haven
     and London: Yale University Press, 1986), John W. Bennett and Seena B. Kohl's
     *Settling the Canadian-American West, 1890–1915: Pioneer Adaptation and Community
     Building: An Anthropological History* (Lincoln and London: University of Nebraska
     Press, 1995), and Janet Floyd's *Writing the Pioneer Woman* (Columbia: University of
     Missouri Press, 2002).

in systematic fashion" (75). In addition, although she noted that "more is known about the first fifteen or so years of the twentieth century," Anderson warned that scholarship on Saskatchewan women in that period still presented "an exceedingly general picture" that required further and more complex investigation, the "personal record" being "highly desirable" in that regard (75–76). Similarly, in Susan Jackel's 1987 "stocktaking" of available resources in prairie women's history, the author referred to the existence of a vast body of "settlers' accounts by the wives, sisters and daughters of male preachers, farmers, ranchers and townsmen," "a considerable number" of which "have taken book form" (*Canadian* 6).[4]

More recently, assertions of the need to regard women's "accounts" of prairie life as legitimate historical source material are articulated in collections of essays that have been gathered in an effort to more fully flesh out the lived experience of all women in the prairie region. For example, in a 1993 essay titled "Remembering Together: Reclaiming Alberta Women's Past," Patricia Roome suggests that "since women's voices are seldom recorded in standard historical documents, pioneer women's accounts remain an invaluable source for understanding women's experience" (179). Similarly, in Aileen C. Moffatt's 1995 essay "Great Women, Separate Spheres, and Diversity: Comments on Saskatchewan Women's Historiography," the author, in reference to the popularity of the Barr Colony as historical subject matter, makes the following statement regarding Mary Hiemstra's largely

---

4 Jackel goes on to give two examples of such "book form" texts, *Of Us and the Oxen* (1968) by Sarah Ellen Roberts and *Two White Oxen: A Perspective of Early Saskatoon 1874–1905* (1974) by Barbara (Hunter) Anderson, both of which are included in my study. It is interesting to suggest that Jackel's own choice of words in acknowledging the existence of such texts may well be part of the problem in attracting critics to them as a worthwhile source of study: for example, I would mention especially the implied passivity of the female author in the suggestion that the accounts themselves "reach print" and "have taken book form," which detracts from any notion, as I contend in my study, that these women deliberately sought public articulation of their own experience in their own words. Jackel's acknowledgment also appears debilitating in that she gives primacy to the women's relationships to men – "settlers' accounts by the wives, sisters and daughters of male preachers, farmers, ranchers and townsmen" – when, as I see it, the very act of writing and seeking publication for such a text indicates the female author's assumption of personal importance as a participant in settlement history in her own right.

neglected memoir of that experience, *Gully Farm: A Story of Homesteading on the Canadian Prairies* (1955):

> Perhaps because Mary Pinder Hiemstra was not a "great" woman, historians have largely overlooked her memoir. This is unfortunate because this type of personalized account is invaluable to historians. Ordinary women and men are central characters in Saskatchewan's history. Historians need both to fully utilize these sources and to consider new ways of examining everyday life in order to more completely explicate the Saskatchewan experience. (15)

It is not a matter of mere coincidence that both Roome and Moffatt assert the "invaluable" nature of women's personal accounts of prairie life; rather, this doubled claim is testimony to the need for such texts as the published memoirs gathered in this study to be recovered from obscurity and reconciled to the historical record. Most recently (and excitingly), recovery and reconciliation has begun in the work of Nanci L. Langford, Sheila McManus, and Brigitte Georgi-Findlay (all of whom examine a variety of genres, not just memoir), but there is certainly more exploration to be done.[5]

While women's published memoirs of prairie settlement have only just begun to be used, however, the subject of prairie women more generally has certainly been fruitfully examined from a variety of perspectives. As the anthologies which include Roome's and Moffatt's essays attest to, the last three decades have witnessed a renewed interest, not only in the daily reality of women's lives, but also in getting a clearer and less universalized notion of that reality through various non-traditional, first-hand sources. In fact, much

---

5   See specifically Nanci L. Langford's "First Generation and Lasting Impressions: The Gendered Identities of Prairie Homestead Women" (Diss. University of Alberta, 1994), Sheila McManus's article "Gender(ed) Tensions in the Work and Politics of Alberta Farm Women, 1905–29," in *Telling Tales: Essays in Western Women's History*, ed. Catherine A. Cavanaugh and Randi R. Warne (Vancouver: UBC Press, 2000, 123–46), and Brigitte Georgi-Findlay's article "Women in the Canadian-American West" in *Zeitschrift für Kanada-Studien* 22, nos.1–2 (2002): 26–42.

of this work has been an explicit attempt to juxtapose lived experience with a static Prairie Woman image, as seen, for example, in Eliane Leslau Silverman's *The Last Best West* (1984), for which the author had "conversations" with 150 women in southern Alberta as a means to get past the "myths about frontier women" that "reduced them to a uniformity of experience" (vii–viii).[6] One of the ways that Silverman manages to bring complexity to the study of prairie women's lives is through her consideration of women who "represent the heterogeneity of ethnic, religious, national, and class backgrounds" (iii). Multiplicity of

---

6   See also Silverman's "Women and the Victorian Work Ethic on the Alberta Frontier: Prescription and Description" in *The New Provinces: Alberta and Saskatchewan, 1905–1980*, ed. Howard Palmer and Donald Smith (Vancouver: Tantalus Research, 1980), which relies on the author's interviews with prairie women themselves as a means to interrogate the notion that reality actually "conform[ed] to the expectations of women's lives that sermons, marriage manuals, political speeches, and school textbooks described and yearned for" (92), and "Women's Perceptions of Marriage on the Alberta Frontier," in *Building Beyond the Homestead*, ed. David C. Jones and Ian MacPherson (Calgary: University of Calgary Press, 1988), in which the author again uses interviews to establish the "participants' perspective" (50) about the institution of marriage and its functioning within a new environment. Also valuable is the work of Mary Kinnear, whose essay "'Do you want your daughter to marry a farmer?': Women's Work on the Farm, 1922," in Volume VI of *Canadian Papers in Rural History*, ed. Donald H. Akenson (Gananoque, ON: Langdale Press, 1988) combines information from two very different sources, "a survey of the work of members of the United Farm Women of Manitoba" and "an essay competition run by the *Grain Growers Guide*," in an effort to come to some conclusions regarding "a livelihood more common than industrial or service work to Canadian women before the Second World War" (137). See also Mary Kinnear's *First Days, Fighting Days: Women in Manitoba History* (Regina: Canadian Plains Research Center, University of Regina, 1987). Finally, there is the work of Angela E. Davis, whose two articles, "'Valiant Servants': Women and Technology on the Canadian Prairies 1910–1940" in *Manitoba History* 25 (Spring 1993): 33–42, and "'Country Homemakers': The Daily Lives of Prairie Women as Seen through the Woman's Page of the Grain Growers' Guide 1908–1928," in Volume VIII of *Canadian Papers in Rural History*, ed. Donald H. Akenson (Gananoque, ON: Langdale Press, 1992), acknowledge the historical importance attached to women's opinions about prairie life and help to further delineate the "daily lives of pioneer farm women" ("Country" 165). As Davis states of the "readers' letters" section of the *Grain Growers' Guide* woman's page, it was "a major outlet for airing their thoughts and feelings about rural life" and it was intended, "from the time Isobel Graham, the page's first editor, asked for their participation, until the end of the First World War," to be a forum for discussion of "all the political, social and economic issues of the day" (164–65).

experience is certainly also the motivation behind Catherine A. Cavanaugh and Randi R. Warne's *Standing on New Ground: Women in Alberta* (1993), David De Brou and Aileen Moffatt's *"Other" Voices: Historical Essays on Saskatchewan Women* (1995), and also Norah L. Lewis's *Dear Editor and Friends: Letters from Rural Women of the North-West, 1900–1920* (1998), in which the editor seeks to recapture the "clear, authentic voices of real women" who hail from "a variety of ethnic backgrounds and geographical locations" (4). Most recently, Cavanaugh and Warne's *Telling Tales: Essays in Western Women's History* (2000) presents a "cross-cultural/multicultural approach to western women's history" while also re-asserting the need to maintain the "basic task of recovering women's stories" and to "broaden" our understanding of western women's lives by including "women's diaries, letters, memoirs, arts and crafts, and oral histories" in our historical perspectives (Introduction 7, 11). Whether dealing with white, English-speaking women or women from different cultural or class backgrounds, the emphasis in these and other studies of prairie women's lives has been to get beyond simple generalizations and, by focusing on the voices of female participants themselves, to illustrate the experience of western settlement as an individual process within a larger cultural pattern.[7]

Similar to Canadian historians, Canadian literary critics have also simultaneously recognized the value of women's first-hand accounts in general as literary documents while neglecting to undertake any concerted study of the memoirs written by white, English-speaking women of the prairie provinces. For example, in the 1983 edition of *The Oxford Companion to Canadian Literature*, Marian Fowler suggested of the vast "field of pioneer memoirs" that "it contains rich insights into the nature of the collective Canadian psyche and its relationship to the land" and recommended "it is high time we turned the first critical sod" (Siddall 923). Fourteen years later, in the 1997 edition of the same text, Gillian Siddall was able to assert some improvement in academic attention to such texts, although she notes that "scholarly enquiry ... has been dominated by an interest in the

---

7   As Bruce Hutchinson suggests in his "Introduction" to Adeline (Nan) Clark's memoir *Prairie Dreams* (1991), "a library of excellent books has described a people who never escape the marks and mental climate of their origin. But, as individuals, they are generally forgotten" (x).

women of the nineteenth century." As a necessary corollary to Siddall's assertion, it should be stressed that scholarly attention to the field of pioneer literature
written by women of the nineteenth century also, by virtue of Canada's historical
pattern of land settlement, means that that attention has been largely confined to
the textual products of *eastern* Canada.[8] For example, Fowler's *The Embroidered
Tent: Five Gentlewomen in Early Canada* (1982) focuses on Elizabeth Simcoe,
Catharine Parr Traill, Susanna Moodie, Anna Jameson, and Lady Dufferin.
Similarly, Lorraine McMullen's 1990 anthology *Re(Dis)covering Our Foremothers*,
a work meant to "recover those [Canadian women writers] once known but now
forgotten and to discover those never publicly known whose diaries, letters, and
autobiographical writings are – or should be – a valued part of Canadian tradition"
(1), devotes six articles to the study of texts by Catharine Parr Traill and/or her
sister, Susanna Moodie. The importance of these first-hand accounts lay primarily
in the fact that, as McMullen suggests, the authors "express a different vision of
Canada and Canadian experience than is conventionally held" (2).

Fairly frequently, literary readings of the texts that encompass this "different vision of Canada and Canadian experience" have tended to adhere to the

---

8   The special interest in nineteenth-century women's writing can be seen, for ex-
ample, in the several New Canadian Library "unabridged reprint[s] of the com-
plete original text[s]" of Catharine Parr Traill's *The Backwoods of Canada* (1989),
Susanna Moodie's *Roughing It in the Bush* (1989) and *Life in the Clearings versus the
Bush* (1989), and Anna Jameson's *Winter Studies and Summer Rambles in Canada*
(1990). Decades earlier, there had already been editions of Anne Langton's *A
Gentlewoman in Upper Canada: The Journals of Anne Langton*, ed. H.H. Langton
(Toronto: Irwin, 1950), *Mrs. Simcoe's Diary*, ed. Mary Quayle Innis (Toronto:
Macmillan, 1965), *The Journals of Mary O'Brien, 1828–1838*, ed. Audrey Saunders
Miller (Toronto: Macmillan, 1968), and Anna Loveridge's *Your Loving Anna;
Letters from the Ontario Frontier*, ed. Louis Tivy (Toronto: University of Toronto
Press, 1972). One recent text that stands out as a starting point for the recon-
ciliation of nineteenth- and twentieth-century writing, and of writing from east-
ern and western Canada, is R.G. Moyles's anthology *'Improved by Cultivation':
English-Canadian Prose to 1914* (Peterborough, ON: Broadview Press, 1994),
which, although it explicitly seeks to "vivify the richness and variety of our pre-
twentieth century prose literature beyond that manifest in recently reprinted
novels" (8) does include alongside the words of Jameson, Traill and Moodie, excerpts from texts published in the early-twentieth century, such as Agnes Dean
Cameron's *The New North: A Woman's Journey through Canada to the Arctic* (1909)
and Georgina Binnie-Clark's *Wheat and Woman* (1914).

traditional either/or image of women alluded to earlier in this chapter. Most commonly, such readings have tended to document the cheerful and relatively unproblematic adaptation of white, English-speaking, women settlers into the "New World" environment. Although I will be discussing her iconic status more fully in Chapter Three, it is important to note Catharine Parr Traill's position as exemplar of the adaptive model: for example, as Elizabeth Thompson suggests, in her non-fiction texts Traill "creates a model of an ideal pioneer woman" (33). Thompson goes on to examine Traill's literary importance in the inauguration of a distinctively female *Canadian Character Type*, one that eventually makes its appearance in prairie fiction. Traill's cheerfully adaptive image, asserts Thompson, spans Canadian literary history and can be traced in its migration from nineteenth-century *eastern* to early-twentieth-century *western* narratives of land settlement. This type of literary mapping of an iconic image of the Pioneer/Prairie Woman across time and geography will certainly be helpful in establishing one portion of the cultural background against which white, English-speaking memoirists had to write their own experiences, especially given that the construction of such an ideal image necessarily means that those writers who do not wholeheartedly subscribe to the adaptive model are so often judged as failures. This complaint has most commonly been laid, at least until recently, against Traill's sister, Susanna Moodie, whose *Roughing It in the Bush* (1852) is all too often and all too simplistically read as being "a condemnation of [settlement] life by someone who found herself to be unfit for it" (McCarthy 3).

For many readers of women's first-hand accounts, however, the either/or readings described above did not accommodate the reality of human experience, which usually rests on a continuum.[9] It is only fairly recently, though, that literary

---

9   A similar rejection of either/or cultural images in favour of "mediated realities" occurs in Carol Fairbanks's *Prairie Women: Images in American and Canadian Fiction* (1986), a transnational perspective on prairie fiction written by women whose works indicate that "there was a sense of having a story to tell that had not been told before" (5). Asserting that no one single historical/literary image can account for the wide variety of women's experiences of prairie settlement, Fairbanks suggests that when female authors eventually chose to take up their pens and "publish their own stories about the frontier," they did so as an act of agency, for they "wanted to undermine or, at a minimum, modify the public's image of the lives of women" settlers (25).

critics have begun to examine the possibility that white, English-speaking women who chose to write about their land settlement experiences might be capable of describing a reality that is simultaneously within and beyond cultural ideals. Women's personal narratives, even those written by women whose background positions them as part of the dominant colonizing culture, are capable of some-times subtle subversions of conventional expectations. In *Mapping Our Selves: Canadian Women's Autobiography* (1993), for example, Helen M. Buss exam-ines "Two Exemplary Early Texts," Moodie's *Roughing It* and Anna Jameson's *Winter Studies and Summer Rambles in Canada* (1838), and suggests that these two women authors consciously and adeptly manage to negotiate the narratives and discourses of Anglo culture as a means to represent their own stories/their own selves. Moodie, writes Buss, effectively inscribes her "own narrative strand to be interwoven with other narratives, an enabling mythology intertwined with many other mythologies" (94), while Jameson manages in her text to "inscribe her own desire by using the discourses of the patriarchy, brilliantly and subversively, against the grain of their own habitual functions" (95). By reading for the ways in which these early women writers mediate in their writing between personal need and cultural expectations, Buss creates a more dynamic background against which to examine the personal accounts produced by a long history of Canadian women writers, including the prairie memoirs gathered in my study. In fact, in *Mapping* she places her critical explorations of texts by nineteenth-century women such as Elizabeth Simcoe, Susan Allison, Moodie and Jameson alongside those by twentieth-century prairie women such as Mary Hiemstra, Georgina Binnie-Clark, and Nellie McClung.

It is my desire as a reader of the prairie memoirs gathered here to reconcile these lost or ignored texts with their historical/literary heritage and to amend the relative lack of critical attention from both historians and literary critics.[10] More

---

10 This lack can be seen in the fact that, although Susan Jackel's 1982 collection, *A Flannel Shirt and Liberty: British Emigrant Gentlewomen in the Canadian West, 1880–1914*, provides excerpts from a number of life writing texts by women who experienced prairie settlement, and although there have been republished edi-tions of such western "classics" as Binnie-Clark's *Wheat and Woman*, Elizabeth B. Mitchell's *In Western Canada Before the War: Impressions of Early Twentieth Century Prairie Communities* (Saskatoon, SK: Western Producer Prairie Books, 1981), Edith

specifically, I aim to read them as points of intersection with idealistic images of white, English-speaking women's participation in prairie land settlement. By "intersection," I mean to suggest the ways in which these texts simultaneously *confirm* and *challenge* cultural images of the Prairie Woman, as well as images of the goal/process/importance of settlement itself, thereby preventing complacency with simplistic either/or dichotomies that deny the reality of individual experience. My assertion that women's prairie memoirs can be productively read as narrative disruptions of cultural images thus necessitates some consideration of the possible reasons why these texts have continued to be overlooked in Canadian scholarship. Central to this discussion will be a generic consideration of the memoir form itself as an all-too-often unrecognized site of narrative intersection, particularly conducive to playing with/interrogation of cultural norms of representation.

Perhaps one of the reasons for the lack of academic attention to prairie memoirs is that the form seems to defy easy categorization and to subvert the expectations of different types of academic readers. Speaking in 1977 to the exclusion of memoir "from serious critical attention," despite the resurgence of "academic interest in forms of self-literature" at that time, Marcus Billson suggests that it is the form's generic instability that produces critical distrust: as he states it, "literary critics have faulted memoirs for being incomplete, superficial autobiographies; and, historiographers have criticized them for being inaccurate, overly personal histories" (259). For many readers, then, memoir texts appear to suffer from a lack of critical depth; they contain neither the fully developed and central Self-consciousness traditionally desired in autobiographical texts nor the objective distance traditionally assumed to be the priority of the professional historian, with the inevitable result that neither discipline wants to lay claim to such a field of works. In fact, the truth of memoir lies somewhere at the intersection of history and autobiography; somewhere between disciplinary misunderstandings of the form as being either too personal or not personal enough.

Hewson's *We Swept the Cornflakes Out the Door* (Regina, SK: Bradley Publications, 1993), and Mary Hiemstra's *Gully Farm: A Story of Homesteading on the Canadian Prairies* (Calgary: Fifth House, 1997), extensive critical treatment of such texts, with the exception of Buss's work, has lagged far behind.

In autobiographical terms, the "I" of memoirs is meant to be less Self-centred, less focused on the development of the unique Self, because it represents a self "*being*-in-the-world rather than *becoming*-in-the-world" (261; emphasis added). In contrast to traditional understandings of autobiographical self-representation wherein the author is assumed to "oppose himself to all others" and to privilege "individuality" over an "interdependent existence" (Gusdorf 29), the memoir represents a self "locate[d] ... in a history, an era, a relational and communal identity" (Buss, *Repossessing* xiv). In historical terms, then, "memoirs are *of* a person, but they are 'really' of an event, an era, an institution, a class identity" (Hart 195); indeed, as Billson suggests, "historicity is the mode of the memoir" and such a text "recounts a story of the author's witnessing a real past which [she] considers to be of extraordinary interest and importance" (268, 261). In the representation of this "real past," says Billson, the author implicitly acknowledges the impossibility of an absolutely objective perspective and, accordingly, adopts a complex narrative position as "the eyewitness, the participant, and the *histor*" (271). Writing as both an eyewitness to and a participant in history, the author establishes her "authority to narrate" on any given event. I was there: I saw, I did, so I can speak to this historical moment. In acknowledgment of the implicitly personal nature of these positions, however, the author also undertakes to play the role of "*histor*,"

> whenever [she] narrates events [she] has not seen with [her] own eyes, whenever [she] tells what [she] has overheard, read about, or accumulated by research through historical records, or whenever [she] provides background material to elucidate the narration or to set the stage for [her] story. (278)

Perhaps the most inclusive sense of the term "memoir" is enunciated by Kate Adams, as follows:

> In general, what does a memoir do? It encapsulates, through the telling of an individual's story, a particular moment or era. A mix of the personal with the contextual, an autobiographical narrative intersecting with history, memoir gives its readers an author as guide, an informant whose presence lends a unique perspective to

the historical moment or event or actor being recorded; the author's status as participant observer lends the history she chronicles
significance, humanity, insight. (8)

This type of recognition of memoir's position at the "intersection" of autobiography and history – of self and social/historical context – becomes especially
important as a means to preserve such texts from pronouncements of failure
according to the traditional expectations of either category.[11]

---

11 An illustrative example from a Canadian context might be helpful in understanding
how memoir texts are often misread as *either* autobiography *or* history. Specifically,
Nellie McClung's two personal volumes, *Clearing in the West* and *The Stream Runs
Fast* (both of which are subtitled "My Own Story") have been misread as failed
attempts at producing traditional autobiographical texts, largely because in both
volumes the author "deflects attention away from herself and towards her family,
her colleagues, and her domestic life" (Dean 88) rather than fully embracing a Self-
centred focus. This kind of narrative deflection was recognized by some contemporary readers, as seen in McClung's own worry that her second volume, *The Stream
Runs Fast*, may be judged as "too introspective," a worry that stemmed from her
"good friend" Laura Goodman Salverson's reaction to the earlier volume, *Clearing
in the West*.

> Apparently, Salverson said I had not revealed myself in that book. I was
> too objective, too concerned with events, conditions and developments.
> Autobiography should have in it the mind and soul of the writer. "Be more
> personal in your new book," she said. "Break down and tell all! We want
> to see you and know how your mind was working." (McClung, *The Stream*
> 145)

In Salverson's desire for McClung to "be more personal," we see the truth of Francis
Russell Hart's suggestion that "memoir is the autobiographical mode that thwarts
generic expectations in readers who go to autobiography for 'that extra degree of
privacy'" (195).
    Clearly, McClung's "autobiographies" may more fruitfully be read as examples
of the memoir genre and, in fact, I have chosen to include McClung's first volume,
which deals with her family's emigration from eastern to western Canada, in this
study, for it seems in the spirit of the author's own life philosophy that her text
should not be held as something sacrosanct, something valued above the body of
works produced by women who were either her contemporaries or her successors in
the desire to document white, English-speaking women's lived experience of prairie
life. Certainly we cannot ignore McClung's own tendency to deny self-importance
beyond "events, conditions and developments."

In terms of the memoir authors who form the basis of this study, I would assert that they all adopt, in one degree or another, Billson's scholarly "*histor*" element; that they all in one way or another have conscientiously "taken the effort to inform [their] personal experience[s] with research" (Buss, "Memoir" 205). For example, Beulah Baldwin notes in the "Acknowledgements" page of *The Long Trail: The Story of a Pioneer Family* (1992) her use of several textual sources when recreating the history of settlement in the Peace River region, as well as the help that she received from "the Provincial Archives of Alberta" (ix). Similarly, in the "Dedication" page of *Land Across the Border* (1978), Donnie M. Ebbers expresses her gratitude to "Mrs. Bert Hodges for history books and material sent from Saskatoon, Saskatchewan" (3) to help the author complete her reminiscence of prairie life. In *Porridge and Old Clothes* (1982), Eileen M. Scott documents her scholarly frame of mind when she writes, "by way of dedication, my thanks goes out to the folks in the research department of the West Vancouver Memorial Library for their patience in answering my endless questions" (n.p.). Katherine Magill provides an entire chapter titled "Historically Speaking" in *Back o' Baffuf* (1977), in which she documents her efforts at "doing a local column for the weekly newspaper" (30). For this column, Magill researched and wrote about the history of the local place, including subjects like the Barr colonists' experiences and Native Indian legends. Anna Schroeder writes in the "Introduction" to *Changes: Anecdotal Tales of Changes in the Life of Anna Born, 1888–1992* (1995) that "the story of the century forms a background to the family history and it seemed good to at least hint at the events that shaped the 19 hundreds, hence the headlines and the price lists" (ix).

Despite the authors' efforts to provide a sense of historical context, however, another dismissal of these texts centres on the charge that memoir representations of prairie life suffer from nostalgia; that the authors as "participants" and as "eyewitnesses" too often exhibit a yearning for "the good old days." For example, as Jacqueline Bliss suggests of personal accounts by Saskatchewan women,

> Written in retrospect, these documents have their limitations.... Memoirs and reminiscences were generally authored by those who

became successful … and thus tend to offer a one-sided view of the pioneer experience. They also suffer from the temptation to view the past through rose-coloured glasses, but do contain useful material, as long as these limitations are borne in mind. (84)

While certainly a healthy skepticism is needed when reading any individual personal account, I believe that through examination of several such accounts a reader is able to discern when biases of perspective hinder understanding of a fuller picture of prairie life. In reading the prairie memoirs gathered here, for example, there is no overwhelming experience of "success" in agricultural terms. In fact, many of the memoirs end on a bittersweet note of mere comfortable survival or even a sense of failure. Another related dismissal of these texts results from the fact that many of them are visions of the authors' *childhood* experiences of prairie settlement, thus making them especially problematic for some academic readers:

> Since children generally do not write autobiographies, nearly all the accounts we have of childhood on the frontier were written by mature or aging adults years later, usually when the individual had moved away from the settlement district. The majority are rather-wistful, nostalgic re-creations of what it felt like to be a boy or girl growing up on the homestead frontier. (Bennett and Kohl 94)[12]

---

12 For example, as Wilfrid Eggleston admits in his essay on his childhood experience of homesteading in Southern Alberta:

> When I think back to those faraway homestead days I cannot escape a sort of bi-focal image. I made my acquaintance with the old homestead first through the imagination and later on through the eyes of a sensitive boy. And after sixty-five years those early impressions still dominate. So I see the experience through a romantic veil. There is still an element of dream or fantasy in my memories. (341)

On the other hand, perhaps an author's self-reflexive recognition of the "romantic veil" so often thrown over past experiences should be seen as an ultimate lack of naiveté and an invitation to the reader to be aware of the possibility of critical reflection. For example, Heather Gilead (one of the memoirists studied here) is acutely aware of the effects of nostalgic blindness, an awareness that allows her to provide a critique of the prairie woman image through the intermingling stories of her own

Certainly an initial examination of some of the titles of the memoirs gathered in this study might seem to confirm this tendency towards a "wistful, nostalgic" view – titles such as *Upon a Sagebrush Harp, Crocus and Meadowlark Country, Barefoot on the Prairie,* and *With the West in Her Eyes.* Nevertheless, it is important here to remember that these accounts are memoirs rather than "autobiographies," so that those texts written by women who experienced childhood on the prairie are less concerned with exclusively the writer's experiences ("what it felt like to be a boy or girl growing up") and more concerned with establishing the multiple forces (national/cultural/social/familial) that affected their family's experiences of prairie life. They talk about themselves, to be sure, but as part of a multi-pronged approach to the subject and not always with nostalgic reverence for some golden age of childhood.

The question of nostalgia is important, nevertheless, in terms of understanding the cultural context/probable motivation behind the production of many of the memoirs gathered for this study. As mentioned earlier, these texts were almost all produced between 1950 and the 1980s, decades in which the production of texts and images highlighting the days of white western settlement was taking place in the nation and in all three prairie provinces. As Carole Henderson Carpenter wrote in 1979, "the many 'birthday' celebrations of recent years, especially the centennial of Confederation, have fostered interest in both pioneer life and Canadian cultural heritage in general" (63).

---

childhood experience of prairie life and the very different experience of her mother bringing up a family in central Alberta in the early-twentieth century. In *The Maple Leaf for Quite a While* (1967), Gilead provides the vignette of an Englishman and his German wife coming to Canada in 1960, after a first visit nearly thirty years prior (in 1933) by him: first she says, "he was lyrical about the prairie harvest and summoned such excitement and sweetness from it as I had not remembered for many a long year," then notes, "it was curiously touching to hear this agreeable, well-spoken stranger conferring romance upon that world of my childhood. I had not, until then, realized how remote that world had become, how utterly banished from my conscious mind – and indeed from the collective conscious mind" (65, 66). Gilead then warns against a totally romantic recall of prairie life with the critical reflection that the Englishman "had, incidentally, apparently not noticed that this world he was extolling was tolerable only for the young, the healthy and preferably the single" (67).

Similarly, Paul Voisey explains the "phenomenal appearance of community-sponsored local histories" in this period as follows:

> [A]nniversary celebrations of Canada and the three prairie provinces in 1967, 1970, and 1980 ignited much of this growth because governments urged everyone to become more historically minded and provided funds for local history projects ... [and] death began claiming the last of the early pioneers at an alarming rate by the 1960s and 1970s. A desperate sense that important links to the past would soon be obliterated launched many local history societies. (504)

Carpenter reiterates this concern for the centrality of individual pioneers to the production of a prairie heritage when she states that "the popular interest in oral history frequently is a manifestation of a 'get it before it dies' attitude and often is associated with a variety of festivals and celebrations which attempt to portray and recapture life as it once was" (64).[13] Added to the desire for local and oral histories were the calls from such periodicals as *The Western Producer*, *Saskatchewan History*, *Alberta History*, and *Manitoba History*, for completion of survey questionnaires regarding different topics of western settlement, as well as for short narratives documenting homesteading experiences. Speaking specifically of Saskatchewan's fiftieth anniversary of provincial status, Carpenter notes that

> a number of special newspaper editions appeared recounting pioneer life, customs and amusements. Additionally, a series of questionnaires concerning pioneer times was initiated, one of which dealt directly with folklore and several others indirectly through, for example, pioneer cooking or housing. These questionnaires are in the Saskatchewan Archives in Saskatoon. Some of the infor-

---

13   The reality behind this "get it before it dies" attitude is illustrated on the dedication page to Nell Wilson Parsons's *Upon a Sagebrush Harp*, where it is noted that "the author died October 28, 1968, while working on proofs of this work" (n.p.).

mation gleaned from them was used in the preparation of several
articles on pioneer life in *Saskatchewan History....* (61)

On top of it all was the "small explosion" (Buss, "Listening" 199) of reminiscent texts (some of which will be studied here) published by presses such
as Western Producer Prairie Books, Banting Publishers, Fifth House, and
NeWest Press, to name a few.

The inevitable result of this concentrated cultural act of preservation was
an heroic, popular, and generally white narrative of western settlement, one
that has dominated the mainstream Canadian consciousness ever since. As the
Anglo-centric story goes, immigrants arrived in this empty land, settling initially in the east and then, eventually, in the name of empire and nation building, journeying westward in an effort to domesticate and cultivate the vast,
uninhabited, yet resource-rich, wilderness of what would become the prairie
provinces. Nothing so simple as making a living here; rather, immigrants to
the prairie region were the lynchpin presence in no less than the construction of a New World. Of course, the prior presence of First Nations people
and the eventual arrival of and reliance on peoples of non-western-European
background was not a central part of this particular version of the settlement
story, which was originally constructed as an explicitly Anglo-centred effort.
Although the reality is now widely understood to have been multicultural,
the mid-twentieth-century passion to preserve a prairie heritage inevitably
resulted in a predominantly white, English-speaking version of history. This
kind of narrative homogenization is not unexpected, for as Katarzyna Rukszto
suggests in a discussion of the Canadian heritage movement and the production of history, "heritage ... is about re-telling, re-imagining and entrenching
the idealized and selective renditions of the past" (16).[14] In addition to being
a predominantly white story, for a long time another "selective" feature of the
prairie settlement story was its inherent masculinity. As recently as 2005, the
editors of the anthology *Unsettled Pasts: Reconceiving the West through Women's*

---

14   Rukszto's study is of the popular "Heritage Minutes," the "series of television com-
       mercials aired as part of the CRB (Charles R. Bronfman) Foundation Heritage
       Project" (2), of which series two "Minutes" represent prairie history.

History still found cause to make the following assertion: "After nearly three decades of increasingly sophisticated work in women's and gender history, popular and academic narratives of the West continue to privilege the masculine and to be dominated by the powerful images of the whisky trader, Indian chief, cowboy, Mountie, missionary, stalwart pioneer, farmer, and politician" (4). Indeed, the image of the individual and heroic prairie farmer (always assumed to be male) could be said to have attained membership in the exclusive world of "Canadian iconography" (Rukszto 9), and when he was given a female counterpart, it was one half or the other of the Prairie Woman dichotomy who generally stood by his side.

The heroic and homogenized vision of prairie settlement does seem consistently present in the memoirs, especially within the dedicatory and prefatory pages of the texts. Reverence for the people and for the task undertaken by them is paramount. For example, Nell Parsons's *Upon a Sagebrush Harp* is dedicated to "Papa and all those other forgotten homesteaders who toiled to make the Prairies the land of their dreams for future generations" (n.p.). Similarly, Beulah Baldwin writes the following in the "Acknowledgments" page of *The Long Trail*:

> As a child listening to my parents talk of their adventures along the Grouard Trail, I never thought of them as remarkable people. Nor did they see themselves as anything but ordinary.
>
> It was only after I was grown, and later when I was working on this book, that I began to recognize them, and their contemporaries, for what they were. True pioneers! People with the courage and fortitude to follow their dreams. They came and, more importantly, they endured, staying to settle a new land. (ix)

The claims made by Parsons and Baldwin about early immigrants following "dreams" and "settling a new land" seems relatively humble in comparison to Franklin Foster's "Foreword" to Mary Hiemstra's *Gully Farm*, in which he poses the rhetorical question, "What is it like to create the world?" then continues on to suggest that "the settlement pioneers of western Canada came as close as any humans are likely to come to this experience" (vii). This potentially ethnocentric assertion aptly conveys the heroic underpinning of heritage projects.

It would appear that the memoirs gathered here are at least partially motivated by and can be read as the authors' desire to enter into the ongoing conversation about and construction of a prairie heritage.[15] Writing such a memoir is to seek after "historical validation" (Silverman, *The Last* viii). It is to claim one's personal experience – or one's mother's or grandmother's experience – as having been intertwined with an important cultural moment, especially when the author of such a text belongs to the dominant culture being represented within the heritage discourse. That sense of belonging certainly illustrates how the memoirists studied here were empowered to write, and why their full-length texts were published. This suggestion of empowerment, in fact, might be seen as being contrary to the oft-repeated opinion within women's historiography that "women have seldom felt themselves to be makers of history" (Rasmussen et al. 8).[16] If we accept this general assertion of modesty as a truism – indeed, I felt its

---

15   I deliberately use the word "conversation" here in order to tap into what is an explicitly oral storytelling atmosphere in many of these memoirs. The authors sometimes directly address the reader, as we see in *The Bridges I Have Crossed* (1973) when Myrtle E.J. Hicks tells about how her father gathered logs for the building of a new barn and says, "I don't know if you younger folks know what a cross-cut saw is," then goes on to provide an explanation (8). In *Rut Hog or Die* (1974), Sylvia Bannert makes the following deliberate invocation of an oral tradition of storytelling: "I was sitting in my old rocking chair and thinking of the past, and what the future holds for me. I hope you will listen to the story of my life. I will try and tell it as I lived it in Monessen, Pa.; Derby, Iowa; Truax, Saskatchewan and Grand Forks, British Columbia" (1). When Anna Schroeder came to write *Changes*, her memoir of her grandmother, she subtitled it *Anecdotal Tales of Changes in the Life of Anna Born, 1888–1992*, and in her "Acknowledgements" page she advises the reader that "if the voices change as the story unfolds, it is because I have tried to preserve the sound of the speaker who told this or that incident" (vii). One of the voices she uses is her grandmother's, who was the subject of an oral interview by schoolchildren in the late-twentieth century. In *Two White Oxen: A Perspective of Early Saskatoon, 1874–1905* (1972), Barbara (Hunter) Anderson also shares a storytelling atmosphere: for example, in a chapter titled "Bonheur's Gift on a Bush Overnight," the author begins by narratively begging her readers to draw near, "That dollars do not grow on bushes has often been averred, but a Gold Coin valued at about $20.00, hung on a bush by the side of a path to the river for at least 24 hours, right in the centre of Saskatoon. Once Upon a Time... This is the story" (83; her ellipsis).

16   We see this reticence to claim significance, for example, in Anna Schroeder's "Introduction" to *Changes: Anecdotal Tales of Changes in the Life of Anna Born 1888– 1992* (1995), which is supposedly "the story of one rather typical pioneer woman's

presence in conversations with my own grandmother – then the existence of this relatively unexplored body of memoirs motivates my further consideration of the effects of these women having undertaken the *extraordinary* act of writing their lives for public consumption. Beyond the desire to stake a claim in the heritage story of western settlement, beyond participating in what is often an explicitly nostalgic undertaking, I would argue that the memoirists studied here are also concerned with fleshing out, or making real, the public and popular version of events. That is, as women – even as white, English-speaking women – the authors of these texts still stand in some degree of opposition to both the traditionally heroic and masculine-centred vision of the heritage story and to the idealized Prairie Woman image that emerged as part and parcel of that vision. It has been said that women's "hesitation about their historical value revealed and reflected the lesson that history is so often about men" (Silverman, *The Last* iii), so that when that traditional hesitation has so clearly been overcome, politicized purpose of one kind or another seems, to me, to be revealed.

Even within discussions of the exclusionary nature of heritage movements there exists the possibility for a more politicized approach to the memoir texts of white, English-speaking women. For example, when Rukszto states that "heritage must construct a past by elevating some events to the status of legends, while omitting, hiding and generally sanitizing any traces of the past that are less than exemplary" (17), she permits the possibility of reading these supposedly nostalgic texts quite differently. Specifically, if we peer beyond what might sometimes be only a surface adherence to the heroic story/the masculine-centred story/the Prairie Woman story, then we might just begin to find some of those "traces of the past that are less than exemplary." Even the nostalgia which is one of the motivating forces behind heritage movements and which is often read conservatively as something "necessarily static and unchanging in its attempt to retrieve a lost utopian space," as something that "upholds the status quo" (Huffer 19), might be more strategically read as a tool or a guise that allows the memoirist to attain a public hearing, with the result that traces of difference in the personal

---

life" (ix). As Schroeder writes of her grandmother Born, she "never thought she had accomplished anything noteworthy."

experience of prairie life might also get heard.[17] In this vein, I would suggest that the "nostalgia" in white, English-speaking, women's memoirs might be most fruitfully read as an ironic narrative and critical veneer through which the representation of a Prairie Woman's life gets "re-visioned," a process that Adrienne Rich defines as "the act of looking back, of seeing with fresh eyes, of entering an old text from a new critical direction" (35). But "old texts" (or images/narratives), and especially ones that have a tendency to dichotomize the Prairie Woman, are often difficult to re-vision. Judy Schultz alludes to this difficulty in her memoir titled *Mamie's Children: Three Generations of Prairie Women* (1997) when she answers the question, "Why hasn't more been written about the role of the ordinary rural woman in the West?":

> Maybe because her frontier-bred, grin-and-bear-it tradition didn't allow for public soul-bearing. To complain about anything more personal than the weather would have been an admission of weakness or defeat, and it wasn't done. On the other hand, a woman had to be cautiously circumspect about even her smallest personal victories because to talk about them might be construed as tooting her own horn, and that wasn't done either. Modesty, like frugality

---

17   Feminist scholarship on the function of nostalgia in women's texts illustrates that "nostalgia" can no longer be simply viewed as "just a sentiment," but must also be read as a deliberate "rhetorical practice" (Doane and Hodges 3). For example, Carolyn Heilbrun suggests that in women's autobiographical texts "nostalgia ... is likely to be a mask for unrecognized anger," an emotion traditionally "forbidden" to women, who then "could find no voice in which publicly to complain" (15). Linda Wagner-Martin examines the function of nostalgia in the work of Edith Wharton, including *The Age of Innocence* (1920). Wagner-Martin notes that after World War I, when Wharton "was in her late 50s" and "in an introspective mood," she chose to write "about New York in the 1870s" because it was a time and place in which "people saw life as promising" (5). Nevertheless, Wharton's use of nostalgia is ironic for she seeks also to suggest that, "in some ways, the age of apparent innocence and propriety had foreshadowed the brutality of the coming war" (6). Wharton thus uses the guise of nostalgia in her historical novel as a means of cultural critique. Another useful reference on the subject of nostalgia in women's texts is Anne G. Balay's "'Hands Full of Living': Birth Control, Nostalgia, and Kathleen Norris," in *American Literary History* 8, no. 3 (Fall 1986): 471–95.

and the work ethic, was an essential virtue in a good farm woman.
(55)

So what is the role of the memoir genre specifically in relation to the act of re-visioning, amongst other things, the seemingly monolithic image of "a good farm woman"? According to Helen Buss, memoir has long been seen as an "attractive form for those wishing to make them selves 'real' in terms of a history and a culture that denies their experience" ("Memoir" 207). In the years since Marcus Billson first sought to theorize the specificities of this "forgotten genre," there have been other critics who have undertaken to provide a more dynamic treatment of this particular literary form that presents a self in historical context. For example, in her 1992 consideration of "The Subject of Memoirs," Lee Quinby provides a re-reading of Maxine Hong Kingston's *The Woman Warrior* (1975), a text that, despite the fact that its subtitle "specifies its genre" as *Memoirs of a Girlhood Among Ghosts*, has been consistently misread as an autobiographical text. Such misreadings are damaging, suggests Quinby, because they "ignore or resist the implications" of an author's specific choice of the memoir form as a means to "negotiat[e] a confrontation with disciplinary power relations" (299). More recently, but similarly, in a 1997 article titled "Memoir with an Attitude" – an article that, like Quinby's, provides a feminist re-reading of Kingston's frequently misread *The Woman Warrior* – Buss highlights the genre's radical nature when she asserts that, because of the author's preoccupation with historicity, the memoir text allows for "'confrontation' with accepted versions of subjectivity" ("Memoir" 206). For both of these critics, "confrontation" is a deliberate rhetorical choice on the part of the memoir writer, although Buss also highlights the importance of an aware reader – aware of the specificities of the memoir form – in discerning where such deferrals from cultural norms and expectations might occur.

Buss's work with other, lesser-known, women's writings also provides a crucial backdrop to my desire to read the prairie memoirs gathered here for the ways in which they "confront" heroic/masculinist/Prairie Woman narratives. In an article titled "Settling the Score with Myths of Settlement" (1997), Buss examines "women settlers' memoirs in archival collections" and finds herself engaged in a process of "unlearning myths of 'settlement'" (167). More

specifically, she realizes that, "although the writers may try to conform obedi-
ently to these heroic stereotypes, they are in fact writing accounts that also
contradict these myths of settlement." Buss goes on to acknowledge that there
is a crucial distinction to be made between the "surface" and "undercurrent"
narrative layers of such texts, a distinction that ultimately reveals "a different
reality than the heroic myths." Discerning this "different reality," however,
demands a particularly active reader, one who is aware of the pressure on writers for seeming conformity but who is also ready to "[seek] the small breaks
in the codes, not obvious on the surface" of the text (168). Buss's explorations
of the gap that occurs between cultural narratives and the "different reality"
that women so often seek to represent in their personal writings, and also
her consideration of the "concern" to at least appear to adhere to those ideals,
is invaluable to my own treatment of memoirs by white, English-speaking
women, especially given the heritage context in which so many of these memoirs were published. As Buss recognizes with archival sources, so, too, it is
time to acknowledge that *published* first-hand accounts of prairie life provide
us with "the opportunity to revise our cultural myths and settle the score for
women involved in the history of the settlement of the West" (182). In seeking
to take up that opportunity here, it is important to note that my background
is literary critical rather than historical or some other disciplinary perspective,
and I believe strongly in the crucial role of the reader in the discernment of
narrative tactics used to "revise" predominant myths.

To "revise," to "re-vision," is to actively engage with or interrogate – indeed, to adhere/conform to *or* to undermine/refuse – those historical narratives and cultural images which have predominated in public representations
of prairie settlement. For white, English-speaking women in the second half
of the twentieth century who desired to write about their experiences on the
Canadian prairies in the late nineteenth/early twentieth centuries, it must
have appeared that there was little room for representations of experience
beyond the homogenous ones of heritage discourse. Between contemporary
propaganda encouraging the settlement of the prairie region, the heritage
movement in Canada, and such cultural imagery as the *Little House on the
Prairie* television series that overarched my own childhood understanding of
prairie life, there must have seemed little chance for the individual woman

writer to give her own story "equal footing" (Buss, *Repossessing* xvii) with more entrenched visions. Nevertheless, it is precisely by choosing the memoir form of writing, and by making that choice in the midst of the national/regional predilection to preserve the heritage moment of prairie settlement, that these women acknowledge their awareness of the historical/cultural contexts that have, in some measure, defined their/their mothers'/their grandmothers' lives while also illustrating the ability of the individual to provide a "different reality" experienced within those contexts. Human beings are not completely self-determining subjects, but neither are they completely subjected to the power structures of the world. As Alison Weir theorizes, for example, we cannot allow the individual the power of agency – or the power of "intervening action" (*Oxford Encyclopedic English Dictionary*; hereinafter *OEED*) – without

> a recognition that subjects, while they do not originate, do *participate* in the ongoing process of the constitution of subjectivity. For of course we are constituted as subjects, but from the time we begin to be constituted, we also participate in our own constitution, through our spontaneous acts and responses to others, through the development of our capacities for reflection, deliberation, and intention, through our constant attempts to make meaning, to understand ourselves and others, to express ourselves to others, to act in accordance with ideals, to account for our failures and our incoherences. (Weir, 127–28)

The prairie memoir text, coupled with the nostalgic veneer of the prairie heritage story, becomes a narrative vehicle through which, in all the ways expressed by Weir, the individual author engages with cultural understandings of what a Prairie Woman is/does and participates in a reconstitution of that image. By simultaneously adhering to the Anglo-centric norms of representation of the prairie settlement story while also engaging in "the expression or realization of one's specificity," the memoir author and the memoir reader, together, find "a capacity for the critique of norms" (187).

The memoirist's "capacity for the critique of norms" is perhaps heightened in the case of those authors who are recalling their prairie childhood. Many of the authors in this study have chosen to reconstruct not only their own experiences of homesteading life (Billson's "participant" role), but also those of their mothers and grandmothers (Billson's "witness" role), those women who may or may not have had the skill, time or desire to enter into the public act of writing. For example, in *Mamie's Children*, Judy Schultz begins her narrative acknowledging that

> this is Mamie's story, it's also her mother's and her grandmother's. It belongs as well to Pearl, Mamie's youngest daughter, my mother. And in a way it becomes my story too because the thread my small, ordinary grandmother began spinning more than one hundred years ago on the Saskatchewan prairies was long and strong. She wove it back and forth among the women who were part of her past and future family, and in the weaving, she bound all of us – together. (12)

As Schultz later remembers, she herself was the "chief audience" for the "stories that passed between [her] mother [Pearl] and [grandmother] Mamie" (104), thus allowing her to pass those stories on to us. The daughter/author does seem to manage a particularly privileged viewpoint in these texts, given that, not only has she been a participant in and eyewitness to the events of prairie life, but she also stands temporally and (very often) geographically distant from the period and place of settlement, which allows her to cast a more critical eye on "the informing contexts that make the personal story a part of a larger cultural framework" (Buss, *Repossessing* 18) – Billson's *histor* role. Through an act of memoir, a genre that is part literature and part history, the (grand)daughter-author is able to combine "imaginative construction and factual testimony" (158) as a means to "look back" with "fresh eyes" (Rich 35), to re-vision, cultural norms of representation.

My readings of white, English-speaking, women's, prairie memoirs for the re-visions they provide will be divided into four chapters. I have chosen to take a thematic approach in order to demonstrate just some of the ways that the texts considered here manage to confront traditional beliefs about and representations of prairie settlement and the Prairie Woman. Chapter

Two will trace the ideas which have dominated our historical understanding of prairie settlement – the heroic story, the masculinist story – as a means to illustrate how the memoirs gathered here simultaneously invoke and reject those ideas in favour of re-visioning our focus from the larger cultural project of land settlement to the more localized concerns of the individual family farm; to effectively move narrative stress from the "stead" to the "home." Chapter Three will trace the female images that have dominated our literary understanding of land settlement in Canada. Specifically, I will examine Catharine Parr Traill's position as cultural icon in a "cheerfully adaptive" model of women's participation in land settlement and then establish the presence of a different model of behaviour available to white, English-speaking women – what might perhaps be called a more "moodified" image based on the less "dauntlessly optimistic" account of Traill's sister, Susanna Moodie. By invoking Moodie in this way, however, I do not seek to construct another false binary, another either/or simplicity, but rather to allow for a more inclusive representation of white women's lived experience of the prairie settlement process. In Chapter Four, I want to examine how gender is constructed within specifically located spaces, including the geographic space of the Canadian west, the physical space of the white female body, and the textual space in which memoir writers represent their life experiences. As I hope to illustrate, contemporary Anglo-centric attitudes focused on the female body as a space reflective of the larger cultural project of land settlement, and the memoir text functions as a temporally safe space in which the female author is able to document the prairie woman's modes of resistance to those attitudes. Finally, in Chapter Five I will turn my attention to the natural environment behind women's memoirs of western "settlement"; that is, I will seek to get beyond those images which are dominant in agriculture – such as the white farmer and his plow set against a backdrop of lush wheatfields – and which effectively result in the absence of "others" in the prairie landscape. By casting an eco-critical eye on this "untilled field" of memoirs, we can acknowledge that the seemingly isolated conditions of prairie life allowed white, English-speaking women a chance to appreciate the presence of the natural landscape, First Nations people, and non-human animals, and thereby to provide a different vision, even a critique, of the land settlement project.

In choosing which texts would form the corpus of this study of prairie memoirs produced by white, English-speaking women, I had to construct a variety of critical parameters as a means to control what could otherwise result in a rather unwieldy (although fascinating) body of texts and an inability to provide close readings of textual passages. First, I am interested in individually-authored, full-length, and *published* texts, precisely because I am fascinated by the sheer number of women who, although we are often reminded of women's reticence to speak, found it necessary not only to write but also to seek (and found acceptance for) publication of their voices. Second, I have chosen to focus on texts written by or about married women, largely because the predominant Prairie Woman image is inherently the dependent of a prairie farmer, whether she is the cheerful or the drudge version of that image.[18] Third, I wanted to maintain a consistent geographic focus, so I have chosen only those texts in which a majority of the narrative treats of an individual's experience of life in rural/homesteading situations in any of the three prairie provinces – Manitoba, Saskatchewan, or Alberta. Although there are many interesting texts which deal with small town life in the Canadian west, I have nonetheless preferred to stay with those women whose families relied upon a farm economy and for whom the female members were instrumental to survival. This has meant that certain texts by prominent Canadian women which have an exclusively urban focus – for example, Fredelle Bruser Maynard's *Raisins and Almonds* (1964) and Annora Brown's *Sketches from Life* (1981) – have not been included in my chosen corpus of texts. My time range, however, is quite vast, with texts that document western land settlement from around 1870 to 1950, this latter period representing the final post-World War II migration northward, most notably to the Peace River regions of both Alberta and British Columbia. Fourth, the texts which I have chosen to rely upon for this study vary considerably in literary quality, with some works being written by sophisticated and experienced

---

18   In her study titled *Land in Her Own Name: Women as Homesteaders in North Dakota* (Fargo: North Dakota Institute for Regional Studies, 1991), Elaine Lindgren begins by documenting "what was to become a common response" to her focus on women who themselves filed land claims, and that was the lack of knowledge about such women and the assumption that women only performed "secondary or 'helpmate' roles" in the homesteading project (iii–vi).

writers (for example, Nellie McClung, Marjorie Wilkins Campbell, Nell Wilson Parsons, and Judy Schultz) and others being written by women with more modest narrative skills. However, each text represents a woman's attempt to articulate, within the realm of her own capabilities, personal experiences of prairie life. Accordingly, any text that has fulfilled the strict parameters of my study has been included for some degree of consideration, although I have not deliberately sought to pay equal attention to every one of the thirty memoirs gathered here. Indeed, I will here invoke the words used by the author of another similarly broad-based study of texts and state that, "given the very considerable number of texts involved ... I have made no attempt to refer to each one individually but have preferred to concentrate on following a line of argument, using the richest and most appropriate texts as illustrations" (Coe xiii–xiv). The central idea here is to bring these texts, these women's voices, to public attention and to illustrate the rich potential of them to continue the scholarly dialogue about issues of prairie history.

Potential can be fostered or lost. On May 6, 1999, when I was first working on this study, I received a phone call from my father telling me that my grandmother Sadie had died after a year of struggling against lung cancer. More than two decades after her husband had died and she had moved westward to live with one of my uncles on the coast of British Columbia, I had only just begun to renew my relationship with my grandmother (mostly by telephone) towards the final few years of her life. My academic interest in prairie women had inspired me to begin to ask questions of the woman whose figure had cut so large an influence in both my personal and professional life. However, ever since her geographical re-placement to the coast, Sadie had seemed to resign herself to a conscious refusal, at least with me, to remember much of anything about her past experience of life on the Canadian prairies. I, in turn, resigned myself to never knowing my grandmother's personal experience. Now, her death has reinforced my knowledge that, while real prairie women will eventually pass on and fade from memory, static images will continue to dominate our understanding, unless we continue the effort to take up their textual remains and read them back into Canadian cultural history.

❊ 2 ❋

"Seemingly Trivial": Re-Visioning Historical Narratives of Western Settlement

Presuming that by force of circumstances the question of a desirable change has come over you, ... the first thought will be "Where shall I go to better my condition?" To such I would say "Follow Horace Greely's [*sic*] advice, 'Go West,' to that magnificent stretch of that agricultural territory, Western Canada, with its millions of free acres, and the British flag for a reserve." Your choice falls on this fair portion of Canada! You have concluded rightly that it offers splendid opportunities, ...

> – "To the British Emigrant," By W.S. Urton (1893)[1]

---

1 This letter was included in the Duck Lake Agricultural Society pamphlet titled *In the Saskatchewan country: Facts about the wheat growing, cattle raising and mixed farming of the great fertile belt: The Duck Lake district of Saskatchewan, Northwest Territories of Canada* (Winnipeg: Printed by Acton Burrows, at the Western World Office, 1893) (Peel #2079). According to Robert Chadwell Williams, Horace Greeley, who was one of the founding editors of *The New-Yorker* in 1834 and who founded the *New York Tribune* in 1841, was a definite advocate of western expansion, although the oft-repeated phrase "Go West, Young Man!" has been possibly erroneously attributed to him (40–43).

Not long ago I met a man who said: "So you are writing a book? What and why?"

"I am writing a book," I replied impressively, "about Canada."

"But *what* about Canada?" he asked.

"The truth, as I see it," I told him.

At that he looked pained. "Why," he said, almost with annoyance, – "why do women always do that?"

"Do what?" I said, fearing that my bright idea had been stolen.

"Tell the truth, of course!"

– Marjorie Harrison, *Go West – Go Wise!*
A Canadian Revelation (1930)

Funny how sometimes it takes fifty years to understand something seemingly trivial.

– Nell Wilson Parsons, *Upon a Sagebrush Harp* (1969)

In order to understand the "re-visioning" potential of prairie memoirs written by white, English-speaking women, it is important to map out, at least briefly, those narratives/images which dominated representations of western land settlement in the contemporary moment of expansion.[2] The timeline covered

---

2   As there have been several studies done regarding contemporary views of western settlement, it is not my intention here to provide a lengthy and detailed history of Canadian immigration policy and its cultural effects; rather I seek to extract what I consider to be certain dominant narratives of western settlement, ones which are most often reproduced in the memoirs which form the focus of this study. For a more detailed analysis of western settlement, see, for example, the following: Jean Bruce, *The Last Best West* (Toronto: Fitzhenry & Whiteside, 1976); Linda Rasmussen et al., *A Harvest Yet to Reap: A History of Prairie Women* (Toronto: The Women's Press, 1976); Doug Owram, *Promise of Eden: The Canadian Expansionist Movement and the Idea of the West 1856–1900* (Toronto: University of Toronto Press, 1980); R.G. Moyles and Doug Owram, *Imperial Dreams and Colonial Realities: British Views of Canada, 1880–1914* (Toronto: University of Toronto Press, 1988); Ronald Rees, *New and Naked Land: Making the Prairies Home* (Saskatoon, SK: Western Producer Prairie Books, 1988); R. Douglas Francis, *Images of the West: Changing Perceptions of the Prairies, 1690–1960* (Saskatoon, SK: Western Producer Prairie Books, 1989); and R. Douglas Francis and Chris Kitzan, eds., *The Prairie West as Promised Land* (Calgary: University of Calgary Press, 2007).

by the memoirs included in this study is lengthy, ranging from approximately 1870 to the very final stages of land settlement in the western provinces after the Second World War. Although the most intense period of immigration to · the Canadian West occurred from 1896 to 1914, it was in the middle of the nineteenth century that the rhetoric surrounding the agricultural potential of the region first became a significant cultural narrative. From the beginning, prairie settlement was conceived of and expressed in large-scale terms: indeed, if we are to believe the back cover commentary for Beulah Baldwin's *The Long Trail: The Story of a Pioneer Family* (1992), the early settlers were filled with "a sense of participation in a huge and magnificent undertaking" (n.p.). One might even say that the ideological magnitude inherent to the hopes and dreams of Canadian expansionists was matched only by the geographic immensity of the prairie region itself, a region constructed as a "New World" Garden of Eden and as the "fount" of both "national and imperial greatness" (Francis, *Images* 73–74).

As a consequence of a series of mid-century expeditions, including those led by Henry Youle Hind and Captain John Palliser, "between 1856 and 1869 the image of the West was transformed in Canadian writings from a semi-arctic wilderness to a fertile garden well adapted to agricultural pursuits," and it was this transformation that "allowed the West to be seen as the means by which Canada could be lifted from colony to nation, and, eventually, to an empire in its own right" (Owram, *Promise of Eden* 3). The domestication of the Canadian west – its transformation into a "promised land, a garden of abundance in which all material wants would be provided and where moral and civic virtues would be perfected" (Francis, *Images* 107) – necessitated a concerted promotional campaign. Enthusiasm for the region grew throughout the 1870s and early 1880s, largely as a result of the writings of John Macoun, a botanist who, "in the spring of 1880," was "ordered by the Department of the Interior to return to the West in order to investigate further the lands of the southern prairies" (Owram, *Promise of Eden* 152). The result of Macoun's trip was that he became an ardent convert to the expansionist cause and in his writings he "romanticized homestead life, minimized problems, and created a utopian vision" (Rollings-Magnusson 224) that became firmly entrenched enough to survive the initial failure of western immigration to match expansionist expectations. When the largest influx of settlement began around 1896,[3] the explicitly utopian imagery and mythic potential of the region continued to be reproduced. Indeed, settlement literature promoted material success as a seemingly inevitable result of residence in the new Garden of Eden: "It was a 'land of opportunity' where almost anyone and everyone could succeed because the conditions for success were intrinsic to the region" (Francis, Introduction xi). These "conditions for success" were seen by prospective settlers, for example, in the "papers, posters, folders [which] showed men standing in lush wheat fields, amidst grain that rose shoulder-high" (Brown 51).[4]

It was this fertile Garden of the Canadian west which, once populated, would become the "cornerstone in the Confederation scheme" (Conway 12). The mere fact of Confederation in 1867 had not immediately secured

---

3   Indeed, during those first decades of western land promotion, settlers merely "trickled" into the prairie region (Rasmussen et al., 12). Gerald Friesen quantifies this "trickle" as follows: "in the thirty-two years from 1867 to 1899, only 1.5 million immigrants entered Canada; by comparison, 5.5 million entered the United States in the 1880s alone and 2.5 million entered Australia between 1879 and 1890" (*The Canadian* 185). At least part of the explanation for this initial lack of interest in prairie settlement was a general economic depression in the West after 1883 and lasting until about the mid-1890s. Nevertheless, says Friesen, "Canada had made a start" and "firm foundations had been established for the flood that was about to commence" (185–86). See Chapter 11 of Friesen's *The Canadian Prairies: A History* (Toronto: University of Toronto Press, 1987) for a more detailed account of the reasons for the largest "infusion of immigrants" in the period 1897–1929.

4   In *Upon a Sagebrush Harp* (1969), Nell Wilson Parsons notes the propaganda "booklets" which "claimed fabulous things for the north," including wheat that "yields sixty bushels to the acre" (5). Perhaps the most hyperbolic image occurs in Donnie M. Ebbers's *Land Across the Border* (1978), in which the author refers to a pamphlet promoting wheat-farming in Canada to potential American immigrants: "Another picture Papa liked, showed John Bull (the man symbol of Canada then) and Uncle Sam standing by a big field of tall wheat, John Bull was asking, 'Well, Sam what do you think of Saskatchewan?' Uncle Sam answering, 'Fine country, John, fine country, good land! But I can't see the land for the wheat!'" (9–10). Sometimes the reality of hard work in achieving economic prosperity was admitted, but still the image of material success remained paramount: "It is true Canada is not exactly a Utopia, Ltd., for there is rough, hard work to be done before homes of comfort or affluence are built. But, on the other hand, the Old World farmer will find ... [that] [h]e will be his own landlord, or, if he likes the title better, a lord of lands" (Ferguson, *Janey* 204). In Parsons's *Sagebrush Harp*, too, it is optimistically admitted that "hard work was all that was needed to turn endeavour into success" (106).

Canadian national identity for, even after British Columbia joined the union in 1871, there still remained the "vast underpopulated hinterland" of what was to become the prairie provinces. Importantly, population influx into the western regions would "permit the development of a British North American nation with enough power to withstand any hostile pressures from the south" (Owram, "The Promise" 24). Thus, when combined together, individual farmers and their families were not simply filling a geographic space, but rather were seen as the linchpin to the confederation dream of a new and strong nation arising from sea to shining sea.[5] Prairie agriculture, undertaken at the level of the individual farm, in addition to contributing to the security of the nation against the United States, would also ultimately accrue to the benefit of the larger national economy and would allow Canada to take its place, first as the bulwarks, and later at the masthead, of the British Empire. Variously labelled as "The Granary of the Empire" (Ferguson, *Open* 22–23) and, as the subtitle of a 1903 book published by the Department of the Interior suggests, "The Granary of the World" (Bruce 61),[6] Canada was promoted as being on the stepping stone to becoming an Empire in her own right: "if imperial Rome could have grown sufficient wheat in Italy to feed her legions, she would still be mistress of the world. But her glory has vanished, and the rulers of the world are they who have the mastership of wheat. It is a big bid Canada is making" (Ferguson, *Janey* 146).[7]

---

5   Indeed, national dreams were concretized in the numerous policies which ensured that the federal government retained control over "prairie land and natural resources," a situation that had not occurred with any other geographic addition to the confederation (Friesen, *The Canadian* 181).

6   In this way did Canadian farming take on mythic proportions in the popular imagination, as seen in a discussion of the Winnipeg Grain Exchange in Douglas Durkin's novel, *The Magpie* (1923): "Here was the great funnel through which a billion bushels of grain passed annually from the broad acres of the Canadian prairies on its way to the nations of the world" (44).

7   Elsewhere, speaking to the state of the Canadian Parliament buildings in 1912, Emily Ferguson (the pseudonymous Janey Canuck) suggested that "changes or additions" would have to be made to the inadequate structure in the near future, for "mayhap, by that time Great Britain will have decided to make the Anglo-Saxon race predominant for the coming centuries by moving the Capital of the Empire from England to Canada" (*Open* 217).

The "big bid" narrative of Empire-building ensured that the Canadian west was also promoted as a human community wherein "moral and civic virtues would be perfected" (Francis, *Images* 107). As Elizabeth Mitchell specified in 1915, the region was meant to provide "a fresh start," a "healthy society" that could only be "successfully erected" by "men of British tradition" (108–9). Indeed, while the reality of western settlement, over time, established a cultural mosaic on the Canadian prairies, the underlining desire for the creation of a distinctly Anglo regional and national identity was early evident.[8] Ideally, whatever the actual cultural backgrounds of immigrants to the Canadian West, the project of prairie settlement was ideologically based on what would be the reconstitution of Anglo norms of "civilization" in a radically different geographic space; it was based on the belief that "the Anglo-Saxon peoples and British principles of government were the apex of both biological evolution and human achievement" and that "Canada's greatness was due in large part to its Anglo-Saxon heritage" (Palmer 311). Indeed, Canada's physical greatness was particularly appropriate to "build up a nation on the British plan" for only "the vast territory of the West offered a canvas large enough to be appropriate for the moral grandeur of British institutions" (Owram, *Promise of Eden* 126).[9]

---

8   As Owram suggests about the early expansionist spirit, it "originated in English-speaking circles in Canada West and even after 1870 its strength derived from this particular linguistic-cultural group. In essence, these English-speaking and largely Protestant, enthusiasts sought to shape the West according to their own cultural values and economic aspirations" (*Promise of Eden* 5). The cultural bias of prairie settlement was not simply a facet of the early stages of immigration, either, for even by the 1930s "the cultural standards of prairie society remained British; social and economic leadership rested firmly in the hands of the British Canadian; and, even in politics, where notions such as socialism and social credit were bandied about, British institutions and principles were as yet unshaken" (Friesen, *The Canadian* 273).

9   The sheer numbers required for western settlement necessitated that "other" cultural groups would have to be inspired to emigrate to Canada and then be naturalized to the new society being created. Although Clifford Sifton, who held the position of Minister of the Interior from 1897 to 1905, "was critical of policies since 1905 that had focused more on ethnic compatibility in immigrants and on sheer numbers, rather than on the sort of immigrants who could succeed in settling new and challenging agricultural frontier," and although it was during his time as Minister that "large numbers of immigrants from Scandinavia and eastern Europe began to arrive in Canada" (Hall 90), assimilation was the "one principle" agreed upon by everyone,

The exclusionary nature of the western settlement project can be seen in the fact that "the existing population" of native peoples were "not central to the expansionists' vision for the future" (Owram, "The Promise" 4). Despite the large-scale focus upon the reproduction of "British institutions and principles," however, the everyday reality of prairie settlement would be predicated upon "a North American regard for progress and individual achievement" (Bruce 13).[10] Settlement of the prairie west relied upon the success of independent

---

including Sifton (92). Frank Oliver, who succeeded Sifton in 1905, was "staunchly British" in his thinking, and thus "he was more inclined to reduce the recruiting activity in central and eastern Europe and to increase it in Great Britain, including its cities, in order to preserve the 'national fabric' of Canada" (Friesen, *The Canadian* 246). Nowhere is the assimilationist nature of western expansion better expressed than in Ralph Connor's *The Foreigner: A Tale of Saskatchewan* (New York: George H. Doran, 1909), in which the author provides the following prefatory note:

> In Western Canada there is to be seen to-day that most fascinating of all human phenomena, the making of a nation. Out of breeds diverse in traditions, in ideals, in speech, and in manner of life, Saxon and Slav, Teuton, Celt and Gaul, one people is being made. The blood strains of great races will mingle in the blood of a race greater than the greatest of them all.

This same philosophy is less romantically stated within the text itself, as one of Connor's characters remarks about the presence of a colony of "Galicians" that they "'exist as an undigested foreign mass. They must be digested and absorbed into the body politic. They must be taught our ways of thinking and living, or it will be a mighty bad thing for us in Western Canada'" (255).

10   This regard is evident in Georgina H. Thomson's *Crocus and Meadowlark Country: A Story of an Alberta Family* (1963) when the author refers to a neighbour who liked to speak about socialism and who "found it wasn't a popular subject with the homesteaders who were mostly of the rugged-individual type, and thought socialism meant taking all the wealth in the country and dividing it equally among the people" (65). Writing about homesteading in northern Alberta in the early 1920s, Peggy Holmes states in *It Could Have Been Worse* (1980) that "it was every man for himself, working against time" (90). Ida Scharf Hopkins gives visual reality to individual prominence in the homesteading project when she writes in *To the Peace River Country and On* (1973) that

> a man may become part of a city and not be unduly noticed, but when he plants himself in the middle of a half mile square of land he can't help but become an individual. His qualities or lack of qualities are exposed to the world to see. His ability to stand on his own two feet and yet cooperate with his neighbours could make the difference between success or failure. (73)

landowners, so that the heroic stature of the hardworking farmer would inevitably become the rhetorical norm in representations of land settlement. For
those in charge of immigration and land settlement policy, individual character
would determine national character, so that, for example, Clifford Sifton was
"a true believer in the North American creed of progress through individual
achievement" and "also a nationalist" (1). As individual settlers accepted the
clarion call of the Canadian government to take up prairie homesteads, they
quickly became enveloped in a mantle of extraordinary virtue. Contemporary
literature designed chiefly for the promotion of western settlement sought to
represent farmers who were in alignment with western notions of material
progress in a golden halo; to envelop them in the glow of heroic achievement.
As a result, "pioneers were the heroes of the prairie agricultural epic" (Friesen,
The Canadian 301).

In early historiographical treatments, the heroic renderings of the prairie
settlement project were largely maintained, with images of individual farmers out to conquer an untamed landscape for the benefit of national/imperial
prosperity. The heroic individual in these early narratives was necessarily
masculine while the woman settler was largely absent from most representations. Although referring specifically to the situation of Saskatchewan history,
nevertheless the suggestion of Ann Leger Anderson that early provincial histories "rarely mention women" ("Saskatchewan" 66) seems an apt description
of early prairie histories in general.[11] Early works were not the only texts to
construct a narrative of western settlement that neglected the important role
of women, however, as seen most recently in Gerald Friesen's *The Canadian*

---

11 This "herstorical" lack is by now so well-documented that, since it is beyond
the scope of this study to provide any substantial overview, I would suggest
that the reader examine the following sources, which, although they purport to
be concerned with a Saskatchewan context, nevertheless document a number of
general prairie histories which neglect women's presence: Ann Leger Anderson's
"Saskatchewan Women, 1880–1920: A Field for Study," *The New Provinces: Alberta
and Saskatchewan, 1905–1980*, eds. Howard Palmer and Donald Smith (Vancouver:
Tantalus Research, 1980), 65–90, and Aileen C. Moffatt's "Great Women, Separate
Spheres, and Diversity: Comments on Saskatchewan Women's Historiography,"
"Other" Voices: Historical Essays on Saskatchewan Women, eds. David De Brou and
Aileen Moffatt (Regina, SK: Canadian Plains Research Center, 1995), 10–26.

Prairies: A History (1987), a seemingly comprehensive text that came under fire from feminist historians concerned with documenting women's lives. For example, Susan Jackel states that Friesen's text is a "major work of historical synthesis" wherein "class, ethnicity, native peoples, urbanization and the arts share the spotlight and attest to the modernizing of the prairie saga, but where women figure fleetingly and infrequently in the narrative and do not even rate an entry in the index" (*Canadian* 3). In a similar vein, Aileen C. Moffatt explains that, "because of Friesen's emphasis on western socioeconomic development, women do not appear as significant actors" (14) in his work. The implications of this lack of attention to gender are vast, suggests Anderson, for Friesen's is "the book most likely to be identified with Prairie West history since its [original] publication in 1984" ("Canadian" 53).

As late as 1992, Friesen himself suggested regarding "the history of women or of relations between the sexes in prairie society" that "these matters have been given very little attention by students of the region" ("Historical" 15). However, he also noted that "the realization that much of this story, typically written by males, created a picture of a male-oriented world, has encouraged a belated rethinking of the prairie past" (12). In noting "the implications of male historians' cultural blindness" towards women's participation in prairie society (15),[12] Friesen neglects to mention the amount of "dramatic revision" of prairie history which had already begun (by the date of his article) to take place in Canadian women's historiography. Indeed, as noted in Chapter One of this study, since the 1970s feminist historians have methodically sifted through the androcentric rubble of traditional historiography in order to examine the lives of prairie women more closely and to reveal the multi-layered reality of settlement life.[13] This is the work that has enabled the deconstruction of those

12 Certainly such a charge can no longer be issued, as attention to the role of women and comments such as the following are increasingly the norm in male historians' treatments of prairie life: "Women were probably more important than any other factor to a homesteader's survival" (Waiser 164).

13 One early example of this archaeological effort was the pioneering text *A Harvest Yet to Reap: A History of Prairie Women* (1976), which is presented in a non-traditional format of exploration and discovery, combining snippets of text, photographs, reproductions of old promotional pamphlets, etc. For more information on the study

static images "that obscure differences between individual women's experiences" (Sundberg 71). When prairie women were mentioned within early histories of western settlement, they were often absorbed into the heroic version of the prairie story, the masculinist story, which generally relegated them to a "hagiographic presentation" (Langford, "First Generation" 1) from which it has taken them decades to escape. The only real alternative was the tendency to thrust all women into the other side of the Prairie Woman coin – the image of the reluctant emigrant/drudge.

Early efforts at recovering women's experiences of western settlement tended to re-entrench such static images. As Dave De Brou and Aileen C. Moffatt suggest, Canadian women's history has been characterized by "three historiographical stages," the first of which was the "celebration" stage, wherein the heroics of individual, exceptional women's achievements were recognized; the second of which was the "exploitation" stage, wherein the collective and universal nature of women's victimization was averred (3–4). But De Brou and Moffatt recognize a third stage in Canadian women's historiography, being that which promotes women as "active agents" and rejects the "women as heroines/victims" model as too "limiting" (4–5). In this stage, scholars seek to discover the ways that women "resisted, devised strategies and accomplished much on their own terms" (5). One of the ways in which feminist historians have attempted to get past the false front of the Prairie Woman image is to utilize some previously ignored sources of information about settlement life, such as memoirs, diaries, letters – sources which help us to confront those images which effectively deny the actual physical/emotional presence of women on the prairie landscape and which help us to re-vision mainstream historical narratives. Indeed, it would seem imperative to use these sources, precisely because so many of them were produced prior to or simultaneous with the feminist revolution of historical scholarship in Canada in the 1970s, and thus they represent an early non-academic attempt to insert women's voices into the gender gap of western Canadian history. Sometimes the voices of white, English-speaking women illustrate narrative adherence to official versions of

---

of prairie women's lives to date, refer to those works noted in Chapter One of this study.

prairie history, but we must also be willing to look for those "undercurrents" of "confrontation" lurking beneath the surface conformity of their texts. While it is certainly true that these women, in the general performance of their domestic responsibilities (including motherhood) were ultimately complicit with the nationalist/imperialist project, it also needs to be recognized that, through their memoir focus upon individual experiences, they allow us the possibility to re-vision key elements of the traditional story of western settlement. Specifically, they allow us to re-vision our focus from the ideological *space* of the Canadian prairies as it was constituted in the heroic and masculinist narratives of western settlement to the specific *place* in which the individual settler woman experienced the daily and not always optimistic reality of life on the Canadian prairies.

Western settlement was dominated by the optimistic ideology of "future plenty and success," an oft-repeated rhetorical credo that underpinned the nationalist/imperialist expectations discussed earlier and that was taken up as an article of faith to be repeated during good times and, most importantly, bad times. The "North West of the expansionist was that of the future" (Owram, *Promise of Eden* 192), as illustrated in the following account given by the Countess of Aberdeen regarding the arrival of Scottish settlers to Manitoba in the late 1880s:

> But the spirit of the country soon fell upon them; there was work and hope in the atmosphere; by the second year actual crops gave earnest for the future, and by the third, with its excellent harvest, indolence and grumbling had been completely pushed aside and forgotten, in habits of hard work and confidence in a future of plenty and success. (105)

The very "atmosphere" of the Canadian west was suffused with the element of "hope"; the very ground in which crops were grown was suffused with the elements of "earnestness" and "confidence" for a better way of life.[14] The use

---

14   Literary characters in prairie fiction certainly felt this "spirit of the country," as seen in Frederick Philip Grove's *Fruits of the Earth* (1933): arriving in Manitoba in 1900,

of such keywords as "plenty and success" most often denote expectations of material gain, as seen in a 1903 "cartoon book published by the Department of the Interior" to promote immigration to Canada, a book that suggests that potential settlers from the United States were coming to a land "where the crops show large and profitable yields" (qtd. in Bruce 61). At the very beginning of a memoir titled *Upon a Sagebrush Harp* (1969), Nell Wilson Parsons provides a poem titled "Fulfillment" that combines the optimism and economic potential inherent in the earth:

> Listen, in the twilight
> When winds sink to a sigh;
> The murmurs of wealth from golden fields
> Where precious wheat stands high.
> The settler felt the promise,
> Huddled beneath his tattered tarp,
> Hearing siren wind-music
> Strummed upon a sagebrush harp.

This kind of idealization of prairie potential is also reflected in Winnie E. Hutton's memoir titled *No "Coppers" in Saskatchewan!* (1973), which documents her family's move from (ironically) "the Village of Eden" in the "County of Elgin in Ontario" (3) and which also begins with a decidedly critical tone:

> In our family there had long been talk of going to the North
> West. Brochures we received used flowery language to tell of the
> "Wonderful West" which was opening up. There were photos
> of nice homes being built after only a short time, giving the

---

Abe Spalding chooses his homestead carefully, motivated in part by the fact that "with his mind's eye he looked upon the district from a point in time twenty years later; and he seemed to see a prosperous settlement there" (16). Similarly, in Sinclair Ross's short story, "The Lamp at Noon," Paul realizes that, in contrast to the experience of his wife, "so vivid was the future of his planning, so real and constant, that often the actual present was but half felt, but half endured. Its difficulties were lessened by a confidence in what lay beyond them" (20).

impression that we would be rich in a few years. They never mentioned the words drought, frost or hail. (1)

That most settlers believed (in varying degrees) in what they saw and read is suggested in the fact that "virtually all [homesteading] accounts emphasize economic opportunity" (Bennett and Kohl 48) as a primary motivation for settlement upon the Canadian prairies. In *Gully Farm: A Story of Homesteading on the Canadian Prairies* (1955), Mary Hiemstra suggests of the Barr colonists who emigrated to Saskatchewan that "the trip was hard but [the men] seemed to enjoy it, and most of them were still looking forward to the rich land they were going to find, and the fortunes they were going to make" (98).

Unfortunately, the narrative of "future plenty and success," after the harsh realities of prairie life had taken their toll, quickly became translated into the popular contemporary phrase used to describe the region as "Next Year Country."[15] When the women memoirists studied here bring up that phrase, they do so in a deliberately confrontational manner, for it is always clear to the reader that "next year" never comes. In *Upon a Sagebrush Harp*, Parsons speaks directly to the effect on women of the "Next Year" philosophy. Writing about her family's experience homesteading from 1907 near Lang, in south-eastern Saskatchewan, Parsons recognizes the painful reality for her mother Annie Wilson: "Looking back now I understand that Mama's life was a wait-ing period ... waiting for fall and harvest ... waiting for next year and a few small luxuries for the shack ... lace curtains, perhaps, and a dress length, and a rocking chair" (31). When the family's second crop proves "poor," Parsons's father says with philosophic optimism, "By next year we should begin to see daylight, start cleaning up on our debts" (98). In the third year, the author says, "There had been hail damage to our crop. The yield was poor," and her father's response is more predictable than the weather: "'Next year will be better,' Papa said. 'Hail can't hit us every year'" (110–11). As the author sums

---

15   As Barry Broadfoot defines it in *Next-Year Country: Voices of Prairie People* (1988): "I found the western farmer and his counterpart in the town to be optimistic. They are firm believers in next-year country, or, in other words, how can it get any worse?" (xii).

up about the "Next Year" philosophy, what she calls the "homesteader's will-
o-the-wisp!": "That was a pattern of prairie life ... windbreak ... firebreak ...
backbreak ... heartbreak. But a homesteader dreamt on. Oh, next year would
be great!" (127, 128). Not much had changed for Beulah Baldwin's family
homesteading in the Peace River country of Alberta in the 1920s: as she
writes in *The Long Trail* about the end of yet another harvest and her father's
decision to go away to help build a bridge as a means to "earn extra cash,"
"Always an optimist, Dad left with a smile and a reassurance that things
would be better in the spring. Mother was beginning to appreciate why they
called this 'next year country'" (207). Kathleen Strange also discovered the
devastating reality of the "Next Year" philosophy when farming near Fenn,
Alberta, in the 1920s. After a major hailstorm that ruins the family's entire
crop – along with some important personal plans of the author's – Strange
writes the following scene that oscillates between stoicism and anger:

> Yes, everything was gone, wiped out as if it had never been.
>
> "What can we do about it?" I asked despairingly, looking at my
> husband's tragic face with tears in my own eyes.
>
> "There is nothing to do," Harry said. "We just have to start
> all over again, I guess. I'm afraid, too, you won't be able to go to
> England – not this year, at any rate."
>
> "Of course not," I agreed, striving to keep the disappointment
> out of my voice. For I was bitterly disappointed. I had so looked
> forward to the trip and now, as on many other occasions, this
> country had crushed my hopes. I felt that I hated it. Sometimes
> I had imagined myself being drawn to it, but now it had thrust
> me away again. It was only by a great effort that I kept the bitter,
> resentful words that surged to my lips from escaping.
>
> Of course, I had to think of Harry. His disappointment, his
> misfortune, was so much greater than my own. Not only was he
> facing a complete loss of this year's income, but he was also facing
> the entire loss of four years' work. The careful, painstaking work of
> seed selection was ruthlessly undone. Right back to the beginning
> again for him.

There was a long silence between us, and then Harry said: "After all, this is a country of 'next years.' That's what we've got to remember. There's always next year and the promise of what next year will bring forth."

Next year! How sick I got of hearing those words. They are a common expression among all Western farmers. Yet perhaps it is because of it that he is able to carry on. Perhaps it is because of his eternal faith in the morrow that there is any West at all. (249–50).

While this passage ends with an optimistic tone and seems to reinforce faith in the very philosophy that frustrates her, as a reader I feel that Strange is ultimately being disingenuous. The scene as narrated illustrates her adherence to cultural norms of stoicism at the time of the hailstorm itself, but in the reminiscent act of writing/representing that scene she reveals that her seeming adherence belies an undercurrent of disappointment and anger. Most tellingly, we see the gap that exists between the image of the author here with "tears in my own eyes" and the title image, the positive image, of the memoir itself – *With the West in Her Eyes*.[16]

Judging from the relative lack of narrative attention paid by women memoirists to documenting agricultural-focused issues, female settlers were apparently unable, unwilling, or uninterested in subscribing wholeheartedly to this "monomaniacal concentration on the future at the expense of the present" (Friesen, *The Canadian* 313). Indeed, rather than adopting a narrative of "future plenty and success" that focuses almost exclusively upon agriculture and its economic remuneration, women memoirists devote more narrative space to the immediate, day to day, physical/psychological survival needs of the familial and local community as opposed to the larger national/imperial/masculinist ones. While men daydreamed about future prosperity, women settlers were of necessity engaged in a very different economy of need and production as they struggled to keep their families comfortable in what for some was a radically foreign environment. In her study of how women in Manitoba

---

16   For more examples of "next-year" philosophy, see also Bannert 67; Raber 37; Roberts 124; and Scott 9.

"disposed of their labour during the century from 1870–1970," Mary Kinnear uses John Stuart Mill's "definition of domestic economy" as a "useful starting point" in understanding women's daily lives: "Domestic economy, wrote Mill in 1844, was an art: the 'maxims of prudence for keeping the family regularly supplied with what its wants require, and securing, with any given amount of means, the greatest possible quantity of physical comfort and enjoyment'" (*A Female* 4). The prominent place that issues of domestic economy have in white, English-speaking, women's narratives of western settlement is inevitable given what is now widely understood to be the culturally sanctioned position of Anglo women of the nineteenth and early twentieth centuries within the middle-class ideology of "separate spheres." This ideology deemed woman's proper sphere of activity and influence as being the home place,[17] and the women memoirists studied here certainly, in large part, adhere to that spatial concept. Their attention to domestic detail can thus be read as complicity with the "civilizing" influence that white women were expected/constructed to bring to the western settlement project. As Sarah Carter asserts about contemporary cultural images,

> Both in the press and in the literature of colonial settlement, white women were projected as essential to the creation and reproduction of the community. They were cast as the moral and cultural custodians of the new community. Their influence was clearly to be seen in "brighter and better homes, a higher standard of morality, and the introduction of the refinements of life." (*Capturing* 6)

---

17   In an Anglo context the separate spheres ideology manifested itself in the "Angel in the House" image of wife/mother, while in an American context this idea gained expression as "The Cult of Domesticity." For further information regarding these gender constructs, see Chapter 11 of Joan Perkin's *Women and Marriage in Nineteenth-Century England* (Chicago: Lyceum, 1989), Barbara Welter's article "The Cult of True Womanhood: 1820–1860," in *American Quarterly* 18 (1966): 151–74, and, for a Canadian context, Chapter 6 of Alison Prentice, et al.'s *Canadian Women: A History* (Toronto: Harcourt Brace Jovanovich, 1988). For a complete discussion of the evolution of the image of "separate spheres," see Linda K. Kerber, "Separate Spheres, Female World, Woman's Place: The Rhetoric of Women's History," *Journal of American History* 75 (June 1988): 9–39.

On the other hand, it must be understood that cultural images of white women in western settlement were constructions, and that such images "bore scant resemblance to the real lives of the women" (10). In the detailing of the "domestic economy" of their sometimes quite meagre and usually quite isolated prairie homes, then, these memoirists often serve to undercut cultural images as much as to illustrate adherence to them. In addition, when we keep in mind the larger cultural focus of the prairie settlement project as tending to highlight agricultural production and expectations of monetary reward by male settlers, I would suggest that the women memoirists' attention to daily reality, including the immediate results of female labour that were necessary to survive (physically as well as psychologically) on the prairies, forces us to turn our collective attention inwards; to re-vision from the ideological space of the prairies to "the messiness of real life" (Ryden 37). They illustrate for us that humans cannot exist on mere faith in the future alone; that, "sooner or later, we pull our eyes away from the horizon and turn them to the dirt under our feet and the neighborhood which surrounds us."

One of the most immediate and important domestic issues for the white, English-speaking, female emigrant to the Canadian prairies is contained in the very word "Homestead" itself. This word that dominated the settlement process is a construct composed of two smaller words, very cleverly positioned in an order that conceals what was often the reality of settlement life in favour of a romantic image of domestic contentment. Despite the fact that "Home" comes first in this equation, the focus of the Homesteading project for most male settlers was upon the "stead" – defined as "property or estate in land; a farm" (*OEED*) – portion of prairie life. In both *Janey Canuck in the West* (1910) and *Open Trails* (1912), Emily Ferguson uses the word "stead" (or some derivative of it) frequently, often as a means to distinguish its meaning as a designation solely of land ownership.[18] Ferguson's contemporary, Elizabeth

---

18   For example, she says that

> these prairie steadings will never be homes in the best sense of the word
> till tree-planting prevails. Men will rape the soil and pass on, as all no-
> mads do, till they have planted trees and harvested them either in the
> form of boards, fuelling, or fruit. Then they become bound to the land;
> they set their stakes well and truly, deep and foursquare. (*Open* 170–71)

Mitchell, also advises her readers about the reality of homestead life when she delineates "what 'a homestead' is in North Saskatchewan – a quarter-square mile of grey-green prairie grass, with a tiny lake perhaps (a 'slough,' pronounced 'slew') and patches of small poplar wood. There may be no road, quite possibly no track, and no neighbours" (25). As Wilfrid Eggleston realistically puts it in his reminiscence of growing up on the prairies, "'Free Land' was, of course, the magnet which drew hundreds of thousands of immigrants to western Canada in the early years of this century" (340). Many of the women memoirists included in this study are acutely aware that, for their husbands and fathers, the true meaning of the word Homestead did, indeed, revolve around the acquisition of landholdings; that the word meant "free land, a quarter section, 160 acres of your choice," and "this was the heart of the matter … owning land was the triumph of it all" (Broadfoot, *Next-Year* ix–x). In Parsons's *Sagebrush*, for example, when her father relates his intention to "homestead" on the Canadian prairies, the then eight-year-old author asks, "What's homestead?," to which her mother knowingly responds, "Free land" (4). Writing about herself in the third person, Donnie M. Ebbers notes in *Land Across the Border* (1978) that, while her father's "conversion" to Baptism made him "less cranky and more considerate," nevertheless "his first consideration still seemed to be for the 'farm work.' Donnie had sometimes thought Papa's first and *only* love was for 'the land'" (94).

This cultural focus upon the "stead" portion of western settlement is reflected in the Dominion Lands Act of 1872. This policy deemed that "to secure their land, prospective homesteaders had to visit the nearest Dominion Lands office, choose their 160 acres, or quarter-section, and pay a ten-dollar registration fee" (Waiser 157). The requirements for "proving up," or taking clear title, or "patent," to one's landholdings, seemed to negate the ultimate importance of the "Home" value of western settlement, in that

> homesteaders had to meet certain basic requirements by the end of
> three years: they had to live on the land for six months each year,
> erect a shelter, and cultivate at least fifteen acres. Raising twenty

head of cattle and constructing a barn for the animals was an acceptable alternative. (158)[19]

The residence requirement, which in the original construction of the policy in 1871 was set at a period of five years, had been reduced to three by the time of the official Act, which already seems to minimize the idea of settled residence by making it feasible to fulfill the cultivation obligations of the federal govern-

---

19   As Susan Jackel clarifies in her discussion of the "homesteads-for-women movement" of the early-twentieth century, Section 9 of the Dominion Lands Act of 1872 inherently excluded most women – at least until 1930, when all three prairie provinces took control of their public lands – from taking up homesteads: it read that "'every person who is the sole head of a family' could apply to take up one hundred and sixty acres of homestead land in the surveyed portions of the west, subject to the usual conditions of entry fee, residence, and improvements. Furthermore, any male eighteen years of age or over was similarly entitled to apply" (Introduction xxi). Jackel notes that this left "three categories of women qualified to enter for homestead lands: widows, divorcées, and, in scrupulously documented cases, separated or deserted wives." In 1915, Mitchell felt optimistic about the "homesteads for women movement" on the prairies, a movement that she regarded as being of vital importance to the question of female equality at the level of individual experience: as she states,

> the most interesting suffragists are the prairie women. They have good minds, and they are accustomed to be serious, and they do think about these things, and so there is a very noticeable movement on the prairie, quite free from any exasperation at all, and quite likely, I think, to succeed soon, so far as the Legislatures of the prairie provinces are concerned.... The special trouble which has turned the prairie women's minds to politics is connected with the land. The woman so obviously shares with her husband in making the "improved farm" out of the 160 acres of original prairie that it is felt to be an injustice that this product of their joint labour becomes the sole property of the man, and that he *can*, if he chooses, sell it and break up the home without his wife's consent. (56)

For more on the subject of married women's property rights, see Sheila McManus, "Gender(ed) Tensions: Alberta Farm Women," in *Telling Tales: Essays in Western Women's History*, eds. Catherine A. Cavanaugh and Randi R. Warne (Vancouver: UBC Press, 2000), 123–46, and also Catherine A. Cavanaugh, "'No Place for a Woman': Engendering Western Canadian Settlement," in *The Prairie West as Promised Land*, eds. R. Douglas Francis and Chris Kitzan (Calgary: University of Calgary Press, 2007), 261–90.

ment without actually having to invest one's fulltime attentions to farming as a way of life. In addition, phrases such as "erect a shelter" also seem to minimize attention to "Home"steading, in favour of the cultivation of land, which was a difficult undertaking in and of itself.[20] Some time later, the idea of residence as a primary feature of "settlement" was reduced again:

> Up to 1884 at least six months' residence a year for three years (instead of five, as in the United States) was exacted before title could issue. In that year, however, the concern of both government and railway for settlement at any cost was such that even these meagre requirements were modified. Residence was waived, except for three months preceding the application for patent, while the entry could be "proved" by cultivation, building, or stock. (Martin 405)

This exclusivity of focus upon the agricultural potential of the region was also reflected in the less than stringent regulations of the "Dominion Lands" policy regarding the type of "shelter" required to be built upon the homestead site. Writing about his father, Wilfrid Eggleston states that, "in order to keep his claim alive he had to get down there within a few weeks to begin occupation, to build a residence, to fence it off, and make plans for cultivating part of it" (341). The language here is telling, as he uses the distinctly legal terms "occupation" and "residence" rather than relying upon more nuanced words, such as "living" and "home." Chester Martin quotes a contemporary observer who suggests that often "the 'habitable house' was a shack that could be put on a wagon and drawn any place, one shack would do duty for a dozen different applications for patent" (405–6). Indeed, when "residences" were built by male settlers, it was very often precisely their lack of "home"-iness which attracted the attention of contemporary writers such as Emily Ferguson, who wrote of the "newly-arrived homesteader" that "he is a queer fellow," not the least because "you may readily see that his ill-proportioned house is an after

---

20   As Bill Waiser notes, "two out of every five homestead applications in the three
     prairie provinces between 1871 and 1930 were cancelled; the failure rate actually
     climbed above 50 per cent during the last two decades of the program" (158).

consideration" (*Open* 133).[21] In addition to the rather rudimentary images of what "Home" need look like, the system of land survey chosen for the Canadian west promoted – assumed? – the eventual increase of the settler's landholding:

> If a settler homesteaded an even-numbered section, he would often find an odd-numbered section for sale next door when he wished to expand his operation. From 1872 to 1894, and again after 1908, the land regulations actually encouraged a settler to think in terms of a larger farm by permitting a 'pre-emption' to be filed.... Thus, the systems of pre-emption and sale reinforced the trend to larger farms by making these sale lands readily available to homesteaders. (Friesen, *The Canadian* 184)

This "trend to larger farms" is also present in the women's memoir texts studied here. In *Crocus and Meadowlark Country: A Story of an Alberta Family* (1963), for example, Georgina H. Thomson notes her father's taking advantage of the quarter-section land system when she says, "a few years later Father bought this [adjoining] quarter, which was C.P.R. land, and we called it 'Twin Butte Farm'" (58). Similarly, in *Pioneering in Alberta* (1951), Jessie Browne Raber notes that, after seven years of homesteading, her family's farm "was getting better and bigger. Dad bought a C.P.R. quarter section, next to our place and intended to raise cattle for market" (150).

While the acquisition and cultivation of land was prominent in the male settler's dream of immigration to the Canadian prairies, for many white, English-speaking women the "Home" was the more valuable side of the

---

21   At face value, the homesteading laws appeared to be more conducive to bachelor immigration to the Canadian West than the settlement of family units intent upon a farming lifestyle. Indeed, as a Department of the Interior pamphlet titled *Twentieth Century Canada* (1906) stated it, "Canada is a man's country, from the fact that all new countries first attract men, because the labour required for early settlement calls for that of man rather than that of woman. In Manitoba there are 21,717 and in Saskatchewan and Alberta 57,851 more males than females" (qtd. in Bruce 22).

"Homestead" coin.[22] In contrast to the male settler's future-oriented vision of the prairie, "for the women, the Garden depended upon its domestic possibilities, its ability to produce a comfortable home that would keep the family together" (Drake 126). While the privileging of domesticity is certainly an adherence to traditional Anglo constructions of appropriate femininity, nevertheless within the heroic and masculinist narrative of white western settlement the detailed documentation in women's memoirs of the expectation of, anxiety about, desire for, and disappointment in achieving a Home on the prairies is a re-visioning of an otherwise "stead"-centred project. This re-visioning begins with the very first glimpse of the new family home, a much-anticipated, although often disappointing, end to the long migratory journey. In a memoir about homesteading outside Carstairs, Alberta, from 1904, Clara Middleton expresses an unusually content reaction to her arrival at the homestead site: as written in *Green Fields Afar: Memories of Alberta Days* (1947):

> I remember thinking, home was never like this, yet I was not depressed. The week of worry and waiting was over. The boys were well again, the air was fresh and sweet, we had 160 acres of good land which would grow anything, and we knew how to work – and like it. So it was in a surge of cheerfulness that I saw beyond a shining slough a tent set on a rise above a little creek bed. (5)

However, several of the memoirists included here, many of whom were children at the time of emigration, explore the question of what exactly constitutes a "Home"-stead and thereby create a cultural-personal confrontation, often by clearly juxtaposing the different visions of fathers and mothers. If the Home

---

22   It is here interesting to note that, in a recent article by Bill Waiser on the construction of Saskatchewan as a "land of opportunity," when the author speaks to the attraction of promotional materials to prospective settlers, three out of four of the contemporary voices he provides are male (156). When he moves to the moment of arrival on the homestead site, the moment when the "hard reality of the situation started to sink in," however, two of the three voices he provides, the ones that take up the majority of the paragraph, are female (160).

2: SEEMINGLY TRIVIAL

is a sort of custodial centre in and from which white women could launch
their moralizing/civilizing influence, then by questioning what constitutes
an appropriate Home place these women would seem to expose the gap between cultural images and their real life experiences. After all, as part of the
promotional effort to bring male settlers and their wives to Canada, the nation was promoted as a "New Homeland," and a plethora of pamphlets were
produced with titles such as *Free homes in Manitoba and the Canadian North
West; New homes, free farms in Alberta and Saskatchewan, Western Canada*; and
The new settlements in Canada: homes for millions. Such pamphlets were often
accompanied by idyllic photos of already established farms, images that surely
led many hopeful immigrants to believe that physical manifestations of the
ideological construct of Home-land would already be present or be achieved
with little effort.[23]

Writing in *Pioneering in Alberta* about her childhood experience of immigration to a homestead near Lacombe, Alberta, in 1894, Jessie Raber is able
to use her temporal distance to construct a rather comic scene describing her
family's first view of their new Home:

> As we jogged along, we children were getting rather tired and
> restless, riding so long in such cramped conditions. Then, all at
> once, Daddy called out, 'There! There is our new home.' We got so
> excited, some of us nearly fell out [of the wagon], trying to stretch
> our necks to get a glimpse of our new home. And sure enough
> there it was. That is, Daddy said it was, but all we could see was a
> little white speck away off in the distance surrounded by green....
> We got nearer and could begin to see it really was a house. As we
> drove up to the door it didn't look much like the houses we had
> lived in before but it was to be our home. (27)

---

23   All of these titles are taken from promotional materials reproduced on the Peel
      Bibliography website at http://peel.library.ualberta.ca : *Free homes in Manitoba
      and the Canadian North West* (Winnipeg, s.n., 1886) (Peel #1566), *New homes, free
      farms in Alberta and Saskatchewan, Western Canada* (Winnipeg: Osler, Hammond &
      Nanton, 1893) (Peel #2100), and *The new settlements in Canada: homes for millions*
      (Canada: Government of Canada, 1898) (Peel #10537)

The excitement felt by the children and Mrs. Browne, who is subsumed as part of the arriving "We" in this scene, when the father makes his declaration, "'There is our new home,'" is palpable to the reader. However, the patriarchal authority suggested in the phrase, "Daddy said it was," is clearly undermined here by Raber's description of their "new home" as being "a white speck" and not "much like the houses we had lived in before."

By the time that Marjorie Wilkins Campbell gets to the end of the first chapter of her memoir *The Silent Song of Mary Eleanor* (1983), which represents her mother's sometimes arduous journey to the family homestead in the Qu'Appelle area of Saskatchewan in 1904, the sympathetic reader has become equally anxious as the settler woman to see Home – meaning that the reader is also perhaps equally disappointed by the "agonizing letdown" (24) of the end result. Campbell recreates her mother's and father's arrival as follows:

> It was not yet midday by her watch when he led them away from the rutted trail and its endless blanket stitching of telegraph poles. The sun burned her [Campbell's mother's] back and shoulders, and she longed for a parasol to protect herself and the children from its heat. Her arms ached from the weight of the heavy, whimpering baby. Too weary to regard it as more than a casual repetition of the gesture that usually signalled a stop, she saw father push back his hat. She could see no reason for a stop, and it was still too early for lunch. There was no house, no stable, nothing. To her amazement he halted the oxen, and his "Whoa, there" sounded like a paean of satisfaction and thanksgiving.
>   We were home. (21–22)

Campbell's sarcasm here – indeed, that small but heavily nuanced phrase "We were home" seems so incredibly vulnerable standing alone – highlights the difference between male and female viewpoints of what makes a Home, for Mary Eleanor's "amazement" at Mr. Wilkins's arrest of their journey suggests her lack of "satisfaction and thanksgiving" at what she actually sees versus how her husband names the empty piece of land. As Campbell begins the next chapter,

No typical lady of the day would lightly accept a long wearying journey behind a yoke of oxen that ended without a semblance of a house or an excuse for the omission, certainly not mother. Struggling to hold back the tears of fatigue and bewildered disappointment, she asked the simple, halting question that every pioneer woman under similar circumstances has asked.

"Is – is this it?"

"This is it. Welcome home! Down you get...."

But she did not move. Still struggling for words, almost in a whisper, she asked the next obvious question: How did he know this was home?

Again, as he had done at her immediate lack of approval for the equipage, he faced her, amazed at the dismay she could not disguise. This was the moment he had planned for for so long, the achievement that was all he had hoped for. Eager for her approval, anxious to reassure her, he reached into his vest pocket for his compass and the document stamped by the Department of Immigration, and he compared the two.

"North-west quarter Section 12, Township 25, Range 14, West 2nd Longitude ..."

Had she not noticed the surveyor's four holes and the marker? She had not, and if she had recognized the marker she would not then have realized that it constituted the sole means by which a settler identified the acres he had chosen or been alloted by the immigration authorities. (23)

While Campbell suggests that this reaction is "typical," thereby playing into universalized notions of what a Prairie Woman is/does, nevertheless the re-created scene of confrontation between mother and father highlights the facility of the memoir form for re-visioning cultural norms. Specifically, Campbell's mother enters into dialogue with her husband, questions his authority, on the matter of what exactly can be said to constitute a Home, and thereby questions cultural authority as well. When questioned, her husband immediately refers to two items that secure his sense of ownership in the "stead" portion of the

western settlement enterprise – the compass and the document – and begins to
read out and refer to the land survey system markers that identify the Wilkins
family as participating in a larger cultural movement/moment. Her mother's
reaction to this seeming evidence of arrival at the family homestead – she "had
not"/"would not" – negates the legitimacy of this vision of Home, so far as the
female emigrant is concerned.

In *With the West in Her Eyes*, Kathleen Strange aptly illustrates the discontinuity in men's and women's perceptions of "homesteading" life when she
describes her first glimpse of her new prairie dwelling:

> At the top of this hill the farm buildings stood. Before them the
> car stopped.
>
> My husband jumped out of the car, held out his hand to me,
> and cried: "We're home, dear!"
>
> Directly in front of me I saw a small wooden shack, unpainted
> and decidedly weather-beaten, with a door in the centre, and a
> single plain window at either end, one facing north and the other
> facing south.
>
> Outside the door was a large, square hole, spanned by a piece of
> board, across which one had to walk to enter the house. Into this
> hole had apparently been thrown an accumulation of rubbish. At
> first it seemed to me to be an extraordinarily unsanitary method of
> disposing of garbage, but I learned soon afterwards that the hole
> had been dug with the intention of making a cellar, over which
> the shack could be pulled. The digging, however, had never been
> completed and the idea had been discarded altogether when the
> owner had made up his mind to sell out.
>
> Behind the shack was a row of some five or six granaries – the
> small, portable wooden buildings which are used for holding
> threshed grain in the fall. They reminded me of a line of large
> sentry boxes.
>
> "What are they for?" I asked my husband.
>
> He smiled as he replied:
>
> "Those, my dear, are our bedrooms!" (19)

Despite her husband's exclamatory enthusiasm, Strange appeals to her reader's sympathetic response by stating, "it will surely be understood how difficult it was for me not to feel shocked and repelled at what I saw, particularly as it was in such striking contrast to the pleasant and congenial surroundings I had always enjoyed in my home in England and since coming to America" (20). The author here enunciates a common thread in many of the memoirs gathered here; that is, that the determination of what could appropriately be accepted as Home was largely based on an explicit comparison to what had been experienced prior to emigration to the Prairies. Clearly, for white English-speaking women, there was an expectation of "the importation of 'civilization' intact from the home they have left behind" (Floyd 4). For Strange, a "shack," and especially one that accumulates such descriptive words as "small," "unpainted," "weather-beaten," "plain," "rubbish," "unsanitary," and "discarded," cannot constitute a Home, at least in her culturally specific understanding of that word. Most importantly, Strange repudiates the equation of agricultural, or "stead," purpose with Home, as seen in her abhorrence of her husband's proposal that "the small, portable wooden buildings which are used for holding threshed grain" be used as bedrooms. For Strange, there can be no overlapping purpose to these buildings, especially if one intends to make an actual Home on the prairies. Indeed, she admits that, for their "predecessors," who "had been in the habit … of moving into the near-by town of Stettler for the winter months, and had consequently found the shack adequate for their simple needs during the working season," the shack may well have "become dear to them … since a home, however simple it may be, is treasured because of its associations." However, given that her "more extensive family" – two adults and three young boys – "intended to make the farm [their] permanent quarters the whole year round, the shack was altogether inadequate except as temporary shelter" (21–22). Strange invokes here the painfully conventional sentiment that says, "Home is where the heart is," which would seem to negate her concern for what her new domicile looks like, but then she rather deftly manages to assert the "inadequacy" of her husband's meagre vision compared to her own.[24]

---

24 For more examples of the settler woman's eager anticipation for a first glimpse of "home," see also Ebbers 30–31; Gilead 13; Hicks 6–7; Holmes 75–80; Inglis 23- 24; Parsons 18–19; and Thomson 19.

The fact that women's conception of Home so often did not immediately translate to the new space of the Canadian prairies was a potentially frightening prospect, given that "A woman's responsibility was for the comfort of her family. When her home did not permit her to extend that comfort, she would see herself as somehow failing" (Drake 132). Certainly, the loss of one's Old World home at the moment of emigration meant a potential loss of role and function: in effect, a traditional script remained in hand, but there was no longer a familiar stage upon which to perform. Speaking specifically of women settlers, although in the American context of the Overland Trail, John Mack Faragher suggests that "the loss of a sense of home – the inability to 'keep house' on the trail – was perhaps the hardest loss to bear, the thing that drove women closest to desperation" (170). As already noted, western settlement was conceived of as a "civilizing" project, and the women memoirists here seem to illustrate their participation in that project when they document anxiety about a lack of feeling "at Home." As Yi-Fu Tuan suggests, "the built environment clarifies social roles and relations. People know better who they are and how they ought to behave when the arena is humanly designed rather than nature's raw stage" (*Space* 102). While the prairie farmer tended to look at the "empty" landscape around him and eagerly anticipated – indeed, envisioned – "future plenty and success," thereby imaginatively eliding current reality, prairie women seem to have felt reality more intensely, more fearfully even, and they actively attempted to reconstruct the old in the new. We see this, for example, in *Gully Farm*, when Mary Hiemstra's mother finds herself on an isolated homestead in Saskatchewan in 1903 without a "proper" domestic space over which to preside. Feeling fearful about the lack of human presence on the vast prairie landscape, Mrs. Pinder reacts to her husband's enthusiasm as follows:

> ... "Just imagine! A hundred and sixty acres, and it's all ours."
> Mother looked at the wide sweep of land around us and sighed.
> "It's so big it frightens me," she said. "I could do with a hedge here
> and there, and walls dividing the fields the way it is in England.
> But all this land without even a cart-track! It's that lonely."

"There'll be plenty of roads soon, and people, too. Land like this won't be vacant long." Dad untied the horses, and holding a halter rope in each hand he led them to the nearby slough to drink. Between the big dark animals he looked very short and thin, but there was pride in his square shoulders, and exultation in his feet. Mother, always neat, put the tent in order. She hung a clean towel on a nail driven into the tent-pole, put the iron kettle on the back of the stove, and set the box that held the pans behind the stove out of the way, then she began to slice bacon for supper. (109).

The perspective is somewhat split here, with Hiemstra's father face-forward to the future, and her mother both looking back to "the way it is in England" and feeling intensely the lacking state of her present surroundings. Stuck between her loss of the old way and the disconcerting new landscape, we see Mrs. Pinder attempt to re-create "order" by foregrounding, within the very limited space provided to her, two of the main domestic responsibilities of the white, English-speaking lady: cleanliness and the feeding of her family. Home might be where the heart is, but it's also the place in which you have the security of knowing who you are so you can contend with where you are. As Elaine Lindgren writes in an American context regarding female homesteaders, "it would be a mistake to judge the adaptation of settlers to the plains by their initial reaction" (15). Indeed, Mrs. Pinder's seeming capitulation to convention does not necessarily indicate complete hostility towards participation in the new reality of the western settlement project; in fact, the backwards glance of settler women most often resulted in psychological preparation (a sort of shoring up) for the work needed to engage in the work of homesteading. As noted by Sheila McManus, "a desire to reproduce whatever sense of the home she had left behind also gave a woman a familiar base from which to face other challenges" (124). I would suggest that the initial desire to reconstitute Home on the prairies be read as partly ideological adherence and partly an empowering psychological response to a new environment.

The security of having some semblance of a Home place was important for the psychological comfort and security, not only of the prairie woman, but also of her family members, and especially the children, who would lend their contribution to the new life. For example, in *Land Across the Border*, a memoir of homesteading near Prince Albert, Saskatchewan, Donnie M. Ebbers writes about a house fire in which her family appears to lose everything and has to move temporarily into a less than ideal place:

> Several years before, Papa had built a one room log house with two small windows, half way between the house and the barn, in which to smoke meat. Though it was seldom used for smoking meat and became a sort of "catch-all store house" it was always called "the smoke-house." Papa and Joe went to work clearing out the tools and whatever else was stored there, cleaned it and set up a small old cook-stove in the north-east corner, built a bedstead of poles and scrap lumber against the west wall and a table in the middle of the room. That was to be "home" until Papa and the boys could get a new house built.
>
> Gertie helped with enough pots and pans for Mama to cook in, and before the middle of April Mama set up house-keeping in "the smoke-house."
>
> When Jackson and Ottie came home from the logging-camp they were shocked to find they had no home, at least there was no house there, and their bed-room would be in the granary for the summer, but Ottie said, "Well, home is where Mother is!" And "Mother" was there! Cooking the same good meals for them, even in the smoke-house, planting garden, and doing all she could with the little she had, to make her family comfortable and happy; as she had always done and would always do, no matter what happened. (82)

Ebbers seems to have considerable play with language in this passage, with "home" having both literal and emotional signification: the "smoke-house" is only re-created as "home" in a theoretical sense, at least until a new "house" is built; the author's brothers come "home" to find they have no "home," or at least not a "house"; in fact, "home" is still present in the person of the Mother, who can still perform all of the domestic tasks that make manifest the emotional security of being Home.

Sometimes the ill effects on a woman from a lack of domestic comfort and security could not be discerned until that same woman was displaced into a vastly different setting. In *The Maple Leaf for Quite a While* (1967), Heather Gilead writes about a 1960 trip she took with her octogenarian mother to Iowa to visit her mother's dying brother. On the way to the small town in which the brother lives, the two women stop and stay with an Aunt Minnie, who works as a housekeeper for a female doctor, whose home – described as "a substantial white frame house" (113) – is opened to them for the duration of their visit. As Gilead recognizes, her mother's movement to this new place elicits a different way of being than could ever have been achieved in the place provided for her family to live in on an Alberta homestead. Referring to the doctor's home, Gilead writes,

We set about the business of Making Ourselves at Home. Indeed my mother *was* at home. I have never seen anything like it, and it was not without poignancy. The doctor's house was spacious, correct, impeccable, comfortable even. Nothing ultra modern. It had no graces. Pictures and bric-à-brac, which might have brought the middling good furniture and curtains into line, brought instead the stale odour of air-conditioned department store "galleries." Comfort and decency were necessities, but aesthetics suspect. But it was a much better house than anything my mother had ever had, or could have aspired to even in her moments of extreme optimism on those prairies where so large a fraction of all effort went into just keeping warm seven months of the year. However briefly, my mother simply appropriated this house, revelled in it, assuming a formality and gentility of which I had indeed seen flickerings upon occasion, but which I had never before seen effortlessly sustained. As the days went by in that house I became more and more convinced that given easier circumstances my mother would probably have been infinitely easier to live with; that the thorns and jagged edges with which she seemed to have become afflicted over the

years were largely barnacle growths – foreign bodies settled upon
her from the environment, rather than emanations from herself.
She did not appear to pay much attention to what went on around
her in the house. She just settled herself somewhere, passive and
beatific, radiating a contentment which was pathetic by its rarity.
(114–15)

The doctor's house is not tasteful, in the author's assessment. Nevertheless,
the words "comfort and decency" loom large as something absent from her
mother's experience of prairie life on a homestead "some seventy miles from
Red Deer as the crow flies" (11). Earlier in the memoir, Gilead describes the
"Home" her mother first came to in Canada from the United States: "The
curtainless windows, the walls innocent of paint or paper, the coarse grey
blankets (some of which were still extant as saddle blankets in my day), the
splintery wooden floors, bare even of linoleum and so cold that the tracked-in
snow would just lie there, unmelting" (14). In her childhood, Gilead took a
negative view of her mother, whose "thorns and jagged edges" seemed such a
contrast to her steadfast father's presence, but in this reflective moment, seeing
her mother in a very different domestic environment, the author is able to
acknowledge how intimately "Home" affects a woman's emotional well-being.

The "thorns and jagged edges" which "afflicted" Gilead's mother stem not
simply from the lack of comfort in the family home, but also from another
side effect of the "future plenty and success" narrative that dominated western
settlement. Indeed, it has become almost a cliché to say that many prairie
women had to wait sometimes interminably for their husbands to turn their
attention away from the needs of the "stead" and towards the construction of
a more substantial home than was initially provided on arrival at the family
property. Most immigrants to the prairies arrived believing that taking up a
homestead meant establishing one's roots in the new country – settling down
on the landscape, agriculturally and domestically. However, a constant complaint on the part of white, English-speaking prairie women was the constant
deferral of settled domestic arrangements. Certainly, this waiting game is well
documented in prairie fiction: in Frederick Philip Grove's *Fruits of the Earth*
(1933), for example, the reader learns that Abe Spalding's "increased acreage

demanded an ever-rising investment in implements; and [his wife] Ruth was
plainly getting impatient about the house" (38). After threshing his first phenomenal profit, Abe finally turns his attention to the new house to be built,
realizing that "it was meant as a consolation; as conveying a sense of his own
shortcomings; he was sorry that he had left Ruth in such surroundings for so
long. He had been an unconscionable time in fulfilling his promise. After all,
she had had to live in the place; to him, it had been just a lair to go to at night"
(110). In the memoirs written by prairie wives and mothers, and also those
written by prairie daughters/grand-daughters, we do not often get to see the
regret felt by husbands who failed, for whatever reason, to provide the comfort
and security of a "proper" Home. What we do get is an enunciation of either
the joy felt by women who were so provided – even if to a lesser degree than
what was hoped for – or, more commonly and overwhelmingly, the frustration
of those women who learned to live with the lack. In Gilead's text, the author
makes the following acknowledgment of the gap between domestic idyll and
reality:

> Within a few years two tiny houses which had belonged to departed
> pioneers were hauled up and tacked on to the existing three rooms.
> These, which were roofed with tarpaper, would become sieves in a
> matter of minutes during a brisk hailstorm. It was as well that we
> lived in a sort of narrow corridor between two hail-prone belts, for
> although my father always had a vague intention of putting cedar
> shingles on those roofs in place of the tarpaper, nothing came of
> it. Indeed for a considerable time he intended, I believe, to build
> a new house for my mother. When I was very small there was
> still a book of potted house plans lying around, but I think she
> was already communing with it more as the reliquary of deceased
> dreams than as imminent possibility, for 1929 was already past and
> Hard Times were upon us. I know that her choice had fallen upon
> one with dormer windows upstairs, and a dining-room separate
> from the kitchen, and with a proper basement in which a furnace,
> to heat the whole of the house, could have been installed.

In 1911 she had probably accepted cheerfully enough all those temporary discomforts, inconveniences and compromise solutions. Forty-five years and seven children later they were still there, grown into her world. (14)

It is painfully inevitable to see Gilead's mother, inhabited in a dwelling that literally reflects/incorporates the false bottom (for so many prairie families) of the "future plenty and success" narrative, have to confront on a daily basis the passing of her dream for domestic comfort. I cannot help but read a change in Gilead's tone when she moves in this passage from her somewhat equivocal "belief" about her father's good "intentions" to provide something better for his wife to her much firmer "knowledge" about her mother's solid and hopeful "choice" of what constituted Home. With her final two small sentences, the daughter-author seems to confront the image of the Prairie Woman as "cheerful helpmate" when she highlights her mother's conformity to idealized gender roles – she does, after all, exist "cheerfully enough" at the beginning, despite the negatives – and then exposes the painful reality behind that image when she so heavily stresses her mother's endurance of a less than utopian reality through "forty-five years and seven children."

When Barbara (Hunter) Anderson and her family arrived in the Saskatchewan Valley in July of 1883, the setting seemed to auger well for the family's comfort and security, as seen in *Two White Oxen: A Perspective of Early Saskatoon 1874–1905* (1972) when the author represents the end point of their journey:

> ... The sun was at our backs, a little to the right-hand side and the mist was rolling up from the valley below. It seemed to stand like a wall behind us, shutting out all our past, and before us a beautiful green valley dotted over with sparkling sloughs, full of water in which myriads of ducks and some geese could be seen. Away in the distance we could see the banks of the South Saskatchewan River winding away to the further north. Two little squares of bright green were the growing grain, growing on each of the five acres broken on our homesteads according to homestead regulations. (27)

On the "stead" side of things, all was well for the Hunter families (the author's aunt and uncle were also homesteading). However, in the next chapter – ironically titled "Home" – Anderson begins the much more arduous journey towards achieving a comfortable Home. Their first home would be less than ideal: "Father pointed out to me our home by the one little square of lighter green. There was a black spot and two white tents by it" (29). The "black spot," it turns out, was a shed, which had been made out of "the lumber intended for the floor of our new house." As we learn elsewhere, the Hunter families had emigrated as part of the Temperance Colonization Society,[25] an organization that was supposed to provide homes, "but the lumber did not arrive until November [of 1883] and it was wet and icy when unloaded from the scows" (30), and thus was not immediately useable for the building of a proper Home.

It was quickly determined that tent life was not feasible to endure a Saskatchewan winter: writes Anderson, "the first frosts came on the fourth of September," which made for a "very chilly" time. By October, Mr. Hunter was busy providing a domestic improvement common on the Canadian prairies for settlers from a variety of class and cultural backgrounds – a "sod house":

> Mother and we children had started digging, while Father was away, and he soon made a good sized cellar of the hole where we had started to work. Next he set posts in the ground and put a long plate on them, mortised, to hold them in place and we started sod walls under these plates, in a straight row. Three feet thick at the base. Twelve by twenty-four feet was the size of the room. Walls were seven feet high and tapered to two feet six inches at the top.

---

25   Dawson and Younge quote Robert England's *The Colonization of Western Canada* (London: 1936) regarding the origins of the Temperance Colonization Society, which was formed in 1882

> at Ottawa chiefly by capitalists and prominent prospective settlers from Toronto, Hamilton, and the surrounding country. This company purchased from the Dominion Government several townships, comprising one million acres, for one dollar per acre. Saskatoon became the central point, or capital, of this block of land. (13)

> One door and two windows were next put in place and sods built
> closely around them. (30)

There's something so delightfully ironic about a home built from the very
ground that underlay the utopian dream of western settlement; an immediate
and practical survival tactic that had nothing whatsoever to do with dreams of
"future plenty and success." Although we never hear what the author's mother
thinks of her family having moved away from Cayuga, Ontario, to live in a
house made of prairie sod, certainly Anderson herself remains philosophical:

> ... true the sod walls were rather dark and unattractive, but after
> living in a tent for five months who would not welcome even a sod
> house. This one was better than some in that it had two double-
> sash windows and a real door with knob and lock like real houses
> had, and the windows could be opened by raising the lower sash,
> and there were such nice broad window sills for the sod wall was
> three fee[t] thick at the base. The floor was better, too, than most
> sod houses for it was covered with lumber, not just the ground, and
> a real cellar was under the floor that would make more room, but
> even then it would be a very small residence for seven people to live
> and work in. Altogether it was a wonderful new house and we were
> all so thankful to be able to move in. (34)

It is important to note that Anderson's appreciative tone is comparative here –
to what they lived in before and to the state of "most sod houses" – but there is
no doubt that the new house represents an attempt to re-create a more permanent and proper sense of what Home means, an attempt that is celebrated by
the Hunter family in an evening "concert, or 'house warming'" (34).

Nevertheless, the sod house was not the end of the domestic journey, for
Anderson, like so many of the memoirists gathered here, spends a great deal
of narrative space documenting her family's Home un-settlement. About six
years after they arrived at that first homestead site, the family moved once
again: in the spring of 1889, says Anderson, "My father was entitled to a
second homestead, having completed his duties on the first in the allotted

time. So he took his second six miles north of his first – 4/38/4. The first
was on 4/37/4, as it was on the river, and would be near water for the stock at
least" (105). In terms of landholdings, this event was a step forward; however,
in terms of living standards, it was most decidedly a step back. As the author
acknowledges,

> The moving and work to get settled there, took all summer. First,
> the corral to keep the stock in; the tent house to live in; there was
> the milk house and pigs' pens to build; then haying. There was
> plenty of grass to cut but so far to haul it, and when the weather
> began to grow cold, we had to build a piece on the milk house to
> live in, as there was not time to build a house, though we had a lot
> of logs ready. Then there was the stable – a poor affair – but we got
> by the first two years on the new homestead, and got at building
> our new log house.

Finally, in "the summer of 1891," with Anderson and her sister Jennie helping,
the family built and moved into their new log house. At the time of building,
however, Mr. Hunter was quite ill, so that, "when finished, it was a comfortable
place, but not as it would have been had [he] been well enough to carry out their
plans" (154) for a real Home.

Clearly a major factor in the comfort and security of a prairie home had
to do with "a sense of permanency" (Langford, "First Generation" 95). After
what was usually an extended journey to the Canadian west, and given the
magnitude of what had been left behind in one's country of origin, taking up
residence in one single place was needed for an abiding sense of settlement. As
with the contentious first sightings of the Homestead site and the sometimes
rather rudimentary versions of Home detailed above, some memoirists' documentation of the often arduous journey to obtain a permanent Home seems
to actively repudiate the western settlement propaganda materials that not
only promised almost instant agricultural success, but also the fixed and stable
"New Homeland" image referred to earlier in this chapter. For Jessie Browne
Raber's mother, getting a home built is not the difficult task, but rather getting to stay in one for longer than a few months. The Browne family arrive at

their first homestead site near Lacombe, Alberta, in the summer of 1894 and move immediately into their new wood board house, then they build a log house before winter sets in, only to end up moving into the home of a bachelor Englishman, Mr. Folger, who "was to leave and spend the winter in England" (73). The author describes this dwelling in idealistic terms:

> Well, we were all in our new home at last. It was such a pretty place. We could see for miles to the south. The view was beautiful with hills, valleys, trees and fields of grain, which the farmers were cutting as fast as possible for winter was nearing now. Some fields were yellow with the stubble, and dotted with cattle and horses picking up what was left. In the back and west side were woods, but all the underbrush had been cleaned out, which made it look clean. Barns were filled with hay and grain. It was a well sheltered place, so the wind didn't get such a sweep onto us. We all felt at home, as we had visited up there many times. (74)

Despite feeling "at home" in this Home, only pages later Raber notes that yet another move is in the works:

> When we moved up to this place of Mr. Folger's, Dad's intentions were to stay there, pay, in time, for the improvements and raise more cattle. He and Mother talked it over for months, but decided it was too far from school. But Dad had found a nice quarter section, if he could get it, where we could move again to a permanent home. We were rather sorry to hear all this in a way. This was such a pretty place. This new place would be only eight miles from town and one and a half or two miles from the school. (79)

While registering some degree of disappointment over moving to "this new place," the author nevertheless takes the philosophical approach and ends this section of her narrative with a stress on the positive aspects of the move, a fairly typical approach to difficult subjects by the memoirists studied here.

A few pages later, though, an indication of Raber's true feelings about the family's new move breaks the surface narrative of childhood nostalgia:

> Daddy had planned with Mr. Folger to live at this place, make our home here. So we children had planned out what flowers we would plant in the spring, as we liked to live here. Dad changed all our plans when he said we would be moving in early spring. So Dad, Billy and Jack were very busy, going over to this new place, finding the lines and then had to go to Red Deer to file on it. Then the house would be built, and things started for our permanent home at last. (82–83)

The tone here is not excessively critical, but clearly there is frustration over the degree of unsettlement experienced by the author's family. The sense of relief is palpable when, almost three full years after their arrival in Alberta, the Browne family finally appear to have found their place:

> April 15th, 1897, we moved onto our new farm, which was to be a real farm now. It was a warm day and we were all excited, all anxious to see the new home, but it was nearly dark when we arrived so there was no chance to see much. It was some job, even if we didn't have much furniture, getting supper, finding places to sit, then fixing beds for the night. We all slept on the floor that night. Even at that, we had a rather contented feeling, being in our own home. (88)

For Annie Keyes's mother, Anna Schultz, the wait for a stable home is seemingly interminable. In July of 1905, the author's father, whose own family had moved from South Dakota to Saskatchewan in 1901, filed for his own homestead, which was "situated across the North Saskatchewan River...south west of the Petrofka Ferry ... now the Petrofka Bridge" (9). Just over a year later, he married a woman from South Dakota and brought her to Canada to live permanently. As the author imagines in her "Forward [*sic*]" to a memoir titled *Down Memory Trails with Jip* (1972), "I am sure their hearts were full of joy … full of dreams for their future together when they moved to their Homestead. A home and land all their own." From that moment on, however, Keyes documents a series of impractical decisions made by her father, for whom homesteading appeared to centre upon migratory agricultural activities as opposed to the creation of a settled home life. For example, only one page after describing her family's first and rather rudimentary home on the prairies, Keyes ends her first chapter by advising the reader that "Father got an offer, to trade his homestead for a Steam Threshing Outfit, which he did" (11), then begins her next chapter saying, "Now they were without a home" (12). This inauspicious beginning is followed by a seemingly endless state of flux: as Keyes notes, "Living in rented homes now, we had to move quite often" (13). Added to the lack of a constant sense of Home is the fact that the author's father is often "away working, threshing, doing custom work for other farmers." At one point early on, the author reveals that her father's gamble on engaging in agricultural work rather than homesteading is to the detriment of any possibility of settlement for his family:

> Father had made a down payment on this farm. As it happened the steam threshing outfit father got in trade for his homestead had a lot of breakdowns. So that he could not earn enough money to make another payment on the place and THE OWNER FORECLOSED. They lost the place and were forced to move again. (14)

After this loss, there begins for the family a migratory cycle that reminds one of the biblical exodus. After four failed moves, the last of which sees the family living in a granary rather than stay in a house full of bed-bugs, the Schultz family finds itself completely unsettled:

> When fall was drawing closer we knew we could not stay in that granary, and we surely did not feel like moving in with those bed-bugs again. Father was buying a Steam Threshing Outfit from Mr. Ed Ewert who lived between Lockwood and Drake, Sask. With his earnings there, father was paying for the outfit. He had

threshed in Drake area in the fall of 1915. So in the fall of 1916, after the summer in the granary, he decided to take his family along. (24)

Preparation for the trip is "flurried" and, despite the author's childhood joy at the prospect of "camping out" in October, she is well aware that "for mother this was quite an ordeal" (24).

After the threshing season is over and the family are "on [their] way home" (to no home, really) Keyes provides a narrative contrast between the domestic ideal experienced by some homesteaders and the cold reality of a night camping out on the late fall landscape:

> Having made camp for the night close to a small lake one evening. It was getting dark before they found this place. Arnold the baby, about 18 months old did not like this camping life much, he sure cried that evening. Mother was trying to get things organized to make supper – while the men tended to the chores of the horses. Mother must have been tired from the days journey, then trying to cope with the crying baby, while getting the meal ready. For I'm sure we were all very hungry by that time. All of a sudden, we saw two people coming towards us through the bush carrying a lantern. It was the mother and her grown up daughter from a farm home just beyond the bush. They had heard the baby cry. They insisted that mother bring the children to their house. I was a little past nine years old. I do remember, that we walked to their home, into the kitchen where the lamp was lit. I have a shimmering recollection of their kitchen, but I cannot remember now whether they gave us some supper and bedded us for the night, or whether mother looked after Arnold and fed him … and that then we went back to our wagon for the night? (26)

As a reader of Keyes's text, I cannot help but be disappointed by the memory gap that occurs about what happens for her family that night, but nevertheless it seems significant that it is two women who emerge from the bush to provide the author's mother and her children with a safe and warm haven, a "shimmering recollection" of what Home should be like – what the author's father can't/won't seem to provide – centred within the domestic space of the kitchen. But the sanctuary is only temporary and the homelessness continues for several more years. As the author states, her "parents were so anxious to get a home of their own again, so we would not always have to move at a moments notice. Mother was so tired of that" (34). Here I see strategic significance in the move from saying her parents are together "anxious" to achieve a stable Home, to the stress on her mother's emotional condition. Finally, sixteen years after Mr. Schultz filed on his original homestead, in the spring of 1921, the author's family found itself renting a farm situated "close to the river, east and north from the Petrofka ferry crossing" – a return back to origins accompanied by a very modified optimism: "We had a hard beginning here. First of all, the house was so very dirty. Mother and I soaked and scrubbed and disinfected the rooms, before they were fit to live in. It was in poor condition. Some of the inner walls only had lath over the studding. In time we could make improvements, and it was quite comfortable" (39–40).[26]

The mere building of a home or the making of "improvements," however, did not guarantee physical or psychological comfort for, "in general, houses are not designed by women.... As a result there is frequently a poor fit between the needs of women and the design of houses. Women must often adapt their behaviour to fit the environment or suffer the costs of 'making do' in a space that makes their work difficult to carry out" (Wekerle et al. 11). As Eileen M. Scott writes in *Porridge and Old Clothes* (1982), a memoir of homesteading life in Manitoba in the late-nineteenth/early-twentieth centuries, her newly wed mother, Jeannie Henderson Thomson Scott, "had designed a step-saving bungalow during her short stay at the Winnipeg Agricultural College, which she dearly wished to have built. However, her father [the author's grandfather] and Ed Gray [a builder] thought they knew best, built a two-storey house

---

26   For more examples of the sometimes interminable wait for a proper home, see also Baldwin 187–89; Campbell 29–31; Ebbers *passim*; Hewson *passim*; Magill 4–9; Parsons 29; Roberts *passim*; Schultz 61–62, 103; Strange 133; and Thomson 222–23, 274.

with a very inconvenient plan" (19). In most women's memoirs, the major issue regarding home construction has to do with a lack of space and, hence, a lack of privacy. In *No "Coppers" in Saskatchewan!* (1973), a memoir of her homesteading childhood in the Strongfield district of Saskatchewan in 1908, Winnie E. Hutton provides a rather extraordinary – although probably not completely unusual – illustration of how the needs of the agricultural side of the Homestead coin could come into spatial conflict with the privacy needs of women:

> When harvest time arrived I was asked to help Mrs. Kennedy with the feeding of the threshers. The day arrived and Mr. Kennedy came to get me. The threshers were expected for the noon meal and I found every thing pretty well ready. The roast in the oven, vegetables pared, and the long table was set for twenty or more men. That did not leave much room around the outside as it was a typical homesteaders' house, with two small bedrooms roughly partitioned off at one end. My heart missed a beat tho, when I found Mrs. Kennedy in bed with labor pains. Dr. Monkman who had recently come to the country and practiced for a short time in the new town of Hawarden, before settling permanently in Loreburn, was sent for, but did not arrive in time. Here was Mr. Kennedy and myself, who was as green as grass about such matters and scared stiff as well to welcome this new arrival, a little girl who brought a sister along, so here on October 15th, 1908 the first twins were born at Strongfield. Shortly after, Grandpa Kennedy arrived with a dear old lady, Mrs. Taylor, who took over and let me get back to the dinner. (23)

Such an amazing overlap of interests in a farming situation: one of the most vital of agricultural moments (threshing days) and one of the most vital days for the civilizing project of western settlement (childbirth). In the description of this scene, Hutton makes her reader aware of the incredible vulnerability of prairie women who found themselves giving birth in less than safe or comfortable conditions.[27] But also, in the juxtaposition of male and female labouring in this scene, we see that the female need for domestic privacy is treated as a relatively minor interruption within the larger cultural pattern. The imperative of getting "back to the dinner" becomes most important as the end to this scene plays out as follows:

> The threshers had almost been forgotten in the confusion. Messages had been sent from time to time, to try to keep on threshing as there was a birth taking place in the house and it was not convenient to have the men in then. It was past noon, the men were hungry so finally some of them set their pitch forks in the ground and said, "We have to eat." The thresher came knocking at the door and asked if it was all right to come in for dinner now. It was, so I got the first meal over. There was lunch in the afternoon and supper at night, to look after, and then tomorrow. (24)

Kathleen Strange also relates the less than ideal spatial conditions of childbirth for some prairie women in a chapter purporting to be concerned with paying "tribute" to "the splendid examples of unconscious heroism and courage that go unremarked, unrewarded and unsung" in relation to "the figure of the Canadian country doctor":

> Many farm homes on the prairies are poorly equipped; even the best of them are seldom equipped for the emergency of sickness. The general lack of electricity, running water, and even adequate space, are some of the difficulties with which he has to cope practically all the time.

---

27   For a detailed discussion of the experience of childbirth for prairie women, see Nanci L. Langford's "Childbirth on the Canadian Prairies, 1880–1930," in *Telling Tales: Essays in Western Women's History*, eds. Catherine A. Cavanaugh and Randi R. Warne (Vancouver: UBC Press, 2000, 147–73). For a memoir example of the sometimes frightening realities of childbirth in homesteading conditions, see Middleton 48–51.

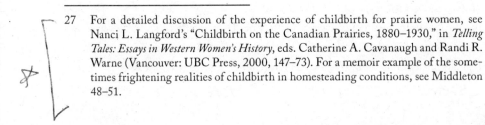

I myself was once in a home where there was but one single room, and in this room, in the middle of winter, and in the presence of several other children, a woman was delivered of a baby. It was too cold to send the little ones outside, so they were herded into a corner, as far away from the scene of the birth as possible. There I attempted to hold their attention while the doctor and the woman's husband ministered to her.

The large double bed sagged so badly in the middle that the doctor found it impossible to continue his work properly. Ignoring the husband's protests, he finally had the patient moved onto the kitchen table, where, after an hour or so, she was finally successfully delivered of a husky male child. All her other children, by the way, had been born without the services of either a doctor or a nurse. Two days following this birth, against the doctor's orders, the mother was up and about again. Apparently she suffered no ill effects, either. (175–76)

Although we are ostensibly meant to be focused on the difficult working conditions of the country doctor, nevertheless I cannot but read this passage more for its documentation (confrontational or not) of the incredible gap that exists between the grandiose construct of white women as "reproducers" of British culture (it should be noted that the woman's cultural background is not specified) with the actual and often deplorable conditions in which many women had to literally perform this role. While Strange herself may have attended hospitals for the birth of her children, and thus inhabited a fairly privileged version of the reproductive role, I would suggest that, especially in the litany of amenities lacking in the home at the start of the narrative – the characterization of the "several other children" as being "herded" like animals, the husband's "protests" against the doctor's intervention in the state of affairs, and the wife's rejection of the doctor's order to stay in bed post-partum (a female brand of heroism? or the necessary reality of being a farm wife?) – there exists an "undercurrent" of accusation against a reality that so often precludes respect for, or sharing of, women's labouring.

Lack of space and privacy was not just a concern in the event of childbirth, as there were other, more regular, needs of the female body that had to be met despite the cramped lifestyle, as seen in Marjorie Campbell's memoir *The Silent Song*. Writing about her uncle Leo's and her father's occasional day-long trips "to the Touchwood Hills for pine and other hardwood to burn," the author notes that the absence of men about the homestead provided her mother with the space to attend to certain personal details of female life:

> Most of all during the first winter, she welcomed those relatively few hours that were so comforting to her sense of modesty, the opportunity to wash and dry the neatly hemmed squares of winceyette on which many women depended before the emergence of commercially available sanitary napkins. That feminine chore had been one of her most embarrassing problems ever since the arrival of father's young brother, and even of living in such close quarters with her husband. (39)

As a woman writing the sometimes intimate story of another woman, Campbell has an amazing capacity for understanding/imagining her mother's need for privacy. Indeed, she finishes the above scene saying, "Above all, she welcomed each monthly reminder that she had escaped a pregnancy she dreaded under their present circumstances."

Sometimes married couples and their families were accompanied in the journey westward by other travellers, and the presence of other men could cause issues for prairie women, issues having to do with limited space and limited privacy. For example, despite the fact that Clara Middleton expresses contentment in *Green Fields Afar* about living in a tent when she arrives at her and her husband's homestead site in Alberta in 1904, there are adjustments that need to be made to an originally masculine space:

> While the boys were unhitching I made an inspection. Here was a bell tent, such as the soldiers at home used on Carling Heights, supposed to accommodate eight men, at a pinch. The range had been put up, half in and half out, with the pipe sticking up crazily

and far enough away from the canvas. A double-bed mattress was supported on a rough frame of two-by-fours and our red couch stood about two feet from it, on the other side of the main pole. I dragged a piece of carpet out of one of the packing cases and pinned it up, separating the bed and the couch. So we had a two-room apartment, suitable for any married couple, with an understanding brother-in-law. And there we slept the sleep of the just and the weary while awaiting the building of a proper house. And the blessed sun shone every day. (5–6)

In *The Long Trail*, Beulah Baldwin offers up a humorous account of the effects of a lack of space/privacy in prairie dwellings when she documents her parents' journey to the Peace River region of northern Alberta in 1913. Staying at a stopping house overnight, Baldwin's mother Olive Freeland, has the following, less than proper, visual experience as a result of the rather cramped space in which human bodies are placed:

> She heard someone struggling into clothes and in the dim light cast by the dying flames recognized Robert Andrews as he approached the fireplace.... She could see him plainly now as he turned to warm his back, and she thought how handsome he looked with the firelight softening his features. It was then she realized he had pulled his woolen shirt over his union suit but had not bothered with his trousers. Suppressing a giggle, she thought how shocked Aunt Em would be if she knew her Ollie was gazing at a man in his underwear. (71)

What is particularly compelling about this scene is that Mrs. Freeland does not recoil at the sight which a lack of privacy provides, but rather takes a light-hearted view of the gap between old world morality and new world reality.

Later in Baldwin's text the author also illustrates that the often rudimentary architecture of the prairie home disallowed "purpose-specific rooms" (Radke 238) and necessitated and made a priority of multi-functionality over any accommodation of personal space:

> I was too young to remember those first winters, but do remember, of later years, our farm kitchen on a winter morning – firewood stacked near the stove, a bucket for slops near the door, coffee perking on the back of the big range, my father shaving at the kitchen table, and I in my petticoat, washing my neck and arms at the corner washstand, while Mother stirred the porridge and eggs sputtered in the frying pan. Farm kitchens had to be functional, not beautiful. Ours was bathroom, dining room, laundry, and in the early days, the dairy. Each in turn and sometimes all at once. (189–90)

Private spaces could be creatively constructed, however, as we saw with Middleton, and as we see when Baldwin notes that "chintz drapes ... were strung on wires across the interior and served as room partitions during the first year in the new house" (205). Jessie Raber's mother was similarly creative within a small home:

> All went along well, and on Monday, the twenty-first of October, 1895, we moved into our new house. We found it much warmer and more comfortable. There were a few things to do to finish it and Mother put up the partitions, some of her rugs tacked along the poles. We were all quite proud of our new house, with the sod roof. (44–45)[28]

For many white, English-speaking women, a sense of Home was symbolized by "sacred objects,"[29] or those domestic or personal items that migrated with

---

28   For more examples of the uncomfortable architecture of first prairie homes, and the creativity of women in dealing with it, see also Middleton 16; Nelson 41; Parsons 21; Schroeder 64; and Thomson 20–21.

29   I borrow this phrase from the autobiography titled *Sketches from Life* (1981) by Canadian artist Annora Brown, who provides a description of a woman named Mrs. Hunt: "a very special kind of person – new to my experience. She was what is commonly called a 'home body'. She gave me the impression that she drew the walls of home about her like a warm cloak, to ward off the tempest outside. Her stove, her table, her china were sacred objects" (150).

them from "back Home." As Kathleen V. Cairns and Eliane Leslau Silverman suggest in their exploration of the kinds of "treasures," or "valued objects," kept by women from a variety of backgrounds, such items provide "meaning and coherence" to women's lives (x). Most significantly, "possessions are a portable self that provides security when the world is in flux" (7), and "flux" is certainly the most unifying experience for women in the early stages of homesteading. On the one hand, the objects that women describe in their memoirs often symbolize or reflect the role of white woman as "civilizer" in the Canadian West, and certainly the use of such objects within the Home suggests a desire to mitigate the perceived threat to domestic purity in the early experience of homesteading, as well as to reassert a woman's adherence to cultural images. On the other hand, these objects often simultaneously reveal to readers that many female emigrants suffered from loneliness and isolation that could only be relieved by surrounding themselves with tangible symbols of connectedness to others. As suggested by Cairns and Silverman, a woman's valued objects usually hold "emotional significance" (xiii), especially in their role in "the preservation of a personal and a family history" (xv). Given that one of the main narratives of western settlement centred on the idea of the prairies as being a land of "new beginnings," or a "fresh start," which in some measure suggests a repudiation of one's past, then the attention paid by women memoirists to "sacred objects" that symbolize the past, continuity and stability, seems to, once again, provide us with a subtle re-vision of such narratives.

In *The Long Trail*, Beulah Baldwin describes the ritual act of unpacking one's sacred objects from "back Home" for placement within the new Home, a "neat cabin, fragrant with the clean odor of new wood and bright with sunshine" (205), as a moment of wonder. Indeed, after nearly seven years of following her husband's migrations, the moment of unpacking for Olive Freeland marks achievement of her own dream, a stable Home for her family:

> Mother's wedding gifts were the first to be unpacked. The most prized was a cut-glass bowl of heavy leaded crystal, a gift from her Aunt Em. We were not supposed to touch it, but we sometimes watched a sunbeam as it caught a point of crystal, setting it afire with brilliant colours. Another possession we children loved was

a cupid carved from wood, holding a large red heart. Mother said it was a memento from a young man she nearly married. Then there was my father's silver cigarette box. Although he hardly gave it a glance, Mother and we children loved it. Engraved with the Queen's initials, it had been presented to him for outstanding service during the Boer War. (204)

The gifts here delineated are certainly symbolic of Olive Freeland's sense of family connection: the "heavy leaded crystal," a gift from her Aunt Em, a woman who had raised Olive until the age of 16, after the girl's family had broken up, and who represents domestic stability, strength of character and emotional support; the "cupid" (probably from her husband's younger brother, whom she had known first and who was once in love with her) as a reminder of a romantic time of life, and perhaps even of choices freely made; and her husband's "silver cigarette box," a sort of narrative gesture towards dedication to the imperial cause.

While still on the trail to their Saskatchewan homestead site in 1904, we see that Marjorie Wilkins Campbell's parents have together taken care to incorporate their past spiritual life within their dreams of the future:

> Last night they had been within less than a mile of Fort Qu'Appelle and all the usual, usually muffled after-dark sounds of two to three hundred people. Across the Narrows, as dusk fell, the coulees echoed the deep-throated voices of the Oblate Fathers at Lebret as they chanted their vespers, and the high, thin voices of Indian children at one of the earliest residential Indian schools in the West. Incredulous, and awed by what they must have felt to be some sort of omen, father and mother had listened to the *"Kyrie Eleison"* that reminded them poignantly of the summer Sunday a few months after they were married when they visited Ely Cathedral and father had made the photo of the choristers chanting the ancient "Lord Have Mercy Upon Us." They had brought the photo with them, a souvenir of the former home that was to become part of the new. (18)

This initial reflection on a sacred object is optimistic, as it comes as a result of being close to "civilization" in the form of religious ritual. Spiritual comfort is still available to the author's parents as they recognize traces of the old life in the new landscape. However, I cannot help but read the horrific irony of this moment as we see the ideal British emigrants being comforted and soothed on their journey into the "wilderness" of the Saskatchewan prairie by Indian children who are actively being "civilized" by one of the main assimilationist tools, the residential school. The complicity of the Wilkins in the displacement of native peoples as a result of white western settlement cannot be more agonizingly apparent. Nevertheless, throughout Campbell's memoir the author deliberately focuses the reader's attention on the experience of Mrs. Wilkins, who ultimately gains sympathy because she is, after all, only one single woman who is struggling to cope in unfamiliar territory. Later in the journey, in fact, when the family has travelled well beyond the presence of human habitation, Campbell's mother feels so overwhelmed by the unfamiliar vastness that surrounds her that she turns to a sacred object for solace:

> From her high perch, hour after hour, mother had searched the horizon for another settler's shack or another stable that might suggest that they were getting near some sign of civilization. Though she tried not to look at the little garnet-rimmed watch pinned on her blouse, her eyes involuntarily sought it as a relief from so much space, the countless sloughs and poplar bluffs, the ocean of grass, and the rutted Touchwood Trail that threatened to go on to the very end of the world. (21)

Here we see the prairie woman literally re-visioning from the larger "space" of the Saskatchewan prairie, a space that in 1904 had only been ideologically "civilized," to focus upon a "little" but sacred object that she carries on her person as symbol of her former life and that provides her with psychological "relief" as she nears what, for her, feels like "the very end of the world."

Once arrived at the family homestead, the Wilkins family construct a new home and the author represents the moment when her mother unpacks her belongings and rediscovers the means by which she will recreate a Home feeling:

Seated on the kitchen floor on a hastily unrolled and still unread copy of the overseas edition of the London *Times*, she laughed and cried as box after box revealed familiar treasures, holding each up for their appreciation. She unwrapped the silver cruet and the china pastry cup she used for making beefsteak and kidney pies, sauce pans, and the children's silver mugs.

But she could not stay at any chore for more than a few minutes. Every item roused nostalgic memories, and she wanted to see everything at once. With the baby clutched against her hip, she reached down to a half-emptied crate and found the antelope horn they had used at home for a hat rack; it could be hung near the door beside father's sjambok. From the crate clearly marked *first needed* she lifted carefully wrapped china and cutlery, only momentarily sad when she came on several pieces that had not survived months of handling. (34)

In the process of unpacking, Mary Eleanor finally retrieves some other sacred items that are integral to her stable sense of identity, but items that nonetheless have to be temporarily laid aside as being non-functional in the early days of prairie settlement:

It was the heavy parcel in the same sturdy crate, also sewn into a sheet, that forced her first, and only, nostalgic cry that day, the heavy parcel of her music, the scores of operas she loved and popular songs, the arias and her favorite piano works. With tears blurring the inscription she had so carefully written to identify the contents, she laid it on the lower shelf of the what-not. Like the leopard skins, music belonged to some future time. Now she must not think about it, nor about her piano. (34–35)

As Campbell later writes about her mother's music, "for her no treasure meant more," and, although "she had no means of playing any of the favorites, merely to have those sheets and collections eased some of the pangs of nostalgia they evoked" (53).

In Campbell's narrative we can see the "sacred object" as highly ambiguous symbolism, providing both connection to one's past and simultaneous reminder of the loss of that past. For Nell Wilson Parsons's mother, some objects just simply could not be out in the open, although they could not be entirely discarded with either:

> Mama's barrel-topped, iron-bound trunk had arrived six weeks after we were in the new house. She unpacked it to get out the underwear we needed, some extra "pinnies" and our dolls. She removed a few other things from the top of the trunk, then replaced the tray and shut down the lid. There was nowhere to put the things, and most of them left unpacked were of no use on the homestead. "It belongs to another place, another time," Mama would say when we children crowded around asking, "What's that green wool?" and "What's that lace?"
>
> Whenever Mama opened that trunk to get something, she would reach quickly for what she sought, and resolutely close the lid again. (35–36)

The sadness surrounding "sacred objects" is not always about the loss of connectedness to the Old World; rather, those objects that make the journey to the Canadian prairies, or the loss of them during emigration or after arrival, are sometimes used to represent the vulnerability of Home in so isolated a landscape. Writing about the terror of a house fire in *Land Across the Border*, Donnie Ebbers illustrates the emotional importance of certain objects which her mother Nannie Yokley Cummins brought from Missouri to the family homestead, which was located "about thirty miles west and north of Prince Albert – in the Shellbrook area" (21). Desperately trying, and ultimately failing, to save some of her family's belongings while being pulled from the fire by a male neighbour, Mrs. Cummins makes one final effort as she goes out the kitchen door:

> Mama reached back and took the glass sugar bowl, cream-pitcher, and butter-dish off the table. They were only press-cut, in imitation of expensive cut-glass, but Mama had kept them washed and shining so they sparkled like real expensive ones. They were all Mama could reach to save from the flames. She sat them in the snow on a flower bed, but when she went to pick them up the next day, each one was in two pieces, broken by the heat of the fire and the cold of the snow. (80)

Although Ebbers notes that the items held no real material value, she goes on to illustrate the momentous personal significance of such items for her mother's sense of personal history and stability. Noting the family's retreat to the barn for cover from the fire and winter wind, she writes about her mother's reaction to witnessing the shattering of a prairie dream:

> Through the open top-door of the feed-way, Donnie and Mama watched their home burn to the ground and the burning logs and roof fall into the cellar. Then Mama said, "I have seen all I have worked and saved for twenty-five years, *go* in twenty-five minutes." (Mama and Papa had been married twenty-five years the October before). (80–81)[30]

---

30   The sacred object as symbolic of a woman's shattered dreams of prairie life is seen in Grove's *Fruits of the Earth*, in which Ruth Spalding's deviance from her husband's settlement plans is represented by her lack of attention to the details of good living:

> she was getting less and less careful with regard to the common amenities of life. At first, she had omitted the white table-cloth only when Abe was absent from a meal. Why go to unnecessary trouble? ... she had a good dinner-set; but, when pieces were broken, she replaced them with heavy white crockery, saving her better dishes for social occasions which never came.... Then she left the white table-cloth out altogether, preferring oilcloth. The room took on a dingy appearance. (46)

Annora Brown also documents this loss of vision when she writes about a prairie rock pile, "though this stone pile was not a dumping ground, except for rocks, we often found bits of beautiful old china or glass there – fragments of vase or goblet that had been brought from the Old Country as a special reminder of home and

The treasured "sacred objects" that women so reverently produced when some semblance of a permanent Home had been achieved are part of the process of transformation women engaged in to make "'home' move beyond a merely functional use of space and become a comfortable and attractive place" (McManus 124). Many items could help a woman achieve the standards of "comfortable and attractive," but one of the most frequently noted items are curtains, which were hung over the windows of even the most rudimentary of prairie homes as an attempt to preserve domestic respectability (Radke 234). Indeed, I believe this is one detail of the domestic economy that seems to represent a most unambiguous adherence to cultural constructs of appropriate femininity (especially when it is done even in conditions of extreme isolation), as recognized by both contemporaries of western settlement and the memoir writers studied here. Curtains were a universal marker of female presence on the prairie landscape, as Emily Ferguson suggests when writing about a trip she took outside of Edmonton and noting that "most of the houses we see are inhabited by bachelors. A traveller does not need genius to know this. Where the one Incomparable She holds sway there is a clothesline in the yard and a curtain at the window" (*Open* 7).[31] Ferguson's capitalization of "Incomparable She" here is certainly a manifestation of cultural constructions of white femininity just as the phrase "holds sway" most certainly alludes to the concept of "separate spheres." Elizabeth Lewthwaite assures her readers of her adherence to domestic norms when she writes about visiting her brothers' prairie home in 1901 and staying in a "small building, about twelve feet square, used previously as a granary": as she notes, however, "some curtains, a few photographs I had with me, and a book or two, soon gave the little spot an air of Home" (712). In *Crocus and Meadowlark Country*, a memoir of homesteading "in the Parkland district of Southern Alberta," Georgina H. Thomson makes clear

---

that had arrived shattered from the long journey across an ocean and a continent" (41). For more examples of the importance of sacred objects to the settler woman's creation of a Home, see also Magill 11–12 and Thomson 20.

31 In Grove's *Settlers of the Marsh* (1925), Niels Lindstedt envies the domestic comfort of his friend, Lars Nelson's, house after the latter man's marriage: specifically, "nothing struck Niels so much as the pleasant look of the white-curtained windows in the house" (61).

the difference between a house and a Home when she describes her father's first building as being "a bare, unpainted wooden house" that features "two as yet uncurtained windows above and one window and a door below" (19). Not only could the mere presence of a woman be determined by curtains on the windows, but also a woman's character could be ascertained, as seen in Nellie McClung's *Clearing in the West* (1935) when, at the start of their trip west, the Mooney family stop at Silver Inlet to visit with a female cousin "who had the name of being a bad housekeeper. She read novels, paper-backed novels, day and night and would neither knit nor sew" (42). Thinking that "maybe she had done better in her new home," the family are disappointed to see that little has improved: "We trailed up a long hill, with a narrow sidewalk of two boards and houses standing one above another. We found Lucy's house quite easily. There were no curtains on the windows and boards in the steps were broken" (although that latter sign of neglect of duty is attributed to the husband). In McClung's story, where the woman in question lives in a town environment, we see that adherence to domestic norms was not only a duty of the individual, but also that it was "collectively and strictly enforced by other White women in the area" (McManus 124).

"Comfortable and attractive" could be difficult to achieve in the isolated and often impoverished conditions that many prairie women faced in the early years of settlement. In consequence, a main facet of the principle of domestic economy was "a woman's ability to use whatever resources were at hand, scarce or ample, to create a more pleasant living environment for herself and her family." We see the creativity of women come to the fore in their perform-ance of the domestic role, both as a means to be "appropriately domestic and expressively individual" (Lindgren 84). For example, Beulah Baldwin provides the following scene in *The Long Trail* when depicting her family's journey from Edmonton to Grouard in the Peace River country:

> They left Edmonton behind and soon approached the first farm. Neat white buildings with green roofs stood before a bluff of spruce and birch, protection from the north wind. In a short while they were passing another fine group of buildings. "I've been told," Dad said, "that these well-to-do farmers have homes as fine as

any in the city." Mother agreed, saying, "You're right Wilbur, I'd never have believed it." Watching her out of the corner of his eye as they approached the next farm, he was not surprised when she exclaimed, "Their first home!" while pointing out a small log cabin with a sod roof. They were soon passing the farms of the more recent settlers. Although they were not as large or elaborate; built mostly of neatly dove-tailed logs, the small windows were bright and clean and hung with gay curtains. These small homes appealed to Mother. Looking up with a bright smile, she said, "Wouldn't it be fun to peek inside and see how these women have managed to create comfortable homes, with very little to work with?"

She glanced proudly at the warm patchwork quilts she had made from clothing left behind by customers at their hotel – woollen jackets and shirts, tossed carelessly aside by men anxious to leave for a warmer climate and an easier way of life. Like many thrifty wives of that era, she cut the material into small squares, creating a checkerboard pattern, and lined the quilts with carded wool that Dad purchased from Father Lacombe's mission. Sewn by hand, the coverings had taken many months to complete. (5)

So much is going on in this passage, illustrating both adherence and confrontation modes. Baldwin begins her reconstruction of this scene by having her father take her mother on a scenic tour of homesteading that seems reminiscent of the promotional pamphlets that brought so many prospective settlers to Canada in the first place. Looking at the homes of farmers who have been successful, the Freelands are able to get a glimpse of the dream of an agricultural life in Canada, something that Mrs. Freeland would "never have believed" had she not seen it with her own eyes. Then they move to the homes of "more recent settlers," where Mrs. Freeland is able to see symbolized, in the form of "gay curtains," the domestic economy which she herself may soon be able to achieve. In fact, the very sight of the curtains inspires her to "peek inside" and see more tangible evidence of female success. In that final paragraph, however, we see Baldwin "proudly" illustrating her own mother's adherence to domestic norms when she reflects on the creatively inspired "warm patchwork quilts" – both "comfortable and attractive" – that lay in wait in the family wagon. When Baldwin provides an explanation as to the origin of those quilts, I cannot help but read some confrontation happening, for the material used comes from clothing left behind by men, probably single men, who apparently gave up; who repudiated the lifestyle that the Freelands are walking into and that Mrs. Freeland seems particularly capable of succeeding at, thus undercutting the narratives of western settlement that privilege the masculine/heroic role.

Later in the memoir, when the Freelands move into a Home of their own, the author's mother proves up her ability to be domestically successful:

> Waylaying the Aikens on their way to town, Mother asked Beulah Aikens to buy two packages of dye with thread to match. Seeing what Mother was up to, Beulah offered the loan of her treadle sewing machine. After the first lesson, there was no holding Mother. From her stock of white sheets she produced window curtains, a cover for the single bed that served as a couch, and several cushions. She dyed them all a deep forest green and trimmed them with the same flowered chintz she had used for the substitute partitions.
>
> We were no sooner settled in when the Lawrence family dropped by to inspect Dad's straw barn and our new cabin. When they saw Mother's handiwork made from the sheets and drapes Dad had wanted to leave behind, they were impressed. Johnnie said with a laugh, "You're not doing badly for a couple of green-horns." (205)

In addition to a deliberate memorializing of her mother's obvious ingenuity and artistic talent, I would suggest that Baldwin works here to advance an alternative vision of what makes a homestead. For example, she suggests that the Lawrences came to see both the barn and cabin built by her father, but then she goes on to stress how "impressed" they especially were with "Mother's handiwork," and she takes care to note especially that the handiwork was achieved only through use of materials that her father has previously seen as expendable to the project of settlement.

One of the domestic objects studied most often by folklore experts and others interested in women's cultural history is the quilt, "an immediate feminine point of reference" by which is "implied the real or imaginary gift of creative power in the face of adversity" (Barnes and Eicher 3). As we saw earlier with Beulah Baldwin's representation of her mother's skill in making quilts, it was "an art of scarcity, ingenuity, conservation, and order" (Showalter 228). As I read through the memoirs gathered for my study, I found that the women have documented several everyday art forms which, like quilting, have the same effect of simultaneously showing feminine adherence to domestic norms while also illustrating that women's domestic labouring was an integral component of survival in often adverse circumstances. Rag-rug-making appears to have been one of the most common household activities which combined economy (everyone, after all, has access to rags), artistry, and a sense of familial community, as seen in Nell Parsons's description in *Upon a Sagebrush Harp* of rug-making during cold winter evenings in Saskatchewan:

> Mama had promptly made over the garments [Papa] had brought home in the fall. In the process she had accumulated a considerable heap of woollen scraps, and in the long evenings we worked at rug making. We all had a hand in it, sitting close around the rectangular rug frame Papa had made to hold the burlap base taut. Three worked with the clumsy, homemade wooden hooks, while the fourth read aloud to the workers. We took turns, hour after hour, while the reader sat where the reflector of the bracket lamp on the wall could be focussed on the pages.
>
> We needed rugs. But the one we children wanted first to finish was the narrow runner to lie between the beds in the crowded bedroom. The floor was always icy, but Mama did not believe prayers effective unless delivered in a degree of discomfort. (80–81)

Annie Wilson's domestic economy here demonstrates the homesteading principal of "making do," for she has taken old clothes given to her by a neighbour and, after making clothing for her own children, she sees the scraps as an opportunity to provide further items of comfort for her family. This manual and communal activity also supports an intellectual one for the Wilson family, whose "reading was varied" and included "a fabulous family-type weekly called *The Family Herald and Weekly Star*" and a book "on the life and explorations of Kit Carson" (81).

Rag-rug-making and other domestic arts often were particularly conducive to fostering a sense of connection to community, sometimes the one to be left behind, sometimes the one developed during the experience of settlement. As Winnie Hutton describes in *No "Coppers" in Saskatchewan!*, the decision to emigrate could be productive of an artistic housecleaning of sorts: as she notes of her own family's preparation for homesteading life, "Everyone was excited and busy. Property had to be disposed of, decisions made about what to take and what to sell. In the house the women tore up every old garment not fit to take, into long strips for carpet rags. We sewed carpet rags like mad, then took them to a lady in the village who wove them into nice rag carpets to take with us" (2). In this description Hutton displays a conventional division of labour along gender lines, but more importantly she captures a form of domestic production that moves out from the family home and into the larger community of female labour. Towards the end of Donnie Ebbers's *Land Across the Border*, the author provides the following scene showing quilting as a time and space to rejuvenate a sense of community and belonging:

> She and Frances [the author's niece] were glad to be back home with Mama again. On the cold winter days she and Mama pieced quilts and Mama taught her how to quilt them and how to use patterns. They sewed, talked and laughed together. Mama told funny stories of her own girlhood days. They made dresses for themselves and Frances. (98)

What is particularly poignant for the author in this scene is that it represents her arrival home after spending the winter away to attend "the Business College in Prince Albert," which was a life choice made for her by her father and which was in opposition to the career she wanted in education. Her main supporter for that latter career was her mother, so the return Home and the shared creative moment is emotionally significant.

In spending so much narrative space on the documentation of women's domestic and artistic skills, the memoirists demand equality of attention and valuation in consideration of what "Homesteading" really meant. In answering the related questions, "What criteria should be used to judge a 'real homesteader'? Does doing 'women's work' disqualify one from this distinction?" (221), Elaine Lindgren acknowledges that domestic activities have always been "devalued" and made less important culturally than "men's plowing their fields." Nevertheless, argues Lindgren, settler women were not merely dependents of men, for certainly men relied on the "essential" domestic and other work of women to "sustain" them in the settlement enterprise (223), thus making the work of "Home"-building as important as – as foundational to, really – the work of "stead"-building. This re-valuation of women's domestic productions can be seen, for example, in Mary Hiemstra's *Gully Farm*, as the author gives her mother's lace-making skills narrative value equal to her father's construction of a family home. In the memoir, the author as youngster is clearly in awe of her father's creative abilities, as evidenced by her choice of vocabulary in describing the "new house":

> I, however, was as proud of the new house as Dad was. I thought it the most wonderful house in the world, and I found something new to admire every time I looked at it. The bulges in the walls were perfect shelves for my collection of small stones. I thought it pure magic that the ridge-pole stayed up. As for the door, I opened and closed it so often Mother finally told me to stop or the leather hinges would be worn out.
>
> But the most wonderful thing about the house was the fact that we had built it. Not so long ago there had been nothing at all on this spot, and now our house stood there. We had caused it to grow. With our own hands we had put it together using the things we had found on the prairie, and I had helped. I had held that log while Dad notched it, and I had stuffed clay into that crack near the floor. How smart Dad was to know just how to build such a

perfect house! I looked at his thin young face, and wonder and
pride filled my small chest. My dad, I was sure, knew everything.
(171–72)

The repetitive use of the word "house" here is important when leading towards
her narrative turn of attention to the Home-making skills of her mother:

> The brown walls and floor were still very drab-looking, and to
> brighten them Mother brought out a pink and white spread for the
> bed, and draped an antimacassar over the glassless window. "That
> does it and no mistake," Dad said when he saw the bed-spread.
> "Sally, this is the nicest home on the prairie."
>
> When Mrs Metherell saw the antimacassar she said it was far
> too lovely for a log shack. It ought to be put away and saved for a
> better house some time in the future. Mother, however, said she
> had plenty of antimacassars and she was going to enjoy them while
> she could. The future might never come. And how sensible she was!
>
> Mother had crocheted the antimacassars before she was mar-
> ried. They were a little over a yard long, and about two feet wide,
> and hours of work had gone into them. I used to marvel at the pat-
> tern, and at the number of stitches in them, for though I couldn't
> crochet I could knit, and knew the tedium of hand work. "How
> long did it take you to make one?" I asked, and when Mother told
> me I knew she was just as clever as Dad. Beauty, however, wasn't
> the antimacassars' only virtue, they were something nobody else
> had. The Metherells' house had two rooms, and Mr Gardiner's
> little house had a pole floor, while the Claxtons' house was said to
> have two windows. None of them, however, had antimacassars,
> or even curtains. That hand-made lace draped so gracefully over
> our little window made our house unique, and gave it a touch of
> elegance even the bachelors noticed. "You have a nice place here,
> Mrs Pinder," they said, looking around the little room. "It's real
> homelike." (172–73)

This passage certainly can be read as illustrating Sally Pinder's Home-making skills as an essential part of the "civilizing" project of western settlement (seen in words like "beauty" and "elegance" and also in the response of the bachelors), but I also read here another narrative concern, which is the author's wish to give her mother's "Home"-building "equal footing" (Buss, *Repossessing* xvii) with her father's "stead"-building. Her exclamatory statements of parental worth in each case (her father is "smart" and her mother is "clever") help to rebalance the unequal attention traditionally paid to the respective genders.[32]

Another facet of "domestic economy" that was central to women's contribution to "Home"steading had to do with the more immediate needs of the family unit. It has long been recognized that the prairie Home was not simply decorative; that it in fact constituted an economic centre that could ultimately be the linchpin of a farming family's level of success. Often, cash was in scarce supply while waiting for the production of crops to become a viable income source, a reality that made a woman's presence on the homestead of vital importance. As Susan Armitage asserts in relation to the American "frontier," "household sustenance" was "work which contributed directly to the family economy by making cash expenditure unnecessary" (469). Nell Parsons illustrates the importance of "household sustenance" when she writes about the hardships wrought by successive crop failures and the "Next Year" philosophy that predominated in the face of such failures:

> Next year … homesteader's will-o-the-wisp! Prairie town businessmen understood farmers must pay bills after harvest. Crop failure worked hardship on them, too. And prairie wives tried frantically to keep grocery bills down by exchanging butter and eggs, when they had any. (127)

Similarly, in *Barefoot on the Prairie: Memories of Life on a Prairie Homestead* (1989), a memoir of homesteading near Bruce, Alberta, in the second decade of the twentieth century, Ferne Nelson describes a family trip to the "old-

---

32 For more examples of women's home craft production, see also Anderson 29; Johannson 107; and Raber 56, 64.

fashioned store" in town where her Mother's productions were given monetary value:

> Russell Kennedy would have totalled up the bill by now, deducting the value of several dozen eggs and several pounds of butter that Mama had brought in. If we had any cash, he would be paid; if not, the bill would be filed on a spike behind the counter. There were lots of bills on the spike to be paid in the fall when the crop came in. (12)

Difficult years for agriculture served to amplify the essential nature of women's domestic contributions, which sometimes could make the difference between survival and foreclosure of the family farm: as Ida Scharf Hopkins remembers in her memoir *To the Peace River Country and On* (1973) about her parents' farm near La Riviere, Manitoba, in the late 1920s,

> Farm crops were on the decline. Yields were down and so were prices. The only cash crops were from products raised on the farm, not from the grain. I know my mother looked after the family and ran the house with the money from the cream cheques, eggs and the turkey sale in the winter. (13)

As can be seen from the passages provided, prairie women contributed as "manufacturers in their own homes" (Sundberg 81) and could even be said to be "more centrally involved in providing subsistence for the farm family than men" (Faragher 50).[33]

We can glimpse women's centrality to the homesteading project in Arthur E. Copping's anecdote about the anonymous pair, Mr. and Mrs. C---, the former of whom "had caught the back-to-the-land fever about as badly as a

---

33   Grove's *Settlers of the Marsh* illustrates this point when Ellen Amundsen tells Niels Lindstedt that "during the first few years it is really the woman that makes the living on a pioneer farm. She keeps chickens, cows and pigs. The man makes the land" (74).

man can catch it" and decided that "[he] must at once sell up [his] small possessions and start farming in Canada" (227). Unfortunately, Mr. C--- arrived
in Canada with no knowledge of farming, but he also arrived with a "wide-
ranging" ambition burning within him, so he "bought a solid square mile of
farm land" (229). Predictably, the couple failed miserably, at least until their
"grand transformation," "all due to Milly," who took it upon herself to learn
butter-making, dairying, and poultry and hog management (230). After Mr.
C---'s decision to follow his wife's lead and take up "learning," success was
theirs: as Mrs. C--- states it, "'we are beginning to make such a lot of money!
We had bumper crops last year; our wheat graded No. 1, and we took a first
for oats. I suppose I ought not to say "we,"' she added in a merry parenthesis,
'though I did lend a hand with the stooking'" (231). It is interesting to note
that, despite Mr. C---'s admission of his wife's central importance to their
eventual success at the business of farming, Mrs. C--- documents that success
at the level of agriculture only, and then devalues her own role in achieving
that success by questioning her use of the pronoun "we." As this anecdote
illustrates, "woman's work was dominated by the omnipresent awareness of
the immediate usefulness of her product" (Faragher 64), but there was no
publicly available discourse to express the value of that work. Meanwhile,
"the flavor of male work was quantitative: acres, fields, bushels – all measured
a man's work" (65), so clearly an accounting of how men's work measured
up was more immediately recognizable to readers. Historically, the value of
women's work in the larger context of the agricultural enterprise has seldom
been tallied: the prairie woman's "economic contribution has been ignored, a
reflection not of the reality of her work, but of the larger society's view of the
role of the housewife as 'non-work' – that is housewives who are not paid do
not produce commodities of value to the economy and are dependents of men"
(Kohl, "Women's" 52). In fact, speaking of a "social landscape marked by a
specific spacing of women and men," Kathleen Storrie notes the private/public
dichotomy and some of the "other 'mapping' dichotomies usually intertwined
with it," including those of "housework/work," which translates into the binary of "consumption/production" (2–3).

However, the reality was that prairie kitchens routinely functioned
as production centres that eased the economic burden of a farm family's

consumption needs. One of the first consumption needs was a physical one, for food. An oft-noted food product manufactured by the settler woman was Home-baked bread, a literal product that served the immediate survival needs of the farm family unit, and sometimes the larger community, and therefore seems to pose a delightful confrontation with more abstract cultural notions of prairie agriculture transforming Canada into "The World's Bread Basket."[34] Not that homemade bread stayed entirely literal; indeed, in the cultural relegation of women to the domestic role, the ability to bake bread took on sometimes symbolic and even mythic proportions. There was even a contemporary verse that ran, "A man well fed/ On Home-made Bread/ Will be proud of his wife/ And love her" (qtd. in Rasmussen et al. 98). No matter what culinary delights the prairie woman produced at table, home-baked bread became a seeming icon of Home on the prairies. Although Marion Cran notes a prairie meal that is "fragrant with the steam of good coffee, the taste of clover honey and wild-strawberry jam, eggs so fresh that they are creamier than cream itself, golden bannocks and home-made bread," it is only the latter to which she ascribes, with emphasis, the valuation of being "the crown of every settler's table!" (133). A prairie man's homestead might well be his castle, but the kingdom, it would appear, gained its value from the presence of a prairie wife who could produce home-baked bread. Annora Brown writes about a woman's successful effort at breadmaking that there is "something so nearly sacred about the achievement, that the cook seems to be bathed in a special radiance as she performs the rite of lifting the fat, golden-crusted loaves from the oven" (151). In such descriptions, we see an almost "hagiographic presentation" (Langford, "First Generation" 1) of Prairie Woman as domestic goddess reinforced. We see this as well in some of the memoirs gathered here, as, for example, in Nell Parsons's *Upon a Sagebrush Harp*, when the author ironically notes that "to the homesteader, the word 'professional' had no meaning. He did everything for *him*self" (emphasis added), then goes

---

34   Taken from page 8 of a pamphlet titled *The granary of the British Empire: The western provinces of Canada: Manitoba, Saskatchewan, Alberta, British Columbia.* Calgary: Canadian Pacific Railway, Department of Natural Resources, 1914. (Peel #3998).

on to indicate how bread-making was a marker, like curtains, of adherence to domestic norms:

> Our distant town had no bakery, but a hard-pressed bachelor could buy bread at the Chinaman's restaurant. Papa had only contempt for baker's bread, and Mama would have scorned being caught short of bread. A housewife who ran out of bread was only slightly less shiftless than the one who could not take needle in hand to mend a garment, to retrim an old hat – or to fashion new garments from old. (30)

Although no direct cultural commentary is made here on the attitude to bread from the "Chinaman's restaurant," the suggestion that only the "hard-pressed bachelor" would buy bread from such a place certainly reinforces that not being such a bachelor was a desirable thing, as underscored by the equation of bread-making with evaluations of female character.

Later in Parsons's memoir, the author also indicates the importance of the discourse of bread-making (as well as domestic culture in general) to the transmission of knowledge as to how to perform the domestic role:

> One feature in the *Weekly Free Press*, which Mrs. Burnside kindly passed on to us when opportunity presented, was a Home Loving Hearts section. It was a section of letters from homesteaders' lonely wives across the land. Some contained recipes, others cherished poems or bits of philosophy from every province in Canada.
>
> Perpetual bread starter was one popular subject, along with ways to keep the week's bread from drying out. (84)

In the naming of such women's sections of the newspaper – "Home Loving Hearts" – there appears to be only a reinforcement of women's domestic role, but the actual function of such sections – to provide an ongoing dialogue with others about the details of domestic life – also provides a means of confrontation with the isolation wrought by the geography of agriculture, an aspect of western settlement that women could not control. The sharing of domestic experiences/ideas also seems to me to be an acknowledgment that such skills as bread-making are not simply a matter of being female; they are not inherent to female biology. Rather, such skills are usually passed on from generation to generation, as seen in a humourous anecdote from Barry Broadfoot's *The Pioneer Years*. In this story, Mary Watson of Weyburn, Saskatchewan, tells of her inability to make bread, something which her husband said "a family needed" (200). Having written to a farm paper for help, Watson states that,

> Next morning there is a knock on the door and I look out and there's a Mrs. Ratigan on the stoop. I knew her. She was one of the coarse ones. Irish. A big woman and even though I didn't have much to do with her on our street I believed her to be capable....
>
> When I opened the door she just barged in and said, "Mary Watson. Weyburn. Bread. I read it," and she sat down. Then she said, "Nobody ever learned to make bread out of a book. It takes a mother to teach her daughter. Where's your mother?" I said in Guildford in England and she said, "Fine. Leave her there. I'll be your mother this morning and we'll make bread." (201)

What I particularly like about this kind of presentation of the transmission of knowledge is that it effectively points out gender as a social construct. Women do not necessarily come ready-equipped to bake bread or perform any other domestic task, but rather they learn through trial, and even sometimes error, when society deems it appropriate for them to do so. In fact, stories abound in pioneer culture about male settlers who, out of sheer necessity, managed to become perfectly adequate, even esteemed, bread-makers in the absence of women.

Many of the memoirists gathered here allow us to engage as readers with the idea of gender as social construct. For example, for Katherine Magill, whose family moves in the mid-1940s to the *Back o' Baffuf* (1977) (or near Vermilion, Alberta) as part of the wave of returning WWII veterans, bread-making becomes an act that dominates her sense of herself as a modern Prairie Woman, although in her memoir she chooses to document her initial failure to succeed at this role with characteristic humility and good humour:

There was the matter of the bread dough. Jim's mother was an excellent cook – a farm wife of many years and much efficiency. Her home-baked bread was a gourmet's delight, light and crisply crusted. This was one standard I would attempt to reach. My first batch of bread just wouldn't rise. Perhaps the yeast had been scalded. Perhaps it became chilled. The dough sat there, sullen and triumphant, a leaden blob.

There could be only one reaction, some loud and lengthy teasing. The boys would join in, and Ron would add his infant glee to the uproar. It was a day of tender easily-bruised moods, fraught with numerous small irritations. This was one mistake I would bury, and make another batch of bread.

I carted the lump out of the edge of the bush, hollowed out a suitable hole deposited the offending object deep, and covered it well. I even, rather cleverly, I thought, scuffled dry leaves over the spot so it might appear undisturbed.

"Rest in Peace," I said with satisfaction, as I gave it a last pat. I made biscuits for supper, and later, loaves risen to a glorious height, I baked the second batch of bread. (14)

The next morning, Magill, who is feeling self-congratulatory, gets a performance review of sorts:

...I poured myself a reward cup of coffee, and carried it outside. The air was like nectar, a warm fragrant nectar, with faint odors of earth and blossoms, tang of barnyard, rich loam, poplar smoke. From my perch on the back door step, I surveyed my private domain. There had been bonuses this spring. A family of Rocky Mountain bluebirds had moved into a poplar tree, occupying the vacant home of a woodpecker. These are a lovely bird. Unlike the Eastern bluebird, with its rosy breast these birds were truly blue, a clear and vivid azure above, fading to softer shades below. A crazy grouse drummed somewhere in a hidden glade, courting.

> I glanced around the perimeter of the houseyard. I must send to
> the experimental farm for some evergreens, I thought. They were
> fresh and pleasant additions to the poplars in many plantings.
> The grove was fine now, but in winter it added to the greyness of
> the days, and when winter winds blew, their grey trunks rattled
> like dry bones. Maybe some blue spruce there, I thought, there a
> Scotch pine, there --
>
> There where the Scotch pine was programmed, something
> had been added. A large tannish thing, like a mutant mushroom
> swelled. There were no rocks in the yard. The ice age had ground
> everything to silt. This could only be one thing.
>
> My guilty secret was no longer buried. The yeast hadn't been
> dead, just resting. Warmed by the good earth, it had truly risen.
>
> It became the most buried mistake of the year. I piled fresh dirt
> on it. Gathering to the challenge, all those yeast spores thrust it
> upward, to burst forth again. By noon I had decided this was one
> mistake too funny to conceal. The effect had dimmed a little, as
> the inevitable collapse came. When the rest of the family had seen
> it, we buried it again for the last time. (14–15)

This humorous and self-reflective anecdote ultimately contains a revealing lesson for the prairie memoirist who writes about her own experiences against a
cultural background that privileges nostalgic narratives and silences "traces of
the past that are less than exemplary" (Rukszto 17). What a well-constructed
confrontational scene! Magill first makes clear that she is aware of "standards"
of femininity in farm culture that need to be adhered to, then she acknowledges that domestic skills such as bread-making are not necessarily inherent to
being female by presenting her readers with her initial failure to perform well.
On the second try, when she does manage to achieve the "glorious heights"
of appropriate femininity, she first toys with the image of herself as domestic
goddess in control of her "private domain" (which simply must be read as an
allusion to the continued dominance of the separate spheres ideology) and
then illustrates the awful reality underpinning those heights as being persistently present and rupturing through the surface idealism.

While everyone was waxing rhapsodic about women who could produce a metaphoric golden loaf, many settler women found it both necessary and personally fulfilling to turn this domestic skill to literal economic advantage. For example, as Nell Parsons notes, "many of the newcomers who settled within a five-mile radius of us were bachelors. Almost at once, Mama had the opportunity to earn a little cash by baking bread for these men. They brought flour in one-hundred-pound sacks, and paid a fixed sum per sack for having the flour converted to loaves over the weeks" (55). Remuneration for this particular female skill becomes much more than mere "pin money," though, as Parsons later acknowledges that her mother's productive abilities in the Home equal greater productive ability on the "stead":

> We were on section thirty, with section twenty-nine east of us. In Canada, sections eleven and twenty-nine are set aside as "school sections" – that is, to provide funds for schools. The fact that section twenty-nine, a school section, adjoined our land, was a lucky circumstance for us. It could not be homesteaded. It was not likely to be sold soon. Therefore it provided good free grazing for our stock. But its real importance came from another detail. There was a lush coulee running the full mile across that section, and good redtop grew there.
>
> Such government land could be leased for a nominal sum. Our first winter the necessary fee was painstakingly saved out of Mama's bread-baking money. In due time the fee was mailed in and the lease came back. Happy day! Now Papa was assured of good hay and might have a surplus to sell. (91)

Mary Hiemstra's mother also turns her bread-making skill to economic advantage for her family by providing for others: as the author writes in *Gully Farm*,

> Now and then new settlers looking for land passed our house, and one day a man asked Mother to sell him some bread. "The children

haven't had a thing but porridge for a week," he said. Mother gladly sold him a whole batch of bread, and that gave her an idea.

We still had several sacks of flour stacked in the corner, and Mother was afraid they would spoil. Every time it rained water seeped through our sod roof, and though we set pans to catch the drip there was no telling when a new drip would start when we were not looking. But if the flour was made into bread and sold the danger would be over, and there would be a tidy profit to boot. Mother immediately baked a huge batch of bread. Sure enough a bannock-weary bachelor dropped by that afternoon to bring us some mail. Through the open door he eyed the bread standing brown and fragrant on the packing-box table. "Will you sell me a loaf or two?" he asked, licking his lips. Mother disposed of most of our flour that way. She could have sold it all and much more besides, but she had to keep enough to last until fall. (280)

Sally Pinder's decision seems to be merely practical; however, her entrepreneurial undertaking comes at a time when her husband is away "looking for work," looking for a way to provide for his family in the temporal gap between initial settlement and viable agricultural production. Here we see the truth in Bill Waiser's assertion that many farming families "faced the double challenge of bringing the land under cultivation and trying to survive in the meantime" (160). It was so often "in the meantime" that women's domestic productions preceded and provided for the continuance of the agricultural project.[35]

As seen with women's craft skills, cooking, too, often became aligned with social respectability; it was, very often, a scale on which to judge female value within the "civilizing" project of western settlement.[36] Specifically, "setting a

---

35 For more examples of the importance of bread-making to prairie life, see also Campbell 35; Hewson 19, 148, 186; Holmes 61, 69–70; Keyes 31; McClung 230; Scott 37; Strange 222; and Thomson 23–24, 52.

36 Contemporary writer Emily Ferguson makes an interesting comparison of public versus private skills of individual achievement when she says, "up to date, I have been president of thirteen women's societies or clubs, but it required infinitely more boldness, more accurate calculation, greater finesse, and deeper insight to tackle the pie art" (*Janey* 32).

magnificent harvest-time table was part of the regional definition of womanliness: a farm wife who did not, observed the Prairie feminist Nellie McClung, was 'almost as low in the social scale as the woman who has not a yard of flannel in the house when the baby comes'" (Thompson, John Herd 82–83).[37] Just as the production of worthwhile (meaning well-graded) crops garnered the prairie farmer social esteem, so too did the settler woman's preceding act of setting a "harvest-time table" to enable that production have social repercussions beyond the confines of the family farm. As McClung remembers in *Clearing in the West*, culinary competition was felt right down to the gustatory details:

> There was considerable friendly rivalry in the matter of feeding the threshers and there were dark stories told of certain places where they got no raisins in their rice pudding and nothing but skim milk to eat with it, and where the pies were made of dried apples even though at that time we were able to get barrels of gravensteins from Nova Scotia and northern spies from Ontario. (368)

In *With the West in Her Eyes*, Kathleen Strange, not yet feeling fully adequate to playing the role of a prairie wife, remembers her first experience of intense social scrutiny:

---

37   The meaning of "magnificence" as used here by McClung, of course, refers to the culinary delights presented, but Jessie Raber describes a humorous incident in which some "new neighbors," the Campbells, who were "right from Scotland," gain a "magnificent" reputation "during threshing," although not so much as a result of the food prepared and served:

> the men were rather amused, for Mrs. Campbell had the dinner table laid with beautiful table cloths, all linen, which hung clear to the floor and her best silver and dishes. Someone told her she didn't need to use her best. She said, "Why, I think men that work like these are of the best, so my best is none too good for them." That put the Campbells on the elite list of the neighborhood and they were liked by all. (142)

> One night Harry came in with the tidings: "The threshers will be
> on our place tomorrow morning. Have plenty of food!"
>
> A neighbour girl had come over to give me a hand and it was
> under her guidance that I had stocked up with the necessary abun-
> dance of food to cope with this anticipated visit. I was decidedly
> nervous, however, at the prospect of having to feed between twelve
> to fifteen hungry men three times a day, but I was also determined
> to go through with it as to the manner born, and to earn, if pos-
> sible, compliments rather than complaints.
>
> "Yes, I'm ready," I said grimly. "Let 'em come!" (85–86)

It should be noted that in Strange's passage, as with the subject of bread-making
earlier, the ability to cook for large gatherings of men is not a skill inherent to
being female, as seen in her need to take "guidance" from a neighbour girl who
clearly has already been schooled in the domestic arts. Once again, as with
Magill's bread-making passage earlier, this kind of narrative humour seems to
expose the gap between domestic ideals and individual realities, for Strange
definitely gives the impression that she is going to be playing a part – she is,
after all, "determined to go through with it as to the manner born" – and that
the possibility exists that she might not succeed. In *Of Us and the Oxen* (1968),
Sarah Ellen Roberts gives us more than the possibility of failure. In fact, in
this memoir of homesteading near Stettler, Alberta, in the first decade of the
twentieth century, the author writes fairly explicitly about her failure to adhere
to any of the traditional functions of the settler woman. For Roberts, just the
prospect of entering into harvest mealtime competitions is daunting enough
to make her simply step out of the field, thrusting her incapability to the fore:

> The threshers came early in October. It was my first experience
> with them and I had been dreading it for days. In Alberta, as in
> Illinois, each housewife vies with the others in demonstrating her
> ability as a cook, and I was almost in a panic. I finally decided that
> I would give them plenty of good food, but would not compete
> with the other women around in a line of work in which I did not
> excel. (222)

It did not have to be harvest time for a woman's ability to cook (or inability) to affect her social standing. As Ferne Nelson suggests in *Barefoot on the Prairie*,

> poor cooks were known all over the community. Their lack of skill at the stove was reported by all the bachelors, whose errands to neighbouring farms invariably coincided with mealtime. Mama was a good cook, and we always had lots of these "old batches" dropping by for her fried chicken and country gravy, sopped up with the airiest baking powder biscuits ever. (104)

Nelson does not indicate how her mother felt about all of these "drop-in" customers, but it certainly appears that the daughter-author feels her mother's culinary abilities to be a point of pride. Sometimes seeming narrative compliance with finding pride in maintaining standards of respectability through cooking allows for a reading which is more subtly confrontational with the goals of "future plenty and success." For example, when Jessie Raber notes on page 117 of *Pioneering in Alberta* regarding Christmas of 1899, "with our new kitchen there was so much more room that Mother invited some of the bachelors over. A merry time was had. Plenty of everything to eat: turkey, chicken and pork, pies, fruit cake, cookies, rolls and good homemade bread, also candy and nuts," it is important for the reader to remember that on page 114 the author has told us that, as a result of a lack of ready cash, her father had found it necessary "to work in town for awhile" as a bookkeeper for a store. We are also told that on the farm "there wasn't a great deal of grain" (115), so that perhaps Mrs. Browne's lavish meal is meant as a material banner of her own productive accomplishments, and/or maybe even a cover for the family's continuing state of economic crisis. In any case, by giving us a more total story than that suggested by the well-laden table, Raber is clearly allowing her readers to read beyond cultural narratives of inevitable prosperity. There is certainly a sense of having been cheated palpable in Raber's later statement that "life went along as usual – Dad in town, and the rest of us running the farm" (120).

These passages by Nelson and Raber bring up another myth of prairie life. Considerable nostalgic attention in cultural reminiscences of homesteading

life is given to a special brand of "prairie hospitality" that featured the unannounced arrival of dinner guests, for whom the settler woman would, without
complaint, provide culinary delights. I have to admit to a personal sense of
mistrust regarding these stories, and a desire to know what the busy prairie
woman *really* thought about the unexpected arrival of yet another mouth to
feed, the need to peel yet another potato. In her examination of women who
farmed in Alberta and Saskatchewan from 1880 to 1930, Nanci Langford
alludes to this myth of prairie hospitality:

> The requirement to be the sole food producer and preparer, in
> combination with the reality that it was the women who stayed on
> the farm more than the men, inevitably created a new work role for
> farm women, as a host. The work involved in entertaining visitors,
> in many cases on a daily basis, was relentless, at times enormous,
> and often resented. ("First Generation" 60)

In most of the memoirs studied here, prairie hospitality is both mentioned
and adhered to with good cheer. However, in Edith Hewson's *We Swept
the Cornflakes Out the Door* (1980), a memoir of the author's mother Katie
Cameron McDougall and the experience of homesteading in Saskatchewan
in the first three decades of the twentieth century, one chapter begins in the
following less than nostalgic manner:

> "Drat the luck! There's someone coming in the gate!" Kate put an-
> other plate on the table, and another kid shoved over on the bench.
> These complaints and the ensuing actions were a daily thing in
> her house. She rarely questioned the "rule of the plains" – "Feed
> all who come to your door at mealtime". This maxim demanded
> without saying it that a farm wife must give without question her
> fresh baked bread, her home-made pies and an open door hospital-
> ity, but required nothing from the recipient in return. There was no
> dearth of recipients at Kate's table. (176–77)

While she insists that her mother "rarely questioned" this "open door" policy of prairie living, nevertheless Hewson very strategically begins this scene with her mother's less than pleased voice and continues on to give a fairly critical reiteration of that policy. Further, Hewson goes on to imply that this policy is only to the benefit of men (and especially unmarried ones) and results in an increased workload for the prairie wife, who is essentially asked to play the wife and mother role on a grand scale:

> The prairies were a man's world. Men poured across the land by the trainload; labourers, harvesters and homesteaders. They came from the "old country" and after a lifetime of seeding and reaping the prairie still spoke with the their Newcastle-on-Tyne drawl, their Yorkshire twang, or their monosyllabic middle European accent. Young marriageable teachers were always well-courted, and lost little time after arrival before they were wooed and carried off by the lucky men who won them. But many men were never quite up to grabbing the pretty prizes, or convincing them that a shack on an undeveloped prairie farm was heaven on earth.
>
> To each farm family came these lonely ones who stopped as regularly as they had to pass by. The hunger in their eyes for human warmth was offset by the satisfied hunger after a meal at their neighbour's. Every Christmas, New Year's, Easter or Thanksgiving found one or more of these bachelors with their feet under the family table. They never left anything behind, like chocolates, perfume, or a gift for Kate; except if they stayed the night. Then often their unwelcome contributions had to be boiled and frozen out of the bedclothes, if Kate was lucky and caught them. (177)

A little bit later, Hewson shows the gap between her mother's surface adherence to the hospitality policy in terms of social niceties and the private reality of her own desire for freedom from the extra work:

Kate treated them all with the same cordiality she used with her
best friends, and demanded the children do the same or she would
"know the reason why!" when they were gone.

"I'm so tired of hired men, hired men, hired men! Just for once
it would be nice to sit down to a meal with only the family around
the table." Kate's wish was never to be granted. The hired man
was as much a part of the prairie farm operation as the horses or
machinery.

In *Porridge and Old Clothes*, Eileen Scott also writes critically on the topic
of prairie hospitality when speaking of the experience and from the perspective of her grandmother Agnes (Agabella) Rutherford Thomson:

> It seemed to Agabella that she never got a rest, not even on the
> Sabbath, because hoards of friends and neighbours would descend
> upon her. They would even come for their annual vacations. She
> didn't have a washing machine at first and everything had to be
> scrubbed on the scrubbing board. True, some of her visitors would
> give her a hand but she carried the main load. No wonder she suf-
> fered from stomach ulcers. I suppose her cooking was just too good
> and people from near and far knew it. Even the peddlers stuck
> their feet under Agabella's table. (10)

In Marjorie Grace Johannson's memoir of homesteading near Elfros,
Saskatchewan, at the beginning of the twentieth century, the author in-
corporates within *The Pink House on the Hill* (1986) actual entries from her
mother's diary, some of which make clear the prairie woman's disaffection for
impromptu visitors:

Monday, August 7 –

> "George started to work on the Government road today with
> his team and plough, $4.00 a day. I preserved my blueberries
> and a big basin of rhubarb. Mr. Rourke was here for dinner

and I had to fly all afternoon to get the dishes washed (they were all dirty) and get the house kind of tidy. Rained about 5:30 and old Bellamy came in here. He stayed for tea, then he and George talked reciprocity till after nine. I was nearly batty, then he went home rain and all. It rained all night and the blame roof leaked all night." (30)

As with bread-making, cooking more generally also became a matter of female cultural heritage; an intimate link between generations of female family members who were often separated geographically by the persistently futuristic focus of a masculinist culture. For example, when Ida Hopkins and her husband left southern Manitoba in 1929 to homestead in the Peace River country, as she notes in her memoir *To the Peace River Country and On*, it was only at the final moment of departure that the author realized the magnitude of their undertaking in terms of the familial/cultural community to be left behind:

Now the goodbyes. We hadn't anticipated how hard this would be. We suddenly realized that we would not be back for many years, and many of our friends would not be there. One final stop was to say goodbye to my ninety year old Grandmother. She walked around the truck with tears streaming down her face saying, "I wish I could come with you, I wish I could come with you". How we would have loved to have taken her. She went into the house and brought out her special cookie recipe, one that she had never shared with anyone and gave it to me. In her Irish Brouge she called them, "Ruzed Cakes". This is still one of my prized possessions. (17)

In lieu of her real presence, then, Hopkins's grandmother provides the young settler woman with a culinary heritage. As suggested by Anne Goldman, women sharing recipes both "provides an apt metaphor for the reproduction of culture from generation to generation" as well as "figure[s] a familial space within which self-articulation can begin to take place" (172). In this case,

Hopkins is enabled to journey to the Peace River country and start a new life, a new "self-articulation" beyond the depressed prairie inheritance of her own and her husband's family farms, precisely because she takes with her a tried and true culinary heritage.

For Judy Schultz, writing a memoir about the experiences of both her grandmother and mother homesteading near Wood Mountain, Saskatchewan, from the second decade of the twentieth century, it is inevitably necessary for her narrative to centre around female cooking. In *Mamie's Children: Three Generations of Prairie Women* (1997), the author notes that her grandmother Mamie once undertook an act that had positive personal significance for the author's own understanding of her maternal heritage:

> She had done the unthinkable for a woman of her day: She'd gone out to work, as a cook on the sprawling Metzger ranch, where two thousand head of cattle roamed the grassland and thirty-five hungry ranch hands pulled up to the table for five meals a day. Depending on the season, she'd feed a few more or a few less – less when they were out on cattle drives, more when everybody was in residence. Her cooking stories were part of my childhood mythology, for she and I both found her tales from a ranch kitchen far more entertaining than *Mother Goose. My, but those boys could tuck away the food. Land sakes, I was never finished – hot cakes and ham for early breakfast, steak and eggs for second breakfast, roast for dinner, cakes for afternoon, roast for supper, cakes before bed....* Between regular meals she baked a daily batch of bread and biscuits, made enough cakes and pies and cookies to stock a small bakery, and washed all the dishes by herself. (27–28)

After her grandmother's death, Schultz is able to maintain her connection with this "childhood mythology" through reference to an intimate record of female experience and knowledge, extending even beyond Schultz's own family:

> Mamie's Cash Book was full of recipes. The recipes were a legacy of other women, secrets of flavor and texture, these vital formulae

that were passed from friend to friend, mother to daughter, one generation of women to another. For many of them, the daily business of cooking was far more than an unavoidable chore. It was part science, part art, possibly the most useful art of all, and there was considerable personal satisfaction in setting a good table and in growing, harvesting and storing what went on it.

Mamie's Cash Book contained her recipe for her most memorable dish – chicken soup with fresh noodles. Years and years later in a kitchen in Bologna, Italy, I watched an Italian chef make noodles exactly the way Mamie had eventually taught me to make them back in Saskatchewan. The chef chattered away while she made a cone of flour on the breadboard, but it was Mamie's voice I heard, talking to my nine-year-old self.

Start with a good pile of flour, she'd tell me. *Thump the middle with your elbow to make a hole, just like that volcano in your book. See? Now break in some eggs.* (92–93)

Here, in the use of the familiar agricultural words "grow," "harvest" and "store," we see Schultz begin her literary confrontation, her recuperation of domestic labouring that needs to be privileged alongside the narratives representing the masculine heroics of agricultural life. She represents domestic labouring that makes commitment to the larger project of land settlement possible, for "the kitchen was both heart and nerve center of the rural home, the room you entered cold and left warm, entered hungry and left well-fed, ready to take another run at the world outside" (94). Indeed, Schultz tips the descriptive scale in favour of prairie women's contributions:

Men might run the farm that produced the grain and livestock – and when called upon, the women would work beside them – but the planting, growing, gathering, cooking and preserving of enormous gardens, the laying of the table, the baking and cooking and serving forth of the feast, and the cleaning up afterward were women's work. Simple things, but not easy.

The rewards were tangible, and like gardening, cooking had a
definite sensual quality. Most women of Mamie's day would have
been scandalized if they been described as sensualists, yet nobody
knew better than a farm woman the intense pleasure to be found
in the smell of rising bread or the little flutter somewhere behind
her ribs when the first lettuce made its appearance as a faint green
line across the garden on a spring morning, or the deep satisfaction
of putting the lid on the last of 120 sealers of wild plum jam. (93)

Unlike the yearly agricultural cycle of hope and, all too often, disappointment – a reality that created the "Next Year" philosophy described earlier
– the female labour listed here by Schultz indicates at least the possibility of
immediate personal satisfaction, of concrete results, in a world built largely
on speculation. Pulling her reader's eyes "away from the horizon" and turning
them "to the dirt under our feet," Schultz provides an intimately imaginative
account of the settler woman's daily reality.[38]

Another important area of home production undertaken by women in
order to control and provide for the consumption needs of the family, and thus
avoid economic strain on the family purse, was in their "complete responsibility for all manufacture, care, and repair of family clothing" (Faragher 53).
Sewing – as opposed to sowing – is foregrounded as a central factor in the farm
economy. As Barbara Burman states, "some historians have regarded clothing
as peripheral to historical enquiry, as too ephemeral or too everyday to warrant
attention"; however, it is through the efforts of those academics intent on "the
enlistment of previously neglected sources" that we can begin to "recover and
clarify [home dressmaking's] historical significance" (Introduction 2). On an
individual level, certainly for the women memoirists in this study, Burman is
accurate in her suggestion that home dressmaking appears to have "special
resonance and potency" in terms of "individual memory and life stories" (5).

---

38   For more examples of the importance of women's cooking to reminiscences of prai-
     rie life, see also Baldwin 66; Bannert 86–87; Clark passim; Ebbers 49–54; Hewson
     passim; Hopkins 10; McClung 107–8; Middleton 18; Moorhouse 18, 21, 29; Nash
     passim; Parsons 43, 116; Raber 110; Scott 59–60; Strange 128–29; and Thomson
     72.

Specific items of Home-made clothing are personal locators of time and place in prairie reminiscences. On a social level, as with other of the domestic arts, "the making, repair and alteration of clothing in the home was a transformative activity crucial to keeping up appearances and to sustaining all the possibilities inherent in the notion of respectability" (11). For example, in *Crocus and Meadowlark Country*, Georgina Thomson remembers a mother who, with "slender resources" to work from, was forced to provide for the material needs of younger children by "making over," making new, the clothing of older members of the family: "Fortunately Mother was a clever dressmaker, and she would rip and make over the clothes of our older sisters for us, adding a touch of velvet or braid for trimming" (169). However, Burman notes that "we cannot assume that home dressmaking always brought pleasure in either its making or its wearing" and that "accounts of childhood are full of instances of the special discomfort which home dressmaking can cause" (Introduction 12). As Jessie Raber notes, the economics of home dressmaking often frustrated her attempts at being seen as an individual as opposed to simply identifying as one of many in the Raber family: "Mother was busy, trying to get some sewing done for us. Every fall, Mother bought a whole bolt of dress goods, so we girls all dressed alike. I was getting old enough to want something a little different, but didn't dare say anything, so took what I got" (110). In Nell Parsons's memoir, we can see the mixture of contempt for and admiration of a settler woman's skill at making clothes for her family members, especially when those clothes were derived from previously worn garments. Home dressmaking "included extensive work to repair and remake clothing for basic needs as part of a fluid clothing survival strategy" (Burman, "Made" 36). As Parsons indicates,

> Mama made all our clothes. We had a remote-control touch with the world of English fashion. The aunts in England sent us, monthly, a fashion magazine known as *Weldon's Ladies Journal*.
>
> It was a miracle magazine, filled with recipes, needlework patterns, homey women's articles. But its most exciting feature was the free pattern each issue contained. In autumn, the pattern was a winter coat or a jacket. The following issue probably contained

patterns for skirt and blouse. Later would come underwear patterns
The spring issues looked toward spring outfits and Easter.

Summer issues brought patterns for challis and voile dresses,
with an evening dress thrown in now and then, a dress to be
made in rich moire, or even velvet; "This style being worn on the
Continent this season," captions informed us. The patterns were
always size thirty-six. For sending sixpence, one could obtain
other sizes. But who had sixpence?

Indeed, who had new goods from which to create the fashions?
Everything we wore was a make-over or a hand-me-down from
England or from Iowa.

"We can claim all our garments are original models." Mama
would smile in an irrepressible way she had. Original models!
Weldon's magazine sometimes mentioned "original models."

"Dressmaking from new material is no trick at all," Mama used
to declare. "Anybody can do that. But making something attractive
from old garments takes ingenuity and imagination." (116–17)[39]

Here we see the settler woman, rather than simply dreaming of a future in
which the family economy would allow for something better (something, one
might say, more "civilized," being what's worn "on the Continent"), eschewing

---

39   In her "Introduction" to an anthology devoted to *The Culture of Sewing*, Barbara
     Burman notes that

     a recent text on popular magazines dismissed a paper-pattern manufac-
     turer's monthly home dressmaking magazine of the 1920s (Weldon's
     Ladies' Journal) as "mindless" because it prioritized patterns over edito-
     rial, despite the fact that it was a bestseller with a circulation figure of
     442,631 a month. The purposes it served for all those readers are not
     considered. (3)

     Certainly it could not have been considered that some of those subscribing readers
     would have forwarded the magazine on to family members in the colonies as a
     practical and psychological aide to women's domestic economy.

role models in preference for viewing the situation in a self-reflexively positive light.

In difficult years economically, dressmaking for older girls who wanted something more fashionable meant a considerable level of creativity, especially when using materials which carried the possibility of social embarrassment. For Annie Keyes going *Down Memory Trails*, empty flour sacks evoke remembrance of the poverty of her family's agricultural dreams: as she writes,

> During the first years when we lived down by the river, we really were hard up. No money to buy print for dresses. I wore some that were given to us. The flour at that time came in a light blue fine checked cotton print bags. So mother sewed a dress for me of the flour bags. It was such a light color and soiled so easily. Mother told me later that for six years she had not been able to buy new cloth for any bedding. She sewed all sheets and pillow cases and slips of the white flour bags. Of course that always meant a lot of work before we had them ready for any sewing. The name print on those bags were so hard to get out. (42)

In *We Swept the Cornflakes*, Edith Hewson notes that her parents' "dominant concerns for their family were first food, then shelter" and that "clothing came off a poor third" (166). Like so many of the prairie women represented in these memoirs, Katie Cameron McDougall also finds it necessary to use "empty flour bags" in order to clothe her fourteen children, an economic reality that, as Hewson remembers it, had social implications: ordered to hang flour bags on the clothesline to blow out the excess flour, the young author questions her mother, "Mama! Why don't you buy Five Roses flour, like the Potters do?" (169). Initially "stumped," Kate asks back, "Why don't you like Robin Hood flour?," to which Hewson responds, "It's not exactly the flour, Mama. Frances Potter always has roses on her pants. I just hate Robin Hood on mine!" She then goes on to provide a humorous image to end this story, one which effectively profanes "King Wheat" as icon of prairie culture: "Robin Hood's male proximity to one's backside, and the direction he pointed his bow and arrow were embarrassing."

In the early 1930s, Ida Hopkins found it necessary to economize by learning to spin wool and make clothing for her family. While working with a neighbour homesteader who "was an artisan and should never have been wasting his time trying to farm," Hopkins's husband makes his wife a spinning wheel to set her on her way to home wool production: as she writes in *To the Peace*, "the first efforts were pretty rough, but it was used for socks. I know I made all the mistakes that could be made; such as winding two strands of yarn together the wrong way, and then trying to figure out why it all kinked up instead of lying flat. After many trials and errors I finally ended up making passable yarn" (53). With this "passable yarn," she fills in some crucial gaps in the family wardrobe:

> First I knit socks, mitts, sweaters and vests. Then Bill's [her husband's] underwear was getting thinner and thinner and the weather seemed to be getting colder and colder. There was no money to buy new sets so something had to be done about it. I had knit him long socks, to his knees, and thought perhaps I would knit a long sweater. This seemed a bit silly. Why not join them! I had used the softest wool we had; and spun quite fine wool. Now I cut up the old suit on the seams and laid it flat on the floor. I started at the ankle plaining and pearling in the regular way to form the leg cuff. Then as the leg got bigger I just added on more stitches, kept laying it on the pattern as I went along and measuring so it would not be too sloppy or small. In about three weeks I had knit a darn good pair of "Long Johns". With pure wool mitts, socks, and now underwear, he could now stand almost any amount of cold. They were not as bulky as commercial made underwear. Altogether I knit four suits. (53–54)

Noting that she "did not knit [these suits] for anyone else," nevertheless Hopkins advises that her homemade wool and knit products became a source of extra income, for she "made socks and mitts for the unmarried men" (54). As with women and bread-making, female labour within the domestic sphere so often underscores the larger agricultural project. Like Hopkins, Georgina

Thomson documents in *Crocus and Meadowlark Country* that home clothing manufacture sometimes exceeded domestic boundaries and became an economic survival tactic when the dream of "future plenty and success" had died. Thomson provides us with the image of Mrs. Linton, who "was very skilled with her needle," so much so that "when her husband Ebenezer or Eben, as she preferred to call him, died in his prime and left her four children to support, she started a sewing class for young ladies, teaching them the many beautiful embroidery stitches which she did so expertly herself" (106). Thus, domestic skills were not only a woman's key to survival in "Next Year Country," but also an essential insurance policy when next year failed to arrive.[40]

By thus turning our focus from the relatively undisturbed landscape of traditional narratives of western settlement in order to sift through prairie memoirs written by white, English-speaking women in search of the details, or "the slight events" (Jeffrey 8), of everyday life, we see that the "Home" gains equal ground with an otherwise "stead"-centred project. Faced with a vast and often sparsely populated landscape, such women (re)turned to the domestic routine of the Home not only as a retreat to the safety of clearly defined gender roles, but also as a source of strength and self-knowledge – a personal re-grounding during a time of flux – that would help the individual woman face the challenges about to come her way. In the performance of traditional domestic duties, as well as in the meeting of domestic challenges unique to the prairie environment, the prairie woman and her Home ultimately became the linchpin of a farm family's survival.

Although Gerald Friesen suggests that "the work week of farm women varied so much that normal or typical routines did not exist for them" (*The Canadian* 307), in fact, judging from the memoirs gathered here, a prairie woman's life was a series of cyclical markers: times of day, days of the week, seasons and years, all of which were constant reminders of her investment in her family's daily survival. For women settlers the homesteading experience was punctuated by the (seemingly) trivial and routine activities of everyday

---

40   For more examples of the economics of women's home clothing productions, see also Baldwin 221–22; McClung 96, 111; Parsons 66; Raber 50; Schroeder 60, 88; Schultz 38, 101–2; and Scott 9–10, 43–44.

life rather than the (supposedly) large-scale heroics of agricultural pursuits; indeed, such activities provided an essential buffer zone for all members of the family unit against the vagaries of an unstable economic enterprise. As Davidoff et al. suggest, "the essence of domesticity in the daily round, the weekly and seasonal rituals within the home, emphasized the cyclical and hence timeless quality of family life in opposition to the sharp disjunctive growth and collapse of commerce and industry" (156). Unfortunately the very words "trivial" and "routine" may suggest experiences which do not merit scholarly attention, but given "the rise of a feminist scholarship that considers the study of women vital rather than trivial" (Kimball 2), we are now able to recover the domestic realities of prairie life as a means to re-vision traditional settlement narratives, and sometimes even to confront ideals of the Prairie Woman herself.

❋ 3 ❋

"Dauntless Optimism"/"Perverse Endurance": Re-Visioning Literary Narratives of Settler Women

Over these abominable corduroys the vehicle jolts, jumping from log to log, with a shock that must be endured with as good a grace as possible. If you could bear these knocks, and pitiless thumpings and bumpings, without wry faces, your patience and philosophy would far exceed mine; – sometimes I laughed because I would not cry.

> – Catharine Parr Traill, *The Backwoods of Canada* (1836)

How ardently we anticipate pleasure, which often ends in positive pain!

> – Susanna Moodie, *Roughing It in the Bush* (1852)

Optimism is more contagious than measles.

> – Elinor Marsden Eliot, *My Canada* (1915)

To compose a work is to negotiate with these questions: What stories can be told? How can plots be resolved? What is felt to be

narratable by both literary and social conventions? Indeed, these
are issues very acute to certain feminist critics and women writers,
with their senses of the untold story, the other side of a well-known
tale, the elements of women's existence that have never been revealed.

– Rachel Blau DuPlessis, *Writing Beyond the Ending: Narrative
Strategies of Twentieth-Century Women Writers* (1985)

The production of life writing texts by Canadian women settlers represents a
long-established tradition in our literary culture; however, somewhere along
the line, the western half of that tradition has largely been lost, from academic
attention, at least, if not from the popular imagination. In fact, scholarly
attention to Canadian literature dealing with the issue of land settlement has
ranged in focus from non-fictional texts written by eastern Canadian women
to fictional texts written by western Canadian authors. Canadian literary criticism has produced no concerted examination of the relatively large body of
prairie memoirs written by white, English-speaking women who participated
in western land settlement in the late-nineteenth and early-twentieth centuries. The inevitable result of this critical lack, I would suggest, is the transpos-
ition of experience from east to west and from fiction to real life; that is, given
the lack of attention paid to western settlement memoirs, readers interested in
the topic of prairie women's lives must either assume a similarity of experience
of "pioneering" in any region and time period of Canada and/or they must
assume the reliability of fictional representations of prairie land settlement.

The potential problem with this critical situation is a heavy reliance upon
cultural image in our understanding of prairie women's lived experience.
While we might easily recognize that fictional women are image productions
of a specific cultural moment, it is also important to consider that those eastern
Canadian women whose texts have received intense critical treatment in the
last few decades have arguably become larger than life figures in our national
culture – have become iconic images heralding the advent of a tradition of
white women's mental/emotional/physical responses to "pioneering" a nation.
For example, Elizabeth Thompson's *The Pioneer Woman: A Canadian Character
Type* (1991), the only full-length academic study of the "Pioneer Woman" in

Canadian literature to date, begins with Catharine Parr Traill's life writing and fictional texts to establish a "Canadian Character Type," or image, that can be traced across region and time period. While both Traill and her sister, Susanna Moodie, have found their place in the Canadian literary imagination, the critical tendency has been to consider the two women separately as polar opposites in personality (very much like the "cheerful helpmate"/"reluctant emigrant" binary referred to previously in this study), with readers especially "captivated by Catharine's sunny temperament" (Gray x), her more positive self-representation. The inevitable result of creating a (false) Traill/Moodie binary against which all other settlement texts are judged is that the female "character" will be seen *either* to uphold those qualities initiated by Traill, *or* to fail to do so, and their texts will be judged accordingly.

As in Chapter Two, in which I sought to re-vision the large-scale narratives of western settlement to a more localized focus upon women's lived experience, I am primarily concerned here with the function of cultural narratives in the representation of settlement life. Specifically, I am concerned with how the narrative of "dauntless optimism," encapsulated in the figure of Catharine Parr Traill, dominated the self-representation of settler women in the century following her work. The purpose of this chapter, then, is to re-examine the ideal of the "Pioneer Woman" as established by Traill's texts, to trace the degree to which this ideal has been transposed to western settlement texts, and to propose a sort of "moodification" of Traill's iconic image. In this way might we "write beyond the ending" (DuPlessis, *Writing* 5) of white, western, settlement narratives we have been given to believe in lieu of women's own voices. Certainly many of the authors studied here, most of whom published their texts several decades after the experience of prairie life, and often as daughters memorializing the painful experiences of their mothers, literally wrote "beyond the ending" of the cultural moment of land settlement; wrote from an historical moment that was caught in the waves of nostalgia that were the heritage movement in Canada, and that, for many, was in the midst of feminism's radical second-wave, when confrontation was a vehicle for social change. We as readers also need to get beyond conventional characterizations of the Prairie Woman – to get to what DuPlessis in the epigraph above calls "the other side of a well-known tale" – and to do so necessitates that we put

the Traill ideal in dialogue with her less culturally idolized sister, Susanna
Moodie, whose own writings will help me to establish the other end of a
continuum of white, English-speaking women's responses to settlement life.
In this project I take my cue from the most recent biography of Traill and
Moodie, Charlotte Gray's *Sisters in the Wilderness: The Lives of Susanna Moodie
and Catharine Parr Traill* (1999), an interwoven treatment of the two "literary
archetypes" that finally works to get past the "personalities" that have been
"deduced ... from their published works"; to discover that "there is much more
to both of them than they ever allowed their own readers to know" (xiii–xiv).

Elizabeth Thompson writes that *The Pioneer Woman*'s "creation was, in
fact, grounded in the actuality of the pioneer experience, and on details of the
experience that were reconstructed and reinterpreted in fiction, often through
a moralistic or idealistic filter" (3). The Pioneer Woman is encapsulated for
Thompson in the figure of Catharine Parr Traill, who "becomes the single
most important contributor to the creation of this new, Canadian, concept of
women in both an historical and a literary sense" (5). Traill, who emigrated to
Canada with her husband Thomas to Lakefield, Ontario, in 1832,[1] produced
two non-fiction texts on the subject of land settlement in the colony, *The
Backwoods of Canada* (1836) and *The Canadian Settler's Guide* (1855). What
makes Traill's writing, and especially these "two most important and accomplished works," unique, suggests Thompson, is Traill's ability, rather than
to lament the "gentlewoman's plight when faced with the exigencies of the
Canadian frontier," to attempt to "fuse the two divergent ways of life"; to
combine "the real physical necessities of life on a frontier both with her own
personal system of values and with her continued perception of herself as an
English lady" (32–33). Taking a stalwart approach to her isolated situation
beyond the fringes of "civilization," Traill manages to paint the "picture of
the typical pioneer woman" as being a "self-assured, confident woman, one
who adapts cheerfully to adverse circumstances, one who is capable and active
in an emergency, one who plays a vital role in pioneering" (4). Indeed, in *The
Backwoods*, Traill answers the question, "What are necessary qualifications of

---

1   Both Traill and her sister Susanna Moodie emigrated in 1832, a year in which "the
     flood tide of emigrants to Canada was at its peak" (Gray 51–52).

a settler's wife[?]" as follows: "[A] settler's wife should be active, industrious, cheerful, not above putting her hand to whatever is necessary to be done in her household" (149).

The one word repeatedly used by critics – Thompson among them – in describing Traill's philosophical stance is "cheerful," a word with a fairly simple aspect, yet one that eventually takes on mythic proportions even in Traill's own writing. In her Introduction to *The Backwoods*, in which she outlines her purpose for writing as being a sort of defence, based on lived experience, against the wide-scale and misleading propaganda surrounding the topic of Canadian immigration, Traill displays practically no trace of anger regarding the reality "of the trials and arduous duties she ha[d] to encounter" in the Ontarian backwoods (9). Rather, she writes to combat descriptions of Canada as a "land of Canaan" (85), descriptions which were far too appealing for those younger sons of the gentry, such as her husband, whose future as half-pay army officers had been blighted and who found themselves part of the upper class in name only. It was for such emigrants, and most especially their wives, "the person on whose responsibility the whole comfort of a family depends," that Traill felt she must write, "honestly representing facts in their real and true light" (9–10). Traill's purpose, then, is not to inhibit the desire to emigrate to Canada, but rather to ensure that, once the journey has been undertaken, the female member of the household would approach the project with the "high-spirited cheerfulness" necessary for her family's success and happiness. This type of gender prescription eventually permeated narratives of Canadian settlement, as seen in N.P. Willis's 1842 text *Canadian Scenery*, in which the author advises, regarding the many and various "occupations of an emigrant's wife," that "if a female cannot resolve to enter upon them cheerfully, she should never think of settling in the woods of Canada or New Brunswick" (qtd. in Abrahamson 4).

As Thompson recognizes, the stoic ideal represented by Traill contrasts sharply with Traill's own sister, Susanna Moodie, whose constant "complaining tone" (46) shows her disaffection for, rather than cheerful adaptation to, settlement conditions. Susanna, who emigrated with her husband John W. Dunbar Moodie in the same year as the Traills, also wrote two texts about her experiences in Canada, *Roughing It in the Bush* (1852) and *Life in the Clearings versus the Bush* (1853), the former of which was, like Traill's text, meant to contradict the tradition of "pamphlets, published by interested parties, which prominently set forth all the *good* to be derived from a settlement in the Backwoods of Canada; while they carefully concealed the toil and hardship to be endured in order to secure these advantages" (13). Unlike her sister, however, Moodie does not hide her anger and deep sense of betrayal; she does not easily adopt the cheerful veil recommended in her sister's texts. Put succinctly, "Moodie did not idealize pioneer life" (Thompson, Elizabeth 32). In the first 1852 British edition of Moodie's text, we can see the full extent of the author's anger in the final chapter, in which she states, "If these sketches should prove the means of deterring one family from sinking their property, and shipwrecking all their hopes, by going to reside in the backwoods of Canada, I shall consider myself amply repaid for revealing the secrets of the prison-house, and feel that I have not toiled and suffered in the wilderness in vain" (489). Not exactly "high-spirited cheerfulness."[2]

These distinctions in tone between the two sisters' texts are commensurate with their very different generic formats. In *The Backwoods*, Traill's "Pollyanna cheerfulness" (Gray 62) probably stems at least in part from the fact that the text began its life as "daily journals and letters to her mother and friends in England" (Fowler 62), written as a means to assure them of her survival beyond the fringes of "civilization." Unlike her sister, Traill *is* eminently capable of hiding her fears and anger about the reality of settlement life. As Charlotte Gray suggests, "at one level, Catharine's enthusiasm was genuine," but there was also "a bleak self-justification underlying [her]

---

2   It should be noted that in the first 1871 Canadian edition of Moodie's text, there was provided a new "Introduction," which, although still primarily negatively-inspired, illustrates the author's attempt to soften the tone of her narrative "warning to others" and dissuade her Canadian readers from the "most unjust prejudice … felt against her book" (527–28). Although at the time of writing *Roughing It*, she "[gave her] opinion freely on a subject which had engrossed a great deal of [her] attention," Moodie assures her Canadian readers that, after almost twenty more years had passed, "my love for the country has steadily increased, from year to year, and my attachment to Canada is now so strong, that I cannot imagine any inducement, short of absolute necessity, which could induce me to leave the colony, where, as a wife and mother, some of the happiest years of my life have been spent" (528).

upbeat tone. Catharine knew that her mother and elder sisters would find Upper Canada appallingly primitive, and that they would be disgusted at the lack of regard for social status" (112). In addition to her concern for the sensibilities of the audience back home, her letters "brim over with the same cheerful enthusiasm that, by now, Catharine had decided it was her marital duty to provide for her husband" (82).[3] Thomas Traill, as it turned out, was particularly ill-suited, physically and psychologically, for settlement life, and "the most unnerving fact for Catharine was the way Thomas sank into gloom" (62) from the moment of their Atlantic crossing. Says Gray, knowing that "if she allowed herself to linger on the discomforts of their new life, she would be falling in with Thomas's pessimism," Catharine "resorted to playing the role she had so often played within the Strickland family: the resilient optimist, who raised everybody's spirits" (113, 62). For example, in reference to a letter received from back home, Traill acknowledges to the author that "Your expressions of regret for my exile, as you term my residence in this country, affected me greatly. Let the assurance that I am not less happy than when I left my native land, console you for my absence. If my situation be changed, my heart is not. My spirits are as light as ever, and at times I feel a gaiety that bids defiance to all care" (*Backwoods* 166).

The publication of Traill's "journal letter"[4] as a sort of public "advice" or "conduct" manual[5] in 1836, only four years after her arrival in Canada, ensured her literary and historical position as icon in Canadian culture. As Gray

---

3   In contrast to Traill, Moodie's letters home oftentimes "described [her family's] circumstances with grim realism" (Gray 89). Traill, too, had outlets for her problems: as Gray notes, when she wrote to Moodie she "poured out her worries" to an extent unknown in her published works, and even to long-time friend, Frances Stewart, Traill "reluctantly confided her own bouts of despair" (181, 188).

4   A "journal letter" is defined by Kathryn Carter as being a "diary written in installments and explicitly addressed to a particular person or set of persons. Generally, it features periodic diary entries addressed to distant loved ones in the form of an extended letter" (51).

5   "Advice" or "Conduct" manuals in Britain were books written by both men and women that "prescribed the way in which a woman should behave in all circumstances, and often gave very detailed guides to personal conduct, from sexual behaviour to appropriate reading" (Buck 437).

notes, both Traill and Moodie had publication histories that included "poetry, romantic fiction and children's stories that fit into the Regency tradition of women's writing," meaning that "most of it was insipid and conventional" (x). Traill's letters appeared suitably "conventional" to her sister Agnes, who edited them into an "attractive publication" in which the author's "sunny personality almost leaps off every page" (114–15). Traill creates a precise recipe for settlement success: as "aliens and wanderers in a distant country" (12), she chooses a method of "adaptation/adoption" in order to negotiate her survival in the backwoods of Canada – that is, she found it necessary to "adapt" much of her British assumptions about life to her new surroundings and to "adopt" ways of being in her new home place to survive in a reality for which she had not been prepared by her inherited cultural knowledge. Significantly, "advice literature" often counselled a woman to "adapt herself to circumstances, and particularly to her husband" (254), so that, in providing advice to potential emigrants, Traill obviously knew that she had to practise what she preached, which no doubt also dictated the cheerful tone of her writing.[6] As Doug Owram suggests regarding "European man's" struggle to survive in the wilderness of the New World, "the person who did adapt became, in the natural course of things, an almost heroic figure" (*Promise* 19). This is an effect attributable to Traill, as seen, for example, in E. Blanche Norcross's *Pioneers Every One: Canadian Women of Achievement* (1979), which "tells the story of a number of women who played an outstanding part in the Canadian adventure" (7). Notably, in the section called "Women of the Frontier," Traill is given a chapter while Moodie is not. The need for cultural icons of female behaviour is evident in Norcross's assertion that the women she chose to include in her textual tribute "were heroines who succeeded against great odds. They showed other women what could be achieved" (7).

---

6 Traill obviously understood the importance of narrative adherence to one's own philosophy, as seen when her brother, Samuel Strickland, with whom the Traills spent time while awaiting the construction of their first home in the backwoods, states, "My pass-words are, 'Hope! Resolution! and Perseverance!'," to which Thomas Traill replies, "This ... is true philosophy; and the more forcible, because you not only recommend the maxim but practise it also" (108).

The immediacy of Traill's letters is in contrast with the reflective distance of Moodie's text, which was not published until 1852, some twenty years after her arrival in Canada and "a decade after she had lived through these experiences" (Gray 209), an adequately long time for the stewing of authorial anger. Unlike Traill, whose "upbeat pretense, for Reydon [the family home in England] consumption, about her less-than-perfect marriage and precipitate decision to emigrate now became the gloss over the hardships of pioneer life," Moodie "was able to put some distance between herself and her life. She was candid about the hardships of the immigrant life" (115, 209). For far too long her "candidness" has been negatively read as evidence of, in contrast to her iconic sister, a bad-natured personality,[7] with the end result that, at least until very recently, readers have often missed the complexity of her cultural critique.[8] The situation of the Moodies was in some respects the inverse of the Traills; that is, while Moodie tended towards the gloomy nature of her brother-in-law, John possessed a "blithe optimism" (Gray 84) that often anchored his wife's resolve. To suggest that John Moodie was cheerful, however, is not to suggest that he was any more capable of success at home-steading than Thomas Traill, and it was inevitably Susanna's psychological strength, often fuelled by her anger at the reality of an emigrant's life in the backwoods, which ensured her family's survival. That anger, that real-ity, suffuses the pages of Moodie's public self-representations. Little wonder, coming from one of the two Strickland sisters (the other being Agnes) who, says Gray, "pushed at the limits of convention" (24) in her published writing. *Backwoods* was no different, for in it the reflective author "was at pains to show the dark underbelly of experiences that her own sister Catharine had

---

7   As seen, for example, in Agnes Strickland's reaction to *Roughing It*: "In [Agnes's] eyes, Susanna's discovery of her own 'Canadian' voice was simply a whining account of past wretchedness which would have been better forgotten" (Gray 214).

8   For example, in 1979 Dermot McCarthy, although finding the book "fascinating and significant," nevertheless felt that "as writing, it is aesthetically flawed; on the whole, mediocre. Moods, sentiments, attitudes are overstated, cloying, and contra-dictory; the style, or styles, are uneven" (3). See Misao Dean's chapter on Susanna Moodie in *Practising Femininity: Domestic Realism and the Performance of Gender in Early Canadian Fiction* (Toronto: University of Toronto Press, 1998) for an overview of critical readings of the text.

written about with gentle joy" (Gray 206).[9] Critical respect for exposing that "dark underbelly" was a long time coming. As Alec Lucas asserted in 1990, Moodie's text "has seldom received the credit it merits as a work in which themes, characters, and narrative form a coherent whole" (146). Specifically in relation to the many embedded character sketches, Lucas suggests that "critics fail to recognize" that "the autobiographical sketch was the only way, other than the essay, open to Moodie to write realistically and imaginatively of her experiences in the backwoods" (146).

Although there has been critical acknowledgment that Traill's philosophical strengths "may be too idealistic for practical application" (Thompson, Elizabeth 32), nevertheless her narrative cheerfulness all too often finds its place as an ideal of female behaviour, with Moodie perennially consigned to the "other" end of the settler woman spectrum – the negative end, whereby women settlers are judged as failures if they do not uphold Traill's more positive vision. The either/or-ism of the Pioneer Woman image has also affected our understanding of white, English-speaking, prairie women, especially given what has been a too limited focus upon *fictional* transpositions of that image. As settlement of the Canadian landscape moved westward, the Pioneer Woman migrated from *The Backwoods* and adapted herself so well that, according to Thompson, she became institutionalized as an "accepted and essential aspect of female characterization in Canadian fiction" (3):

> [T]he longevity of the pioneer woman as character type in English-Canadian fiction and her recurrent use as a metaphor for Canadian femininity indicate that the character appeals to some common perception of a woman's role in Canadian society, and that the role for women proposed by the early emigrants was indeed an appropriate choice for the Canadian frontier, *regardless of the location and nature of that frontier*. (3; emphasis added)

---

9   As Gray notes, Agnes's distaste for Moodie's book even affected her response to
     Traill's proposal for her second volume aimed at female emigrants to Canada, *The
     Canadian Settler's Guide*, for in a letter she suggested, "Be sure you warn ladies not
     to make the worst of everything" (237), clearly an indictment of Moodie's work.

While the Traill typology was becoming entrenched in fictional representations of western settlement, real-life women were still confronting the actual western landscape as they emigrated to the prairie provinces, and the extent to which their memoir texts recreate the Traill ideal (or the "cheerful helpmate" ideal, as discussed in Chapter One) reveals how surely cultural image becomes what DuPlessis calls a "literary and social convention." As Sheila McManus notes in her examination of farm women in Alberta,

> Characteristics such as uncomplaining perseverance and adapting to a challenging new environment were generally praised and occupied a central place in these farm women's construction of appropriate femininity. Not possessing these characteristics or actively displaying their reverse, set a woman firmly outside what was acceptable. (128)

We can see the impact of such binaristic thinking, and its specific importance for women of Anglo background, in many of the memoirs gathered in this study. For example, we can see the invocation of a decidedly Traill typology at the end of Kathleen Strange's *With the West in Her Eyes* (1945):

> I feel sure that any modest success, and certainly the great happiness, that I myself have enjoyed in this country has been mainly owing to the fact that I possess one particular quality – a quality that is possessed in a high degree by all people of British stock – that of *adapting* myself. I reminded myself from the outset that Canada was to be my permanent home. It was to provide the means of my husband's livelihood. It was to become the birthplace of my children. I must accept it as my own country. And I did. (292)

In Franklin Foster's "Foreword" to the 1997 edition of Mary Hiemstra's *Gully Farm* (1955), we can see that the cultural embrace of the Traill typology as a palatable mode of being during western settlement necessitated a rejection of a more Moodie state:

Generations of Can. Lit. students have been exposed to Susanna
Moodie's *Roughing It in the Bush* for its rare account of a woman's
daily life in the backwoods of pioneer Upper Canada. *Gully Farm*
deserves equal rank. It speaks strongly to western Canadians, and
Hiemstra avoids the underlying outraged frustration that colours
Moodie's recollection of what seemed to her a period of exile on a
stump farm north of Belleville. Little Mary Pinder recognized the
hardships of pioneer life, but she quickly accepted them as part of
the sacrifice necessary to build the new and better life her parents
and so many others sought. (x)

In order to get past such extreme either/or thinking, we must, as Gray's biography of Traill and Moodie works to do, put these behavioural binaries in
conversation as a means to get at the more complex reality lying behind the
idealistic veneer of the Prairie Woman image. By rejecting the either/or construction of prairie womanhood in order to see a reality of experience that
rests and ranges on a continuum of possibility, we will be able to discern the
ways in which white, English-speaking prairie women "act in accordance with
ideals" and also "account for [their] failures and incoherences" (Weir 127)
with those ideals. The point is not to contend with the predominance of the
Traill image by suggesting that prairie women fit the Moodie model instead;
rather, the point is more simply to examine how the memoirists studied here
represent issues/behaviours that allow for a more complex understanding of
the Prairie Woman as exhibiting a range of responses to western settlement.
It is here again important to note that many of these memoirs were written by
daughters/grand-daughters with varying degrees of distance from the cultural
convention of the Prairie Woman, both in experiential and temporal terms,
which allows them a greater chance at confrontation in their texts. While it
is certainly true that "written descriptions or artistic-literary expressions of
experience, authored both by participants and by observers, contemporary or
historical, will be influenced by the images they possess" (Stoeltje 26), it is
equally important to recognize the individual's ability to "participate in [her]
own constitution" (Weir 127) through articulation of her own experiences.

Traill's "cheerfulness" may have been the ideological starting point for prescribing female emigrants' behaviour, but that single word soon evolved into a cultural myth that has permeated the production and study of women's settlement texts – something I will call (borrowing a phrase from one of the memoirs included in this study) the myth of "dauntless optimism" (Roberts 37).[10] As Thompson suggests, Traill's writings display a consistent and "determined optimism," and "an ability to bow to the inevitable" (39). As Traill herself puts it in *Backwoods*, "nothing argues a greater degree of good sense and good feeling than a cheerful conformity to circumstances, adverse though they be compared with a former lot" (150). It is always difficult to discern a woman's part in the decision to emigrate to Canada, but it has been popular to assert both Thomas's central role in making the Traills' decision to leave and Catharine's extreme enthusiasm for Thomas's decision.[11] However, enthusiasm for a fate already decided seems less than purely inspired; rather, as Gray notes, "although the Strickland girls were raised to respect intellectual achievement, they were also brought up to be docile wives to whomever they might marry" (27). We can discern this upbringing in Traill's *Backwoods*, in which the author indicates her adoption of a Ruthian ideology of female behaviour: indeed, Traill explicitly invokes the biblical image of Ruth when on a visit to "the house of a resident clergyman, curate of a flourishing village in the township of ———" (220): speaking of his wife's "decision" to join him in emigrating to Canada, the clergyman states that,

> when I named to her the desire of my parishioners [who were emigrating en masse], and she also perceived that my own wishes went

---

10   Using this phrase in a discussion of Traill's work seems particularly apt given the assertion in Moodie's text that "The Scotch are a tough people; they are not easily *daunted* – a few difficulties only seem to make them more eager to get on" (261; emphasis added).

11   For example, as Audrey Morris represents the scene back home in England, Thomas, who was "twelve years older than Catharine," "announced not only his own plans for an early departure in the spring to Canada, but also that he was taking Catharine Strickland with him as his wife" (29). Norcross suggests that "Catherine [*sic*] was thirty years old, just married, and eagerly looking forward to a new life in Canada" (47).

with them, she stifled any regretful feeling that might have arisen
in her breast, and replied to me in the words of Ruth: –

"Thy country shall be my country; thy people shall be my
people; where thou diest I will die, and there will I be buried: the
Lord do so to me, and more also, if ought but death part thee and
me." (224)[12]

Subtly implying that perhaps she had been feeling less than enthusiastic about
her life in Canada, after this scene, Traill assures her readers that "the pas-
tor told us enough to make me quite contented with my lot, and I returned
home, after some days' pleasant sojourn with this delightful family, with an
additional stock of contentment" (227).

While Traill's adaptations thus appear to be biblical in nature, Moodie
appears to be unable to perform the adaptation of the "British gentlewoman"
image or the "dutiful Ruth" image to the physical reality of life "in the bush."
Initially at least, Moodie does appear to adopt this role, as seen in her acknowledgment that it was her husband who "finally determined to emigrate
to Canada" (72),[13] a decision with which she concurs, saying she had "bowed
to a superior mandate, the command of duty" (194). Although nowhere in her
text does Moodie explicitly invoke the image of Ruth, nevertheless at several
points she paraphrases the sentiments of that image.[14] However, the reality

---

12   Despite the fact that I am relying here upon traditional distortions of the Book of
     Ruth as "reinforcing repressive stereotypes of docile and angelically 'good' women"
     (Kates and Reimer xx), a distortion to which Traill and many of the prairie mem-
     oirists included in this study obviously subscribed, it is important to point out the
     considerable feminist scholarship that has attended to this and other female-centred
     biblical stories in recent years. On the Book of Ruth in particular, see, for example,
     Reading Ruth: Contemporary Women Reclaim a Sacred Story, eds. Judith A. Kates and
     Gail Twersky Reimer (New York: Ballantine, 1994).

13   As Moodie clarifies in the 1871 Canadian edition of her text, her husband, "not
     being overgifted with the good things of this world – the younger sons of old
     British families seldom are – he had, after mature deliberation, determined to try
     his fortunes in Canada, and settle upon the grant of 400 acres of land, ceded by the
     Government to officers upon half-pay" (525).

14   For example, she writes that "emigration may, indeed, generally be regarded as an
     act of severe duty, performed at the expense of personal enjoyment, and accompan-

behind Moodie's Ruthian self-representation is quite different: as Gray notes, even before she and John were married, Moodie's rebellious nature rose to the surface: "In January 1831, while John was still in Scotland [visiting relatives], [Susanna] abruptly broke off the engagement: 'I have changed my mind. You may call me a jilt or a flirt or what you please.... I will neither marry a soldier nor leave my country for ever....'" (32). Suggests Gray, "the prospect of emigration appalled Susanna. She did not want to leave England" (43). In addition, Moodie provides a scene in *Roughing It* in which a male emigrant remarks upon the unfairness of subjecting women to the conditions of immigrant life, then she uses the scene as a subtle means to criticize her husband's own decision to emigrate to Canada. Having attended a lecture on the merits of emigrating to Canada, from which Susanna is certain her husband will return "quite sickened with the Canadian project" (64), John Moodie arrives home accompanied by a friend, Tom Wilson, who makes the following less than optimistic prediction of their chances for success at life in the colonies: "we shall both return like bad pennies to our native shores. But, as I have neither wife nor child to involve in my failure, I think, without much self-flattery, that my prospects are better than yours," a statement that Moodie upholds when she advises her reader that "there was more truth in poor Tom's words than at that moment we were willing to allow" (72). If we accept that "Moodie's narrative of Tom's story becomes a strategy by which she may say things, realize things about her husband that cannot be said, cannot even be thought, inside the wife's discourse" (Buss, *Mapping* 89), then it is apparent that Moodie's narrative rejects her sister's Ruthian cheerfulness.

The contagious nature of "dauntless optimism" – which, as will be seen, is reflected by a number of synonymous terms – in the decision to emigrate, its particular attraction for potential male settlers, and the woman settler's role in spreading the infection, are all aspects of land settlement in Canada

---

ied by the sacrifice of those local attachments which stamp the scenes amid which our childhood grew, in imperishable characters upon the heart" (11). The concept of female duty is also present in her "Lament of a Canadian Emigrant," in which she writes, "And the babe on my bosom so calmly reclining,/ Check'd the tears as they rose, and all useless repining./ The stern voice of duty compell'd me to roam,/ From country and friends – the enjoyments of home" (85).

which eventually migrated to the prairie region. For the institutions which promoted western settlement, the myth of "dauntless optimism" functioned as a dominant cultural narrative and, at least according to the considerable number of prairie memoirs I have read, it was a myth that was initially most attractive for men. In his discussion of promotional materials for western settlement while Clifford Sifton was Minister of the Interior, David Hall says it was "a masculine audience to whom the writers appealed; the assumption clearly was that men were making the decisions about settling in the West" (85–86). There has been considerable debate about which gender was most likely to choose emigration. For example, while Sara Brooks Sundberg suggests that "the lure of cheap land, the chance for economic independence, captured the imaginations of women as well as men" and that, "in fact, women were sometimes the first to recognize the opportunities inherent in western land" (73–74), John Mack Faragher's study of women on the Overland Trail makes the contrary observation:

> In their diaries and recollections many women discussed the way in which the decision to move was made. Not one wife initiated the idea; it was always the husband. Less than a quarter of the women writers recorded agreeing with their restless husbands; most of them accepted it as a husband-made decision to which they could only acquiesce. But nearly a third wrote of their objections and how they moved only reluctantly. (163)

While the truth of the matter is that the decision-making process was a complex one, affected by individual personality, family economics, gender ideologies, etc., nevertheless what is beyond doubt is that the promotional literature aimed at settlement presented the Canadian West with a distinctly seductive air, as seen especially in the "profusion of pamphlets with alluring titles" (Bruce 4), such as "The Last Best West" and "The Granary of the British Empire."[15]

---

15 This propaganda campaign was initiated by governmental sources and represented an amazingly vast undertaking: "The chief function of the federal Department of Agriculture from 1867 until 1892, when the responsibility was transferred to

A sort of romantic wooing was undertaken by the pamphleteers, who no doubt understood, as did Emily Ferguson, that male readers in particular would be "caught and lured by colour, atmosphere, the hidden, the desire for the new, the ache for adventure, the something behind the hills" (*Open* 111).[16] For example, in *Gully Farm*, Mary Hiemstra represents a conversation between her mother and her Uncle Sam, who says about Mr. Pinder's enthusiasm for emigration, "'He seems *quite smitten* with Canada'" (7; emphasis added). Nellie L. McClung writes in *Clearing in the West: My Own Story* (1935) that her eldest brother Will was the first in her family to be taken in by the tide of western immigration: feeling restless about the "narrow gauge" of life on a farm in "The County of Grey," Ontario (29), Will began to pay attention to the books and letters being produced in the late 1870s about land settlement in the Canadian west. As McClung writes, "the majority of the farmers were skeptical ... but men, particularly young men, who worked on stony farms listened eagerly" (30). When a young male emigrant comes back home for a time to get married, he has "many tales to tell" about life in the

---

the Department of the Interior, was the promotion of immigration.... Starting from a faith in the importance of free land, the branch spent large sums on maps, pamphlets, prospectuses, and other printed advertising material in a wide range of languages – probably at least a million pieces per year after 1870" (Friesen, *The Canadian* 185).

16 The assumption that male emigrants would respond most enthusiastically to promotional materials is evident in Ferguson's sarcastic description of the special brand of optimism inspired by such materials:

> [I]t is natural that in a land where despondency is unknown, the whole lion-hearted generation should be addicted to magnifying themselves and their wonderful country.
>   A lie is nothing serious to a Westerner. He need not check his reputation on such occasions. His "stretchers" are mere natural ebullitions arising purely from rewarded toil, prosperity, and a singularly ozonated atmosphere. (119)

A rare and more realistic consideration of the virtues of Canadian homesteading occurs in Heather Gilead's *The Maple Leaf for Quite a While* (1967), in which the author says of her father that "he had a thorough instinctive mistrust of all fast bucks, all easy money, all short cuts to wealth and/or the millennium," so he chose a "semi-desirable farm which would yield a living if you treated it right, but never much more than a living" (12).

West, such as that there are "hundreds of acres of land, without a stone, or a bush, *waiting to be taken*" (31; emphasis added). The result is inevitable, for the young men of the community "could see the sea of grass and the friendly skies above it, and they could feel the intoxication of being the first to plant the seed in that mellow black loam, enriched by a million years of rain and sun." As McClung acknowledges, "Will caught the fever," and he became the touchstone for the family's future: "Will would go at once and if he liked it we would all go in a year" (38). At the beginning of the twentieth century, Winnie E. Hutton's family began to "talk of going to the North West": as she describes in *No "Coppers" in Saskatchewan!* (1973), "brochures we received used flowery language to tell of the 'Wonderful West' which was opening up. There were photos of nice homes being built after only a short time, giving the impression that we would be rich in a few years. They never mentioned the words drought, frost or hail" (1). As with McClung's family, Hutton's brother Roy Sinden is the first to go west, and his "enthusiasm" upon return is so infectious that both the author's "father and brother-in-law decided they would also get homesteads. They were each able to file on a ¼ section adjacent to the one Roy had, and the business was completed in the East" (2). The land having been taken sight unseen at the time, Hutton's retrospective and subtly sarcastic account of the family's arrival at the homestead sites calls into question her brother's original optimism: "We were happy to arrive at the homestead and see the rest of the family. We had to get accustomed to the flat prairie with no trees, but we were not going to let a little thing like that dampen our enthusiasm. After all, we were looking forward to the wealth we had read about in the brochures" (4).[17]

While "dauntless optimism" was initially highly attractive – or highly contagious, depending upon the chosen metaphor – for male immigrants, the philosophy also required that women settlers submit themselves to the infection, incubate it, then renew its strength from time to time as the positive vision was dimmed by reality. Indeed, the male settler did not always and easily

---

17   For more examples of male enthusiasm about western settlement, see also Baldwin
      21–31; Campbell 3; Ebbers 9; Hiemstra 2; Holmes 44; Moorhouse 5; Parsons 5–6,
      68; and Schultz 31–37.

maintain an air of "dauntless optimism" for the homesteading project; on the contrary, as Helen Buss states it, the male settler's enthusiasm "flags easily" ("Settling" 173). Thus it was of the utmost importance for a prairie woman to stiffen her husband's resolve; to magnify his own surety of himself in relation to the homesteading project. Indeed, contemporary writer Arthur E. Copping illustrates the settler woman's importance to "dauntless optimism" as he recounts the following meeting with a prairie farmer: "'Looking for a jarb?' shouted the bronzed man in the blue shirt and great floppy wide-awake; and, as the buggy drew up, I noticed that the woman's face reflected her husband's eagerness" (37).[18] Later in his text, Copping asserts that Canada is, in fact, "a nation of optimists" (262), and he provides a chapter specifically on the topic of "Women Settlers," in which he advises, "out on the prairie I met many English housewives. If asked to classify them, I should be tempted to say: a small minority are grumblers; a large majority are optimists," the latter of whom (like Traill before them) take "everything very good-naturedly from the outset" (221–22, 226).[19] Copping goes on to provide an illustration of the female "optimist" by referring to a Mrs. Fisher, "the ideal prairie housewife" (226), in the following tableau:

"Lonely!" echoed Mrs. Fisher in amazement. "Lonely? What, when we are surrounded by such nice neighbours, and I'm always driving round to see them, and they're always driving round to see me! And when we have so many whist parties at this house and musical evenings at their houses! Lonely – no, that's quite impossible out here. I pity anybody trying to be lonely with five children

---

18 Nellie McClung's meeting with a female suffragette confirms Copping's mirror image – with a twist: says Mrs. Brown, a widow left to run the family farm alone, men "want women to be looking-glasses, howbeit false ones that make them look bigger than they are" (305). In *We Swept the Cornflakes Out the Door* (1980), Edith Hewson provides an image that suggests that the prairie woman also reflects an optimism inherent in the landscape itself: she says that the prairie town of Wapella "was the centre of a rapidly widening wheat country, golden with promise that overflowed *across the face* of western Canada" (1; emphasis added).

19 Writing about Catharine Parr Traill, Gray states that, "Catherine [*sic*] rarely indulged in grumbles" (189).

about. And if they might be at school, and there was nobody at
home, and I wanted to talk with somebody but hadn't time to go
out – well, there is always the telephone. I don't mind telling you, I
often have a chat with my friend Mrs. Knight – when I'm waiting
for the bread to rise, and she's doing the same three miles away."

When Mr. Fisher next came in – to join us in the pretty parlour
– I found myself regarding him with a new interest. For I now had
a clue to the smile of placid contentment that seemed never to leave
his face. (69)

On pain of being read in the category of "grumblers," I admit my own distrust of those too-insistent exclamation marks used at the beginning of Mrs.
Fisher's speech; after all, we have only Copping's translation of her voice (assuming she actually was a real personage), and we must remember the title of
Copping's text, which is *The Golden Land*.[20]

Other contemporary writers also insisted upon the value of a settler
woman's optimistic outlook, even above more practical achievements: for example, in 1901 Elizabeth Lewthwaite advised readers of her article "Women's
Work in Western Canada" that "a cheerful, happy temperament will be worth
all the technical knowledge in the world" (717), and as late as 1925 Howard
Angus Kennedy purportedly met with a prairie "house-wife" described as
"singing as she comes to the door" and who, although she "admits when asked"

---

20 A year after the publication of Copping's text, Emily Ferguson published *Open
    Trails* (1912), in which the author provides what I would suggest is a slightly more
    sarcastic image of the enthusiastic settler woman:

    The Frau, who is a Norwegian, tells me she has been in town but once
    in six years, on which occasion she spent two months in the hospital.
    Previously she lived at Lac Sainte-Anne, where she rarely saw a white
    woman. On account of the bad trails it took six days to reach Edmonton,
    and one could only travel on horseback....

    But hear, O world, and wonder! The Frau says she was never un-
    happy. It would seem that she whose heart is wisely blithe has an endur-
    ing holiday. Or it maybe [*sic*] this Norwegian had the assurance of things
    hoped for, the evidence of things not seen. The vision of the pioneer,
    unlike other visions, is one that makes for contentment. (39–40)

that "she and her husband have had difficulties" in their new life, "brushes them lightly aside for cheerful topics" (198). For Marion Dudley Cran in 1910, the prairie woman becomes a physical embodiment of the "dauntlessly optimistic" vision of prairie life, as seen in her presentation of a feminine ideal who "makes beds and rushes from room to room like a Utopian whirlwind that leaves order in its train" (133–34). Meanwhile, those women who dared to deviate from the "dauntlessly optimistic" script were regularly taken to task for their ideological (and thus practical) failure. Arthur Copping's portrait of a female "grumbler," for example, is only referred to as "Mrs. Y---," as though he cannot even name that which will hurt the propaganda purposes of his travel narrative. Copping tells of his visit to "a beautiful quarter-section of rich soil in Southern Alberta" (which immediately implies, how could you fail to prosper there?), where he meets Mr. Y---, "a dissatisfied chemist in England, and scarcely knowing a horse from a cow," whose wife was unable to adapt to the new environment and who, suggests Copping, "ought to be deported" (222, 226). While not making light of the husband's ineffectiveness as a prairie farmer, nonetheless it is the wife who suffers the harsh judgment of banishment from the Promised Land.[21]

Female characters in western Canadian fiction tended to fall in line with this either (optimist)/or (grumbler) dichotomy. One of the true heroines of western literature, Nellie McClung's Pearl Watson, is most notable for her "contagious optimism," her "optimistic vision" (*The Second* 104, 159). In *The Second Chance* (1910), McClung writes about a Mrs. Cavers, who possesses the "good gift" of "hid[ing] her troubles" from her sister and mother back home in eastern Canada: indeed, in the spirit of Traill, Mrs. Cavers's letters "were cheerful and hopeful," and she herself was "a brave woman and faced the issues of life without a murmur" (313). In Harold Bindloss's *Prescott of Saskatchewan* (1913), heroine Muriel Hurst, who visits western Canada from

---

21 For women who even dared to "grumble" publicly, the powers-that-be were everpresent to enforce silence. Once again, Emily Ferguson makes this point humorously clear when she says, "If I, waxing bold, send an article to an Ontario, or even to a United States, magazine, and mention the fact of noticing alkali in the soil, the editor – profligate fellow – promptly blue-pencils it. I do not know the reason unless he, also, has real estate to sell in the North-West" (*Open* 9).

Britain and falls in love with the title farmer, feels an immediate sense of confidence about prairie life, a confidence that emanates from the landscape itself: "Last had come the prairie – the land of promise – which seemed to run on forever ... its vastness and openness filled the girl with a sense of liberty. Narrow restraints, cramping prejudices, must vanish in this wide country; one's nature could expand and become optimistic here" (13–14). Later, when asked what she thinks of "the country," Muriel responds, "[I]t's delightful! And everybody's so energetic! You move with a spring and verve; and I don't hear any grumbling, though there seems to be so much to do!" (32). The "wide plain and sense of freedom" of the prairies "banished moody thought" (Bindloss, *Prairie* 181–82), and, accordingly, the "grumbling" woman is often subject to censure in fictional texts: for example, in Bindloss's *Prescott*, the less than feminine ideal Ellice, whose "slight accent suggested the French Canadian strain, though Prescott imagined that there was a trace of Indian blood in her," is once described (significantly for the topic of this chapter) as being "moody of late" (27). Ellice, whose status as wife to an unsuccessful wheat farmer named Jernyngham is under question, acts as the anti-ideal to the Ruthian image, for she is suspected of taking advantage of those men capable of providing for her material needs rather than participating with them in their "dauntlessly optimistic" quest. When the narrator of Arthur Stringer's *The Prairie Wife* (1915) finds herself far removed from city life in New England and becomes the wife of prairie farmer Duncan Argyll McKail, she resolves *not* "to be a Hamlet in petticoats" (66), and "especially" not to become another Mrs. Dixon, a "sad-eyed soul" who "seemed to make prairie-life so ugly and empty and hardening" (69).

The contemporary message was painfully clear: to be acceptable in the context of the decision to emigrate to the Canadian west meant to be "a contented wife, submissive, self-sacrificing, retiring, and resigned" (Rasmussen et al. 88) – to be, as Traill's adaptive philosophy dictated a century before, a Ruth on the prairie. The Ruthian role was a natural one for women settlers, whose "leaving was activated by the things women believed and expected of themselves. Their own social and personal values demanded that they be loving and obedient wives, faithful and ever-present mothers" (Faragher 174).[22] The image of Ruth and commitment to that icon of obedience sometimes occurs explicitly in the memoirs included in this study, as in *With the West in Her Eyes* (1937) when Kathleen Strange explains her decision to emigrate with her husband by saying, "[A] woman has to follow her mate. With Ruth I had said: 'Whither thou goest, I will go ... and where thou lodgest, I will lodge'" (273). Similarly, in a memoir titled *Mamie's Children: Three Generations of Prairie Women* (1997), Judy Schultz makes clear that it was her grandfather who was "seized" by "the Canada-or-bust euphoria," a feverish desire to emigrate north and westward, against which Mamie Elizabeth Harris had no recourse: "[W]hat could Mamie say? She did as she was told and started packing" (36). Writes Schultz, it is "doubtful that, given a choice, Mamie or any other woman would willingly leave a home she knew and possibly loved for the danger and uncertainty of a foreign frontier, yet women did it, willy-nilly, in the faithful thousands" (32). What Mamie is "faithful" to is a traditional marriage script wherein a woman's "duty was clear" and that faith, for Schultz's family, at least, had repercussions for generations of female experience:

> She would follow Ernest. Like some latter-day Ruth, she believed the scriptures had clearly marked the path for women like her: "Wither thou goest I shall go, whither thou lodgest I shall lodge, thy people shall be my people forever...." (It was one of her favorite passages from the Bible, and many years later, after my own father had announced that we were moving yet again, I heard her repeat it to my exasperated mother, who was near tears at the very idea of another move. When I married, the Song of Ruth was part of the ceremony at Pearl's suggestion.
>
> Though she didn't say so, I knew it was for Mamie.) (35)

---

22   In fact, even outspoken feminist Emily Ferguson humorously admitted about her emigration to northern Alberta in the early part of the twentieth century that "the Padre [her husband] has decided to come to Edmonton to live, and I have decided to remain at Poplar Bluff. We will compromise on Edmonton" (*Janey* 208).

However, the Ruthian image does not always remain undisturbed by contrary behaviour. For example, in *Gully Farm*, Mary Hiemstra is open about the fact that, every time her father expressed enthusiasm for emigration to Canada, Sally Pinder showed herself to staunchly inhabit the Moodie – or the "grumbler" – half of the Prairie Woman dichotomy by making negative comments such as: "Papers don't seem to care what they print these days," "You can't believe all you hear, and only half you see," and "There's drawbacks there just as there are anywhere else" (2–3). After the decision to leave has been made, Sally Pinder's participation in the undertaking is informed by the fact that her husband has promised that they "were not going to Canada for ever. In a year, two at the most, [they] would be back" (23). Her half-hearted adherence to the Ruthian script is thus underwritten by a serious Moodie strain. Once arrived in Saskatchewan, and while searching for a homestead site, the family stops in the "city of tents" known as Battleford, where, according to Hiemstra, the Moodie reality disperses itself more widely amongst the female half of the Barr colonists:

> While we were in Battleford Dad went to the land office and asked about homesteads. He was told the same story: there wasn't much good land left around there. A few fairly good quarter sections might still be vacant a little to the north, but the best land was farther west.
>
> Dad and Mother discussed the matter and decided to go north first. Dad was anxious to get settled, and Mother felt that the sooner we stopped the sooner we would get back to England. In her opinion this long, hard trip was mostly a waste of time, but it was the only way she knew to convince Dad that Canada was impossible.
>
> Most of the other women thought as Mother did, and endured the hardships of the trail for the same reason. (97)

This frank portrayal of her mother as embodying the "reluctant emigrant" half of the Prairie Woman coin, however, is not simply a capitulation to the culturally accepted either/or dichotomy. As the memoir progresses, we learn that being perennially pessimistic is a part of the functioning dynamic between Mr. and Mrs. Pinder, who do share a deep emotional connection. Sally Pinder is genuinely regretful at times about having left her home and life in England, but for all of her seeming moodiness, she is not incapacitated. She does display an incredible practical commitment to prairie life and even occasionally finds reason for happiness. And ultimately, towards the end of *Gully Farm*, she does admit the suitability of the Ruthian script for application to the marriage bond, as we see when Hiemstra writes about a time when her father left her mother alone with the children and when she details some of the ways that the family passed the time, including the following emotionally resonant moment:

> When Mother wearied of the fairy-tales she read the Bible to us. One afternoon she read to us from the Book of Ruth. Her voice flowed evenly until she came to the place where Ruth elected to go with Naomi. "And Ruth said: Intreat me not to leave thee," Mother read slowly, "or to return from following after thee: for whither thou goest, I will go; and where thou lodgest, I will lodge: thy people shall be my people, and thy God my God: Where thou diest, will I die, and there will I be buried: the Lord do so to me, and more also, if ought but death part thee and me."
>
> Mother's low voice faltered as she read, and when she came to the end of the verse she stopped reading altogether and looked at the little window for a long time, then softly and as if speaking to herself she said: "It ought to have been written about marriage." (261)

The invocation of the Ruthian script at this late point in Hiemstra's memoir when Mrs. Pinder is seriously concerned about her husband's survival on the prairies, reflects an emotional change from her mother's seeming incoherence with that script throughout the earlier parts of the text.

Even where Ruth is not mentioned by name, language reminiscent of the cheerful and dutiful wife still dominates women's narratives; competes with instincts and feelings to the contrary of the "dauntlessly optimistic" script. It is no coincidence that Nellie McClung's novel, *Sowing Seeds in Danny*

(1911), is "lovingly dedicated to [her] dear mother" (n.p.), who is included in McClung's memoir *Clearing in the West* as being in that category of "typical" pioneer women described as "calm, cheerful, self-reliant, and undaunted" (82). Although I suggested earlier that it is McClung's brother, Will, who first initiates discussion of westward immigration, nevertheless it is the author's mother who enunciates the masculine privilege of land ownership and adventure and ultimately inspires the family to leave home:

> Strangely enough, my mother was more impressed than my father with Red Michael's story. She questioned him closely, and unlike some other questioners, listened when he answered. I think Michael liked talking to her.
>
> "We'll have to go some place, John," she said one night to my father. "There's nothing here for our three boys. What can we do with one-hundred-and-fifty stony acres? The boys will be hired-men all their lives, or clerks in a store. That's not good enough!"
>
> Father was fearful! There were Indians to consider, not only Indians, but mosquitoes. He had seen on the Ottawa what mosquitoes could do to horses; and to people too. No! It was better to leave well enough alone. Had any of us ever gone hungry? And now when we were getting things fixed up pretty well, with the new root-house; and the cook-house shingled, and the lower eighty broken up, and a good school now, with a real teacher, and an inspector coming once a year anyway, and a fine Sunday-school too, and all sorts of advantages....
>
> We all knew mother was agitated as she went around the house, for she banged doors and set down stove-lids noisily. And she kept everyone going at top speed. Even I knew she was in some sort of tribulation of spirit.... (32–33)

What a delightfully confrontational scene! First of all, it presents a repositioning of the traditional gender constructs with the author's mother being the one "impressed" by tales of prairie life, as told by a young settler who has come back to marry before returning west, and the author's father hyper-inhabiting the "reluctant emigrant" role usually reserved for women. But it is also confrontational in another key way, for Mrs. Mooney is originating enthusiasm for the settlement project rather than adhering to Ruthian notions that settler women merely follow/reflect their husbands' enthusiasm as a point of obedience.

What I particularly enjoy about McClung's portrait of her mother, however, is that it shows the real prairie woman as having a variety of responses to the issue of western settlement, triggered by a variety of personal experiences. For example, the family's first winter dampens Mrs. Mooney's spirits a bit, as seen in a letter to a female friend from back home: drawing her concerns clearly along gender lines, she writes,

> I get worried sometimes about my own health and wondering what would happen to the little girls, if I should be taken. Boys can always get along but it's a hard world for girls; sometimes I blame myself for coming away so far. There's no doctor closer than Portage, which is eighty miles away. I can't say this to anyone but you, I don't blame Willie; he is a good boy, if there ever was one. It's at night, when every one is asleep and this great prairie rolls over, so big and empty, and cruel. (78)

Mrs. Mooney's letter acknowledges that in the contemporary moment of settlement a woman's expression of fear was antithetical to cultural ideals; was something unintelligible beyond the privacy of personal correspondence. However, by including this letter in her memoir, McClung seeks to move beyond the predominance of the "undaunted" image she has already drawn for her mother. Later in the memoir, when writing about her eldest sister's serious illness that first winter, McClung indicates that even "typical" prairie women could experience a sense of failure and a wavering of faith in the inherent optimism of western settlement:

> My mother, who was a wonderful nurse, had tried every remedy she had, but there was not one flicker of response. Hannah and I were doing what we could to get meals ready, but on this worst day

of the storm, no one wanted to eat. It was like a horrible dream. The storm tore past the house, and fine snow sifted through the walls.

Mother came out from behind the quilts which hung around Lizzie's bed, and sitting down in the rocking-chair buried her face in her hands.

"I'm beaten, John," she said. "I can't save her! I am at the end of my resources!"

Her shoulders shook with sobs and it seemed like the end of everything. No one spoke. Behind the quilts, that labored breathing went on, hoarser and heavier.

"My little girl is dying for want of a doctor, in this cursed place – that never should have been taken from the Indians...."

"The Indians have their revenge on me now, for it's tearing my heart out, to see my little girl die before my eyes.... We shouldn't have come John, so far – so cruelly far – What's money? – What's land? What comfort can we have when we remember this – dying for want of a skilled hand – the best child I ever had." (79)

As McClung recreates the scene in her memoir, her mother's anxiety manifests in an overt critique of the purposes ("What's money? – What's land?") and the inevitable result ("never should have been taken from the Indians") of western settlement, as well as of her own infection with the spirit of the project. However, narrative compliance with cultural ideals is restored when McClung goes on to note the timely and divinely inspired arrival of a new Methodist minister: writes McClung, "[F]rom the moment he entered the feeling of the house changed. I saw the fear vanish from mother's face. *She was herself* in a moment" (80; emphasis added). Nevertheless, Mrs. Mooney continues to be subject to "low spirits," and is sometimes found to "sit drooping and sad under the pall of loneliness that wrapped [the family] around for many months in the year" (172). McClung's honesty about her mother's fluctuating enthusiasm for prairie life becomes a lesson in the need to reconcile the Ruthian typology characterized by Traill with the less than perfect response to settler life represented by Moodie. Indeed, looking one day into her mother's face, the young author reaches the following understanding, one that speaks well to our re-visioning of the settler woman's life: "some glimmering of life's plan swept across my mind. Sorrow and joy, pain and gladness, triumph and defeat were in that plan, just as day and night; winter and summer, cold and heat, tears and laughter. We couldn't refuse it, we must go on. We couldn't go and sulk in a corner and say we wouldn't play" (143–44).

One of the least Ruthian prairie women represented in the memoirs studied here is Marjorie Wilkins Campbell's mother Mary Eleanor: indeed, in *The Silent Song of Mary Eleanor* (1983), Campbell reconstructs the significant and telling moment – a moment reminiscent of Susanna Moodie's own initial reaction to the subject of emigration – of her family's arrival at their homestead site by providing an adequate tableau of her parents' different responses to prairie life:

Out of the mass of typical pioneer homecomings, each settler came to cherish his own peculiar memories, the little events that colored that memorable day; like a wedding night, joyous or tragic, it could never happen again. Of the scores of such occasions remembered by scores of old-timers, one scene remains clear in my imagination: the man looking up from beside the loaded wagon, the woman cradling their children and trying to control her emotions as she looked down to him.

In their particular moment he must have recalled her spirited opposition to his suggestion that they emigrate to one of the colonies and the scene that triggered their first quarrel. She as vividly recalled his equally spirited retort that if she felt that way about it he would go to Africa alone, neither of them believing that he actually would book passage to Cape Town.

Under the hot noonday sun, marooned on this sea of grass, as she contrasted his eloquent descriptions of life in Canada with the reality, mother wished she had refused the pearl engagement ring and later the wedding ring he had brought her from Africa. Father, content with every promising aspect of his quarter section, in that long assessing moment wondered why he had written the fulsome diary addressed to *My Dearest Nellie* and now faced the possibility of having to transform 160 acres into a productive, prosperous farm with so seemingly hostile a wife. (23–24)

Campbell's use of the word "marooned" in relation to her mother, and her insistence on the "contrast" of "reality" from "description," clearly undercuts the vocabulary associated with her father, words such as "promising," "productive," and "prosperous." Mary Eleanor's "seeming hostility" is an open contradiction of the expected Ruthian role. As Campbell explains about her mother, unlike her husband's futuristic visions of a land of plenty, Mary Eleanor "could not see what he saw. She could not match his enthusiasm" (25). No wonder, given that Campbell also remembers her father as a man who "never actually admitted to anything but a bright future" (54). The imagery in Campbell's text is in direct contrast to that provided by Beulah Baldwin in *The Long Trail: The Story of a Pioneer Family* (1992). Baldwin's father is clearly the one who made the decision to emigrate to northern Canada; however, he is also the first one to experience misgivings about what he and his family are undertaking. Even at the moment of departure from Edmonton, while Mr. Freeland is harnessing the horses, he "could not help but worry how his young pregnant wife and eighteen-month-old son Carlton would endure the long, tedious hours sitting cramped and cold in the horse-drawn sleigh, and the discomfort of primitive accommodations along the way" (2). Not much optimism in these words, yet, as Baldwin assures her readers, Olive Freeland's presence works as a reflection of her husband's original eagerness to undertake the journey north:

> Dad need not have worried. The young woman who stood watching from the upstairs window had a look of determination and courage in her sparkling blue eyes. She was small, just an inch or two over five feet, with golden brown hair piled high on her head. When her husband looked up and waved for her to join him, she waved back, and the answering smile that broke across her face made her truly beautiful. (2–3)

Having accepted the necessity of her family's emigration to Alberta at the start of the twentieth century, in *Of Us and the Oxen* (1968), Sarah Ellen Roberts advises that the homesteading project is secured by the family's unwritten agreement to maintain a deliberately optimistic spirit when entering, as she herself sarcastically calls it, "the 'promised land'" (16). At any point that some "calamity," some literal contradiction of imagined promise, befalls the family, the members gather together and renew in one another the spirit of "daunt-less optimism": for example, having lost their first successful crop to hail, she writes,

> I could never tell what that destruction meant to us. To under-stand, one must remember that we had no means, that we had been through three summers with constant expense and that this was to be our first crop. For myself, I must say that I had watched that grain from the time the first tiny green blades appeared until the very day of the tragedy – for tragedy it truly was. I had feasted my eyes upon its beauty and fed my soul with the hopes that were centered in those beautiful billowy golden acres. Bound up in that grain was almost an entire summer's work and our winter's supply, and as it neared harvest time, it promised to pay for the one and be ample for the other. Then in less time than it takes to tell it, it was annihilated.
>
> I didn't go out into our field until the next day. I just couldn't. When I went, I went alone. I did not want anyone to be with me when I went to view the wreck of the summer's work and the winter's hope, for I knew it would be my hour of weakness. And it was. I wondered indeed, whether we wanted to "cast in our nets in these barren sea waters" again. But when we were all together no one admitted discouragement. Disappointment there was, but each of us did all that he could do to fortify the courage and resolve of the others, and we all asserted with a confidence which was no doubt assumed, that we would have better luck next time. (124)

As indicated by her suggestion that "courage and resolve" had to be "fortified,"
and that the guise of "confidence" was merely "assumed," Roberts and her
family are struggling to maintain a "dauntlessly optimistic" role that women
themselves were meant to quite routinely exhibit in the face of sometimes
extreme adversity. If an entire family cannot maintain that role together, what
chance does a single woman have? For Roberts, no chance at all. From the
moment she arrives and sees the rather rudimentary housekeeping conditions
in which her husband and son have been "batching" while awaiting the arrival of the rest of the family unit, Roberts finds herself confronted with the
practical futility of optimism within a homestead environment. When she
arrives, she is literally sickened by the sight of the family tent, but she notes her
"resolve" that "as soon as [she] was able to work, 'things would take a turn'" (6).
Significantly, that last part of her sentence, "'things would take a turn'," which
indicates her attempt to reproduce the air of optimism with which the "adventure" was undertaken, is placed within quotation marks, almost as though she
is marking her knowledge that the phrase works better as a theoretical than a
practical goal. In the end, although Roberts has earlier asserted that she does
not mean to present her memoirs as "a calamity wail" (29), she nonetheless
makes the following confession to her reader:

> If I could have been an enthusiastic optimist and could have said
> and believed, "Oh, everything will be all right in the end," I might
> have been spared most of this anxiety. But however desirable such
> a state of mind might have been, I was not able to make it mine,
> nor can I see how such a mental attitude could have caused a rise
> in temperature or have opened the windows of the heavens and
> brought the rain that was so greatly needed. (204)[23]

As evidenced already from women's use and intermittent rejection of Ruthian-
type language, and as I've already indicated about Traill's "cheerfulness," the

---

23   For more examples of the invocation and rejection of the Ruthian typology, see
     also Gilead 14–15; Holmes 15, 73–76; Hopkins 20–23; Magill "Dedication," 2;
     Moorhouse 5, 8; Parsons *passim*; and Schroeder 94, 101.

mere adoption of the philosophy of "dauntless optimism" does not preclude
the presence of contrary feelings. In fact, I would assert that Traill's upbeat
attitude sometimes betrays an underlying sense of the author's own experiences of personal/psychological disjunction with her New World environment. For example, as the epigraph from Traill's *Backwoods* at the head of
this chapter illustrates, the ideal of the Pioneer Woman relied upon a sort of
"hypnotized confidence" (Mitchell 174) – a deliberately engineered program
of emotional self-denial. When I read Traill's avowal, "sometimes I laughed
because I would not cry" (97), I imagine the presence of a very real emotional
distress lying just below a thin veneer of "cheerfulness" – after all, Traill states
that she "*would* not cry" rather than that she "*could* not cry." The corduroy
road over which Traill travels threatens to dislodge the stoic Pioneer Woman
from her perch as it becomes representative of the sometimes "jolting" reality of backwoods life,[24] a reality that, as Gray illustrates in her biography,
Traill so determinedly attempts to deny as a source of personal discontent.[25]

---

24 Peggy Holmes begins *It Could Have Been Worse: The Autobiography of a Pioneer* (1980),
a memoir about settling in northern Alberta, with a chapter titled "Undaunted
Optimism," in which the author undergoes a similar experience to Traill:

> As I tried to relax on the hard, springless wagon seat, jogging over the
> rough trail taking me to my new life in Canada, I glanced up at my hus-
> band.
>   Could this possibly be the man I'd married only four years ago in
> England? Even though I knew he owned property in northern Alberta,
> I had never had any burning desire to be a wild west pioneer, and when
> I repeated my altar vow, "For better, for worse", such a drastic change in
> my lifestyle was beyond my wildest dream. (15)

After a narrative explanation of how she came to find herself in this position,
Holmes comes back to the moment of emigration and notes that "after sitting all
day, or one should say rolling, on a hard wagon seat with no springs, my enthusiasm
was at a low ebb. I was sore in both body and spirit" (74).

25 Early in *The Backwoods*, Traill is able to make a similar judgment about other emigrants to the one which I am making of her here: speaking of the "house[s] of
public resort" in Montreal, a stop-over on the journey to their homestead site, she
first notes that "the sounds of riotous merriment that burst from them seemed but
ill-assorted with the haggard, careworn faces of many of the thoughtless revellers,"
then, in a line that forms its own and purposeful paragraph, she states that "the contrast was only too apparent and too painful a subject to those that looked upon this

In fact, denial of the sometimes agonizing reality of settlement life is often a primary feature of recollective texts, which "seem to imply that hardships were actually ennobling experiences – proof of pioneer character – rather than sources of trouble and suffering" (Bennett and Kohl 56). Underneath the myth of "dauntless optimism," there was "trouble and suffering," in varying degrees. For myself as reader of settlement memoirs, the question that inevitably arises from the jolting scene in Traill's text is, at what point does the romantic notion of "dauntless optimism" devolve into a less idealistic contagion we might call "perverse endurance" (Silverman, "Foreword")? Judy Schultz provides an interesting image that encapsulates what I wish to invoke in this latter phrase when writing in *Mamie's Children* about her great-great-grandmother Magdalena. Imagining Magdalena's experience of emigration from old Bavaria to the United States in 1840 in "steerage class," Schultz says regarding the terrors of such an ocean journey, "I've tried to fit the woman who was my ancestor into this picture, and in my mind she always ends up on deck, facing the storm and in some perverse way enjoying it, if only because she was surviving it" (19). I would suggest that through recovery of this "perverse way" of enduring the conditions of western settlement we are able to continue the confrontation of the Traill typology's mythic proportions and achieve a less idealistic, hence more realistic, picture of women's experiences.

Annora Brown's *Sketches from Life* (1981) supplies me with a particularly apt illustration of the "dauntless optimism"/"perverse endurance" dichotomy of which I speak: regarding a group of trees, "old pines and firs," she notes "their roots pinched by rocks, their branches tormented by incessant winds from the [Crow's Nest] pass, these trees have developed distinctive characters. As we worked [at sketching them], such titles as *Where Life is Hard, Undaunted, Valiant, Stout-hearted* came to mind" (156). Moodie's text, I would suggest, in all its narrative deviation from the myth of "dauntless optimism," inspires a re-evaluation of women's settlement texts for the presence of "pinched roots" and "tormented branches" – of "perverse endurance"; it aids us in getting beyond the happy ending of the Pioneer Woman "Traill" to begin to answer some of

---

show of outward gaiety and inward misery" (39). Does this "too painful a subject" betray the author's own experience of "the contrast" in question?

critique of settlement project in general

the questions posed by Sara Brooks Sundberg back in the early stages of the recovery of western women's lives:

> The image of the stoic, hardworking helpmate not only homogenizes prairie women's experiences, it leaves some experiences out altogether. What about the women who could not cope with frontier life on the prairie? What factors made the difference between success and failure? We lose part of the story of women who stayed, when we ignore those who left. (86)

cheerfulness as ideological tool

Some historians would caution against this approach to women's settlement texts, as does John Mack Faragher:

if you're not cheerful you're in sabotage the colonial project

> If we are to trust and respect their revelations in their diaries and recollections, the greatest struggle of women on the trail was the struggle to endure the hardship and suffering without becoming bitter and resentful, without becoming the carping wife, without burdening their marital relationship with the bad feelings that burned inside them. If we are to judge them not by our standards but their own, we will not resurrect and applaud every little act of womanly resistance and mean feminine spirit but examine and attempt to understand the powers of endurance that permitted them to act out the role of good wife through the whole hated experience. (174)

Remembering that, in fact, "their standards" were only theirs insofar as they lived within a specific society in a specific time period – even Faragher allows that settler women were forced to *"act out the role* of good wife" – I would suggest that Faragher's caution resounds with condescension ("every little act of womanly resistance and mean feminine spirit") and ignores the fact that these women may have had legitimate reason at times to feel "bitter and resentful," to "carp" and "burden," to "resist" and show "spirit." It also ignores the fact that these kinds of supposedly negative reactions did not necessarily mean that a woman was stuck exclusively in a Moodie mode of being, and that they could, in fact, represent ways and means of coping with "trouble and suffering" and thus form an essential part of the process of settlement in a new land, rather than simply being a threat to that process.

For example, after spending years away from the family farm, in her memoir *The Maple Leaf for Quite a While* (1967), Heather Gilead is explicitly on a personal journey to understand her mother's experience and she does not demure in representing a certain level of domestic tension in her family household; indeed, she is fairly condemnatory of her mother, at first, for being the cause of that tension. As the last of six surviving children, the author, invoking the Traill script, first states that "home was a cheerful enough place as I first recall it," then revises that declaration by acknowledging the uniqueness of her position in the family, a position that facilitated her emerging awareness of the reality lurking beneath the surface "cheerfulness":

> My sisters got on rather well together. They were twelve, ten and eight years older than I. Then there were my two brothers, four and five years older than I. But all too soon my sisters were away at school, then married or working. The boys were early engaged in men's work, as farm boys used to be. I might almost have been an only child about the house then.
>
> And so, by the time I was eight or ten, the house was too quiet, too free of distraction, for me to remain unaware of my mother's chronic unhappiness which she had converted into specific grievances. (2)

After telling her readers about her parents' continued night-time amours, she goes on to describe the daytime reality as follows:

> But, come the dawn, and nothing much remained but recriminations on the one side and, on the other, the door quietly, definitively closing. No sooner had [my father] gone out, shutting the door behind him, than my mother would start muttering to herself as she worked, rehearsing the next grievance to be aired so that no

time need be lost in delivery when my father should appear in the doorway again. (4)

Unable at the time to understand her mother's reaction to what would now be labelled her father's "passive-aggressive" behaviour, one morning the young author, at "the sensitive age of thirteen or so," takes an emotional stance against what she sees as her mother's incessant "nagging":

> As he closed the door on it one day I rounded on her – it must have been shocking, like being savaged by a bunny rabbit – and announced, "If ever I speak to my husband like that I hope he beats me!" Then I stood awaiting the wrath to come. She turned her back. I thought at first that she hadn't heard, and wondered if I should ever get enough courage screwed up to speak out again. She resumed her work about the kitchen. After a few minutes I realized that she was silently weeping. I crept off, appalled. I doubt if she had wept since the death of that infant son so many years before.

This is a very compelling scene, not the least because Gilead and her mother essentially duplicate the domestic tension of the household, this time with Gilead playing the nagging, confrontational role of the mother, who is not being "heard," and the mother reacting by "turning" away as the author earlier describes her father doing. It is in this moment, told in retrospect, that Gilead begins to understand the extent of her mother's painful reality living on an isolated farm with a husband who never listens, never reacts, never responds. Gilead's decision to openly represent in her memoir her mother's almost ritual acts of "carping" and "burdening" represents her mature understanding of the settler woman's desire for some type, any type, of human interaction. As she now knows, her mother, who had grown up in a small community in the United States, was showing a fairly reasonable response to the conditions she faced:

Seal bats' ears with wax, release them in a space fraught with obstacles around which they have been accustomed to navigate without difficulty, and they will promptly clobber themselves on every obstacle in sight and be reduced to squeaking, quivering disorientation. Marriage must have been something like that for my mother, except that instead of being released into the midst of obstacles she was, so to speak, released into the midst of infinity, so that none of her emitted signals were ever bounced back to her. (4–5)

As Gilead concludes, her mother "had not been born a nag," she had simply lived "without an adequate supply of perpetual, direct human relationships." The inevitable result, "it must have left her as bruised and baffled – and as shrilly resentful – as the sealed-up bats" (6). This new awareness about her mother forces Gilead to tentatively re-evaluate her heroic feelings about her father, as well:

How many years it took her to become a sort of broken record, reiterating a catalogue of peripheral grievances, I don't know. That marriage had endured twenty years before I became aware of it and decided to be bruised by my poor father's martyrdom.

Martyrdom! This quiet, courteous, tranquil little man was not one to excite outrage. Besides, by the time I learned that his serenity was not a brave and stoic performance, but the Real McCoy, he was long since in his quiet prairie graveyard. No, not outrage: I didn't feel outrage. But that he should have lived with that woman all those years and never even noticed her pain! And he was a kindly, generous man – it would have grieved him, I'm sure, had any measure of it registered.... (7)

Gilead's attitude towards her father is a balancing act between kind words on the one hand and incomprehension at his absolute lack of sympathy for her mother's "pain!" on the other. In the middle, the reader discerns an implicit understanding of the "trouble and suffering" that underlay her initially "cheerful" memory of a prairie childhood.

Gilead's text is a good example of the fact that, unlike Faragher, I am not dealing with immediate diary accounts, but rather with texts that were written at a far remove from the settlement experience, often in response to a cultural desire for nostalgic representations of Canada's prairie heritage, and often by the less-constrained daughters of prairie women, so that evidence of alternative images to the Traill ideal may be read as a speaking out against, a confrontation with, conventional scripts. Thus, recovering the process of "moodification" at work in these texts is not intended to glorify some victim image of white prairie women as simply "reluctant migrants," but rather to suggest that women's involvement in land settlement was far more complex than the narrative of Ruthian adaptation allows. Indeed, I am suggesting that "adaptation" as a coping mechanism is not simply a prescription that can be "cheerfully" fulfilled at will, or not; rather, "adaptation" is a whole process in which the individual experiences a variety of physical/psychological reactions, with the result that, in the end, she has undergone a journey of self-discovery equal to the geographic one of immigration. As Gray suggests of Moodie's *Roughing It*, it "was more than a collection of 'events as may serve to illustrate a life in the woods,' as Susanna modestly claimed. It was the dramatic story of her own journey of self-discovery, as she faced the rigours and disorientation of pioneer life" (208).

So now we return to that image of Traill refusing to cry. As characterized by Audrey Morris, Traill "seldom cried, for she had an innate talent for taking delight out of every occasion" (18). Susanna Moodie, on the other hand, was "given to frequent tears" (19), as illustrated by her text. Having exhorted her reader to "bear with me in my fits of melancholy, and take me as I am" (89), she then shows herself, at various points throughout her text, succumbing to fits of homesickness so that "all [her] solitary hours were spent in tears" and "it was impossible to repress those outgushings of the heart" (337). In fact, Moodie notes the facility of crying when she states that "tears are the best balm that can be applied to the anguish of the heart. Religion teaches man to bear his sorrows with becoming fortitude, but tears contribute largely both to soften and to heal the wounds from whence they flow" (60). Some prairie women

who understood tears as "the best balm that can be applied to the anguish
of the heart" still felt the impulse for self-control – for continued adherence
to the Traill typology – as a matter of maternal duty, as seen when Nellie
McClung's mother writes to a female friend about the loss of the family cow:

> "Our first Christmas was not very happy because we lost our nice
> little black cow.... I can't tell you how I miss her.... She had win-
> some ways, coming to the door and shoving it in with her nose if
> it wasn't latched, or rubbing the latch up and down, reminding me
> it was milking time. I had great hopes of Lady! She was going to
> establish a herd for us, all having her gentle disposition, but that's
> past! You know I do not cry easily but that morning I did. Just for a
> minute, and when I saw I was breaking up my whole family, I had
> to stop, though I would have been the better of a good cry to ease
> my heart, but when a woman has children, she has no freedom, not
> even the freedom to cry." (77)

In contrast, a prairie *Summer Storm: A Manitoba Tragedy* (1985), a memoir of
homesteading near Pendennis, Manitoba, in the second and third decades of
the twentieth century, becomes the vehicle for Velma Inglis to contextualize
the facility of a prairie woman's tears to the restoration of commitment to the
settlement project in the face of personal anguish. As Inglis illustrates through
her grandmother's emotional reaction to the untimely death of a family member, an open and deliberate policy of crying helps the settler woman to cope
with this most painful reality of prairie life and to get back to the practical
needs of the family farm: after the death of the author's Uncle Marsh,

> Grandmother walked up and down the path between the house
> and the barn sobbing and crying in the rain.... She refused to be
> consoled by anyone and said just to leave her by herself, as this was
> the way she handled grief when her daughter Eunice had died five
> years earlier, and that she would be better the next day and she
> was. The grief was still there but she was cried out and was able to
> function and do the many things that had to be done. (67)

I would suggest that, for many prairie women, crying is an emotional release – a "moodie" outburst – which, although temporarily deviating from the myth of "dauntless optimism," nonetheless ultimately allows her the space and time to re-assert control over – to adapt to – her experiences. Evidence of an experiential reality that exceeds the smooth surface of the myth of "dauntless optimism," tears (of either anger or sadness) are a generational rather than an incapacitating force that allow prairie women to get beyond the considerable difficulties of settlement life. Daughter-authors were very often "privileged witnesses" to their mothers' bouts of crying, an expressive behaviour typically performed in moments of privacy within the domestic world, when male family members were absent from home. For example, describing a time in winter when her father was away from home, in *Pioneering in Alberta* (1951) Jessie Browne Raber notes her mother's position at the intersection of the Moodie/Traill as follows:

> One evening, we knew it was the coldest yet, so Mother said she would help us cut more wood. We children had to haul it by hand from the creek, then Mother and Billy cut it, using the crosscut saw. No one was used to it, but we got by for awhile, until Mother said her hands and feet were about frozen. Going into the house to warm up, she rubbed her hands and jumped up and down to warm her feet, crying all the time, saying they hurt her so. We children felt so bad, we worked hard at the wood cutting and splitting. They were only small trees and we were nearly frozen too, but didn't say anything. We cut until it was nearly dark. Mother got to feeling better, talking about what her relations would think if they only knew what hardships she put up with out in Alberta. But Mother wouldn't write to them about it. (55)

In a moment of privacy, away from the eyes of her husband, Mrs. Browne is able to temporarily succumb to feelings that are unproductive of "dauntless optimism," although we are also given the stoic face that she, like Traill, presents in her letters back Home. Besides being a tool through which she manages to "feel better" and to once again face the "hardships" of prairie life, Mrs.

Browne's bout of crying is also practically productive for, as Raber tells us, her father "stayed around a few days and cut fire wood every minute he had to spare after some of the younger children told him about Mother crying" (56).

A good example of this "moodification" strategy also occurs in Beulah Baldwin's *The Long Trail*, in which the author's mother is fairly consistently represented as a "vital" component of her husband's pioneering project. Indeed, in a chapter titled "Mother's Story," Baldwin represents Olive Freeland as having come from a long line of courageous and independent immigrant women. Given this behavioural heritage, one might well expect Olive Freeland to be represented as an icon worthy of Traill herself; nevertheless, Baldwin ruptures the calm surface idealism of her own text when she honestly represents her mother's periodic lapses into incapability and disaffection with the settlement experience. Helping to run a northern Alberta hotel while waiting for her husband to finish work on their homestead site, Baldwin's mother becomes frustrated by the shame she feels while "having to wait on table in her [pregnant] condition, especially as most of the boarders were men," and so, "one lovely Sunday ... Dad suggested to Mother that she escape the noise and confusion of the hotel and accompany him to the homestead where he wanted to repair the fences" (142). As Baldwin continues her anecdote,

> After reaching the cabin, Dad pointed to the far corner of the yard where he would be working within calling distance. Mother decided to rest. With a book in hand, she headed for the small cot in the cabin. But the woods through the open door seemed to beckon to her. She put her book down and walked toward them. Standing at the edge of the clearing, she contemplated the tall trees – untouched except by birds and squirrels, rain and sunlight – the way they had begun in God's mind, tree beside tree, standing at random beneath the blue sky.
>
> Noticing the markings of a trail, she decided to follow it. The trees soon began to thin out allowing the sun to filter through. Ahead, in the bright sunlight, she saw a patch of tall-stemmed wild blue flax swaying in the gentle breeze. Enchanted by this lovely display she picked a few flowers. She stopped to watch birds

nesting overhead and laughed when she heard herself confiding aloud that she was nesting too. Mother came to another clearing covered with spikes of lavender fireweed and Indian paintbrush. She had been told that they were the first growth to appear after the earth was scorched by fire. She began picking them and soon had a big bouquet, pleased at how well the scarlet paintbrush blended with the lavender fireweed and blue flax.

When she decided to go back to the cabin, she looked for the path but could find no trace of it. She had been drawn to the flowers and had not realized that the path had petered out. After wandering around, she discovered a faint trail and followed it until it branched off. By this time she had lost all sense of direction and began to panic but, remembering Dad's advice, she decided to sit and wait for him to find her. (142–43)

This is a critical scene in Baldwin's text on many levels. Initially, the city girl Olive Freeland seeks the possibility of "escape" within the confines of a book, but her perspective changes when she is "beckoned" by the woods beyond the "cleared" area of her husband's farm. Forgiving for a moment her assumption regarding the spiritual origins of the woods, Freeland's "contemplation" of the "tall trees" which remain "untouched" by human hands forms a clear contrast with the activity of her husband, who repairs fences, or felled trees which no longer create a home place for "birds and squirrels, rain and sunlight." Looking beyond the ordered world of the land survey system of her husband's "clearing," Olive Freeland feels the pull of "randomness" towards emotional escape from her husband's visionary migrations, as seen in her change of focus from the "tall trees" to the trail beneath her feet. Her "enchantment" at the "lovely display" of naturally occurring "wild blue flax" juxtaposes the futuristic focus of the large-scale agricultural pursuits of the land settlement project, as does the lush growth of the natural "clearing" in the woods. More personally, her identification with the "nesting" birds in this space, her psychological awareness of this space as an "untouchable" home place, calls into question her husband's delay in providing such a place for her own comfort and security. Most importantly, in the detail of the "growth" that follows when "the earth was scorched by fire," we see the possibility that this place and Olive Freeland's recognition of its inherent value will allow for a sort of rebirth, a ritual renewal of self and spiritual strength in a time of personal crisis. After some initial patience with her situation, we are told that Olive Freeland succumbs to tears: "sinking onto the grass, she sobbed out her fear as well as the frustration and tension that had been building up for months. After a few minutes, she wiped her eyes with her petticoat and realized that she felt better" (144). This brief narrative moment might seem to be a less-than-transformative experience, but it is necessary to reiterate the constraints under which settlement memoirists write, given an agricultural and heritage context in which farmers and their wives are posited as optimistically and heroically "proving up" their participation in the homesteading project. Even the simple act of representing a woman's tears, especially when they are a result of having "lost all sense of direction" (143) with regards to the beaten path of cultural expectations, can be read as "confrontational." Indeed, the facility of a temporary "moodification" for restoring the settler woman's equanimity is apparent in the above scene from Baldwin's text and, in a later period of emotional crisis, when a relative's visit has resulted in "great waves of homesickness" to "sweep over" her and Olive Freeland has her husband (who becomes an unsuspecting emotional midwife) once again drive her to the homestead cabin, for she "wanted to be alone to cry out her frustration" (152). Once again entering the woods, she feels "her faith strengthened" and is "resolved to hang on, no matter how bad the storm."

In *With the West in Her Eyes*, Kathleen Strange, too, undergoes a process of "moodification" as a means to regain her resolve about undertaking prairie life. When Strange and her new husband had originally planned to leave England after the war, they had decided to repatriate to Hawaii, where Harry Strange had previously worked in "a position of responsibility as general manager of a large Honolulu company" (4). However, Strange's husband had been injured in the war and was told by a doctor to "take up some form of outdoor life, preferably farming, in a more bracing climate than that of Hawaii" (8), and they eventually decided upon Canada. Almost immediately upon her arrival at their new Alberta home, the author is confronted by the reality of a rather rudimentary lifestyle: having been told previously by her husband "we haven't any house at all – yet" (18), Strange soon learns that her family will be living in "a small wooden shack" and sleeping in "some five or six granaries" located behind that shack (19). Feeling the disorientation of having come from an urban environment in England, Strange's reaction seems reasonable:

> After some more or less disjointed conversation – for we were all feeling strange – I sought the opportunity of retiring to my own granary-bedroom to commence unpacking.
>
> Once there, I confess, I gave way to an outburst of tears. I thought of how by this time we might have been well on our way to Hawaii. How thrilled I had been at the idea of going there in the first place! My husband had painted many glamorous word pictures of the Islands for me. And now he had brought me to *this*! Disappointment, resentment, and an active dislike of my new home fought together within me. I would be no heroine, I told myself, swallowing my own feelings for the sake of my husband's future. I would tell him just what I thought of the place, and of him for bringing me to it. (22)

Given that (as indicated earlier in this chapter) elsewhere in her memoir Strange represents herself as having an inherently Traill personality type (292), her outright rejection of Ruthian resolve here, as well as her inability to maintain "dauntless optimism" in the face of the first obstacle she encounters with life in Canada, suggests that the process of "adaptation" is not as seamless as cultural constructions of settlement women might suggest. For Strange it comes easier than for others, though, as we see when her husband comes into the room and she writes, "to my utter amazement I realized suddenly that he himself actually *liked*" their living conditions, which makes her hold back her critique. Later in that first day, Strange and her husband take a walk "to a piece of high land to the west of the house" so that they can survey their "domain" (24), and the author represents her return to coherence with the Ruthian script:

"It *is* beautiful," I thought to myself, "but it's, oh, so different!" I wondered if I would ever be able to endure it all and to settle down. Harry's voice broke in upon my thoughts.

"There's something rather romantic about building from the ground up, isn't there?" he said. "We're starting off with practically nothing. We'll put up a fine house and good buildings. We'll look after our surroundings as well as our crops. One day we'll have a garden and maybe, right here where we stand, a tennis court. Of course, it will take time and patience and a lot of hard work and fighting. Yes, fighting, for if there is one thing I've already learned about farming, it is that whatever else a man wins out of the land, at least he can be sure of one thing, and that is a struggle. There's always the challenge to fight. And I love a good fight!"

Despite myself I felt my own spirit catching some of his enthusiasm. I'd fight side by side with him in this battle for a home and happiness. It should be a partnership in every sense of the word. (27–28)

Certainly Strange's invocation of the word "partnership" here suggests something more equalitarian than the note of obedience usually struck in references to the figure of Ruth, and that phrase "Despite myself" sits there in a subtly confrontational manner that moves readers beyond a mere stereotyped understanding of the "cheerful helpmate" image.

Ferne Nelson's mother certainly found it difficult to maintain a cheerful face, especially on a cold and windy "washday" in March: as the author begins Chapter Two of *Barefoot on the Prairie: Memories of Life on a Prairie Homestead* (1989),

How had we got into this mess? Banished to the bedroom, our faces streaked with tears, we scraped away the frost on the little window and watched Mama struggling to hang the clothes on the line outside. The garments froze as her stiffened fingers fastened the wooden pegs. The long underwear and rigid petticoats whipped back against her body as she patiently pushed them back, stopping now and then to beat her cold hands against her sides. Poor Mama. Life was hard on this prairie farm. She worked so hard, and today she looked so tired and worn. How could we have made fun of her just because she had become fat lately? (4)

A rather odd opening to a chapter titled "We Wanted Ice Cream," and one that is clearly meant to erupt through the romantic titular image of childhood joys on a prairie homestead. Life for Myrtle Alexander is obviously less than romantic, as seen in another of the author's descriptions: "Her hair, which had broken loose from the combs that were meant to restrain it, hung limply about her face. She pushed it back with a soapy hand and scrubbed vigorously at a grey sock" (4–5). We are told that the author and her sister are busy drawing pictures on the frosty windows and trying to stay busy because "Mama had been irritable and impatient all day, and with the washing to do, had had no time to invent the usual little games" (5). As the scene continues, Myrtle Alexander's "unrestrained" physical appearance takes on psychological dimensions:

> We continued our drawing, moving over to the other unblemished window pane. Ve drew a very fat lady with a big stomach and wispy hair. Underneath it she printed a word that I could read: Mama. I laughed. It did look like Mama in her big apron with her hair all messy. We both dissolved in giggles. Mama looked up from the washboard and laughed too. She was happy to see that our boredom had disappeared.
>
> Ve flushed with pleasure. She was amusing her little sister and showing off the sophistication she had acquired in a year at school.
>
> "Mama is fat!"
>
> "Mama is fat!" I echoed. I looked at my mother fearfully, sensing that I shouldn't have said such an outrageous thing. Mama hadn't heard us above the monotonous scrubbing.
>
> "Mama looks like a fat old cow!"
>
> "Mama looks like a fat old cow!"

We marched around the kitchen, turning the words into a sing-song chant."Mama is fat! Mama is fat, fat, fat!"

Mama stopped scrubbing. A look of disbelief chilled her pretty face. Then she looked at the picture on the window.

Two girls were slapped hard. Two little girls and their mother burst into tears. Mama went back to the tub, her tears falling into the soapy water. We huddled in the corner, howling. We weren't slapped very often. (5)

Looking back, Nelson realizes that her mother's tears are the product of something more than simply the naive taunting of bored little children; indeed, the sympathetic reader of Nelson's text can feel the tension in this scene mounting from the woman's "struggling to hang the clothes on the line outside," to the "vigorous" and "monotonous" scrubbing on the washboard, to the extra weight (physical and psychological) of performing these tasks with a "big stomach" – the import of which most readers must by now be aware – and right through to the proverbial straw that broke the pioneer woman's resolve, the taunting voices of girl children growing up in a culture that will inevitably try to consign them to the same experiences as their mother. The effect of Myrtle Alexander's crying spree upon the family unit is ultimately solidifying for, after supper that night, Nelson and her sister help with the cleanup and their father attends to bringing the laundry in from outside (6). Meanwhile, Myrtle's maternal equanimity appears restored, especially after the chapter ends with her having given birth to a healthy baby boy, whom the Nelson girls would happily trade for "new shoes, bananas, ice cream – anything to a new baby brother!" (9).[26]

Part of the problem with a woman's crying in the present moment was that it provided tangible proof that her optimism about the settlement process was not entirely "dauntless." Perhaps even less desirable, however, was the act of looking or, worse yet, going back; of grieving the lost past "back Home" and

---

26 For more examples of the presence and facility of settler women's tears, see also Hiemstra 258; Holmes 61–62; Hopkins 56–57; McClung 77; and Roberts 58, 202–3.

regretting the decision to leave that Home. According to Traill, a debilitating attachment to the past was the norm of experience for female emigrants, as she notes when speaking of a group of settlers with whom she was acquainted both in Canada and in Britain:

> The men are in good spirits, and say "they shall in a few years have many comforts about them that they never could have got at home, had they worked late and early; but they complain that their wives are always pining for home, and lamenting that ever they crossed the seas." This seems to be the general complaint with all classes; the women are discontented and unhappy. Few enter with their whole heart into a settler's life. They miss the little domestic comforts they had been used to enjoy; they regret the friends and relations they left in the old country; and they cannot endure the loneliness of the backwoods. (90)

Traill goes on to assure her readers that she does not herself share this "general" trend:

> This prospect does not discourage me: I know I shall find plenty of occupation within-doors, and I have sources of enjoyment when I walk abroad that will keep me from being dull. Besides, have I not a right to be cheerful and contented for the sake of my beloved partner? The change is not greater for me than him; and if for his sake I have voluntarily left home, and friends, and country, shall I therefore sadden him by useless regrets?

Expressing one's "regrets," or "pining for home," continued to be viewed as a potential threat right up to the period of prairie settlement. In Harold Bindloss's *Prescott of Saskatchewan*, for example, the title hero says to heroine Muriel Hurst, "Do you know the secret of making colonization a success? In a way, it's a hard truth, but it's this – there must be no looking back. The old ties must be cut loose once for all; a man must think of the land in which he prospers as his home" (274).

Unlike Traill, Moodie makes little effort to hide her numerous acts of looking back, as seen in one of the most emotional experiences of her backwoods life:

> After breakfast, Moodie and Wilson rode into the town; and when they returned at night brought several long letters for me. Ah! those first kind letters from home! Never shall I forget the rapture with which I grasped them – the eager, trembling haste with which I tore them open, while the blinding tears which filled my eyes hindered me for some minutes from reading a word which they contained. (121–22)

The poignancy of this moment has resonance for our reading of Traill's text, for while she may well have been writing letters home to assure friends and family of her own "cheerful" experience of settlement life, it is important to recognize that Traill, too, is continually receiving letters, so that her "dauntlessly optimistic" prescription for emigration is actually based upon the act of looking back and not the renunciation of family and community as a measure of female "endurance." Indeed, I would suggest the facility of looking back psychologically/emotionally – of keeping the image of "back Home" always within present range – for allowing the female emigrant to settle into the new place and keep her from the really threatening physical act of "going back"; of truly giving up on the prospect of western settlement. As prairie poet Ethel Kirk Grayson wrote in *Unbind the Sheaves: A Prairie Memoir* (1964): "[T]he unpardonable sin, written in the creed of a man with houses and streets and wheat in his blood, was in going back: and in letting nature, the snow, the wind, the drought, the hail, outwit you" (22). Elizabeth Lewthwaite subtly makes this point when writing about visiting her brothers' residence on the prairies with her sister in 1901: "At the end of twelve months our *ménage* had to undergo reconstitution, as my sister had to return to England, partly on private matters, but partly, truth compels me to admit, because the life did not suit her. The atmosphere so bracing to me, and, indeed, to the majority who go there, had an entirely reverse effect upon her" (714). The situation seems not to have changed much in recent years, for in the popular imagination it is most often those women who endured all the negatives of prairie life who secure our greatest admiration: as Barry Broadfoot writes about women's participation in *The Pioneer Years 1895–1914*, "for every woman who quit, there were thousands who stayed with their men and took it" (199).

Some of the memoirists studied here include in their recollections negative images of women going back Home rather than staying and "taking it." For example, on their journey west from Winnipeg, Nellie McClung's family meets up with "a tragic family who had turned back, discouraged and beaten" (58). Specifically we are told in *Clearing* that "it was the wife who had broken down," and certainly McClung's narrative attention to the woman's clothing indicates her temperamental unsuitability for the role of "dauntlessly optimistic" pioneer: "She wore a black silk dress and lace shawl and a pair of fancy shoes, all caked with mud. She would have been a pretty woman if she would only stop crying." In explanation of her attempt to penetrate the western landscape, the woman makes the following confession: "I want to go back to [my mother]; she never wanted me to come, but I thought it would be fun, and Willard [her husband] was so crazy to get land of his own." The meeting with this woman – this failed Ruthian figure – is potentially threatening to the Mooneys' own immigration project, for, as McClung writes about her mother's reaction to them, her "zeal began to flag, 'Take her back,' she said to Willard, 'she's not the type that makes a pioneer'." However, McClung clearly counts her mother among those women who do "make a pioneer," as seen when the other couple moves on and the author represents her mother getting to the heart of the matter by saying that poor Willard "made the mistake many good men have made – he married a painted doll, instead of a woman" (59). In *Of Us and the Oxen*, Sarah Roberts provides more than one image of the danger of going back, seemingly as a means to highlight her own powers of endurance despite strong feelings of homesickness. Roberts's husband was a doctor in the United States before emigration to the Canadian prairies, where he is quickly put to service by fellow settlers in need of medical attention. At one point, a woman neighbour requests that Dr. Roberts attend upon a Mrs. Rosenberg, for it would appear that the latter woman "was not in her right mind, her obsession being that she must go back to her home in Michigan to spend the coming winter. This was in spite of the fact that she had spent the preceding winter there and that her husband had sacrificed much to send her" (135). While Roberts states that her doctor/husband deems Mrs. Rosenberg to be "a very sick woman" and "diagnose[s] her trouble as typhoid, complicated by kidney trouble, uremic poisoning and dropsy," nevertheless the author herself clearly identifies with a different psychological cause for the woman's desire to return Home; that is, "her case was another sad one. From what I heard, I think that she could not adapt herself to the conditions of life on the homestead."

Just over half way through *Upon a Sagebrush Harp* (1969), Nell Wilson Parsons reveals a little secret lurking just behind her mother's seeming adherence to the myth of "dauntless optimism," a secret regarding the family's emigration to the Canadian prairies. First the author explains her mother's presence in North America with a very typical emigration story; however, she goes on to indicate a little wrinkle in the typical narrative:

> Though we had come north from Iowa, where Rena and I had been born, my parents were English. Cecil had been born in England. I had better explain how that happened. Alone in the world at seventeen, Papa had come to the States, where he worked on Iowa farms for ten years. Returning to England on a visit, he met and married Mama. They returned to rent an Iowa farm.
>
> At the end of three years their prospects were excellent. They could have bought the farm they rented. But Mama, homesick for her family, wanted to go back to England. They sold everything and returned.
>
> As so often happens, returning to a place enhanced in memory proved cruelly disappointing. In two weeks Mama realized they had made a great mistake. However, another baby was coming, and it takes a great deal of money to get a family across an ocean, and half across a continent. It took them three years to save enough to leave England a second time. (88)

Annie Wilson's physical return Home as a spur to eventual adaptation to prairie life is the rare case, for it is more usually the ability to look back, to

keep Home within the heart and mind, that acts as a stimulus to psychological endurance. Indeed, Mary Eleanor Elliott Wilkins begins to look back
towards Home the moment that she arrives in Saskatchewan in 1904, a fact
that Marjorie Campbell chooses to highlight rather than obscure, making it
function ultimately as a personality strength in *The Silent Song of Mary Eleanor*.
We see this in the author's description of her mother watching her husband
walk away from the boarding house at which she will stay until their move out
to the family homestead:

> Two days later when he left at dawn to inspect the quarter sec-
> tion, she watched him stride north along the rutted trail, scarcely
> able to recognize his sturdy figure in the unfamiliar breeches and
> high boots. She had never before seen him with a pack on his back
> and the double-barreled gun in the crook of his arm, except in the
> African albums. The very strangeness made her feel lonely. When,
> almost out of sight on the horizon, he turned and waved his hat,
> the loneliness overwhelmed her. Desolate as she had never been,
> she turned and rushed back to the boarding house and upstairs to
> the children who were just awakening.
>
> Missing the rocking chair she had always sat in while nursing
> her babies, now she braced herself on the edge of the bed. When
> she had unbuttoned her blouse and cradled the infant against her
> breast she cuddled the toddler close in her other arm. She told
> herself that of course he would be back again in a week or ten days,
> as he had promised. (8)

Her feelings of "strangeness" at the moment of her husband's departure inspire
Mary Eleanor to engage in a routine maternal occupation as an act of connection with the past and its comforts. Later in that same day, writes Campbell,
her mother realizes that she will have to "face up to her terrifying loneliness,
not easy for a woman accustomed to city life and the close proximity of a
warm group of family and friends. She longed for them all, but particularly for
her sisters." Remembering her past life of comfort and community makes her
mother question, "Why had they left it all for this raw, empty, lonely land?"

(9), but that questioning, after a good night's sleep, is ultimately productive of a renewed resolve: "That early morning she wrestled with her fears and her emotions, 'stood herself up in a corner' as her north country-lowland Scots ancestors would have said." Realizing that "her aversion to leaving home" (10) had prevented her from fully understanding her husband's desire to emigrate, she takes symbolic action to help her face the future:

> Now she was in Canada, Western Canada, and the new life had commenced. Though she sensed that she was poor stuff for a settler's wife, for the first time she wanted to know what he might expect of her.
>
> Quietly, so as not to waken the children, she got out of bed. At the narrow, oak-veneered washstand she poured cold water from the enameled iron jug and in the basin made her first attempt to wash away some of the worst handicaps of her incongruous past.[27]

An even fuller retreat from the philosophy of "dauntless optimism" is a woman's descent into some form of mental illness, the pejorative for which is "madness," a kind of polar opposition to Traill's "cheerfulness." I should note that I am not concerned here with demonstrating actual clinical forms of mental illness, but rather seek to discover those images of women that suggest varying degrees of psychological "incongruity," to borrow a phrase from Campbell, with the myth of "dauntless optimism," from temporary feelings of depression to severe mental breakdowns classified as "insanity." Traill's ability to remain positive stems in large part from her textual philosophy of "adaptation/adoption," a philosophy that contains an interesting paradox. On the one hand, she maintains a panoramic vision of future prosperity in the backwoods of Canada (as a means of personal and cultural inspiration to "dauntless optimism"): for example, everywhere she goes, she looks for the "charms of civilization" which she knew in her home place, such as "open fields, pleasant farms, and fine flourishing orchards, with green pastures, where abundance of

---

27 For more examples of women looking back Home, see also Ebbers 8; Gilead *passim*; Hiemstra *passim*; Holmes *passim*; Middleton 18; and Strange 135, 228–29.

cattle were grazing" (54). On the other hand, she simultaneously narrows her focus to the ocular minutia required by the "hobby" of botany, ostensibly as a means of adapting her vision of herself as a British gentlewoman to the present and often untenable situation of life beyond the margins of "civilization," but also as a defence mechanism against the "monotony in the long and unbroken line of woods, which insensibly inspires a feeling of gloom almost touching on sadness" (63). In this way does Traill both maintain her sense of enthusiasm about the cultural importance of participation in land settlement and avoid becoming overwhelmed by "the gloom of the wood" (70) – avoid, that is, "getting bushed." Given that the word "gloom" not only means "darkness; obscurity" but also "melancholy; despondency" (*OEED*), Traill's ocular avoidance of her rather claustrophobic surroundings suggests a fear of psychological weakness, something to which other emigrants become easy prey.

In contrast to her sister, we might say that Moodie "can't see the forest for the trees": that is, bogged down by the often terrifying present reality of life in a new place, Moodie is unable to wholly sustain an optimistic vision of the future. Indeed, a defining moment for the author comes while still on board ship when, after judging that Gross Isle "looks a perfect paradise at this distance," she is advised by the captain, "Don't be too sanguine, Mrs. Moodie; many things look well at a distance which are bad enough when near" (28). Given that "sanguine" means "optimistic; confident" (*OEED*), the captain's advice has repercussions for Moodie's ability to uphold Traill's long-range and idyllic settlement vision. Unlike Traill, Moodie most certainly enters fully (physically and psychologically) into the bush, a place in which she experiences both the terrors of settlement life and the spiritual peace of a close association with the natural world. Much has been made of how certain character sketches in Moodie's text relate to and reveal certain aspects of the author's own experiences, and perhaps one of the most important self-reflexive characters is Brian, the Still-Hunter, who is described as being "moody," "sour, morose, queer," and "as mad as a March hare!" (176, 175). As Helen Buss points out, Brian, amongst other things, "represents the terror of being 'bushed'" (*Mapping* 91), a reality that Moodie herself experiences on at least a couple of occasions. Although their specific circumstances are distinct, Brian is an explicit example of the madness, or "cabin-fever," which can result when a person is exposed to the extreme isolation of bush life and Moodie's immediate affinity for this man becomes a measure of her own faltering psychological stability (*Roughing* 182–87). As Traill well knew, Moodie certainly had a personality character-ized by something less than "dauntless optimism": in a reflective mood after her sister's death, Traill wrote of Moodie that "her facility for rhyme was great and her imagination vivid and romantic, tinged with gloom and grandeur.… As is often found in persons of genius, she was often elated and often de-pressed, easily excited by passing events, unable to control emotions caused by either pain or pleasure" (qtd. in Gray 337).

For the memoir author who is also writing as a daughter/grand-daughter, representing female madness is a way of staying true to the reality of the diffi-cult conditions of homesteading life, but it might also be a way of documenting some sense of personal loss in terms of a mother's psychological presence. As Faragher suggests, one of the things that "women believed and expected of themselves" was the need to be "faithful and ever-present mothers" (174), so that by exposing what might be termed as "'failed mother' narratives," includ-ing "stories of those mothers who go crazy" (Brandt 162), we again manage to get to, as suggested in the final epigraph to this chapter, "the other side of a well-known tale." The spectre of "madness" is invoked again and again in con-temporary settlement literature, usually as a warning to those who might not possess an appropriately "pioneering" character, one adaptable to the specific conditions of prairie isolation. In the June 18, 1913, edition of the *Moose Jaw Evening Times*, for example, Barbara Wylie writes,

> [W]e are told that Canada is a woman's paradise. It is nothing of
> the kind. A woman's life in Canada is extremely hard, and lonely,
> and it is because of their loneliness that the asylums there are being
> filled with women, who are driven mad by the loneliness. They are
> caged in a "shack" often miles from any populated district. Turn
> your back on Canada." (qtd. in Rasmussen et al. 22)

Similarly, Elizabeth Mitchell's 1915 *Impressions of Early Twentieth Century Prairie Communities* included mention of the effects of "cabin fever":

The prairie madness is perfectly recognized and very common still.... A woman alone in the house all day may find the silence deadly; in the wheat-farming stage there may not even be a beast about the place. Her husband may be tired at night, and unwilling to "hitch up" and drive her out "for a whimsy"; or the husband may be willing and sympathetic, but she may grow shy and diffident, and not care to make the effort to tidy herself up and go to see a neighbour – any neighbour, just to break the monotony. Then fancies come, and suspicions, and queer ways, and at last the young Mounted Policeman comes to the door, and carries her away to the terrible vast "Sanatorium" that hangs above the Saskatchewan. There is still that kind of loneliness on the prairie. (150–51)[28]

Certainly the geography of homesteading on the Canadian prairies was widely recognized as a direct cause of human isolation, for the land survey system that parcelled the prairies into 160-acre quarter-sections inevitably resulted in farms being widely spaced apart.[29] The psychological effect of this system is clearly gendered, as seen in Eliane Leslau Silverman's comment that "the staff at the mental hospital at Ponoka had a label, back in those years, for the women they admitted. They called them 'prairie women'" ("Women" 95).

---

28 The prairie woman's "grow[ing] shy and diffident" as a symbol of her psychological retreat from "dauntless optimism" is also seen in Frederick Philip Grove's *Fruits of the Earth* (1933) when Ruth says to her husband, "Look what this life has made of me. When I am to talk to any one but the children, I am nervous. Rather than go to town and show myself, I stay at home, day in day out, year in and year out" (111). Similarly, in *The Silent Song of Mary Eleanor*, Marjorie Campbell says of her mother's response to the prospect of entertaining guests in her home that she "lost her nerve": "That entire year in which she had never seen another woman had left her diffident and self-conscious, embarrassed because she had so little to offer. She needed all the gallant reassurance father could muster to restore her poise and her innate love of people" (44).

29 That the geography of isolation is culturally imposed is clear when looking at "other" patterns of settlement. For example, Emily Ferguson notes the difference of the "communistic" system of settlement adopted by the group of people who comprised the "Doukhobor village of Vosnesenia": as she states: "[T]here are some very apparent benefits in this Doukhobor method, too. The people are not isolated on lonely steadings miles and miles from any one. This loneliness is undoubtedly the greatest trial our settlers have to endure" (*Janey* 48).

That North American settlement was an arduous process, placing great
psychological and physical demands upon individuals, especially women,
is an oft-repeated assertion, but I would like to leave room for Ann Leger
Anderson's suggestion that "this psychological dimension of oppression needs
study.... Allowed to be 'emotional,' to express feelings more freely than men,
some women did just that, and were perceived as being 'on the verge of insanity,' but these expressions of confinement, isolation, and despair acted as a
catharsis" ("Saskatchewan" 76). While I would assert that the Ruthian image
of the female emigrant (as represented by Traill) does not necessarily "allow"
women "to be 'emotional,'" I also want to borrow from Anderson here and
stress (similar to my discussion of crying and the act of looking back) that
women's narrative deviations from the myth of "dauntless optimism" should
not be read as evidence of their failure to commit to the settlement project;
rather, women's "expressions of confinement, isolation, and despair" become a
necessary and "cathartic" part of the whole and complex process of female survival. "Madness," then, whatever form it takes, becomes one of the experiences
through which the memoirist is able to complicate the Pioneer Woman image.
When Barbara (Hunter) Anderson chooses to write about the effects of prairie
isolation on the settler woman, she does so in a chapter of *Two White Oxen: A
Perspective of Early Saskatoon 1874–1905* (1972) titled "Storm Bound," which
is written very dramatically, reading almost like fiction, with her mother and
father referred to by their first names, Margaret and William. Anderson's
narrative certainly displays an eclectic array of narrative styles anyway, but
one wonders what it is about this particular remembrance that might have
motivated the author's recourse to the fictional mode. The story begins with
a traditional image of prairie fiction; however, very quickly Anderson moves
into a rather unorthodox – physical, although not psychological – positioning
of her female character:

> Snow! Snow! Snow! Its glistening whiteness reached away to the
> horizon, with nothing to break the monotony of its rigid waves on
> the whole expanse of vision.
>   From her point of observation on the top of her shanty home
> with its adjacent outbuildings and hay stack, there was no sign of

other habitation. A wave of intense loneliness swept through the whole being of Mrs. Margaret Hunter as with a sigh, that was almost a sob, she murmured, "Oh, why left I my hame – why, oh why, did I ever consent to come to this wilderness." (94)

The author's mother goes to visit her husband, who is busy working in the stable, and the author recreates their dialogue as follows: having been asked about her outdoor presence, Margaret Hunter replies,

> "Yes, I wanted a breath of fresh air, and oh, how I long for a change; how I hate the monotony of this shut-in winter time; no chance to see a face but our own, it is so long since I've seen anyone," she continued.
>
> "Feeling a bit blue are ye?" her husband asked. "I'd think you would be content with all our nice smart children to see and hear every day, and me having my Sundays at home and not having to leave you and them to go to work as I used to do back in Ontario. Just think! living in our own house, on our own land, and being my own boss. Isn't that worth something – don't you think?'"

It is interesting that, while Margaret Hunter merely suggests the desire for a temporary change of scenery and condition, her husband responds by first diminishing her emotional distress as mere "blueness," then questioning the legitimacy of her sense of isolation on the basis of the presence of children and a husband, before defending the decision to emigrate to the prairies by using the typical masculinist images of propagandists ("living in our own house, on our own land"), which lead to the announcement of the chief masculine motivation ("and being my own boss"). Therein lies the problem, which Margaret Hunter recognizes when she replies by saying, "Oh, yes that's all very well, for you get out to see folks sometimes." As the author continues her less than stoic portrayal of her mother, Margaret says, "'I suppose it will be summer before I can go anywhere and then I won't want to go likely,' said Margaret chokingly, as the loneliness overcame her" (95). In response to his wife's enunciation of her distress, William Hunter suggests that the two of them go alone, leaving the children to care for the family farm and each other, to Saskatoon for a meeting of "the Central Saskatchewan Agricultural Society" (98), to which proposition Margaret Hunter finally agrees. While her husband is in the meeting and Margaret is visiting a friend in town, a "blizzard" begins, but "the ladies were enjoying the evening together, unheeding the snow that was coming down heavily when their husbands returned from the meeting" (99). For a brief moment in time, then, the author's mother enjoys complete self-absorption in the warm circle of female community, but anxiety soon sets in as the parents' journey home to the children is delayed by the poor weather conditions. They have to wait for one whole day; then, with the temperature registered at "48 below!" (100), they head home. Upon their return, when they have assurance that all the children all well, Margaret Hunter is able once again to see clear to the optimistic side of her life on the prairies: "After the children were in bed and asleep, Margaret said to her husband, 'This little sod house is the dearest spot on earth to me'" (102).

Beulah Baldwin alludes to "cabin fever" in *The Long Trail* when she writes about her family's less than ideal living conditions in northern Alberta, overlooking the Smoky and Peace rivers, during the winter months of 1916–17:

> It was the middle of December when Dad moved us into a wooden shack close to where our tent had been. The weather had turned very cold, with strong winds coming off the river threatening to lift the tent from its platform. With the baby expected in a few weeks, we needed a better space. The shack, hastily built, was without insulation except for tar paper on the inside. This made it look dark and gloomy, especially with a thick layer of frost covering the windows, but at least we could now move in some of our furniture. (188–89)

Despite the set-up for a Moodie episode, though, Baldwin comments on the fact that her mother does not lose her equanimity in such surroundings:

> I can not imagine how my mother kept her sanity during those long, cold, winter months ahead – cooped up, everything jammed

in together, along with two active children and a new baby born in January. When the temperature dipped to thirty and forty below, we must have been confined to the bed, as the floor was freezing cold. The worst feature of the tent, according to Mother, was a dripping ceiling during sudden thaws. (189)

A few pages (and a couple of years) later, however, after the family had built a new cabin and started to make minimal economic progress, Baldwin shares a scene with her readers that shows the ill effects upon her mother of a life of toil and successive winters being cooped up:

We children had no idea how worn and depressed Mother had become. But it was not until Grandma and Edward left that a feeling of restless dissatisfaction engulfed my Mother. We returned home from school one wintery day to discover that Mother had left, taking Warren and Marjory with her. Dad said that she needed a rest and had gone to be with Grandma in Calgary. In response to our questioning, Dad told us in a cross voice that we were too young to understand. We were frightened, and when Junior cried in the night I crawled into bed with my brothers and, although we shed a few tears, we were soon asleep.

Our days were mostly bleak and dreary during that time. Not only did we need our mother, we also missed our brother and baby sister. To make matters worse, our good-natured father became morose and harsh, expecting us to cook and do many of Mother's tasks. He even spanked Carlton for not sweeping the rug properly. We hated this task, as clouds of dust filled the air while we swept. Mother was probably away for only a few weeks, but it seemed a long time to us. I was shocked to discover years later, when she tried to explain why she changed her mind and came back, that she had intended to leave for good. If we children had known she had intended staying away, we would have been devastated. (221)

Baldwin's own sense of personal loss as daughter-author is apparent in this scene, and yet it is clearly important to her to document her mother's momentary incoherence with the myth of "dauntless optimism." What brings Olive Freeland back is that one of the children she takes with her, Warren, suffers from a bout of "tonsillitis," which "saved her from making a terrible mistake. When he became delirious from a high fever and she thought she was going to lose him, she realized how much she needed her family" (221). That, and the letter that she receives from one of the sons she leaves behind, saying that "if she was not back soon we would all be as thin as stove pipes," makes her realize her crucial role in the immediate survival of her family, and so she returns, writes Baldwin, thus "setting our world aright again." In a bittersweet retrospective moment at the end of this scene, Baldwin provides her reader with her enduring memory of her mother, one which seems to me to hover in the gap between ideal and real:

> Looking back, I often picture Mother sewing by the fire, the soft lamplight making a golden halo of her hair. For years she had dressed us from the trousseau she had hardly worn. With four pregnancies in six years, she had not much use for lovely garments. (221–22)

Another factor of women's lives that caused emotional distress is the fact that, especially in the early years of homesteading, women often found themselves left alone for a variety of reasons: indeed, as Nanci Langford asserts regarding her study of prairie women,

> One of the unexpected outcomes of this research was to discover the extent to which women lived and worked alone on prairie farms and ranches throughout the settlement period. Popular imagery of the homesteading couple describes them working side by side in the fields or the barn, or getting together frequently throughout the work day to consult and support each other and share meals together. While this did happen for most of the women and men in the group studied, it cannot be considered a consistent way of

life for first generation homesteading couples. The frequency of
men's absences away from the homestead, and often for long periods of time, is astonishing. ("First Generation" 73)

Marjorie Grace Johannson confirms this reality in *The Pink House on the Hill*
(1986) when she notes that

> Lack of money, for many newcomers made it necessary for men and
> even young boys to leave their homes and families a few months of
> the year they tried to get work on the railroads, in logging camps,
> or any job where they could earn money to purchase the necessities
> of life. While the men were away, women and children were left to
> face the hardships, loneliness and difficulties of every day living on
> a new homestead. (92–93)

Left alone with her new baby in a cabin on a homestead in the Peace River
country in 1929, Ida Scharf Hopkins struggles with the spectre of "madness"
when her husband has to work elsewhere in order to supplement the often
tenuous farm family economy: as she writes in *To the Peace River Country and
On* (1973),

> In the later part of summer Bill got a chance to work at a small
> sawmill in Sunset Prairie, about thirty miles away. It meant of
> course that I would have to stay alone with our baby, but we need-
> ed the money. For the first time I realized our complete isolation.
> There was no one within at least four miles, and no roads through
> the bush, just trails. We had built on the bank of the river, actually
> at the top of a cliff, or what was called a "cutbank" above an old
> trail used in the Klondike days called "White Mans Crossing".
> The river was cold and clear, and the source of our water but it was
> a long piece down. The hill sloped up from the back of the house,
> so no matter which way I looked it was either side hill or trees.
> Very pretty, but I soon discovered very lonely.

A roving band of Indian ponies soon discovered our haystacks
and moved in. Our pole fence was no match for their cunning.
During the day I could cope with them, but they soon learned to
come at night. I listened for the crack of poles and ran out with
sticks, stones, and curses to try and chase them away. In the day
time I dressed the baby up, put her in a box to keep her warm,
and started in to try and repair the fence with haywire, pliers, and
nails. The hay was very precious to us because it was the winter
supply for the horses. Night after night it was the same routine.
Some times the horses won; sometimes I won.

It was nearly a month before Bill got home again. By this time
I was nearly "stir crazy". I don't know whether it was more from
loneliness or anger at the horses. Anyway he came back with more
new ideas. (29–30)

Hopkins's use of the phrase "stir crazy" and her reluctance to attribute that
form of distress to simply the spectre of "loneliness" potentially makes less
severe what probably was a frightening experience, a reality that begins to leak
through Hopkins's generally cheerful surface narrative with her final comment
about her husband returning with "more new ideas," a comment that holds her
husband accountable for having provided some less than stellar experiences up
to this point. However, one of the "new ideas" proves valuable for Hopkins's
emotional survival: referring to a male neighbour, she writes,

He had married and was coming back, so now Mr. Bedell was
moving his wife and three boys back to his own homestead in
the Little Buffalo Valley. Land next to him had been closed to
homesteading, but was about to open up. It was not so isolated and
the soil was good. We would have neighbours. They planned on
mutual help. Bill would help him clear land, etc. in return for the
use of machinery we didn't have. His wife and I were already good
friends and each liked the idea of having a 'woman neighbour.'
There was no school as yet so I was to start the boys on school

work. We made our decision. We abandoned the first homestead and gambled on the new land. (30)

Nevertheless, with her husband finding it necessary to take work "at the mill in the winter" (35), Hopkins again experiences isolation and loneliness:

> The days in the winter were very short. It was dark until nearly ten in the morning and by four in the afternoon. One time I ran out of coal oil for the lamps when I was alone. I had to get everything done in the daylight hours and then spend the rest of the time in the darkness. I tried opening the stove door, it helped but it was impossible to read or do any handwork. Even though I was warm and comfortable and had lots to eat, the nights were a million years long. The darkness and the deadly silence nearly got to me. At the end of the week when Bill got home and brought the oil I don't know if I was more glad to see him or the five gallon can of coal oil. (36)

The force of Hopkins's suggestion that "the darkness and the deadly silence nearly got to me" is blunted when she, very typically, finishes with the re-instatement of a cheerful surface narrative by ending the passage with a joke.

In the case of one memoir, a physical disability might partly be read as an outward manifestation of a psychological disability (or at least disinclination) to adapt to the homesteading project, and partly as a manifestation of the emotional incapacitation that occurs as a result of conditions of extreme isolation. In *Of Us and the Oxen*, Sarah Roberts does not scruple to mention the frequently debilitating migraine headaches that force her to withdraw periodically from participation in her family's undertaking. From the beginning, the fifty-four-year-old Roberts makes clear her disaffection for the isolated conditions of land settlement, especially as she is the only woman in her family of five who emigrate to Canada. Her dismay regarding her situation is exacerbated by the fact that she finds herself, especially during the winters, "constantly confined" (65) within her modest sod home. She openly confronts the inherent inequality of the traditional division of labour along gender lines when she points out the key difference between her own and her husband's physical – and hence, psychological – condition. Reflecting on a visit from her daughter and grand-daughter, she writes:

> Alice's visit during the summer meant more to me than I could ever tell. The distance between us and our dear ones never afterward seemed to me so great. And then it was worth so much to me to have a companion in my work. Papa almost always had one of the boys with him – indeed, he hardly ever worked alone – and if by chance they were all away for a few hours, he plainly showed the depression that comes from loneliness; but I worked by myself most of the time. (125–26)

This reflection on the psychological demands of being alone for great lengths of time relates to the headaches from which she suffers throughout her homesteading experience. In fact, towards the end of her memoir, Roberts provides an interesting anecdote that illustrates a complex relationship between her headaches and the extreme isolation that is part of her homesteading experience. However, before she goes into the anecdote itself, she provides the following qualification:

> Now, because this story doesn't put me in a very favorable light, and because I want to be fair, even to myself, I will preface it by telling of conditions which perhaps might be thought of as extenuating circumstances, even if they did not excuse my conduct.
>
> All through these years on the homestead I had had the same dreadful headaches that I had had all my life, but I think they were even more severe than they had previously been and lasted longer, for they usually kept me in bed for two days and unfitted me for any work for at least one more. Of course, at these times, Papa and the boys had to do the housework. (249)

There is at least the possibility here that Roberts's worsening headaches upon her arrival in Alberta, and upon her discovery of the emotional distress caused by the sometimes extreme conditions of isolation, have a psychological component. Certainly her distaste for her domestic routine (made evident elsewhere in the text) gets addressed through these headaches when the male members of the family pitch in "to do the housework." The headaches do not, however, prevent the men from having to leave Roberts alone at times, for, as she confesses:

> As I look back, I know that there was never a time when I was sick that they did not insist that someone stay with me. It was not due to their negligence that someone did not always do this, but was due entirely to my insistence that they go to do their outside work. Of course, I dreaded unspeakably the long weary day alone with no one to speak to or to do a thing for me, but I knew how much work there was to be done and that they could never do it all, no matter how hard they worked.

All of this detail about her headaches and her seemingly self-sacrificing nature ultimately leads to the anecdote Roberts wants to relate about an "episode" she experiences, one that puts her far beyond the Traill typology:

> It was while I was in the throes of one of these headaches that the episode which I am about to describe took place. At the end of the second day, I became very restless and began to wonder why Papa and Brockway did not come, for they were later than usual. They told me afterward, when I would listen, that they had stayed to finish up a particular piece of work. Time dragged along, and night was at hand, yet still they delayed, until it seemed to me that I would go frantic if I had to stay alone another minute. Then, just before the "break" came, I heard them drive into the yard and thought that again the agony that I had endured so many times was past. (249–50)

This experience of "perverse endurance," however, is not the end of the tale for, when the men come inside it is only to inform Roberts that she will be left

alone again as they "must make a trip over to the store yet that night" (250).
As the author goes on to describe her intense reaction to once again being
left alone, she explicitly admits her emotional/psychological incoherence with
"cheerfully adaptive" ideals of settler women:

> The minutes dragged by. It was cold, and I was not only sick, but
> was timid, as I always was at night when alone. Indeed, even when
> I was well, it took all my nerve to stay alone at night in that little
> sod house on the prairie so far away from everyone that no matter
> what my need might be I could not summon help; and now I was
> sick and worn out with two days of loneliness and intense pain. I
> could not understand why they did not come, for it seemed to me
> that they had been gone long enough to have made the trip twice,
> and the old fear that they might have lost the trail and be wander-
> ing around trying to find it, added to the terrors of a situation with
> which, in my weakness, I was unable to cope.
>
> I am sure that there are many heroic women who would have
> thought that an experience which was testing me to the breaking
> point was a light thing, and all I can say for myself when things
> reached this juncture is that my nerves just got the better of me. I
> lay there with my head throbbing and fear chilling my heart; wait-
> ing, listening, and longing, while all sorts of crazy notions flitted
> through my brain.

Given all of the set-up for this anecdote, including her giving the qualification of having a very bad headache at the time of this event, the reader might
well expect that what she is showing regret for is her faltering resolve; her
inability to adapt to the necessary circumstances of her family's homesteading
life. However, as it turns out, the behaviour that she apologizes for and that
she attributes to "intense pain" is the anger she feels (and expresses internally)
against her menfolk before they return from their trip. When the men finally
return home, she diffuses her anger – restores her equanimity – by engaging
in a comical act that seems to embody "madness," but which really is a parody

of what she has already dramatically experienced, as well as being an act of revenge:

> Papa said, "Sarah, where are you going?"
>
> "I'm going outdoors and stand on my head in a snowdrift," I replied.
>
> "Why, Sade," he said, "I believe you're crazy."
>
> "I go you one better. I don't believe it, I *know* it," and I marched out of the house, while Papa and Brockway sank down into their chairs, with their arms lying limply at their sides, and with complete helplessness and hopelessness expressed in their faces and attitudes. And it was no wonder.
>
> When I was out of the house, I went to the west side, where the drifts were piled high. I broke the crust, kneeled down, and stuck my head into the snow as far as I could without smothering. I held it there until it felt frozen, and so did the rest of me for that matter. When I came back into the house Papa and Brockway were sitting exactly as they were when I went out. I believe that neither of them had moved a muscle. (251)

In the spectre of her "madness," the men are as incapacitated as she had been while they were gone. She turns the tables, leaving them inside while she, finally, gets "out of the house," then when she returns things are changed:

> We all learned something from this experience. I learned among other things, that the best cure for a headache is to put your brains into cold storage, and that the same treatment will allay violent, unreasoning anger; and we all learned that it was not well for me to be alone at such times. Always thereafter, someone stayed with me when I was sick. (252)

Some memoirists found less dramatic coping strategies in times of emotional distress. In a chapter of *It Could Have Been Worse: The Autobiography of a Pioneer* (1980) – significantly titled "Chinking" – Peggy Holmes recreates a less-than-satisfying visit she and her husband once made to a neighbouring farm in northern Alberta in the 1920s, a farm where they were going to "board" their chickens for the winter:

> Apart from the relief of getting our chickens looked after, this visit didn't lift my spirits at all. Mrs. Sergonne had been a school teacher and had married a farmer. She was "bushed," had let herself go, and was hopelessly depressed.
>
> Her opening remark was, "Move your chair from the wall. The bed bugs are very bad – I can't keep them down." I did some fast footwork.
>
> She pulled on a cigarette that hung loosely in her sagging mouth. "Take advice from me girl. Get out before it gets you!"
> It was no use sobbing all the way home. The tears would have frozen on my face. (106)

The representation of this visit directly precedes a confession to her readers that Holmes herself struggles with her new life in Canada: "During this time I was getting mail from home telling me about the family parties, theatres, etc. Still suffering from homesickness these letters did little to comfort me" (107–8). However, later in her memoir Holmes makes it clear that she possesses more resolve than the Mrs. Sergonnes of the world and that, although she will certainly experience moments of incongruity with settlement life, nevertheless she is able to devise creative ways to dissipate the psychological ill-effects of living isolated in the bush. For example, as she rather humourously writes,

> One sunny afternoon we had to pick up some supplies from our local store a few miles away, so Harry hitched up the wagon and I climbed up beside him. Skin and Grief plodded along the track and all was peaceful. It was a glorious day – the sort they sang about later in *Oklahoma! – Oh What a Beautiful Mornin', Oh what a Beautiful Day*. In my hazy dream world at that time I was thinking of *Come to Kew in Lilac Time*.

It's strange what this life does to one. Suddenly, for no apparent reason, I let out a bloodcurdling scream. The horses were terrified and bolted as fast as they could go. Using all his strength, Harry tried to pull them up, but no way would they stop. They were going hell bent for leather after such an experience.

The wagon box was somewhat rickety and I was rocked out of my screaming jag. But I really did feel much better. Finally Harry won the day and Skin and Grief slowed up, panting and foaming. "For God's sake, whatever was the matter?" Harry asked.

"Nothing, nothing at all," I replied. "I just felt the urge to scream."

"Well, if you ever get that urge again, go behind the barn and do it – and let me know beforehand or you'll scare the livestock to death." (135–36)

For one brief moment, the joy of the "glorious day" farming in Canada is disrupted by memories of life back Home, causing Holmes to resort to a unique form of self-expression. As she continues, such "mad" behaviour, while ultimately productive, could have negative consequences in a less-isolated environment:

I did this many times and, believe me, it relieves tension. I am sure Freud would have suggested other therapeutic methods, but I can assure you that a jolly good scream behind the barn really helped! I had to curb myself later when we lived in the city. Even one scream in the garage behind closed doors would probably have been followed by police sirens and a visit from the arms of the law. (136)

The good-humoured approach can only get you so far, though, and Holmes goes on to admit to a more serious and more poignant bout of "madness" later in her text, one that requires a more spirited cure:

Busy as I was, I always looked forward to news from home. Letters came telling me about weekends on Harry's houseboat, the *Ariadne*, yachting parties on the River Humber, and family gatherings. It was all meant to cheer me up, but my family's well-meaning efforts often plunged me into the depth of despair and homesickness. Homesickness is worse than seasickness. I've had them both! Seasickness stops when you step off the boat; I could hardly step off the land.

This was particularly hard on Harry. He tried to cheer me up in many ways. But I hit a low that summer; I even got past the screaming behind the barn point. I would saddle Mignon and urge her into her fastest gallop. Riding was not as exciting in the bush country as it had been dashing over the uncluttered ranges east of Calgary, but it was one way to blow my low spirits to the four winds, and I would return telling myself how lucky I was to have my own horse – and who wanted to go boating anyway? (147)[30]

As seen from the above examples, many of the memoirists display moments of "trouble and suffering" endured as part of their experiences of homesteading life. Some of the women overcome these bouts of "madness" easily, while others struggle throughout the process of "adaptation" to the new life. Despite the warnings of contemporary writers, however, none of the women represented in the memoirs gathered here end their narratives unable to overcome their psychological/emotional incoherence. None of them end up like the woman whose story is told in Campbell's *The Silent Song of Mary Eleanor*, wherein the author's father remembers "one particularly unfortunate woman" (58) who arrived in the west all "lovely pink and white and golden" and who soon became "faded and worn," with the inevitable result that "her romance ended in a mental institution, still on the prairies with the wind she couldn't bear" (59). Rather, the endings here are quite a bit more mundane, more real, once again in rejection of the either/or-isms of success or failure that inevitably accompanied the Traill/Moodie dichotomy. From propaganda materials to prairie fiction, the final act in the land settlement drama, as seen in Traill's text, is most

---

30   For more examples of female madness, especially as a result of extreme isolation, see also Bannert 78; Clark 53–55; Hewson 2–4, 80–82; and Schultz 58–59.

often a re-affirmation of commitment to the homesteading project and a re-assertion of the narrative of "dauntless optimism." If we accept the end of Traill's story as represented within the confines of *The Backwoods*, then we might fairly easily understand why T.D. MacLulich wrote in 1976 that the two sisters' texts represent "the complementary halves of a single fable," as seen in their two very different endings:

> One sister finds a likely piece of land, realizes the necessity of swallowing her pride and changing her ways, and settles down to help her husband start a farm; she lives happily ever after. The other sister finds an equally likely piece of land, but refuses to change her behaviour and ideas and is continually dissatisfied at having to do menial labour; finally she and her husband leave the farm, failures, and finish their lives as a minor official and his embittered wife in a small provincial town, far from the bustling capital. (118)

While MacLulich's summation is painfully simplistic, nevertheless it does manage to capture the respective tones sounded by Traill's and Moodie's narrative endings. Given the epistolary format of Traill's *Backwoods*, and the fact that the text was published only three years after the author arrived in Canada, the reader is not really provided with a full ending to the settlement story, so that it must necessarily be concluded that Traill's cheerful enthusiasm will inevitably carry her family on to some level of success. Indeed, as the author assures the recipient of her last letter, "our chief difficulties are now over, at least we hope so, and we trust soon to enjoy the comforts of a cleared farm" (250). Here we see Traill ever faithful to the cultural mythology in which settlement success was inevitable if only the emigrant was willing to work hard and persevere against all odds.

In Moodie's text, there is no linear adherence to the philosophy of "dauntless optimism," no climactic moment when the author is able to declare "the comforts of a cleared farm" as a result of years of stint and save. In fact, Moodie's text runs precisely counter to the linear model, illustrating as it does an endless cycle of hopes followed by disappointments. In a telling moment in a chapter titled "The Walk to Dummer," when Moodie and her friends discover that

their pilgrimage has gone astray of the trodden path and that they must turn
back, she encapsulates the prevailing tone of her own immigrant experience in
the following reflection: "What effect must that tremendous failure produce
upon the human mind, when at the end of life's unretraceable journey, the
traveller finds that he has fallen upon the wrong track through every stage,
and instead of arriving at a land of blissful promise, sinks for ever into the
gulf of despair!" (456). Moodie's awareness of her family's ultimate failure at
land settlement inspires her to an act of self-preservation that most decidedly contradicts the Ruthian image of female behaviour: she writes a letter to
the Lieutenant-Governor, Sir George Arthur, asking for help, with the end
result that her husband is offered "the situation of sheriff of the V – district"
(475). At the end of her story, we see the author's physical and psychological
emergence from the bush, her body carrying the visible signs of her "perverse
endurance" of settlement life: as she describes her less than romantic ending,

> For seven years I had lived out of the world entirely; my person had
> been rendered coarse by hard work and exposure to the weather. I
> looked double the age I really was, and my hair was already thickly
> sprinkled with grey. I clung to my solitude. I did not like to be
> dragged from it to mingle in gay scenes, in a busy town, and with
> gaily-dressed people. I was no longer fit for the world; I had lost
> all relish for the pursuits and pleasures which are so essential to its
> votaries; I was contented to live and die in obscurity. (476)

Not exactly a glowing recommendation of settlement life.

Contemporary literature of western settlement definitely favoured romantic endings. Indeed, the promotional materials created to inspire emigration to
the Canadian prairies were entirely predicated on the assumption of inevitable
success. As discussed in Chapter Two, the text and images of such materials
were visionary, with an eye always to the future and to the achievement of
a utopian paradise. Prairie fiction, too, tended towards the romantic ending. For example, in Arthur Stringer's first novel in a trilogy *The Prairie Wife*
(1915), the female narrator, a city girl, marries a man named Duncan Argyll
McKail, a "Scotch-Canadian" and a "broken-down civil engineer who's

taken up farming in the Northwest" (5). After a series of trials and tribula-
tions, the novel ends on a positive note with Duncan's announcement that
farming success is guaranteed; after all, "*The railway's going to come!*" (310).
As he goes on to calculate the effect of such news for his wife, "And there'll
be a station within a mile of where you stand! And inside of two years this
seventeen or eighteen hundred acres of land will be worth forty dollars an
acre, easily, and perhaps even fifty. And what that means you can figure out for
yourself!" (311). In Douglas Durkin's *The Magpie* (1923), the ending witnesses
the hero Craig Forrester rejecting city life and politics by re-assuming the
"toggery of romance" (6) and becoming a farmer, like his father before him.
The final image of the text strikes the iconic note of prairie optimism: "And
in the sky before him as he walked steadily on, the shafts of gold shot to the
zenith, flooding the earth with the faint glow of early dawn" (329).[31] Harold
Bindloss's 1925 novel *Prairie Gold* ends on a similarly enchanted note, as seen
when a newly married and delightedly heroic couple, Hugh and Alice, have
joined together to become an "invincible" force on the path to success:

> When he had lighted his pipe he leaned against a wheel and
> glanced at Alice on the fragrant load of prairie hay. Her skin was
> brown, her look was tranquilly satisfied, and although she had
> helped Hugh put up the load he saw she was not tired.
>
> In front, the dark-green wheat rippled in the wind. Where the
> spiked heads bent, one saw touches of coppery red, and across the
> summer fallow the oats were going yellow. Soon they would be
> ripe for harvest, and tall stalks and strong color promised a full bin
> of "prairie gold." (310–11)

Prairie memoirs written by or about white, English-speaking women who
would have been subject to the idealistic expectations of such cultural construc-

---

31   Emily Ferguson's description of the "Pit" area of the Winnipeg Grain Exchange
     interestingly corresponds to Durkin's golden image of wheat farming: "When I was
     a little girl I heard tell that the rainbow followed the plough. This may be true, but
     one end of the bow rests on this Pit, and at its foot may be found the proverbial bag
     of gold" (*Open* 188).

tions, however, tend to give the lie to the narrative of "dauntless optimism" by not fulfilling expectations of inevitable economic success or inevitable personal contentment. As with Traill's *Backwoods*, the "well-known tale" of settlement propaganda often belies a more modest reality. Indeed, the ending of Traill's text is not really the end, for, as her most recent biographer notes, Catharine's family lived a "hand-to-mouth existence" (174) as they moved from home to home and failed at successive attempts to "settle" themselves in the backwoods. Writes Gray, "by mid-century, clearly the tables were turned between the two sisters. Twenty years earlier in the colony's backwoods, Catharine had been the strong, sunny-tempered elder sister who reassured and comforted her sibling," but now "Catharine's visits to Susanna were her only respite from worry" (228). While not usually ending on such an extremely negative note as Moodie's text, the memoirs studied here do work to expose "the other side of a well-known tale" by making clear that "success" is a highly mitigated term. In many of these texts the author so often focuses upon other concerns than strictly agricultural pursuits that the reader forgets the overriding utopian purpose of the homestead project and arrives at the end of the memoir only to discover either the family's dismally pathetic failure or ridiculously modest success. Quite often fathers were the ones to decide, either by choice or fate, how a family's homestead experience was going to end. The untimely death of a husband was a fairly common ending to a family's prairie dreams, one decidedly not accounted for in promotional materials. In Barbara Anderson's *Two White Oxen*, the dream begins to fade for the Hunter family when, eleven years after their arrival in the west, the author's father dies in September of 1894. Although he leaves all of his property to his wife and exacts "a promise from his children to love and respect their Mother as they had done" to that point (154), the effect upon the author's mother is ultimately devastating and it is noted that, afterwards, "Margaret seemed to prepare for her own death though she was but 45 years of age." Although she does live for another forty-five years, Margaret Hunter's life is marked by "years of hardship," "pain and sorrow" (155), as well as comfort and family connection, and is an anticlimactic rejection of the myth of "dauntless optimism" with which her family originally set out to homestead.[32] In another illustration of the potential for an unromantic ending to the settlement story, in *Crocus and Meadowlark Country: A Story of an Alberta Family* (1963), Georgina Thomson refers to the Eversfield family who immigrate to Canada from England. As she describes Mrs. Eversfield, she "was a quiet, cultured woman and probably had no illusions as to the life she was coming to, but she adapted herself bravely to the hardships, and was friendly with all the neighbors and well-liked by them, however different their backgrounds might be" (104). However, even successful adaptation on a personal level does not keep the sometimes harsh reality of prairie life at bay, for, as Thomson advises,

> [F]rom lack of experience and for other reasons, their home-steading venture did not prove a success, and its end was tragic. May [the daughter] died while still in her 'teens from lack of proper medical attention as well as the hardships in her life, and [Mr. Eversfield] was found dead one day following an apoplectic stroke. The place was sold and Mrs. Eversfield went to live with Alf [her son] and his wife in Calgary. (105)

The Thomsons themselves certainly cannot be said to have failed at home-steading, but even their moderate level of personal success clearly undercuts the hyperbolic visions contained in the myth of "dauntless optimism." After the Thomson children had all left to begin their own lives, the parents were "left on the homestead alone with what hired men they could get," until the decision was made to sell:

---

32 Although by 1894 the Hunter family had experienced something less than per-sonal prosperity, the cultural optimism carried on, as Anderson illustrates in her "Appendix C" to her memoir, in which she reproduces a "Reminiscence" written by George W. Grant and published in the "Saskatoon Phoenix, Vol. 1, No. 1, Saskatoon, N.W.T., Friday, October, 17th, 1902": the article begins, "The present prospects of the Saskatoon District are sufficiently encouraging, and the indications of the future prosperity are so decidedly apparent that it makes the founders of the settlement, their historic relationship, and the spirit of heroism which characterize them, a subject of new interest to all concerned" (175).

Father got tired of hired men. He had done well through the war
years when the price of wheat was high, and now with the price of
land going up to an unprecedented height, Father, though barely
60, suddenly decided to sell his homestead and the two quarters of
C.P.R. land he had owned for some years. How he could bear to
part with his cherished quarter-section on which he had filed so
proudly, and the horses he loved, I do not know. (274)

Thomson's subtle questioning here of her father's ability to privilege monetary
gain over emotional attachment is heightened when she goes on to specifically
consider her mother's reaction to the end of their prairie story and to confront
male authority in such matters:

I was not at home when the sale took place. I do not think I could
have borne it. Mother did not want to leave the farm. She would
have liked Father to build a more modern farmhouse for them and
let a hired man and his wife have the old one. Many years later
after Mother died I found plans of houses she had designed or
cut from magazines, among her papers. But she never questioned
Father's judgment and authority, though she was much better
educated than he was and in many ways had a better mind. He
was "Caesar in his own house," and she was the yielding Victorian
wife. I think he soon regretted selling the farm, and always spoke
of the homestead years as the happiest in his life.

In contrast to most of the memoirs examined here, in a rare revelatory moment, Myrtle G. Moorhouse writes an ending to her homesteading experience near Swift Current, Saskatchewan, that, although it is far from romantic,
nevertheless ultimately documents a sense of personal achievement. As she
writes in a chapter of *Buffalo Horn Valley* (1973) titled "Hopes Deferred," the
vagaries of prairie farming, especially during the "dirty thirties" (30), could be
devastating to one's sense of promise in the future:

How can I describe the hopes in the spring, only to be sore disappointed later on, year after year, dust storms, horses dying with
sleeping sickness, grasshoppers, wire worms, army worms, no
money, relief cheques which were a mere pittance and had to be
coaxed, begged and wrung out of the authorities.... Cliff would
sometimes put in 200 acres of crop, and a three day blow would
send the sand flying and cut off the small tender blades. He would
walk from window to window crying, with his lungs full of sand
that he had breathed in while seeding. (31)

As a result of such devastation, writes Moorhouse, her husband became de-
spondent: he "couldn't take it any longer and he turned to drink." Moorhouse's
love for her husband is always evident in her writing, but no reader can miss
the bittersweet tone – the deft narrative balance she seeks to achieve between
sympathy for her husband's emotional turmoil and a sense of personal abandonment – when relating memories such as this one:

When our first crop in ten years was showing up, along with fourteen years of debts, he said he was afraid to have a crop, for fear he
would drink it all. Then one day, after a big drunk, he just went out
to his workshop and shot himself. He left a note so I wouldn't be
blamed. He thought he was doing me a favour but poor Cliff, he
never knew how hard he made it for me. (32)

Making the decision to continue on the family farm and raise her three young
girls alone, Moorhouse ends her memoir by noting the monumental nature of
the task she faced, as well as the magnitude of her success:

Then began the job of untangling fourteen years of debts, paying
the most urgent ones, and asking the other people to hold off, until
I could get around to them. I must have convinced them, because
they took me at my word. The man we bought the land from hadn't
received one cent, and he said to me, "I don't know what a woman
with three wee girls wants a farm for, but it's yours if you want it,

no one else will get it, and pay when you can." My sister and her
husband helped with my work, and I let them use my machinery
and tractor on theirs. In three years I paid off three thousand dollars. I milked a cow and raised cattle and pigs. Once I carried a
calf home a mile in twenty-five below zero weather. I finally got
every debt paid, and raised my kids, kept them dressed nicely and
well fed.

Sometimes a family's prairie dreams ended as a result of a father's economic
mismanagement. In Anna Schroeder's memoir of her grandmother *Changes:
Anecdotal Tales of Changes in the Life of Anna Born, 1888–1992* (1995), one of
grandfather Born's children provides a rather diplomatic explanation for the
loss of the family farm:

Father was a good farmer, and they were getting on quite well. He
should have made a success of it, but his heart was too big, and it
tended to overrule his common sense. Some of his brothers wanted
to buy farms, but could only buy them by borrowing. They needed
someone to back their loans.... In the late '20's, as in the '80's,
the expectation was that everyone would continue to prosper, and
no one would be hurt. The brothers failed to make a go of their
farms, the stock-market crashed, the loan organizations which had
been encouraged to over-extend their credit got into difficulty, and
along with about 1,600 other farmers, Father lost his homestead.
(78)

In her selection and placement of anecdotes, Schroeder allows her reader to
go beyond diplomacy in understanding the family's lack of success by highlighting the less-than-realistic outlook of her grandfather in direct contrast to
the more practical personality of her grandmother. In fact, in some ways she
constructs grandfather Born to suit the Moodie version of the land settler. For
example, referring to the onset of the Depression, when "grain prices world-
wide dropped to an all-time low," Schroeder repeats the following story:

Wheat was 25c/bushel, barley was useless. That winter there was no point in trying to sell a granary full of barley, because it would not bring enough to cover the cost of shipping it. That meant, however, that there was no money to buy coal for the stove. The fire was dying down, there was no fuel, and Father was sitting with his head in his hands, at wit's end. They had heard that people were burning grain, but he could not bring himself to do it. Mother took the coal scuttle, went and filled it with barley and threw it in the stove. It burned beautifully, and kept the family warm. (79)

After the Borns are forced to sell out, remembers one family member, "Father considered moving into the town of Winkler and living on faith, on whatever the Lord might send them. Mother was not quite so romantic. She thought it would be better if they did something to support themselves." In the end, the Born family moves a couple of times, from small town to small town, and grandfather Born eventually gets represented as a living embodiment of resignation to an unromantic end:

Father's health had been failing since they left Rosenbach. The situation there had been a devastating blow to him from which he never really recovered. After the move to Gnadenfeld, he was definitely fading. His preaching days were winding down, and he would spend much time lying on the "schlopbenk" brooding. He was 60. (107)

Over time this man becomes "weaker and more lethargic," "quite depressed," and we are told that "he was disappointed in this world, and looking forward to the next." After her husband's death, the more stalwart Anna Born is left with a less-than-ideal ending to her story: "Mother was alone for the first time in her life. And she had no income. Old Age Pensions did not start until age 68 or 70, and there was no such thing as a spousal allowance.... So Mother took in boarders" (115).

For Judy Schultz's grandmother, too, a husband's unrealistic vision resulted in a less-than-utopian ending to prairie life. As the author writes in *Mamie's Children*,

> Gradually, Mamie's family prospered. In the autumn of 1926 they were farming a full section of their own land, plus several rented quarters some distance from the homeplace. By virtue of their position on the edge of the coulee, their bottomland had good topsoil, some of which belonged originally to neighboring farms. Although not every crop was a bumper, Mamie's family had avoided the pitfalls of the monoculture cereal crops by diversifying. (132)

Given this set-up at the beginning of a chapter, the reader cannot help but be intrigued/dismayed when on the next page the expectations of success are thwarted:

> As far as [Mamie] was concerned, her world was unfolding in the best way any country woman could expect. That's why it was such a shock to her when, as she said on those few occasions when she would talk about it, "Everything just started to go to the dogs."
>
> It was the only explanation she ever gave for what happened to them personally in a time when not just they, but their neighbors and the entire southern prairie, especially the area within Palliser's Triangle, would begin to suffer terribly. If the hard times couldn't be erased from her memory, neither did they make their way into her favourite stories.
>
> It was Uncle Ken who had another explanation, one that became as relentlessly familiar on the prairies as the very wind that blew there day after day: "Dad had become a wealthy farmer, but he went into debt." (134)

Eventually the story comes out that Ernest Harris suffered a "personal downfall" (135) through a coincidence of his own land greed, mortgage debt, negative climate conditions, and an unsavoury moneylender. As the debt increased over the course of two years and her husband began to experience health problems, "Mamie felt as though a permanent cloud was anchored over her head" (137). When the farm is finally taken away from them, Mamie suffers indignity and the loss of everything she held dear:

> In a final insult, Mamie was required to sign a co-covenant. The clerk in the Moose Jaw land titles office explained what it meant: Even though Mamie never legally owned so much as an inch of the land for herself – not a stone around her flower bed nor a shingle on the roof of her beloved house – the co-covenant also signed away her right to remain there in any capacity, just in case she was suddenly inclined to become a squatter.
>
> And so, in the blink of an eye it was over. They lost it all. Mamie's Canadian dream had lasted less than twenty years. (140)

The real end of the story rejects romantic versions of the land settlement story even more thoroughly, as we see when we are told that Mamie and her husband moved north to a new farm located "near a clearing in the bush called Etomami," that the "new farm was somebody's else's failure" and that, although Mamie "stuck it out," "she never liked it" (150–54).

The Depression years, as we have already seen with some of the memoir endings above, were a powerful force in the destruction of the western spirit of "dauntless optimism," as seen in Ida Hopkins's poignant image in *To the Peace* (an image informed by personal understanding) of the abandoned settler's cabin:

> There are many abandoned cabins in the bush, their former owners forced out by regulations, hunger, inability to cope, or straight loneliness.
>
> An empty log cabin is a very living thing to me. I can visualize all too well the life of the people who once lived there. They are monuments to unfulfilled ambitions, and lost hopes. (69)

Hopkins's personal engagement with the myth of "dauntless optimism" begins to fade long before the end of her narrative: as she says, "after seventeen years in the Peace we began to wonder if we wouldn't find life a little easier in a milder climate" (118). Life in the Peace River district has most definitely lost its romantic aspect for Hopkins, who makes a gender distinction in terms of the rewards of settlement life:

> A few consecutive years of early and late snowstorms, letters from those who had left making, "Big Money", and stories of daffodils and crocuses blooming when we were looking at three or four feet of snow, started to get through to us, or rather I should say ME. Bill was still very much the farmer. This was understandable because every inch of ground under cultivation had been created to farm land by his own efforts. Every animal was part of him. Homesteading is very much a family affair but in the final analysis a MAN'S WORLD. (118)

As she continues, homesteading provides no real excitement for the woman settler, no romantic sense of adventure, even in the 1940s: "Much as a women [sic] becomes completely involved in the homestead life many of the challenges become repetitive." In contrast to so many of the stories already explored, and as a result of her own dissatisfaction, the Hopkins family "put the homestead up for sale" (119) and eventually hit the road with trailer in tow and with no specific plans for the future. Seventeen years of homesteading labour are thus unceremoniously and unromantically ended in Hopkins's narrative in favour of a decidedly unsettled life moving from province to province and city to city in search of a new place to call Home.

Similar to Hopkins's text, Katherine Magill's *Back o' Baffuf* (1977) contrasts the idealism of rural life with the economic viability of city life. As she writes near the end of her narrative, about eight years after initial settlement, "our time here was coming to an end. An ultimatum had been delivered in the spring. We must meet our back payments on the land" (71–72). Faced with debt which threatens their homestead life, "there was only one solution. Jim must find work, and work as well that paid a fair salary" (72). As a result, Magill's husband leaves her and the children behind to hold down the farm and goes to Edmonton for summer employment, which eventually becomes fall employment. As game as she might have been at the start of their homesteading adventure, Magill now has to face reality: she comes to the "inevitable" conclusion that, while "summer coping wasn't too bad," "winter coping – if not impossible – would be hazardous." The painful decision is made to move the whole family to Wainwright. In the end, Magill provides a narrative reflection on settlement life that openly rejects the spirit of "dauntless optimism" in favour of something more equivocal:

> … I sat for awhile on the doorstep, and looked around the small clearing, that had encircled so much of my life for the last few years.
>
> We had lived here, deeply, often precariously, and we would never be the same.
>
> Perhaps we would be back, I thought. Perhaps this would just be a time of regrouping, fattening our capital a bit. Personally, I would always, I had no doubt, be ambivalent about this brooding austere land. Perhaps that's what it took to endure a vital and challenging relationship. (73)[33]

Magill's is an apt final image to this chapter for, in the (unromantic) end, the one constant shared by all prairie settlers, no matter the individual circumstances that made out-migration a reality, was that they "would never be the same" again after experiencing the ups and downs of homesteading life. The cultural text of "dauntless optimism" favoured a view of settlement life in which, as the dominating figure of Catharine Parr Traill has long symbolized, "cheerfulness" in the face of adversity becomes a necessary personality corollary to survival. However, by reading women's memoirs for the presence of

---

33   For more examples of unromantic endings to the settlement story, see also Baldwin 48–49, 227–30; Campbell 135–43; Ebbers 107–11; Hewson 182–84; Hiemstra 285–88; Holmes 172–90; Inglis 80–81; Johannson 182–90; Nelson 119–20; Parsons 7, 14, 76, 140–44; Raber 58, 65, 169–71; Roberts 259–60; and Strange 262, 286–88.

various "failures and incoherences," we are able to discern the Moodie reality of "perverse endurance" that gives the lie to that culturally designed text as an impossibly romantic vision. However, it should be noted that, as indicated by the forward-facing slash in the title to this chapter, I have not meant to suggest by my use of this latter phrase that settler women who deviate from the "dauntlessly optimistic" script simply encompass the "other" side of some behavioural pairing. On the contrary, to invoke what I am suggesting are representations of "perverse endurance" – such as women crying, looking back, going "mad," and writing beyond romantic endings – is meant to indicate that the experience of settlement life is far more complex than often depicted in our cultural heritage. As Magill suggests, and as Moodie's text affirms, people actually "lived" on the prairie landscape, "deeply, often precariously," and the practical realities of everyday life demanded survival tactics that went far beyond the fever of idealism that so often inspired the decision to emigrate. In writing about "practical realities," the memoirists considered here have risen to the challenge of being true to themselves and to the others whose stories they write, ensuring that their narratives, like Magill and the many settler women who came before her, will "endure."

❈ 4 ❉

The "Precarious Perch" of the "Decent Woman": Re-Visioning the Space(s) of Western Settlement

In the wild west, where men were men and life was hard, women were supposed to be one of two things – commodities or prizes.... We are not here counting the wives of homesteaders, of course. They were neither commodities nor prizes. They were, like anything that was likely to produce, used as devices to prepare the dream of a future.

– George Bowering, *Caprice* (1987)

Dad straddled one wall, I straddled the other, then Dad fitted the log.... The blows of the axe sent shivers up and down my thin arms, and often I almost fell off my precarious perch.

... Mother couldn't straddle the walls the way I could. Her long skirts got in her way, and since no decent woman exposed her ankles in those days she couldn't do a thing about them. She tried sitting sideways on the walls, but that didn't work very well. She couldn't balance both the log and herself, so the log slipped, the

notch was wrong, and the whole thing had to be done over again,
which irritated everybody.

> – Mary Hiemstra, *Gully Farm* (1955)

Space is abstract. It lacks content; it is broad, open, and empty,
inviting the imagination....

> – Yi-Fu Tuan, "Place: An Experiential Perspective" (1975)

The issue of "space" has long dominated studies of the Canadian prairies;
indeed, whether seeking to determine the evolutionary history of a western
"landscape of the mind shaped by the myths, stories, and attitudes" (Francis,
Images xvi) of a culture, or to delineate a trend in fictional representations of
human reactions to the "surrounding emptiness" (Ricou ix), what stands prominent in most treatments of western settlement is the engagement between
the physical vastness – the seeming unboundedness – of the region, and the
limited and culturally specific language used by contemporaries to represent
it. Examination of both historical and literary images of prairie settlement
further suggests that the language settled on to describe this space is often
gendered as female, so that western expansion becomes figured and idealized
as a physical projection of Anglo culture into the fertile prairie landscape as
a means to conceive a new national identity, one that is sustained on an individual level by the (male) farmer's battle to control the productions of the land
through "cultivation" and "improvement." Accordingly, contemporaries posited that the type of "healthy society" being imagined in the Canadian west
could only be "successfully erected" by "men of British tradition" (Mitchell
108–9). The majority (though certainly not all) of these gendered descriptions
of "Man" on the prairies stem from the imaginations of male writers, which
begs the following question: Given that women's implied role in this drama of
prairie settlement was to be "used as devices to prepare the dream of a future,"
is there any difference in the way that the white, English-speaking memoirists gathered here have represented their engagement with this geographic
space, which has attained mythological status as being "blessedly free of most
conventional restrictions" (Stegner 29)?

In an attempt to answer this question, my concern in this chapter is to examine how gender is represented within specific spaces, including the geographic space of the Canadian west, the physical space of the female body, and the textual space in which memoir writers represent their lived experience of prairie settlement. As will be seen in the memoir passages taken up in this chapter, these three spaces are inter-related, so that the memoirists themselves have to negotiate between exhibiting conformity to cultural expectations of the female body in the prairie landscape when representing the moment of settlement, and at the same time using the textual space of the memoir to provide less constricted representations of prairie women; to document female transgressions of cultural expectations, both as they may have occurred in the lived experience of settlement and as new and empowering constructions at the moment of "looking back."

Chapter Three ended with a quote from Katherine Magill's *Back o' Baffuf* (1977), in which the author remarks concerning the moment of departure from rural life in northern Alberta in mid-century, "we had lived here, deeply, often precariously, and we would never be the same" (73). While Magill's use of the word "precariously" highlights the economic difficulties of survival on a homestead, nevertheless that image of living precariously – of moving into a new geographic territory that, as seen in the epigraph from Mary Hiemstra's *Gully Farm* above, challenges conventional expectations of the female body, and specifically the type of work that that body is able to perform – and of being significantly changed by the end of such an experience, erupts again and again within the memoirs included in this study. Through implication, the phrase "precariously perched" suggests spatial location, both the space upon which one is perched as well as the space of downfall below that perch. For many women settlers, even those who emigrated in the first two decades of the twentieth century, "precarious perch" adequately describes the Victorian values that dominated cultural expectations about the type of society being created in the Canadian West, as well as women's (re)productive role within ·that society – the imperative to be a "decent woman." To be "precarious," how-ever, is to be uncertain, without solid foundation, and certainly many of the earliest women settlers discovered that "civilization" in the prairie west was "the dream of a future," and that the isolated conditions of prairie life often demanded behaviour that threatened to topple them into the perilous depths lurking below social/cultural expectations/conventions. And liberation from expectations/conventions was not simply a matter of historical progression, either, for sometimes it was precisely the early and most isolated conditions of prairie life that allowed white, English-speaking women, if they were able to relinquish even temporarily their own internal self-monitor, to embrace physical behaviours that deviated from idealistic cultural images. Ironically, as time and "civilization" marched on and as prairie communities grew, women settlers who had experienced a feminist revolution of behavioural codes in the wider world emigrated to the prairies only to discover that rather Victorian attitudes and values had solidified and become the norm, meaning that women often had to consciously and publicly choose between ascending or rejecting the prevailing cultural perch. The immediate experiences/choices of women settlers remain largely silent within historical narratives; however, women's memoir representations of those experiences/choices provide us with a means to revisit contemporary expectations of female behaviour as well as to discover the "traces of the past that are less than exemplary" (Rukszto 17) in terms of those expectations. Indeed, if we accept Tuan's definition of space in the epigraph above, then the memoir as textual space allows for considerable and imaginative play with the culturally constructed Prairie Woman image; it effectively becomes an "interface between individual and communal identities" (Higonnet 2).

In order to discover the "less than exemplary traces" that might rest within that interface, we must first consider the behavioural norms that dominated the construction of women's experiences in western settlement. That the Canadian West was intended to inspire a rebirth of the British Empire, together with all its perceived superior and "civilized" values, inevitably meant that cultural narratives of western expansion and settlement became inscribed by a spatial politics of gender. As an ideological vision, the Canadian West was figured as a masculine domain: as one Canadian historian puts it, "in constructing and reconstructing the West – from wilderness wasteland to economic hinterland to agrarian paradise – expansionist discourse perpetuated the myth of the West as a 'manly' space, assigning to it a moral and political force that underwrote elite Anglo-Canadian men's hegemony in the territories" (Cavanaugh, "No Place" 494). Indeed, the national project of bringing the prairie landscape under cultivation was seen as a necessarily masculine endeavour, as reflected in the vocabulary chosen by contemporary writers on the subject: for example, as J. Ewing Ritchie phrased it in 1885, "there is a good deal of hardship to be encountered by any who would *penetrate* to the dim and mysterious region we denominate the North-West" (160; emphasis added). For those who would so penetrate, however, the hardships experienced would ultimately enhance one's masculinity, as seen in George M. Grant's 1873 assertion that "a man out West feels like a young giant, who cannot help indulging a little tall talk, and in displays of his big limbs" (87) and also in Thomas Spence's 1880 characterization of the settler "gazing out" across the landscape and "feeling himself every inch a man" (qtd. in Owram, *Images* 126). Similarly, in 1891 Nicholas Flood Davin had a message for potential emigrants from eastern Canada: "The Ontario farmer is a fine specimen of the yeoman, but three years in the North West raises him higher on the scale of manhood" (108).

Meanwhile, the prairie landscape itself – the "garden of abundance" (Francis, *Images* 107) – was usually figured as feminine, as seen in George Livingstone Dodds's 1906 poem "The Canadian West," which ends with the following lines: "Food for the great world's millions/ She pours from her fertile breast;/ This land with a mighty future,/ The fair Canadian West" (39). In 1908, towards the end of her idealistic prairie novel *Sowing Seeds in Danny*, Nellie McClung provides the following (rather violent, I would suggest) postharvest image of the landscape: "The earth had yielded of her fruits and now rested from her labour, worn and spent, taking no thought of comeliness, but waiting in decrepit indifference for her friend, the North Wind, to bring down the swirling snow to hide her scars and heal her unloveliness with its kindly white mantle" (294–95). The designation of the earth as female is a cultural construction that has been noted in a variety of contexts, both geographic and historical. For example, in *The Lay of the Land: Metaphor as Experience and History in American Life and Letters*, Annette Kolodny examines "what is probably America's oldest and most cherished fantasy: a daily reality of harmony between man and nature based on an experience of the land as essentially feminine" (4).[1] Similarly, and with particular importance for our understanding of western settlement in imperial and national terms, Jean Pickering and Suzanne Kehde suggest that "the object of colonial encounters is typically feminized, held to be in want of masculine (imperial) authority. This feminization can be applied both to geography ... and to the colonial population" (6). Prior to the mid-nineteenth-century rise of expansionism, the Canadian West had been figured as a wasteland, a space inimical to human habitation, but the conversion of the region to an Edenic paradise demanded re-figurement along human lines. Thus, borrowing from Kolodny we might say that "to make the new continent [or region] Woman was already to civilize it a bit, casting the stamp of human relations upon what was otherwise unknown and untamed" (9). The "stamp of human relations" can certainly be seen in an 1875 essay titled "The New Canada" by Charles Mair, one of the founders of the Canada First movement, who figures the Empire-building imperative of western settlement in the following way:

> This new Dominion should be the wedding of pure tastes, simple life, respect for age and authority, and the true principles of free government on this Continent. It stands, like a youth upon the threshold of his life, clear-eyed, clear-headed, muscular, and strong. Its course is westward. It has traditions and a history of

---

1   Frieda Knobloch traces this "cherished fantasy" back historically when she writes that "nature was, of course, female and came into the English language at the same time as the plow, in the eighth century, replacing the woman who produced food *in* the field with the woman *as* the field" (74). Although Kolodny notes that "other civilizations have undoubtedly gone through a similar history," she goes on to suggest that they did so "at a pace too slow or in a time too ancient to be remembered" and that "only in America has the entire process remained within historical memory" (8). For the purposes of Kolodny's study, "America" means the United States of America, although a great deal of her conclusions are applicable to the Canadian experience of land settlement. Indeed, Dick Harrison notes that "the identification of woman with the land [in Canadian prairie fiction] is not uncommon," citing Arthur Stringer's *The Mud Lark* (Indianapolis: Bobbs-Merrill, 1931) and Ralph Connor's *Gwen, an Idyll of the Canyon* (Toronto: Fleming H. Revell, 1899) as prime examples (97).

which it may well be proud; but it has a history to make, a national sentiment to embody, and a national idea to carry out. (151).

Mair's insistence on the masculine nature of the "new Dominion" and its need to, as he goes on to suggest, "project into the fertile immensity of the west" (153) as a means to "embody" forth "national sentiment," delineates the contemporary narrative of western settlement as a sort of "gendered romance" (New 107), a "wedding" of Anglo-inspired cultural values and the feminized prairie landscape as a means to achieve – conceive? – a legitimate national identity.[2] Indeed, as one early-twentieth-century author described the advent of spring on the prairies, "the land is clothing herself with verdure as a bride adorning for her husband" (Ferguson, *Open* 72).[3] In the act of carrying out the project of western expansion, the individual farmer as representative of the new nation would play the role of husband by taking ownership of his

---

2   The image of national expansion into the west as a process of legitimation gains significance when contrasted with the words chosen by Canadian imperialist, George R. Parkin, to describe the proposed effect on Canadian identity of continentalism:

> In a Great Britain reorganized as a federation, or union, or alliance, Canada would hold an honorable place, gained on lines of true national development; in annexation to the United States she could have nothing but a *bastard nationality*, the offspring of either meanness, selfishness, or fear. (qtd. in Bennett, Paul W., et al. 303; emphasis added)

It should also be noted that Mair's narrative relies heavily on a rhetoric of constriction: as he suggests, the new nation's "power and cohesiveness are being felt at last, and already it is binding the scattered communities of British America together in the bonds of a common cause, a common language, and a common destiny" (152). In this way, then, did narrative constructions of the Canadian west as both geographic and ideological space seem to preclude individual resistance to/transgression of the common "bonds" of nation and empire building.

3   Compare these romantic images to the language used by Henry Kreisel to describe "the conquest of the land": "into the attempted conquest, whether ultimately successful or not, men pour an awesome, concentrated passion. The breaking of the land becomes a kind of rape, a passionate seduction" (49). Kreisel's suggestion of rape here – which he then rather unnervingly corresponds to "a passionate seduction," surely a subject for a whole separate study – is particularly apt given that western expansion is so often figured as an "irresistible force" (Owram, *Promise* 102).

own section of land, bringing it under cultivation, and making it productive. He would, through hard work and perseverance, unlock "the wonderful,
mysterious promise" which "hang[s] over" the "abundant broad bosom of
earth!" (Stringer, *The Prairie Wife* 220).[4]

Given the sensual directives to the male farmer regarding his possession
and use of prairie lands, one might well ask if there was room for the presence of real women in such abstract narratives of western settlement? Was the
Canadian West really a space where only "strong *men* gathered"[5] and where
the ideal prairie woman, like Martha Perkins in Nellie L. McClung's *Sowing
Seeds in Danny*, could be described as "a nice, quiet, unappearing girl" (199)?[6]

---

4   That the images of fertile abundance illustrated here were an effect of changed cul-
     tural expectations of the prairie region is evident from the fact that, in contrast,
     in the late-seventeenth century, Henry Kelsey, the "first white man to visit the
     Canadian interior," popularized the "mental image of the Prairies as barren and
     unprofitable" (Watson, J. Wreford 15).

5   I am referring here to Douglas Hill's *The Opening of the Canadian West: Where Strong
     Men Gathered* (New York: John Day, 1967). In contemporary "masculinist definitions
     of the ideal settler," says Catherine Cavanaugh, "women's exclusion continue[d] to
     be so taken for granted that it seem[ed] to be less an idea than the natural order
     of things" ("No Place" 504). The implicit bias towards a masculinization of the
     prairie settlement project can also be seen in Dorothy Kamen-Kaye's discussion
     of "The Composite Pioneer," in which she suggests that "a pioneer is an individual
     who blazes a trail into strange territory for others to follow. But they do not refer
     to themselves as 'pioneers', these *men* who came to what is now Saskatchewan" (6;
     emphasis added). Georgina H. Thomson's *Crocus and Meadowlark Country: A Story
     of an Alberta Family* (1963) also documents the typically masculine conception of pi-
     oneering in the west, as seen when she mentions the "First Council Meeting in the
     Parkhill (now Parkland) district" of Alberta, held in "the summer of 1904 before we
     women folk came out" (13). This meeting of "the pioneers of the community" even
     included, writes Thomson, "our 17-year-old [brother] Jim" (14) and was commemor-
     ated by a photograph, provided by the author for the reader's perusal.

6   We can see the "unappearing girl" phenomenon also in Frederick Philip Grove's
     Settlers of the Marsh (1925), in which we are first told about the "hero" Niels
     Lindstedt that in his "longing for the land that would be his," he dreamt of having a
     house of his own and "a wife that would go through it like an inspiration" (39). Then
     it is clarified that

          woman had never figured as a concrete thing in Niels's thought of his
          future in this new country. True, he had seen in his visions a wife and
          children; but the wife had been a symbol merely. Now that he was in the

In many representations of the immigrant family, the main focus was upon the male head of the family – the individual who would undertake the actual process of land cultivation and who, in a marketplace-driven economy, represented an immediate monetary potential to the process of western settlement. The woman settler, on the other hand, often appeared as merely an appendage to her husband. For example, in 1922, the former Minister of the Interior Clifford Sifton drew the following image of what he deemed to be a "quality" immigrant to the Canadian West: "I think a stalwart peasant in a sheepskin coat, born on the soil, whose forefathers have been farmers for generations, with a stout wife and a half-dozen children, is good quality" (qtd. in Hall 90).[7] Leaving aside for the moment the fact that Sifton is enunciating an image that defers from the essentially Anglo-focus of immigration policies during the height of westward expansion, it does seem that the "stout wife" and her children are rendered here as merely part of the implements necessary to a male farmer's success on the Canadian prairies. We also see this construction of women in a Department of the Interior pamphlet titled *Western Canada: How to Get There; How to Select Lands; How to Make a Home* (1902), in which settler W.E. Cooley testifies to the origins of his success as a farmer: as he states it, "My earthly possessions at the time I reached this place were $1.75, a wife and seven children," all of which, by dint of "work[ing] hard and faithfully," he translated into "520 [of 800] acres under cultivation," "12 horses, 81 head of cattle, 15 hogs and all the equipment necessary for a farm," and "as fine a residence as there is" (qtd. in Francis, *Images* 131). Women and children were literally accorded a lesser monetary value than men, as seen in the fact that "the Canadian government paid American railway booking

---

country of his dreams and gaining a foothold, it seemed as if individual women were bent on replacing the vague, schematic figures he had had in his mind. He found this intrusion strangely disquieting. (39–40)

7   Interestingly, Sifton's characterization of what, in his mind, was the ideal settler woman contrasts sharply with a feminine ideal represented in Frederick Philip Grove's *Fruits of the Earth* (1933), in which Ruth Spalding says of her husband "that he had begun to look critically at her. She had caught herself wishing that she could make herself invisible; [*sic*] She was getting stout. Not that Abe said a word about it; but she knew he disliked stout women" (46).

agents a bonus of $3 for every male agricultural immigrant over 18, $2 for
every female and $1 for each dependent child" (qtd. in Bruce 19). Ralph Allen
even increases the value of the male immigrant (by implication) when he
notes that "Sifton sold huge tracts of Canadian government land at give-away
prices to private colonization companies, then paid them a bounty out of
the Dominion treasury for every settler they could produce – five dollars for
the head of a family, two dollars each for women and children" (262), thus
conflating women down to child-size value.

However, as Sarah A. Carter suggests in *Capturing Women: The
Manipulation of Cultural Imagery in Canada's Prairie West*, within the explicitly British-Canadian imperative of western settlement, women occupied a
position of paramount importance: in the late-nineteenth and early-twentieth centuries, the image of the white prairie woman was represented as the
central vessel through which the Anglo ideology of "civilization" would be
replicated in the west. Despite the fact that a Department of the Interior
immigration pamphlet titled *Twentieth Century Canada* (1906) suggested
that "Canada is a man's country, from the fact that all new countries first
attract men, because the labour required for early settlement calls for that of
man rather than that of woman" (qtd. in Bruce 22), women's labour was also
needed in the making of a nation – after all, the prairie woman "was to be the
civilizer and the reproducer of the race" (Carter, *Capturing* 8) in the Canadian
west.[8] In her discussion of early female immigration to rural Manitoba, Mary
Kinnear states the function of women thus: "Women were needed to help
produce crops and goods, and they were needed to swell the population.
Women were in the spotlight both as producers and reproducers" (*A Female*
22). The woman settler's function was thus both metaphorical (as image, in
her role as disembodied reproductive vessel of a culture – a particularly fitting role for the gender who would not be formally declared "Persons" until
1929) and literal (as lived experience, in her real life role as a mother). This

8   Catherine Cavanaugh also suggests that women settlers' role within expansionist
     discourse was to ensure a gender hierarchy of power: "Created in opposition to the
     middle-class ideal of active, conquering manhood, civilizing womanhood is made
     passive and disembodied, thereby guaranteeing representations of men's domin-
     ance" ("No Place" 497–98).

dual function is clearly articulated in contemporary literature on the subject of western settlement: in Marion Dudley Cran's *A Woman in Canada* (1910), for example, the author suggests that, "in the North-West, where wives are scarce, a work of Empire awaits the woman of breed and endurance who will settle on the prairie homesteads and rear their children in the best traditions of Britain" (14–15). In a similar vein, in *An Englishwoman in the Canadian West* (1913), Elizabeth Keith Morris suggests that women settlers could fulfil "their highest and noblest mission in life" simply by becoming "the mothers of Canada," "our true empire builders" (26).[9] Thus does the cultural narrative of western settlement appear to rely upon the population of the prairies as a reproductive act – that is, reproductive of the "best traditions of Britain" – with actual women being represented as the cultural vessels through which the failing greatness of the British Empire would be given new life. The work of the ideal Prairie Woman, then, was a replication of the work of the idealized prairie landscape: re-constitute, hence re-invigorate, the British Empire, and be concretely productive. The connection between the fertility of the western landscape and the fertility of the Prairie Woman can be seen in Marion Cran's poetic description of one of the women she met on her travels through Western Canada: "Here, where they found virgin prairie, she stands; the heavy ears [of corn] lap against her splendid hips, and here and there they tip her breast; round her skirts the children cling, she moves in this beautiful, fruitful land like Ceres among plenty" (137).

The inevitable result of this construction of woman's dual role within the geographic space of the Canadian prairies, notes Sarah Carter, was a rather "limited repertoire of behaviour available to white women" (*Capturing* xv):

> The wise women from the East would exemplify all the qualities
> of the ideal Victorian woman, which included purity and piety. At

---

9   In illustration of the contention that motherhood was "at the center of empire build-
     ing" (Stoler 649), in her memoir *Pioneering in Alberta* (1951), Jessie Browne Raber
     remembers her mother's own numerous productions: "I stayed home every day now,
     for Mother told me, a new baby was to come in February. I thought we had enough,
     but one more didn't make much difference. They were sweet anyway, so we had to
     do our very best to have them grow up to be good and helpful citizens" (140–41).

times it proved useful also to emphasize the frailty and delicacy
of the white woman, as well as her dependence on males, though
these were scarcely the qualities that would ensure stability or success in the Prairie West. (8)

What is clear from the prescriptions on female behaviour as here articulated
by Carter is that "the prairies were not, after all, culturally isolated from the
rest of the world" (Rasmussen et al. 88). Indeed, as already alluded to in
Chapter Two, Carter's "repertoire" is commensurate with the domestic images perpetuated throughout the British Empire and North America, as in
the Victorian "Angel in the House" (Perkin 233) and what Barbara Welter
identified in nineteenth-century American society as the "Cult of True
Womanhood." The role of Prairie Woman as "civilizer," then, was meant
to aid in "the government's purpose of recreating the middle-class domestic
ideal on the prairies" (Cavanaugh, "No Place" 505). This desire for "recreation" of female behavioural norms can be seen in contemporary literature.
For example, in 1901, Elizabeth Lewthwaite contributed an article to *The
Fortnightly Review*, in which she assures potential emigrants that "robust
health in England is not a necessary qualification, though of course desirable,
for the prairie atmosphere is so pure and invigorating that many delicate folk
on their arrival become new creatures; and I have often been amazed at what
fragile, delicate-looking women are able to accomplish" (717). The civilizing
presence of "fragile, delicate-looking women" was also acknowledged in 1913
by Elizabeth Morris, who noted regarding the "shaggy appearance of some of
the [male] settlers" that "these men had become rough through the lack of a
woman's refining influence, but it was a roughness that could be very quickly
rubbed off by a dainty, gentle hand" (25).

In the desire to translate the domestic role to a very different geography,
there was created a paradox to be faced by real women: on the one hand,
they were expected (and usually expected themselves) to adhere to the accepted female role as domestic icon; on the other hand, the practical nature
of their participation in the settlement of the Canadian west would demand
many activities to be undertaken and provide many opportunities to be seized,
that would be profoundly unsettling of that role. Indeed, the demand on

women for "purity and piety," "frailty and delicacy," and a "dependency on males," as Carter notes about white prairie women, had very little to do with the reality of women's lives. There has been scholarly debate about the extent to which middle-class domestic ideals actually influenced the behaviour of white, English-speaking women who emigrated to the Canadian West, with some people laying stress on strict adherence to cultural dictates and others adopting the more individualist idea of the West as a space of liberation,[10] but given a subject with so many variables attached to it (e.g. place and time of settlement; age, personality and personal experience of the settler), it is now more generally agreed that the prairie region was often a highly ambiguous space for women settlers. It was a space in which, once again, extremes often had to be rejected in favour of a continuum of lived experience. As Catherine Cavanaugh puts it,

> But just as seeing women as unambiguous agents of Empire is problematic, it is equally mistaken to assume that the frontier acted invariably as a liberating force in the lives of newcomer women. The West was not a priori a place where established cultural practices and beliefs were easily and readily abandoned; rather, middle-class British women measured the freedom of the West by contrast to the social and economic constraints imposed on them in England. ("Irene" 105)

In the parallel constructions of the prairie landscape and the female settler's body as spaces of "civilizing" potential, I would suggest, we see the female body functioning as "a space of mimetic representation" (Blunt and Rose 5)

---

10   In illustration of the debate that has gone on, in his examination of American women's travel diaries about the Overland Trail, John Mack Faragher suggests that "feminine farm roles had little to do with the fetishized domesticity that was a part of the womanly cult flowering in the East, for in most ways these pioneer wives and mothers were the very antithesis of that antiseptic and anesthetized version of femininity" (171). In *Frontier Women: "Civilizing" the West? 1840–1880*, though, Julie Roy Jeffrey asserts that "frontier images of women were closely tied to images of middle-class women current in the East. The concept of woman as lady, the heart of domestic ideology, survived" (129).

of the larger cultural project. I would further suggest that the universalizing and "limited repertoire of behaviour available to white women" ensured that the female body as culturally inscribed space would be veiled in an "illusion of transparency": as suggested by Henri Lefebvre,

> The illusion of transparency goes hand in hand with a view of space as innocent, as free of traps or secret places. Anything hidden or dissimulated – and hence dangerous – is antagonistic to transparency, under whose reign everything can be taken in by a single glance from that mental eye which illuminates whatever it contemplates. (28)

The "illusion of transparency," then, is a repudiation of difference or of the unknown, which enhances the idea of the domestic ideal as a script, a known "repertoire" of physical/emotional/spiritual behaviours, the performance of which can be unproblematically judged as either appropriate – or not.[11] Most important, at all times the female body as a space reflective of Anglo norms of "civilization" must perform its denial of a "space of the 'impure' beyond [its] own utopian boundaries" (Blunt and Rose 6). The question inevitably becomes then: Is the cultural pressure for "transparency" so overwhelming that the female bodies represented in the memoir texts gathered here remain complicit with domestic ideals, even though they were written sometimes many years after the cultural moment of settlement life? As Rachel Blau DuPlessis clarifies regarding the idea of the cultural regulation of individual behaviour, "sociologists and other students of social practices use terms like 'scripts' to explain the existence of strongly mandated patterns of learned behaviour that are culturally and historically specific, and that offer a rationale for unselfconscious acts" (*Writing* 2).

---

11 Historian Julie Roy Jeffrey suggests that the ability to judge people on the basis of, amongst other things, physical behaviour, was essential to "civilizing" efforts in the American west in the mid-nineteenth century, and "because middle-class white women and men relied on their own cultural standards to judge others, they found many groups deficient and unworthy of social inclusion when they did not adopt white values and standards of behavior" (7).

So to phrase my question another way, are the memoirs written and published by white, English-speaking women produced as "unselfconscious acts" of behavioural complicity? Or do they represent a self-conscious attempt to confront those "strongly mandated patterns of learned behaviour" that still dominate our domestic conception of the Prairie Woman image? If we accept the idea enunciated in Chapter One that the memoir genre is a unique narrative choice for an author seeking to write at the intersection of self and social context, and if we concur with Alison Blunt and Gillian Rose that "there is always a space of some kind for resistance" (15) to the "imposition" of cultural norms, then I would suggest that the prairie memoirs gathered here function to provide just such a (temporally safe) space for the possibility of resistance. We might say that memoir functions to provide "a space of the 'impure'"; it functions as a textual "frontier" in which the woman writer stakes her claim in his-story and embodies forth the possibility of resistance to western imperialism's construction of female behaviour. While these memoir texts tend to represent women's general coherence with domestic scripts, nevertheless they also make clear that the "Prairie Angel"[12] was often required to step down from her pedestal and participate in the daily reality of settlement life, which necessitated a rather less delimited "repertoire" of behaviour from the female body. These texts betray that real women "seized chances, or responded out of necessity, to act, to do more than adorn the hearth or their men's status" (Silverman, *The Last* xii).

One of the ways in which women's bodies were subject to cultural expectations of female behaviour is through the dictates of fashion, including such adornments as clothing and hairstyles, both of which can be seen to function as "an encroachment of social norms upon the body's surface" (Stadler 20). More important to our understanding of Prairie Women as "custodians" (Carter, *Capturing* 6) of the western settlement project, "social identity expressed in dress becomes not only an answer to the question of *who* one is, but *how* one is, and concerns the definition of the self in relation

---

12   For a discussion of the "Prairie Angel" as an example of the "iconography of pioneer prairie women" in North America, see Carol Fairbanks, *Prairie Women: Images in American and Canadian Fiction* (New Haven, CT: Yale University Press, 1986) 76.

to a moral and religious value system" (Barnes and Eicher 2). The connection between outward appearance and morality can be seen in a January 27, 1916, report in *The Calgary Albertan* about a sermon given by Rev. Dr. Fulton "on the subject of 'Wives'":

> He quoted the Bible to show that wives' duty was to "love their husbands, to love their children, to be discreet, chaste, keepers of home, good, obedient to their husbands." He exhorted wives to retain their husbands' affections as it was said that "Love is a wife's only wages".
>
> The question is: How is a wife to get her pay? A great number are not, he said. There are a good many homes where love is stark and dead, but the remedy is in the wife's hands. He advised her to make herself agreeable and attractive, keep herself neatly dressed, hair well in order, and always wear a smile. Keep the home cheerful, clean and cosy. (qtd. in Rasmussen et al. 94)

One of the important points raised in Fulton's sermon is the idea that the major responsibility for adherence to social norms/expectations rests in the individual herself. The imperative to exhibit conformity is thus made an empowering act; a means of achieving public approbation, if you care to take it; if you take care. In many contemporary narratives, female settlers are specifically noted as upholding ideals of domestic femininity, based on outward appearance. For example, Marion Cran provides the following model:

> [T]here she is – my pretty hostess with her young face and grey hair, lighting the kitchen fire for the day's work. I watch her for a little while. She has a contented face and works very neatly; her dress is a pretty blue cotton and over it is a linen apron, the sleeves are rolled to the elbow, her feet are thickly shod, she wears a low collar, her skirt is four inches from the ground, there is nothing to impede her movements, and yet the whole effect is very smart and workmanlike. (130)

In addition to rendering white women's bodies as "transparent," as readable for signs of transgression of social norms, the Anglo bias of fashion (clothing and/ or hair) as moral barometer also allowed for the rejection of non-white/non-Anglo women as not being suitably "pure" enough to participate in the "civilizing" project of western settlement. As Sarah Carter notes, in contrast to the idealized images of white women that were produced during the early phase of western settlement, native women were constructed in an entirely negative way with "images of Aboriginal women as dissolute, dangerous, and sinister" ("Categories" 61). A fictional example of this occurs in Harold Bindloss's *Prescott of Saskatchewan* (1913), in which Ellice, a half-breed woman "married" to a white farmer named Jernyngham, is described as being "a young woman with fine dark eyes and glossy black hair, whose appearance would have been prepossessing had it not been spoiled by her slatternliness and cheap finery" (4). Given that "her character was primitive," Ellice is particularly unfit for the role as "civilizer" of a race, as seen especially in descriptions of her clothing and hair, which form a stunning contrast to Cran's female model given above: "Her white summer dress was stained in places and open at the neck, where a button had come off. The short skirt displayed a hole in one stocking and a shoe from which a strap had been torn" (28). Only a few pages later, when the title hero goes to visit Jernyngham's home, "the clatter of domestic utensils indicat[ing] that Ellice was baking" holds promise for cultural ideals of the prairie woman's role; however, her apparent conformity is interrupted when she appears at the door "with a hot, angry face, and hands smeared with dough, her hair hanging partly loose in disorder about her neck, her skirt ungracefully kilted up" (35).

One can imagine that the desire to be deemed a "pretty hostess" rather than a "slattern" was a major incentive for self-regulation in choices of dress and hairstyle. Here again we see debate about the extent to which women conformed to or confronted Anglo standards of fashion. Seena B. Kohl, for example, seems quite unequivocal about the impracticability of conventional women's clothing, especially in the early days of prairie settlement: as she asserts, "one has only to look at the early mail order catalogues to become aware of the incongruity of urban constraints upon women in their daily lives on the frontier. No pioneer woman could milk six cows, drive a horse team, or plaster her house in the corsets and skirts of that period – and they did not" ("The

Making" 178–79). But Nanci Langford repudiates vast generalizations when she states that "the fact that traditional modes of dress and hair styling were inappropriate on a prairie homestead because of the nature of women's work and the environment in which they lived and performed their work, did not bring about any significant changes in women's approach to female fashion on a broad scale" ("First Generation" 150). Once again, the reality likely rests on some middle ground, with individual women weighing at various moments in their lives the potential social risks of non-conformity relative to the practical needs of homestead work. The balancing act between self-regulation and criticism can be seen in the following "incongruity" noted by contemporary writer Emily Ferguson:

> A woman should never attempt to weed. She is not made that way. Pray consider my difficulties! If I stoop, every drop of blood in my body falls to my head and I thus court death from apoplexy, hæmorrhage, congestion, or a multiplicity of nameless ills. True, this is only a contingency; but as an actual happening, I always break the steels in my stays, and often the laces.
>
> If I get on my knees I soil my skirt, and our village Celestial will charge me $1.25 to starch it again. Besides, this attitude has a disastrous effect on my shoes. It wrinkles them across the toes. To weed with anything like comfort, one must squat after the manner of the monkey eating pea-nuts. I would prefer to let the weeds grow.
>
> Men should be forced to weed the flowers. Women are only meant to wear them. Nature made men ugly of a purpose that they might grub in the dirt and "crick" their backs. (*Janey* 143)

In Ferguson's avowal we see that "She" is explicitly aligned with the "female costume"; that is, while Ferguson suggests that "She is not made that way," meaning "She" is not capable of the physical behaviour necessary for effective weeding, it is, rather, only "She" as constrained by her clothing – her "stays" and "laces" – who is incapable of the exertion of weeding without threat to social standards of feminine fashion, as seen in the "disastrous effect" of being "soiled" and "wrinkled." Ferguson more openly criticizes Anglo standards of "female costume" when, earlier in the same text, she notes of the women in the "Doukhobor village of Vosnesenia" that, "on the whole, their dress spells comfort. Their arm-holes are easy; their skirts do not drag; their bodies are not jails of bones and steels, and they wear no cotton-batting contrivances" (42). She works to deflect her own criticism of Anglo fashion constraints, however, when she continues her observation by noting that, "while I was undressing, the women returned and examined my clothing with apparent interest.... They seemed much pleased with the ribbons running through my underwear, but were shocked and, at the same instant, amused by my corsets" (43).

For many of the earliest female settlers to the sparsely settled Canadian West, regulation of bodily behaviour/appearance was virtually non-existent, except at the level of the individual; that is, for well-socialized women of Anglo background, "the principle of self-surveillance" (McClintock 58), like Lefebvre's "mental eye which illuminates whatever it contemplates," was always in effect, even when living at the very margins of "civilization." To borrow from another theorist, who significantly borrows from the language of land ownership, "a woman must continually watch herself. She is almost continually accompanied by her own image of herself ... she comes to consider the *surveyor* and the *surveyed* within her as the two constituent yet always distinct elements of her identity as a woman.... The surveyor of woman in herself is male: the surveyed, female" (Berger 46–47). Constructions of femininity were so all-pervasive, so thoroughly entrenched in cultural rhetoric in general, let alone in narratives of western imperialism, that it was extremely difficult for early women settlers to the Canadian West to relinquish the "ways of seeing" themselves learned as part of their inherited cultural knowledge. This difficulty is certainly present in Clara Middleton's memoir about homesteading near Carstairs, Alberta, from 1904: as she writes in *Green Fields Afar: Memories of Alberta Days* (1947), even while performing what would be considered traditionally male work, and even when doing so without reservations, a woman had to adhere to appropriate fashion:

> Then came shingling time. Homer was never any good on a roof, or a stack, or any elevation. Ladders were deadly threats, so far as

he was concerned. They made him giddy. So while he kept his feet
on the ground and his hands busy at ground tasks I went on the
roof with Free and helped him lay and nail six or seven "squares"
of shingles. I wore a sweater, an old skirt and a flannel petticoat,
for in those days no woman of taste would have been seen in men's
pants or overalls. There was a time, a little later, when I had a divided skirt for riding, but even that seemed a little less than modest
and decent. (15)

Mary Hiemstra's *Gully Farm* provides us with a glimpse into the difficulties
of maintaining Victorian standards of "purity" as related to clothing and the
behavioural performances of the female body. Prior to the family's arrival on
their homestead, while still on the train ride from St. John to Saskatoon, Sally
Pinder appears to adhere without difficulty to the orderly physical symbols of
her position as a "decent woman": as Hiemstra writes,

How Mother managed to keep herself and three children, one a
small baby, neat and clean on that long trip I don't know, but somehow she did. Her long, lovely hair was never unkept and frowzy.
She always combed it first thing in the morning and twisted it into
a neat, thick roll on top of her small head. Her dress was as tidy as
her hair. There was never a gap between her trim skirt and bodice,
and she never walked about with her shoes unlaced as some of the
women did. (46)

The author is here playing on polar oppositions of order/disorder, such as
"neat," "clean" and "tidy" versus "unkept," "frowzy" and "unlaced." But I would
suggest that it is especially in Hiemstra's insistence upon the symbolic lack of
"a gap between her trim skirt and bodice" that Sally Pinder's body displays
its adherence to cultural expectations of feminine decency. From her meticu-
lously maintained hairdo, right down to her shoelaces, the author's mother has
evidently not yet been "undone" as a result of her journey to the margins of
"civilization." However, once she has arrived in a virtually unpopulated – and
hence "uncivilized" – portion of the region, Sally Pinder finds herself living in

a tent and facing the advent of a prairie winter. Despite her fear of the great outdoors, she is forced by necessity to at least occasionally emerge from the family tent and aid her husband in the construction of their first home on the prairies. As suggested in the scene used as an epigraph to this chapter, Sally Pinder and the then six-year-old author are placed in what Hiemstra calls a "precarious perch" (162) as they find themselves sitting atop the ever-growing walls of the new structure, helping to pull up logs. For the author's mother, especially, the performance of such work places the female body in a position that threatens the maintenance of Victorian values in terms of female behaviour and, as Hiemstra takes care to note, it is only the log that slips and not her mother's strict adherence to ideals of the "decent woman." What is not contained in the epigraph above is the ending to this scene, which suggests that, however much Sally Pinder might prefer to live in an environment that does not necessitate engagement in activities that challenge domestic ideals of femininity, nevertheless she does imagine at times a physical presence that exceeds cultural norms:

> "We just aren't big enough to build houses," Mother said as she struggled to hold the log and keep her balance. "It isn't as if we're going to stay here. We could just as well leave now, and save ourselves all this trouble."
>
> "I started this and I'm going to finish it," Dad said grimly. "You go back to the tent if it's too much for you."
>
> Sometimes Mother took Dad at his word and went back to the tent, taking Lily and Jack with her. When that happened Dad always chopped viciously for a while, and I kept quiet no matter how much the log rolled and the axe tingled my arms. After such a day, however, there was always a better than average supper waiting for us, and Mother often said she wished she was a bigger and stronger woman.

As Sally Pinder's stay on the prairies lengthens and necessity demands an increasingly "indecent," or "impure," repertoire of behaviour, we begin to see Hiemstra construct a textual space of liberation for her mother, a growing freedom from cultural constraints as reflected in fashion. Keeping in mind her orderly image while on the train ride to Saskatoon, we must compare that early image to a later scene in which Sally Pinder participates with her husband and another immigrant couple in chasing a bear. The bear scene occurs while the Pinders are still in the midst of building their first winter home, and after they have spent an entire day cutting, loading, and installing "sods" onto the roof, with both of them ending the day "black and hungry" (166). If it is true that middle-class women "could not bear on their bodies the visible evidence of manual labor" (McClintock 153), then Sally Pinder has now firmly entered the realm of the "impure." The Pinders are on their way back to their tent home when the author's mother sees a bear, for the second time. Earlier, Mrs. Pinder had to endure her husband's disbelief about the existence of the bear, but this time he sees it too, and is ready to take action. After loading his gun, Mr. Pinder takes off into the bush to chase the bear and, to the surprise of her children, Sally Pinder "dashed after him." This seemingly instinctive decision is shocking for the reader, especially given that just a couple of pages previous to this scene, Sally Pinder has remarked as follows on the gender inequality of life in Canada:

> They [men] liked being their own bosses and doing as they pleased. They could work or not just as they wanted, and if they wanted excitement they went to the gully and shot ducks. With a woman it was different. All she could do was stay at home and worry, especially when she had bairns. Canada was a man's country, and if the women were sensible they'd leave. (164)

Two pages later, Sally Pinder seems eager for some excitement herself, and when she decides *not* to "stay at home and worry," it is understandable that her three children are "startled at being left alone" (166). After a period of waiting, Sally Pinder returns from her sojourn in the bush and is described by Hiemstra as follows:

> She didn't look at all like the quiet mother I was used to. She was young and excited, a Diana enjoying the chase. Her cheeks glowed

pink, her blue eyes sparkled, her lips smiled, even her knot of hair
that had slipped a little looked adventurous. A long bramble clung
to her skirt, but she didn't seem to notice. (167)

Hiemstra's description is particularly interesting given what I suggest in
Chapter Three is the most common female characterization of the displaced
settler woman as a modern-day Ruth, the always loyal servant to and fol-
lower of her husband and family, an image that Hiemstra herself utilizes in
her text. As a Ruth, we might well assume that Sally Pinder is following her
husband into the grove as an act of self-effacement, of concern for his safety;
however, by very deliberately invoking an earlier cultural image of female behaviour – and especially by invoking the image of Diana (Artemis, in Greek
mythology), "the huntress, with her golden bow and moaning arrows, who
leaves in her trail howling animals and a shuddering earth, is goddess of the
wild, virgin nature, all the inviolate places of the earth where humans dare
not enter" (Baring and Cashford 321) – the author deliberately represents her
mother in a more self-interested chase after the bear and away from Victorian
concerns of female "decency" and "purity." In details such as the "knot of hair
that had slipped a little" and the "long bramble [which] clung to her skirt" –
not to mention that her self-monitor is off, as she "didn't seem to notice" her
own state of disorder – Sally Pinder's perch seems ever more precarious as her
reflective memoirist-daughter begins to redefine the spatial politics of western
settlement.

Hiemstra clearly constructs her mother's final plunge into the depths of
behavioural transgression in another fiery scene. Although Sally Pinder has
stated that, in the event of a prairie fire, she would be able to do nothing more
than "run away" (183), nevertheless at the first signs of a fire, perhaps as a
result of the previous disorderly pleasures of bear-hunting, she unhesitatingly
plunges into the burning bush. Hiemstra begins her prairie fire scene with
an interesting conversation between her parents, one in which the traditional
spatial politics of female behaviour are simultaneously invoked and rejected:

"What are you doing back so soon?" Mother asked anxiously
when we clattered into the yard.

Dad tried to smile though his face looked pale. "There's a prairie fire coming," he said.

"Where?" Mother looked around. "I can't see any fire."

"You can't see it for the bush," Dad said. "But it isn't far off."

"Well, then, don't stand there looking gormless," Mother snapped. "Let's go and put it out."

"It's too big for that." Dad began taking out the heavy iron pin that held the double-trees to the wagon. "But I'll go and plough a wider guard. You stay in the house with the bairns. You'll be all right."

"The bairns can stay by themselves," Mother said. "I'm going with you."

Dad told her she'd be better off in the house, but Mother paid no attention to him. "Where's them sacks?" she asked, and she ran into the barn and got them.

I helped hitch the horses to the plough, then Mother told me to take Lily and Jack and go into the house.

"You'd better go with them, Sarah," Dad said. "You'll be better off there. All I have to do is start a back-fire."

"Then let's get on with it." Mother's round face looked frightened but firm. (183–84)

Thinking back to Sarah Carter's repertoire of behaviour available to white women in the Canadian West – "purity and piety," "frailty and delicacy," and a "dependence on males" – Sally Pinder's impatient desire to attend upon the scene of the fire and her decision to leave her children alone appears to transgress cultural norms. Hiemstra even seems critical of her mother's decision to again leave her children in a terrifying situation when she enunciates a childhood fear about abandonment and documents the wait that she and her siblings endured, and expresses their feelings of trauma: "[W]e were alone in the turmoil. Mother and Dad had forgotten us." However, when the author recounts her mother's return to the farmyard she works to reconstitute an heroic version of motherhood in which a sense of adventure beyond the confines of domestic duties does not negate prospects for maternal attention.

Indeed, when she finally emerges from the smoke and ash-filled air, Sally Pinder appears ironically cleansed of her complicity with acts of "decency" and now carrying the bodily symbols of her conversion to acts of "impurity":

> Lily and I stood still in the little trail and looked at each other. We were too frightened to speak. The whole world seemed to be on fire. We didn't know what to do.
>
> Suddenly, *as if she knew we needed her*, Mother came out of the smoke, but she looked so unlike the pretty mother we were used to we were almost afraid of her. Her face was black, and her eyes were red. Her hair was singed, and so were her eyelashes and brows. "Where are you going?" she called.
>
> "To the Metherells' away from the fire," I shouted.
>
> "There's fire at the Metherells', too. You'll be burned to death if you try to go there. Go back home, and be quick." And without waiting to see whether we obeyed or not she went back into the smoke. (185; emphasis added)

After her second plunging "into the smoke," Sally Pinder emerges once again, this time represented by Hiemstra in a symbolic tableau of Victorian woman resisting the physical restrictions of her clothing: "Mother was driving the team and doing very well at it. She was running and her long, wide skirts streamed out behind her, and so did the little shawl tied around her neck" (186). It is clear to the reader at this point that Sally Pinder has travelled far away from being merely the "reluctant emigrant." While the author's mother arrives from the Old World initially complicit with cultural norms of female behaviour, the sometimes harsh realities of early prairie settlement often necessitate bodily transgressions of those norms. In the end, the cumulative effect of Sally Pinder's acts of impurity, her adventures beyond the confines of appropriate female behaviour, is significant for, as Hiemstra tells us, at least for a little while after these experiences, "Mother never mentioned going back to England" (189).

Writing in *The Silent Song of Mary Eleanor* (1983) about her mother's arrival on the prairies, Marjorie Wilkins Campbell illustrates one of the

immediate "challenges of space and geography" to the female body in the
following description of her parents' arrival:

> It was the spring of 1904 when William Herbert Wilkins and his
> wife Mary Eleanor Elliott stepped from the colonist car at the
> little South Qu'Appelle railway station that, like every other sta-
> tion they had passed since leaving Winnipeg, had been painted
> deep *sang de boeuf*, the color of dried blood. He carried the baby
> and she held tightly to the two-year-old while the wind tugged at
> her hat and wrapped her skirt about her ankles. (4)

Despite the immediate wrenching at her sense of order (as expressed in her
fashionable exterior), Mary Eleanor's sense of propriety does not immediately
suffer. In fact, her sense of herself as a "decent woman" seems to redouble
despite her feelings of displacement in the new environment:

> For her it had all been too swift and too overwhelming. She
> needed more than a few weeks and months to understand that the
> West cared little for old-world distinctions between a lady and a
> woman. Despite her acceptance of father's trust in her adaptability,
> she could not have helped the slightly disdainful swish of her long,
> modishly dust-ruffled skirt as she followed him along the plank
> sidewalk to their boarding house. (5)

However, Campbell's mother, an "Edwardian gentlewoman brought up under
the restraints of late Victorian middle class modesty," soon experiences a more
severe moment of "consternation" (12) when her husband presents her with the
mode of travel that will be used to get to the family's homestead site:

> But nothing he had said prepared her for the shock of that equip-
> age. She had expected to see a fine team of horses, and perhaps
> some sort of carriage. Never having imagined how they would
> move their belongings from the railway station to the new farm,
> she was utterly unprepared for father's solution. Their equipage –

he obviously savored the term – was a high green wagon box on wheels. Hobbled nearby were two great, heavy oxen, beasts she had hitherto seen only in Dutch paintings at the galleries, or hauling drays. (11)

Faced with a sight which contradicts her class-based "expectations," Mary Eleanor's immediate point of reference, the way that she attempts to make sense of what she sees, has to do with the culture of "civilization" ("paintings at the galleries") back Home. As she soon discovers, however, "civilization" of the prairie landscape is, as noted in the epigraph by George Bowering, "the dream of a future," and in the meantime she finds herself being asked to accept a rather "precarious perch," one that is ungirded by the social/cultural conventions she previously knew and trusted. When told by her husband that "she and the children were to travel on the narrow seat on top of the load," the disjunction between "Old" world expectations and "New" world realities is made apparent:

> Again she was handicapped by her ignorance. She had never seen a woman riding on top of such an equipage, except, perhaps, a Breton fisherwife. Naively, she could not imagine herself in the role of a peasant. She did not know that every pioneer woman would ride to her new home as he had suggested. Nor did she understand that the high seat would be reasonably safe for herself and the children. (12)

Physically safe, perhaps, but a "shock," to be sure, to Mary Eleanor's sense of decency, as evidenced by her efforts to ascend and maintain her perch: as Campbell writes,

> Mother wore the only travelling costume she had until their boxes could be unpacked. Father held the baby while she grasped the long skirt and struggled up onto the high seat. Then he handed up the baby and lifted the toddler to a place beside her. There was nothing he could do, had he tried, to help her with the hat that

threatened to escape its long pins and sail off in the strong, gusty wind.

Without his brief account of that departure I would never have believed it happened.

"No amount of imagination could quite picture the sheer lunacy of that trip. The only excuse is that most explorers and pioneers are considered fools by the sane of their community. Friends and relatives in England would have sought means of preventing such foolhardiness.

"A green Englishman with most of his goods and chattels piled high on a wagon, and, hitched to the clumsy vehicle, a pair of green oxen. The crowning bit of folly was the slim, steady-eyed young woman, attired in her London-made costume, seated with her two children on top of the nearly top-heavy load."

…

Like the boarding-house experience, mother seldom talked about that journey. From the top of the high load the vast countryside looked utterly empty, the horizon endless. The slow, steady swaying of the oxen's broad backs made her feel giddy. Struggling to keep her balance and to hold the two children, she tried to remind herself that they were on the last lap of their journey to the new home.... (13)

Mary Eleanor's British sense of dignity is further breached when the family stops for a rest and she faces the indignity of a foreign geography's effect on her bodily behaviour: facing her husband "in sudden consternation," she asks,

"What shall I do for a W.C.?"

"What the native women do, I suppose," he suggested practically.

"Or the gypsies!" she retorted, trying to accept the situation. Lifting her long skirts in the long grass behind the wagon, she learned how desperately she needed to accomplish what she later saw Indians performing easily and naturally as women have done since the beginning of the species. (14)

In Campbell's description of her mother "trying to accept the situation," we see the Edwardian woman forced, as a matter of physical necessity, to literally behave beyond the confines of private domestic space, as defined by Anglo and middle-class cultural values. In addition, by choosing to represent this event, the memoirist-daughter uses the space of her writing as a means to document ways in which prairie women's lived experience often exceeded cultural expectations and ideals of "civilization." By invoking what "native women do" as a "practical" solution to one experiential problem, the author highlights that Anglo norms of behaviour are constructions rather than divine sanctions, and that a different geographic space affects bodily space and function. What Campbell notes as a "natural" function experienced by all women had long been dominated by cultural expectations demanding silence on issues of the female body, so that her decision to represent this intimate moment becomes a deliberately confrontational narrative re-vision of the Prairie Woman image. Given her mother's silence about this journey, one can only imagine that Campbell's recreation of this scene derives at least in part from her use of her mother's diary account of the homesteading experience, so that a contemporary and private "incoherence" (Weir 127) with feminine ideals becomes the inspiration for a public re-presentation of the gap between image and reality.

Further assaults on Mary Eleanor's external appearance of female decency occur along the trail, as when the family joins up with a local rancher to cross "the bridge across the Narrows between Echo and Lebret lakes" (16). Learning that "the approach was under several feet of water," Campbell's mother prepares for one more adventure beyond the pale of female purity, as reflected in dress:

> Both men ignored her anxious attempt to delay the departure that to her threatened our very lives. While the rancher jumped down from the democrat and helped her up to the high seat, father held the baby and then handed the toddler up to a snug place between them. The rancher in his wide sombrero and high-heel boots

gripped the reins firmly, spoke quietly to his team and they lunged
into the murky, deep, swirling water. Terrified as she clutched the
baby with one arm and held the toddler with the other, mother
saw it rise to the nearest hub. The turning wheels churned the
water like the wash of a fast boat until it sprayed her face. Without
knowing what she did, or why, she braced her feet against the dash
board. Moments later, when the horses' hooves clattered onto the
firm surface of the bridge, she knew she had been so intent on
sharing the ordeal that she had forgotten all trace of her personal
fear. As the wheels rattled over the gravel at the far side of the
Narrows she casually ignored the muddy water that dripped from
the sopping wet hem of her dust-ruffled skirt and her boots. (17)

In the words "forgotten" and "casually ignored," we see, as with Hiemstra, a
transformation occur as the prairie woman begins to realize that the demands
of the new geography necessitate at least a temporary dismissal of her "mental eye," her self-surveyor, as a means to allow for acts of "impurity"; acts of
physical survival in a new space.

    Again similar to Hiemstra's mother, Mary Eleanor, too, experiences
the challenge to female "decency" and "purity" presented by a prairie fire,
an experience once again represented by the prairie woman's state of dress.
Returning home one day after taking "his first paying crop" to the nearest
grain elevator, Mr. Wilkins smells "the first whiff of burning prairie grass"
(64) and arrives at the family farm to witness the following "indecent" sight:
"Between the two rows of ploughed fire guards around the yard mother stood
poised with matches in her right hand, ready to back-fire as soon as uncle Leo
gave his order. Her skirt was hitched up about her waist, a scarf knotted about
her hair, a dripping grain sack clutched in her other hand" (65). Unlike Sally
Pinder, however, Campbell's mother is "saved" from actually battling with the
fire; thus she undergoes no symbolic divestment of her "Edwardian" attitude
regarding female "decency," either in terms of geographic or bodily space, with
the result that her self-confidence about staying and coping with homestead
life does not soon improve. In fact, directly after this scene, rather than being
enervated by physical exertion as Hiemstra's mother was, Campbell shows

her mother to be incapacitated by the stress of the situation as she "fell into father's arms as he jumped down from the wagon, sobbing her relief," and as she retreats to the safety and privacy of the domestic sphere to perform one of the most intimate functions of the female body:

> After the first agonizing moments mother rushed into the house to us two terrified little girls and the baby screaming with hunger. While uncle Leo watered and rubbed down and fed the horses and father quietened Nora and me with bread and butter and jam and milk, mother sat down in the rocking chair and opened her blouse to the nudging, searching infant mouth.
>
> But no milk came. None of the milk that normally by now would have saturated the blouse and her chemise and corset. There was nothing for the baby, and no relief from her own numbing agony that was worse than the worst toothache she had ever known. Her breasts felt hard and tight, the nipples excruciatingly painful. The smell of smoke in her hair and on her clothes sickened her, and the crackling sounds of flames that had been less than a mile away echoed in her ears. Remembering the possibility of having to wade into the slimy slough with the baby in her arms, she felt a terrible shudder take hold of her entire body, and the terror of it made her long to scream, knowing that somehow she must relax her awful tension.
>
> She did not scream. It was the baby who screamed again, frustrated and hungry. Across the room father sat at the table with us two older children. She herself sat in the now familiar rocking chair and as she moved with it from sheer habit she began to croon, not conscious of the melody or the well-known words that were part of her being. Slowly, as the melody took charge of her mind, she massaged her taut breasts and though for minutes she did not realize that the miracle had occurred, she felt the guzzling little mouth draw the first welcome drops. The flood of milk brought unspeakable relief. The gossamer touch of the baby's caressing

hands assured a complete return of the natural function. Some day,
mother knew then, she would sing again. (65–66)

This stunning narrative moment in Campbell's memoir is complex. On the
one hand, as I've offered it up here, this scene seems to represent the prairie
woman's retreat from an activity that forced her to exceed the repertoire of
possible behaviours available to the "decent woman" of the early twentieth-
century to an activity that confirms domestic ideals of femininity. And yet, on
the other hand, in the detailed intimacy of the scene as drawn by the author,
in her narrative transgression of the culturally silenced female body, there
seems to be a desire to complicate even an act of seeming adherence to gendered scripts. As mentioned earlier in this chapter, white women's role in the
Canadian West was reproductive in both metaphorical and literal terms; that
is, in their role as "civilizers," or "moral and cultural custodians," white women
would effectively reproduce the Anglo values and norms that would bring
the Canadian nation into being, thereby re-invigorating the British empire.
Metaphorically, they would nurture a nation. At the same time, they would
literally give birth to and raise children, who would populate, inherit, and
maintain this "civilized" nation. In cultural narratives and images, however,
all of this work of women remains rhetorical and disembodied. In personal
narratives, such as the memoirs studied here, that undertake to document the
literal work of women, what gets detailed are the traditional domestic tasks
such as those examined in Chapter Two. The bodily acts of child-bearing and
child-rearing are only ever mentioned cursorily, and not in the kind of minute
detail that one might represent, say, the planting, growing, nurturing, and
harvesting of crops. The female body may have been constructed, as I said
before, in alignment with the productive capabilities of the prairie landscape
itself, but cultural constraints on representations of female bodily functions
would not have allowed for the same degree of detail in documenting adherence to this particular type of women's labour. The cultivation of crops could
be explicit, but not the cultivation of a nation's future population. While most
of the transgressions of "transparency" in female bodily behaviours occur out-
wardly – outside the constraints of fashion, outside the home, outside the repertoire available to white women – the strength and difference of Campbell's

text, and specifically in passages like the one above regarding the intimate acts of the maternal body, is that the author transgresses inwards. She takes us inward and beyond the surface fashion of the "decent woman" to reveal her "blouse and her chemise and corset," eventually exposing those physiological happenings within a space that is "antagonistic to transparency" because it cannot be "taken in by a single glance" (Lefebvre 28). Cultural narratives of domestic femininity colonize the female body; they effectively bring the unknown under control by disembodying real women. In scenes such as the one given above, Campbell re-presents the prairie woman's physical body and literalizes the metaphorical role, thus ironically transgressing cultural narratives of the "decent woman."

In both Hiemstra's and Campbell's memoirs we are dealing with representations of the adult female body that move us beyond cultural norms of physical behaviour to make space for transgressions. As the epigraph from Hiemstra's text illustrates, however, the prairie girl's body was not as completely constrained by the ghosts of convention as the adult female body, so that many of the memoirists use the "frontiers" of narrative space to document the experiences of obedience and transgression that occur between mother and daughter as the latter gets older and begins to take up the domestic script. Remembering a time when she was a teenager *Pioneering in Alberta* (1951) in about the first decade of the twentieth century, for example, Jessie Browne Raber writes about getting her first lesson in gender ideals as related to an article of clothing:

Mrs. Brown gave mother many clothes to make over for the girls. Black velvet was one thing. Oh, we were so thrilled! Mother made skirts for Margaret and me. That was just about the most wonderful thing that could of happened to us. We certainly were careful with them. Then I had a beautiful blue skirt and with a white blouse, I surely was dressed up. Mother let Margaret and me go visiting over to Pleasant Valley one day. We had a grand time with the family whose name was Holben. They had four boys and one girl, and one of the boys liked me quite well, but I didn't have time for just one boy. We played games and raced. One race was to climb

over a fence and reach the barn first. I won, but discovered I had
a little three-cornered tear in the very front of my skirt. I nearly
died, for we were to go over to some more friends, the Smiths, for
supper. I didn't care if they saw it so much, but what would Mother
say. It was such a pretty skirt. I was so proud of it, but there was the
tear. Well I'd just have to face the music when I got home. (151)

Here we see the prairie girl's simultaneous appreciation for an article of female
fashion and desire for greater physical freedom than that article seemingly
allows. We also see a simultaneous acknowledgment of the mother's probable
negative reaction to what the tear in the skirt would imply about her daughter,
and maybe about her own performance of the domestic role, and the daughter's own confession of unconcern about being read for signs of adherence to
feminine norms. Once she arrives home, Raber waits anxiously for maternal
judgment and rather predictably the major issue for Mrs. Browne is not the
condition of the skirt *per se*, but rather how the tear in the skirt reflects upon
the "precarious perch" of her eldest daughter's femininity:

I still felt guilty over the skirt, tried to mend it but not very satis-
factorily. I stayed home a long time, scared Mother would tell
me to wear my pretty blue skirt. Of course I knew the day would
come, which it did. I was scolded good, for acting so wild, not a bit
ladylike. Mother gave Sis and me quite a lecture on a young lady's
behaviour. I still had to undo the stitches and do it better, but I
felt such a relief to get it off my mind. The tear was mended quite
neatly under Mother's supervision. (151–52)

A few pages later in Raber's text, the author notes another way that fashion
norms hindered the performances of young female bodies:

The summer had been very nice, that is we children thought so, for
we were really getting up into our teens now. Sis and I had to have
our skirts made longer, much to our disgust, as they were in our way
for running. They were all right for going to parties though. (157)

While that last line indicates a change in activities that marks the change of focus from childhood to womanhood, the other issue of running as "unlady-like" behaviour – as a geographic transgression of physical decency – in the early years of settlement is evident in other of the memoirs gathered here. For example, in Nellie McClung's *Clearing in the West: My Own Story* (1935), a memoir about homesteading life in southern Manitoba in the last two decades of the nineteenth-century, the author writes as follows about a community picnic "early in the summer of '82":

> A committee was formed and a program of sports arranged. There was to be a baseball game, married men versus single men; a pony race, an ox race, a slow ox race, and foot races. I was hoping there would be a race for girls under ten, or that girls might enter with the boys. But the whole question of girls competing in races was frowned on. Skirts would fly upward and legs would show! And it was not nice for little girls, or big ones either, to show their legs. I wanted to know why, but I was hushed up. Still, I kept on practis-ing and tried hard to keep my skirts down as I ran. I could see it was a hard thing to do. In fact, I could see my dress which was well below my knees, was an impediment, and when I took it off I could run more easily. I suggested that I would wear only my drawers, (we did not know the word bloomers) I had two new pairs, held firmly on my "waist," with four reliable buttons. My suggestion was not well received. Then I wanted a pair of drawers made like my dress; for that would look better than white ones with lace. Lizzie thought this a good idea, but mother could not be moved. There was a stone wall here that baffled me. Why shouldn't I run with the boys? Why was it wrong for girls' legs to be seen? I was given to understand that this was a subject which must not be spoken of. (106)

This scene surely documents McClung's early feminist inclinations and as a retrospective account it certainly establishes the author's sense of herself as a dissenter from cultural norms of femininity. Just as importantly, as with

Raber's account above, we see here the gap that occurs between mothers and daughters when inculcation in gender construction is being questioned. Like Raber's mother, Mrs. Mooney is portrayed as complicit with contemporary expectations of gender and is presumably the one who "hushes up" her daughter's determined and creative search for spatial liberation; for the establishment of new and different boundaries of "decency" in fashion more suited to transgressive bodily behaviour. Ultimately, of course, the young McClung comes to the realization that cultural norms are difficult to change and the "stone wall" of social expectation will continue, for the time being at least, to dominate her physical performances. Like Raber, however, McClung uses the moment of writing her memoir, an act of self-narration, to confront cultural constraints by representing youthful thoughts/acts of rebellion.

Change would come for little girls who desired to run free, as seen in Nell Wilson Parsons's *Upon a Sagebrush Harp* (1969). In this story of homesteading life in southeastern Saskatchewan in the first two decades of the twentieth century, the author gives a detailed description of the voluminous clothing which female children had to wear: "Over Rena's and my long underwear, flannel petticoats, and heavy stockings, we wore woollen dresses and enveloping aprons Mama called 'pinnies'" (74). Although Parsons notes the efficacy of such clothing on a winter's morning on the Canadian prairies, as the following dialogue with her mother illustrates, she is also aware that the layers of clothing a girl is forced to wear throughout the year have more to do with social convention than real life climatological needs:

> Putting on these petticoats on icy mornings reminded me of a time
> the last summer in Iowa. I had come downstairs for Mama to but-
> ton my dress up the back. It had been a sizzling hot morning.
> "Stop dancing up and down," Mama chided, turning from the task
> of frying sausage at the stove. Her hands stopped moving as she
> began to button the dress.
> "You've left off one of your petticoats."
> "It's so hot, Mama. I could go with no clothes on and not be
> cold."
> "Hush you! No clothes on. The very idea!"

"It's so hot," I insisted. "I don't need but one petticoat. I've got my ferris waist on and the ruffled petticoat and my ruffled drawers. That's enough clothes."

"W---ell, I don't know. A lady has to wear clothes she doesn't exactly need, many a time ..." (74)

Significantly, we are not told how this matter resolves itself, for the ellipses in this passage are the author's own. The effect for the reader, then, of this open end, of the author's mother's obvious final hesitation to re-assert the norms of what "a lady has to wear," especially when combined with Parsons's alignment of the young overdressed girl on a "sizzling hot morning" with the "frying sausage," is to make possible the questioning of cultural norms. Unlike McClung, Parsons is not "hushed up," and the "stone wall" of appropriate femininity appears to have suffered some instability.

In a later scene recounting the family's preparation for a community picnic, Parsons again questions the clothing which she and her sister were made to wear for this public occasion:

Our excitement grew into a suffocating frenzy in the days before the picnic. There was hurried trying on of dresses we had not worn since leaving Iowa, elaborate, lace-trimmed dresses of pink china silk. The dresses for Rena and me were exactly alike. Six-inch lace dripped from yoke and sleeve.

Iowa relatives had thought Mama clever to get a dress for each of us from Cousin Ida's full-skirted, long dress with leg-o-mutton sleeves. Our dresses were, indeed, almost exact replicas of the original. (96)

What is particularly important here is that the young girls are dressed into "exact replicas" of the fashion worn by an adult woman, thus symbolically representing the seemingly inevitable path of socialization to cultural norms of femininity. However, as the picnic anecdote goes on, Parsons notes a gap in her own appearance of conformity:

I think Rena and I must have looked a little peculiar at the grove picnic in those fussy dresses with wide, pink satin sashes, but bare-foot. The town girls all wore white, and patent leather slippers! I envied those girls their slippers, but the enduring memory of that day is the footrace. The prize for my age group was fifty cents. FIFTY CENTS!

One million dollars! Fifteen cents would buy a new hair ribbon from Eaton's catalogue. Twenty cents would buy a tin of new water colors. Painting was my passion, and the paints brought from Iowa were long since used away. What else, with a fortune of fifty cents? I would need the catalogue in hand for final decision. (96–97)

The gap, of course, is between the "fussy" dress and the bare feet, but it is also in the emphasis of the scene itself. While she begins by noting her mo-mentary attachment to an article of fashion (the "patent leather slippers"), the overwhelming emphasis in this anecdote is the young girl's privileging of a physical exertion that could garner economic freedom and indulgence in a private passion. The act of financial independence is only partly undertaken, however, for after having run one race which ended in a tie, the young author is waiting for the deciding race when her own lack of decent clothing becomes an ironic economic advantage:

The wait for the running off of the tie was agony. If I could beat the tall girl ... fifty cents ... fifty cents! The judges were placing my competitor and me for the run-off when the girl's mother came forward and took her daughter's hand. I am not sure, but I think perhaps a fifty cent piece may have been pressed into the girl's palm. She smiled at me, turned to the judge and said, "I think I would rather Cora did not run again in this heat. Give the other girl the prize money."

The prize was mine! A millionaire by default! (97)

What is delightful about this scene is that when the mother of the town girl sees that the young Parsons is not fully appropriately dressed (in social terms), she feels sorry about the symbol of economic lack and throws the race by resorting to a particularly feminine excuse for her own daughter. In the end, then, Parsons's mildly indecent self-presentation is rewarded publicly.

In Kathleen Strange's *With the West in Her Eyes* (1937), a memoir of home-steading in Alberta in the 1920s, we are able to observe that an increase in population and post-war changes in the norms and values of the wider world did not necessarily result in a greater liberation from cultural constraints upon the female body. Strange experienced homesteading as an adult, and in her memoir she arrives in Canada with new behavioural expectations in hand and herself fully marked with evidence of her "impurity," only to discover that the establishment of close-knit prairie communities seems to have consolidated the gender norms of an earlier period. Despite the burgeoning emancipation of women in the larger world, women living in prairie communities, which were now less isolated than when Hiemstra's and Campbell's mothers arrived, seemed to be clinging to older ideals of female behaviour: indeed, as Jacqueline Bliss notes of women in a Saskatchewan context, "as the need for survival skills in Saskatoon women diminished with the growth of the community, women began to revert more closely to the Victorian ideal" (97).[13] Strange's first impression of the small prairie community of Fenn, Alberta stresses her sense of difference and exclusion:

> I felt sure I read a measure of suspicion and disapproval on every face I encountered. I am sure, too, that there were many dark prophecies, when our backs were turned, as to our apparent unfit-ness for farm life. I am equally confident that many of our future neighbours believed then that we would not endure the life very long. Not only did they *expect* us to fail, but I rather fancy they unconsciously *wanted* us to fail. We were so obviously city prod-ucts, and we were, also, by way of being interlopers, since we

---

13   The stifling effect that a small prairie community can have on female behaviour is most clearly illustrated by Sinclair Ross in his novel, *As For Me and My House* (1941; Toronto: McClelland & Stewart, 1957), which Henry Kreisel describes as "contain[ing] the most uncompromising rendering of the puritan state of mind pro-·duced on the prairie" (51).

had come into a community that consisted mainly of one large family from a certain part of Ontario, related, if not by ties of blood, then by ties of marriage and long association. (11–12)

Strange here marks her family's difference as being based on both their status as "city products," as members of a class of people whose values differ radically from rural populations, as well as being imperial "interlopers" in a colonial community that, especially after World War I, was beginning to feel its independence from the Mother country. In addition, by here joining the words "*apparent* unfitness," Strange gets at the concept of transparency introduced earlier, for she documents human culture's tendency to align a person's surface appearance, including style of dress, with a person's character.

While all of her family members are subject to disapproval, however, it should be noted that Strange appears to merit special attention in being judged as appropriate or not for settlement life. As she steps off the CN train, she finds herself immediately confronted with cultural expectations of female bodily behaviour as her family members are made objects of public scrutiny and her body functions as a public symbol, a transparent space subject to cultural judgment. As Strange admits, she does not fare well in her first display:

> A group of people, waiting near the platform, eyed us curiously as we approached. Word had evidently gone forth that the newcomers would arrive on the noon train, and so our future neighbours had turned out in full force to look us over, and to pass judgment on us, as well as to extend to us a kindly if somewhat inarticulate greeting.
>
> I realize now that we must have appeared to them to be rather queer-looking people. I myself, for instance, did not look the part of a farmer's wife in any particular. I was small and none too robust-looking. I was dressed, city fashion, in a tailored suit, and wore a little hat that had its inception in Paris. I also wore high-heeled shoes and the filmiest of silk stockings. To make matters worse, I had my hair cut short, and wore it in a straight Dutch bob with heavy "bangs." Short hair had been a fairly general custom

in England since early in the war, but it appeared not to have penetrated this particular part of Western Canada at all. For some time after my arrival, to tell the truth, I felt very uncomfortable and conspicuous on this account, and was more than once tempted to "grow it out," so that I would not seem so very different from everyone else. (11)

Leaving aside the issue of Strange's apparent physical inappropriateness for "the part of a farmer's wife," we see here that her clothing problem stems specifically from the fact that she is dressed "city fashion," a style apparently too frivolous, too delicate, for the practical necessities of rural life. Like many immigrant women before her, Strange is perched precariously (on high-heeled shoes); she is on the verge of exceeding rural notions of female "decency" and "purity" as reflected on the body through clothing.[14] In addition to inappropriate shoeware, Strange's hairstyle – despite its obvious practicality for women's work anywhere – marks her as "different," as not appropriate enough, to play "the part of a farmer's wife."[15] Despite the fact that, as Aileen Ribeiro notes in her study of *Dress and Morality* in Britain, in the first decade of the twentieth century the fashion "ideal" had become "a young, slim girl with short hair fitting close to the head," "a curious mixture of sophistication and boyishness" (149–50, 154), this style trend had obviously not become the norm in western Canadian society, probably due to the existence of a colonial mentality whereby gendered customs of an earlier period were preserved as a mark of communal stability and identity. On the other hand, as Strange goes on to make clear in the real ending to the above passage, her impure presence in the landscape of the Fenn community does eventually result in accommodation

---

14 Rural disdain for such city fashions as high-heeled shoes is also evident in Peggy Holmes's *It Could Have Been Worse: The Autobiography of a Pioneer* (1980). Holmes, who also emigrated to Alberta as a new bride at the end of World War I, relates an "afternoon teaish" conversation with a female neighbour, who gossips about a "new settler," Mrs. Bright, who is notable for her "fine airs and fancy talk, spiking around on them high heels" (97).

15 Again we can refer to Holmes's *It Could Have Been Worse*, in which the author notes that in 1922 she wore her hair "long, as was the custom" (143).

of difference: "However, one by one the younger members of the community began, somewhat daringly I suspect, to follow my example. Eventually, to my own secret relief, even the older women followed suit, and today, of course, short hair is as general a fashion among prairie women as it is elsewhere in the world."[16] Short hair had become so fashionable, in fact, that by the 1930s in Alberta, Kathreen A. Nash only ever knew her mother with that hairstyle: as she writes in *The Maypo Lea Forever: Stories of a Canadian Childhood*, "I never saw my mother's abundant chestnut hair except in her wedding picture, piled high on her head, and in one lock, which she had saved when it was cut. Even before I was born it was cut short and waved, as old snapshots show, in the fashionable 1920's 'bob'" (100).

Just as with her hair, so, too, with her style of dress does Strange manage ultimately to make her mark on the western Canadian community in which she lives. As Anne McClintock notes about cross-dressing, "clothes are the visible signs of social identity, but are also permanently subject to disarrangement and symbolic theft" (67). Strange does not take long to perform a "symbolic theft"; she does not wait long to challenge both geographic and corporeal space in relation to "decency" in clothing:

> Just before Grandma Strange went away, she and I unwittingly did something that greatly shocked the community.
>
> We had decided that we would both like to do some horseback riding. Good saddle horses were available on the farm and we wanted to make the most of them. I had brought with me from

---

16　The "bob" style had caused considerable controversy in this period, as evident in a contemporary Canadian novel, Douglas Durkin's *The Magpie* (1923), in which Marion Nason, whose hair was "'bobbed' in the latest mode," finds herself subject to expectations of female decency, for, "although her mother had once hinted that longer hair might be more becoming in the wife of Craig Forrester, she had refused to forsake the 'bobbed' hair mode that she had affected before her marriage" (25, 127). Criticism of short hairstyles for women could even take on political connotations, as seen in Durkin's mention of another female character, Rose, the "communist," who is "a disciple of the Thing-that-is-not," as evidenced by the fact that "[she] bobbed her hair before anyone else in her crowd" (162). For more examples on the politics of women's hair in the memoirs gathered here, see also Inglis 39–40; Johannson 163; Moorhouse 28, 33; Nelson 37–40; and Schroeder 88.

California some new riding breeches, in which I felt I looked quite smart. Naturally I put them on. Grandma was induced to wear a pair of Harry's army slacks. They were rather a tight fit, I confess, but we trusted they would stand the strain.

Somewhat gingerly we rode forth, intending to visit a neighbour. Neither of us had ridden a Western stock saddle before. We found them very comfortable, however, and easy to ride.

When we arrived at the neighbour's house we were received with a decidedly frigid reception. We could not understand it at all. This same lady, a short time before, had treated us most cordially. So charged was the atmosphere that we only remained a few minutes and returned home wondering what on earth could be wrong.

We were not left very long in doubt. A few days later a deputation of ladies called at the shack and asked to see my husband alone.

They told him they had called to protest against my wearing breeches. They said that no women had ever appeared in such an immodest garb in that community before, and they wished to inform my husband that I must be stopped from ever appearing in such an outfit again. They did not mention Grandma, though I imagine they considered her appearance equally disgraceful.

My husband listened solemnly to them and promised that he would take me severely to task about it.

When he told me what had happened I was furious.

"What is it to do with any one what I wear?" I demanded. "I shall certainly please myself." (39–40)

In this scene we have one of the best examples of the female body as transparent space, and clothing as a visible sign on that space that can be read as being appropriate or not. While earlier women settlers to the Canadian West had their own self-monitor attuned to the constructions of femininity that prevailed in Anglo culture and could thus judge themselves accordingly (as well as break the rules where necessary, with relative impunity), Strange arrives

in rural Alberta after women's participation in the work force during World
War I had wrought major changes in fashion trends and she arrives apparently
truly believing that, by outside standards, her "new riding breeches" should
make her appear to be "quite smart." In fact, she deems it "natural" to wear
them because in the world she comes from they are appropriate for the activity
she engages in. According to her own self-monitor, she expects to gain public
approbation rather than public censure. What she does not know is that the
boundaries drawn around appropriate femininity in the Canadian West are
tighter than in places like England and California, and in this scene she rides
straight into the gap of competing standards. She ascends her rather precarious perch, only to discover that "the boundaries of appropriate femininity
were also collectively and strictly enforced by other White women in the area"
(McManus 124).

As with the issue of her bobbed hair, however, Strange does not here
acquiesce to charges of "immodesty."[17] In the hair scene, while she indicates
having felt "very uncomfortable and conspicuous" with her "different" hairstyle, she nonetheless adheres to her own barometer of appropriate femininity
and fairly modestly confesses her "secret relief" in helping to bring short hair
within the bounds of acceptability. In this later scene, Strange's response to
the "deputation of ladies" is less equivocal as we are told that she is "furious,"
an emotional response that she uses as "an instrument of cartography" (Frye
93–94) to, once again, map change:

> Defiantly I went on wearing the offending garments, and in time
> apparently wore the resistance down. But it was by way of being
> a hard-won victory, for I had to endure a constant atmosphere of
> disapproval, at least in certain quarters, all of which made those
> early days of mine the harder to live through. (40)

---

17   As Angela E. Davis has noted elsewhere – and as Strange here discovers – prairie
     women "seemed unable to break free of traditional values. Women were 'doomed to
     the skirt,' said one writer, 'any attempt to get away from it has raised a hue and cry
     of immodesty and ridicule'" ("Country" 169).

Strange's use of the word "endure" in this context repeats her earlier usage – when referring to how her neighbours believed "that we would not endure the life very long" – and makes apparent that, at least in the time period in which her family faced settlement, the major antagonistic forces on the prairies were not environmental conditions and hard work, but rather social constraints regarding bodily behaviours for women. Importantly, other women in the community eventually begin to wear "breeches" as well, which suggests that, as with the younger women and the bobbed hairstyle, the desire to trangress and thus rewrite the boundaries of appropriate femininity had existed within the closely knit community for some time, but that only a stranger with the willingness and the privilege to make an "extravagant display of [her] *right to ambiguity*" (McClintock 68) would be able to achieve the feat of fashion change. Dress, says Ribeiro, "act[s] as a kind of social lubricant, to ease contacts between people in society. It is thus a conservative force, and the history of dress can be seen as a constant battle against the introduction of new styles, which may be thought of as 'immoral' until their novelty is muted by the passage of time" (12). Thus, in this one small but effective way, Strange's determination to resist cultural expectations results in cultural change. In the simple act of riding out over the vast space of the prairies "indecently" clad, she destabilizes the boundaries erected on the female body as a culturally defined space and ultimately frees other women in the community to dress in a way that makes their work more comfortable.[18]

Strange's physical defiance in the above scene documents a change in women's physical behaviours across the span of years of prairie settlement on at least two fronts, the wearing of "breeches" and the riding of horses (especially western style), thus bringing together the transgressions of bodily and geographic space. For women in Canada, "the long skirt remained standard until the 1920s when skirts were shortened and clothes in general became more comfortable" (Davis, Angela E., "'Country'" 170). Once again we see a

---

18   For more examples of how prairie women's clothing and hairstyles represent obedience to/transgressions of the boundaries of appropriate femininity in prairie society, see also Ebbers 36–37; Hewson 3–5, 61, 73–75; Middleton 21, 23; Nash 169–79; and Thomson 57–58.

difference between the values and standards of the larger western world and western Canadian society: as Ribeiro notes about women in Britain, "from 1915 women began to work in munitions factories, on the buses, and on the land, and many of them for convenience and comfort began to wear trousers. There were some complaints of indecency, especially by the older women" (152). Clearly this largely urban phenomenon had not affected the values of small prairie communities by the time of Strange's immigration to Fenn, Alberta. In contrast, homesteading in the more sparsely populated area of northern Alberta in the early 1920s seems to have provided Peggy Holmes with the ability to don the latest fashion trend from back Home in England, for at least some activities. As the author writes in *It Could Have Been Worse* (1980) about the labour-intensive activity of clothes washing, "I always had several long skirts and petticoats to wash as there were no jeans in those days, although I wore breeches for riding" (142). Holmes's "breeches," as she explains earlier in the memoir, are a creative gesture towards the fashion trends for women in the larger world: as she states with characteristic good humour, "I felt very smart as I rode around the estate. My parents had sent me a discarded uniform worn by the 'clippies', the wartime bus conductresses – navy blue with silver buttons. With my large hat, turned up at the side, I looked like a relic from Custer's last stand!" (66). Ultimately, however, the skirt, whatever its length, remained an identifiable, or "transparent," marker of appropriate femininity, as seen in Emily Ferguson's assertion that "the unequal distribution of trousers and skirts in Canada makes countless thousands mourn, and so, perforce, the Eastern spinster and Western bachelor sigh vainly for each other like the pine and palm" (*Janey* 28).

Nevertheless, the exterior form of the skirt was not always so transparent an object; it did not always reflect a strict adherence to cultural standards and could, in fact, work to hide something "dangerous" to gender norms. We can see this, for example, in Beulah Baldwin's *The Long Trail: The Story of a Pioneer Family* (1992). When recreating her parents' journey from Edmonton to the Peace River district during the winter months of 1913, Baldwin's description of her mother's restrictive clothing indicates the reality that, where the conventions of female fashion are concerned, "to a considerable degree, the Edwardian period – which for convenience we will take up to the First World War, an event which changed the course of history and ushered in a new age of political and social attitudes – is a postscript to the late Victorian era" (Ribeiro 146). As Baldwin writes, "Mother dressed hurriedly in a skirt and blouse over several petticoats, put on long black stockings, and heavy shoes. Because she was pregnant, she was spared the agony of corsets, then considered de rigueur for every woman, no matter what her living conditions" (16). In her pregnant body, Olive Freeland epitomizes both the biological and social function of her gender, and the clothing with which she begins her settlement journey conforms to and confirms this function. As the Freelands continue on their journey, however, the geographic impracticability of such attire becomes obvious, and Baldwin interestingly documents that her mother's inspiration to deviate from the strict expectations about gender-based fashion, and also culture-based fashion, initiates from the authoritative experience of a freighter who was used to conditions in Northern Alberta:

> Looking at her feet, the man told Mother she would never make it if she had to walk any distance during a storm in the shoes she was wearing. He advised her and Dad to buy Indian moccasins and moccasin rubbers along with heavy knee-length socks. He went on to tell them that when his own wife came out with him, she wore a pair of men's heavy mackinaw pants under her long skirt in the worst weather. (18)

In this scene, Western Canada is clearly being depicted as a geographic space that necessarily allows for some free play with behavioural codes as related to fashion. It is especially interesting, I think, that while the freighter explicitly "advises" Mr. and Mrs. Freeland to deviate from Anglo norms of dress and to adopt "Indian" footwear as a survival tactic, his admission of his wife's own blurring of gender distinctions as they relate to dress is "told," like a story, or a sidelong suggestion of possibility, and one that quickly fades into narrative obscurity when Baldwin quickly moves on in the following paragraphs to a discussion of her parents' continuing journey.

However, later in the text, later in the journey, we learn that, in reaction to the harsh reality of northern Alberta in winter, the author's mother has in fact undertaken her own bodily transgressions of appropriate femininity:

> My parents were glad now that they had taken the freighter's ad-
> vice and bought warmer clothing. They probably would need them
> for the rest of the trip. Dad's extra union suit had been indispens-
> able from the start and was the first article Mother reached for
> in the morning, pulling it on under her voluminous nightgown.
> Although it was a bit long for her short legs, she tucked the cuffs
> into her heavy socks and wrapped her moccasin flaps neatly over
> them to help keep her body heat from escaping.
>   While the men harnessed the teams, Joan said to Mother,
> "On mornings like this, I usually wear a pair of Robert's trousers
> under my skirt." So Mother dug out the pair she had bought at the
> Landing. But when she tried them on, she discovered they did not
> fit over the small bulge of her waistline. She yanked them down,
> only to have them slip past her knees. When they recovered from
> laughing, Mother asked, "Now what do I do?" "Make them fit
> with a piece of string," Joan answered. (72)

What I find interesting here is the fact that, while the author's mother has transgressed as far as wearing her husband's "extra union suit," and while she has apparently not at this point taken the implicit advice of the freighter to wear pants, she has actually bought a pair of pants that are now readily avail-able to her, but only when another woman has (again, not quite explicitly) opened up the possibility of using them. When Joan Andrews acknowledges the hidden item "under [her own] skirt," she makes space for Olive Freeland to engage in the same quietly transgressive behaviour. It is especially delightful that Mrs. Freeland's pregnant body at first rejects the unusual covering, but that the women go on to persist in adapting the masculine article of clothing to the ultra-feminine body. The women in this scene hide their trousers under their skirts, thereby maintaining at least a surface appearance of conformity to cultural standards; nevertheless, as Baldwin continues, "Dad caught a glimpse of the trousers while helping Mother into the sleigh, and smiled his approval. They were both learning to take advice" (73). Clearly, in extraordinary circumstances, exceptions can be made to cultural rules.

Olive Freeland's need to hide her bodily transgressions is not only attributable to the fact of her being an adult, for even memoirists who write about the experience of girlhood on the prairies in the first three decades of the twentieth century often represent the wearing of pants as a private rather than a public behaviour. For example, in *No "Coppers" in Saskatchewan!* (1973), a memoir of homesteading life in "the Strongfield district of Saskatchewan" in 1906, Winnie E. Hutton, who, at the time of her family's emigration west, was "still a school girl" (2), provides the following rather humorous note to a discussion about battling mosquito attacks: "We also put paper inside our stockings as slacks, for ladies had never been heard of" (20). These privately constructed "slacks" are not necessary in a settler girl's *Prairie Dreams* (1991) for, as Adeline (Nan) Clark writes in her memoir of homesteading life near Oxbow, Saskatchewan, from 1918 to 1924, on mornings when her central character Ruth remained within the confines of the family farm, she "hurried out of bed and into her overalls" (50). As Sylvia Bannert documents in *Rut Hog or Die* (1974), even as late as 1936, cultural attitudes towards females in pants remained prohibitive for prairie girls. While the Cooper family had by then moved further west in search of economic success, nevertheless their prairie values apparently migrated with them, as seen when Bannert describes her younger sisters' response to attending school in Grand Forks, B.C.: "Little Dal and Lolie said they liked the teacher but the girls here wore jeans to school and one person was real nice, but they couldn't tell if it was a boy or a girl because of the jeans" (157–58). For Bannert, who spent her teenage years in Saskatchewan from 1911 on, wearing pants was preferred as a private act, although there is one occasion when she unintentionally finds herself quite publicly exceeding conventional boundaries of geographic and bodily space:

> One night when I came home from school, Merlie [her older sister] was asleep and I saw the horses were out. I put on overalls and a cowboy hat. I did not put a bridle on Roy, just the halter. I rounded up the horses and they started for home, hell bent for

leather. Roy started to race with them. Off went my hat, down
came my hair. The horses took off for the hummocks with Roy in
the lead. I prayed he would stop, but I knew I was riding a runaway
horse. He hit the hummocks, over went his ankle, and I was sent
flying through the air. I came down flat on my back. The run was
all out of Roy and me, too. Bees were buzzing in my head and
everything was black. Finally I looked around. Roy was limping
home. I saw Will coming on the run for me. At that moment my
biggest worry was that he would laugh at me in overalls, for girls
did not wear jeans in those days. (83)

Bannert's experience here takes me back to Kathleen Strange's act of fashion disobedience, for both women expose themselves to public censure (or,
in Bannert's case, the possibility of public censure) while riding a horse, a
rather suggestive and voluntary adoption of a "precarious perch" that challenges cultural expectations about appropriate femininity in a variety of ways.
What women wore and what position they assumed when riding, and, indeed,
whether they should ride at all, was a matter of great discussion in contemporary literature, especially as the activity was very often undertaken in public.
For a long time, cultural conventions of female "decency" demanded that
women who rode did so side-saddle, rather than in the masculine posture of
legs astride, or Western style. Nellie McClung is openly critical of this convention for women in *Clearing in the West* when she writes about an experience
she had being thrown from a horse:

> I was not hurt for I fell on the grassy roadside and I was not far
> from my destination. I hoped my friends had gone to bed, and so
> would not know that the sorrel had come home without me. If I
> had been riding the right and natural way astride the horse this
> could not have happened. A side-saddle is surely the last word in
> discomfort for both the rider and the horse; another example of
> life's injustice to women I thought as I hastened along through the
> dark. (309)

In *Land across the Border* (1978), Donnie M. Ebbers remembers such an "injustice" at work during her prairie childhood in Saskatchewan in the late-nineteenth/early-twentieth centuries:

> The next door neighbors had two girls and two boys who were companions for Gertie, Jackson, Ottie and Joe. They all went on sleigh rides and skating parties. There was no one Donnie's age but the oldest one of the neighbor girls was a "good sport." She came over and played with Donnie some afternoons. Donnie remembered one sunny day Kate had taken her around the yard on her little hand sled. Then they noticed a low out-door root or vegetable cellar back of the house. They made a path in the snow to the top of it and tried sliding down on the sled. Then they sat astraddle of the peaked low sod and snow-covered roof, pretending they were riding horses. Kate has whipped the "horse" with a willow and they had laughed and whooped together like cowboys. Later Papa remarked, "It wasn't lady-like of Katie to sit astraddle of that snow-covered roof and get her skirts all dirty." (Thank fashion for slacks today). Donnie had always liked Katie and she liked her more than ever after that fun filled afternoon, which she always remembered. (27–28)

In that last line especially, Ebbers's memoir becomes a narrative space of rebellion against her father's judgment of "unladylike" behaviour, and this particular scene has implications for the reader's understanding of a later event when the author's mother prepares for a day of family berry-picking:

> When they were getting the logs for the barns, Ottie had noticed blue-berry and cranberry bushes growing under the trees and told Mama he thought there would be lots of berries there in the fall. So on a sunny day in early September Mama put Joe and Gertie astraddle the big white mare, gave each a pail, handed Donnie up to Gertie to hold till she could climb on in front with the big pail,

then sat Donnie in front of her, shook the reins and said, "We're off to the berry-patch!" (40).

Perhaps in the earlier scene Ebbers's father is really just concerned about the dirt on Katie's skirt, but it reads to me more as though he disapproves of *the way* the young girls are sitting on the roof of the cellar and "pretending they were riding horses," and specifically doing so "like cowboys." In this later scene, then, there is some transgression of norms going on under the authority of the mother, for not only Donnie and her sister Gertie, but also Nannie Yokley Cummins herself appears to be seated in an "unladylike" manner.

As seen earlier with hair and clothing fashions, however, cultural norms are ultimately fluid, as seen in the variety of attitudes in women's memoirs towards the issue of women riding "astraddle." For example, as Marjorie Campbell writes in *The Silent Song of Mary Eleanor*, in the first decade of the twentieth century there were many behavioural constraints on a girl who would be entering into society:

> Nothing had prepared me for going to school. I had never played with other children who had been to school for that frightening first day. It was the last thing I wanted to do. I hated all mother's admonitions that I must be a good girl; sit properly with my knees together like a young lady and not in the hoydenish tomboyish way Nora and I straddled the leopard's stuffed head; never let anyone kiss me on the mouth and remember that nice little girls kissed people on the cheek. (105)

At about the same time period, however, as Georgina H. Thomson notes in *Crocus and Meadowlark: A Story of an Alberta Family* (1963), sitting "straddled" could be considered a cultural norm. Writing about various visits from neighbours, Thomson notes that "Mr. and Mrs. Til Fisher rode up on horseback the first day too. They had a ranch on Mosquito Creek and Mrs. Fisher rode with her husband there, but we were surprised to see her riding side-saddle. Most of the western women rode astride like men" (35).

When Kathleen Strange and her mother-in-law set out in 1920 to ride their way into charges of "immodesty" while wearing trousers, they did so in "Western stock saddles," which they found "very comfortable" and "easy to ride" (39). The fact that the Strange women's riding astride is not what triggers public censure indicates that, by the 1920s, this position had apparently become a norm of female behaviour. Indeed, as early as 1910, Emily Ferguson was able to openly declare her own sense of liberation in this regard, thereby playing into prevailing contemporary notions of western exceptionalism in terms of social norms for women:

> Off we go! Champ of bit, ring of shoe, creak of saddle, neck for neck, stride for stride in a duel with time and space.
>
> It is a great place this Canada West – the country of strong men, strong women, straight living, and hard riding. Tut! Who wants to go to heaven?
>
> Goldenrod is making a superb run, and his great barrel pulses evenly between my knees, without catch or strain. He is a mighty fine fellow, this Irish hunter, a rare equine unification of fire and steel that always keeps me dubious as to my mastership of him.
>
> Yes! I am riding astride. Most of us do. It is safer, more comfortable, more healthful, and in every way consistent with good taste. Besides, here is the wide and tolerant West; every one knows that a woman's boots are not pinned to her skirts. (*Janey* 213–14)

Increasingly, western women were choosing to "ride astride," and to do so publicly, as Ferguson rather humorously observes in another of her social treatises of Western Canadian life, specifically regarding Jasper Avenue in Edmonton in 1912:

> There are many women who ride on this street. Most of them ride astride, because it is not pleasant or, for that matter, safe for a woman to be hooked to the side of a horse as if she were a bundle of clothes on a peg. The gentlemen from England hide their faces

as the equestriennes go by; but I know they peep through their
fingers. (*Open* 108)

Ferguson here diplomatically equates cultural expectations as they relate to
women riding horses with the general issue of physical safety – after all, as
women have always recognized, being placed on a pedestal of virtue means
that the only place to fall *is* down – but elsewhere she admits her own personal
desire to break free from spatial constraints, both geographic and physical:
having witnessed the equestrienne prowess of a western farmgirl, Ferguson
rather vigorously exclaims, "I would barter my sphere, any time, to be able to
keep my seat and hitch a plunging steer to my saddle-horn. Yes! or I would
barter my hemisphere" (182). Later, after returning from a day in the fields,
she laments her return to "civilization": "We make believe we are valkyries
speeding to Valhalla. For my part, I am Brunhilda on Grani, my great, white
horse. I, Brunhilda, who this day have been a goddess riding a wild horse into
a wilder sky, must ever, hereafter, sink into womanhood. I, a wild valkyrie, to
sit by the fire and spin!" Ferguson's choice of imagery here is informative, for
she privileges horseback riding as an act that, by its very precariousness ("to be
able to keep my seat") becomes a deliberately rebellious perch chosen by the
female rider as a means to achieve bodily and geographic liberation ("I would
barter my sphere") from the constraints of her culture's domestic ideal ("to sit
by the fire and spin!"). I would suggest that, by figuring that domestic ideal as
a sort of downward motion, a "sink[ing] into womanhood," Ferguson uses her
narrative representation of prairie life to invert the "Angel in the House" icon
of Anglo culture and thereby provide a transgressive alternative to cultural
norms of femininity.

For most of the memoirists included in this study, however, the issue of
women riding horses provided a slightly less dramatic narrative space for documenting female rebellion against cultural expectations for female behaviour.
That young girls should learn to ride seems to be generally unproblematic,
even in the earliest stages of western settlement. But as Barabara (Hunter)
Anderson writes in *Two White Oxen: A Perspective of Early Saskatoon 1874–
1905* (1972), for the author and her sister, the lack of horses on the family

homestead in Saskatchewan in the 1880s meant that, if they wanted to ride, alternative modes of transportation had to be found:

> My sister Maggie and I used to ride on Brisk [an ox] and some-
> times on Jock [a bull] and many a rough ride we had if the mosqui-
> toes got bad and made the cattle run. Often I was left behind for I
> was usually helping Maggie to get mounted first. One day she was
> riding Jock, the bull, when suddenly they all went on a stampede
> and when they headed for a deep slough, she slipped lightly off
> his back and waited for me. I had been afraid for her but she was
> alright. (74)

Later in her memoir, Anderson documents the simple act of riding a horse as a means of self-expression outside the family unit:

> The year I was thirteen, my twin brothers were born. I was at
> home from school to help and was persuaded by my Father to try
> and ride Ned, the two-year old colt. I was much afraid at first, but
> he got used to me and I to him, in a few weeks. I have never loved
> a pony as much as I did him. The rest of the family were united in
> the opinion that he was stubborn and balky and it might be that
> was the reason I always favored him. (76–77)

In that last sentence the intended reference for "that" is vague, implying that Anderson either "favored" Ned as a mark of disjunction with her family's collective "opinion" of him or that she did so because his "stubborn and balky" temperament suited her own personality on some level.

Nowhere does Anderson actually suggest that her horseback riding is anything unusual for a young woman on a Saskatchewan farm in the late-nineteenth century; however, her use of the term "escapade" to describe something that she undertook at about the age of twenty-one is suggestive of an activity that exceeds behavioural bounds for women and that secures her identification with the "stubborn and balky" Ned:

Another escapade I got into was when I tried to harness a broncho. My father had bought a mare that was very thin, had been work- ing, and I thought I could ride up from the river on her back. She had no bridle or even a halter on her. Just a rope on her neck. I stood on a big stone and jumped on her back, but I found myself on my back among the stones instead. I walked up the river bank but decided I should be more cautious. The next broncho I tried was a little chunky black mare my Mother and I bought with John Blackley's help. We gave two yearling steers for her. The cowboys caught her and halter-broke her, and we tied her in our stable where I fed her and led her to water every day for two weeks. Burpee said he would come and hitch her up some day before haying time. One day I took her out and tethered her to the clothesline post; she was so quiet I thought I could put some harness on her, so I got a collar and put it on her. She was perfectly quiet and I led her around. Then I took the oxen neck-yoke, straps – large new leather straps – and buckled the two together and put them around her, buckled them up tight, and the fun started. She bucked to get the straps off, and then ran the length of the tether rope, bucking and kicking like mad. The good new rope broke right at the knot at her neck and away she went. I stood looking helplessly after her. Thinking I had lost forty dollars for Mother, and how could I ever repay it. When Mother found out she said, "It's a mercy you weren't killed." I got on Ned's back and tried to follow her but she was far out of sight, and I had no idea where she had gone. (119–20)

Significantly, it is after this scene that we are told by the "discouraged" author that the unwilling mare's name is, significantly, Eve, that icon of female rebel- lion. But our young rebel Anderson is, at least for the time being, chastened of her confrontational behaviour for she tells us that, in the end, "I had to promise I would not try again to break bronchos, and I wouldn't. That was in 1895" (120).

For Nell Parsons, too, there is a certain thrill to be found in playing rodeo cowboy. As she writes in *Upon a Sagebrush Harp* about homesteading life on the Saskatchewan prairie in the first decade of the twentieth century, riding the family's first horse Kit "was one of our chief pleasures" (70). However, while Kit was gentle, Parsons remembers most fondly a slightly wilder ride, one attractive enough for a young girl looking to stretch her limbs over the vast geographic space of the prairies:

> That second summer Dick Sharland, a bachelor neighbor a mile northeast of us, loaned us a wiry bronco with a baleful eye. His name was Buster and he was round enough for comfortable riding. Saddles were unknown to us then. We children liked to ride Buster.
>
> He was faster than old Kit had been. It was a thrill to ride him over the undulating grass, the strong wind in my face. I could whoop and holler and sing at the top of my voice. I could try a dozen voices, from high soprano down and no one to hear me. Papa did not altogether trust the restless bronc. (109)

Here we can see the female author's reflective narrative attention to the intimate connection between body and geography as her act of unconstraint exceeds contemporary expectations of femininity (preferring a "wiry bronco" to safe "old Kit"), as well as paternal judgment. Similarly, for Myrtle G. Moorhouse, whose *Buffalo Horn Valley* (1973) documents her family's experience homesteading near Swift Current, Saskatchewan, from 1910, riding horses becomes a retrospective narrative transgression important in the process of self-identification. Noting at one point in her narrative that "to be a cowboy was the aim of every young lad" (17), Moorhouse elsewhere represents herself as "the rebel of the family," in contrast to her older sister Olive, who is "a dutiful daughter" (11). Two pages later, she provides a number of photographs to accompany her text, and the final one on the page has the following description provided by the author and clearly illustrating the truth of her designation of herself as rebel, especially against norms of femininity: "8. Myrtle Moorhouse, the author, on 'Baldy,'" a pinto pony. "I love this picture, and I loved this horse and his mate 'Bugs,' wise and gentle, and full of pep" (12). The picture itself shows the author as a young girl seated on Baldy, whose forelegs paw at the air under the control of the adventurous rider (13). What is particularly significant about this picture and the anecdote provided by Parsons is that neither girl seems terribly precarious, even while they push at the limits of "decency."

The romance of the rodeo cowboy eventually translated into the romance of the cowgirl, in both the wider social context as well as the horizons of a prairie childhood. For example, in about 1925, Ferne Nelson resolved that she wanted to be a "cowboy" (111); however, as she describes in *Barefoot on the Prairie: Memories of Life on a Prairie Homestead* (1989), there was one major hindrance to this dream, the lack of an appropriate mount, although considerable creativity is shown in her improvisation:

> We were quite young then and weren't allowed to ride Papa's saddle horse, so we had built up a stable of stick horses, which we rode everywhere around the farm. These humble steeds had names and were stabled and groomed continually. We must have been a comical sight astride these sticks as we galloped madly from bluff to bluff and raced our mounts on the dusty roads. We also rode the calves in the calf pen for a while, but Mama discouraged that after Ve fell off one of the frisky young steers and got her face stepped on. (111–12)

The only horse that Nelson is allowed to ride does not bode well for her future riding career, although it certainly allows her and the animal in question to exceed the confines of "proper," or domestic, "function," in contravention of both natural and parental law:

> I had to settle for old Buck, whose proper function was to pull the buggy. However, in my ambition to become a cowgirl, fate played into my hands. That year Ve wasn't attending school, and Rus hadn't started yet, so I had to go alone and ride old Buck. This was perfect. Alone on the prairie, I could perfect my techniques and emerge as a skilled rider.

Every morning I saddled my old blue roan and set off for school, a dumpy twelve-year-old on a reluctant horse that moved at a sedate walk or, at best, a slow trot.

Every morning Papa warned me not to try to gallop old Buck.

"Remember, you keep him at a trot. He stumbles if he tries to go any faster."

"Yes, Papa, I'll remember."

Out of sight of the farmhouse, a metamorphosis took place. No longer was I a lumpish schoolgirl on a tired old nag, but a dashing cowgirl on a fiery bucking horse. In my imagination my chaps were the gayest imaginable, my white hat shaded my eyes, and those bare heels that dug into my horse's flanks were really encased in hand-tooled boots with high heels and twinkling silver spurs. Old Buck wasn't slow or unwilling, but "rarin' to go" – a snorting, unmanageable piece of horseflesh that only I could control. (112)

Nelson's daydream fashion image here might at first appear to concur with what Collette Lassiter and Jill Oakes note was the 1920s "'golden age of the show cowgirl, an innocent time' for the country's rodeo sweethearts" (61); however, the author's narrative representation of the "dashing cowgirl" in "control" of a "snorting, unmanageable piece of horseflesh" defies a spatial politics in which behavioural denominations such as "innocence" and "sweetness" confine female bodies in specific geographic locations (the safety of the rodeo ring, for example). Unfortunately for Nelson, her attempt at maintaining the "precarious perch" of geographic and physical rebellion fails miserably:

But the reality was most discouraging to an aspiring rodeo star. Buck did stumble, regularly. His short bursts of speed always ended the same way, with me sitting on the prairie and him standing by, patiently waiting for me to mount him again. This I would do in complete frustration, muttering my disappointment that Papa wouldn't give me a better pony to ride. (112–13)

In the end, conformity prevails for, as Nelson writes, "Buck and I continued to go to school, at a sedate trot or a fast walk. Both of us knew our limitations" (114).[19]

As implied in many of the examples above, perhaps one of the reasons for limiting women's access to horses had to do with the fact that, once they experienced "control" of such an unpredictable source of power, female bodies quickly responded to the excitement to be found in the transgression of domestic space, both geographically and physically. However, the fact is that most prairie women had little time for experiencing life on the prairies beyond the domestic duties that kept them largely confined to the home sphere, and the inculcation of daughters in the performance of such duties was certainly a norm in prairie families. As Donnie Ebbers notes in *Land across the Border*, her father's expectations for her future assumed a reinforcement of a spatial division of labour along gender lines: as Mr. Cummins advised his teenaged daughter, "Your mother is a good housekeeper and a good cook. She can teach you to keep house, to cook and sew, and even to nurse the sick. She can teach you all you need to know to be a good wife for a farmer" (94). Mr. Cummins's words indicate a certain cultural understanding that to be a "good wife for a farmer" was a teachable/learnable task, a role with definable boundaries into which any willing and hard-working girl could be fitted. Similarly, Kathleen Strange determines to learn the "natural dut[ies] of the farm housewife" (44), Peggy Holmes seeks "to learn how to be a farmer's wife" (58), and Katherine Magill admits her initial failure "in the role of farm wife" (13). In Georgina Thomson's memoir, the author fairly frequently uses the term "women-folk" to designate the female members of their particular family group, a term apparently initiated by the author's father and taken up and repeated by Thomson, first as a seemingly natural category then increasingly as a feminist criticism of categories of women's work. What Thomson's use of the term "women-folk" indicates, and what many of the other memoirists imply, is that in settlement communities there was a tendency towards separation of prairie folk into two

---

19   For more examples of women and girls riding horses, see also Hiemstra 142–43;
      Inglis 41–42, 49; Middleton 29–30, 34; Raber 113, 125–27; and Thomson 21–22,
      34.

sub-groups, men- and women-"folk," whose designated functions in rural culture were clearly separate. Thus, for example, does Thomson remember one of
her family's hired men as follows:

> Harry [Wakeman] hadn't the slightest interest in cows. He fed
> them and cleaned out their stable grudgingly, but he drew the line
> completely at milking them. He didn't know how to milk and he
> wouldn't learn. It was good policy on his part, but it left the milk-
> ing still entirely to the women-folk, as Father referred to us. How
> I hated that term! It seemed to put us in a menial category. (247)

Although Thomson herself has used the term "women-folk" several times
throughout her memoir, nonetheless, after this statement about hating the
term and her relation of it to her father's less-than-liberated view of women,
her use of the term becomes layered with the sarcasm of quotation marks: for
example, speaking of another hired man who did milk the cows, she says, "this
was a break for us 'women-folk,' but we still didn't like his treatment of the
horses" (249).

Although I suggested in the previous paragraph that men and women
in prairie culture appeared to comprise sub-groups "whose designated functions in rural culture were *clearly* separate," in point of fact, while the ideal of
separate spheres seems to have been a fairly common familial/cultural concept,
nevertheless the reality of what exactly constituted the boundaries of women's
work (both in terms of geographic and physical space) seems to have been
constantly shifting. It is one thing to speak, somewhat paradoxically, of the
"*natural* duties" of the prairie woman, but it is quite another thing to achieve
a consensus as to what duties make up that role. When Jessie Raber makes
the statement, "Daddy was a busy man outside; Mother and we girls busy
inside" (89), she reflects the general cultural understanding of how the ideology of separate spheres functioned; however, in the farming context of western
Canadian settlement, the division of labour along gender lines is usually a
little less spatially discrete. For example, certain outdoor chores, because they
were deemed as women's work, can be represented as a penetration of the
domestic sphere outwards into what Sheila McManus calls "the shared space

of the barnyard, the grey area of work that was neither a strictly 'feminine'
nor a strictly 'masculine' responsibility" (134). Activities that were assumed to
require a particularly maternal sense of nurturance for success, such as responsibility for laying hens, turkeys, etc., were thus often deemed as a "natural duty"
of the farm woman. As seen in Georgina Thomson's discussion of hired men
above, responsibility for milking cows – in contrast to the use of and caring for
horses, a breed of animal traditionally equated with masculine power – most
often rested in the hands of women. In *Changes: Anecdotal Tales of Changes in
the Life of Anna Born, 1888–1992* (1995), for example, Anna Schroeder asserts
that "milking was one of the 'girl's jobs'" (58). However, milking cows was not
always viewed as an appropriate activity for female bodies. In fact, at one point
in her memoir, Thomson refers to a Mrs. Hawk, whose "sphere of action ended
at the kitchen door. She never milked a cow, fed a stubborn calf, put a clucking
hen on the nest, hoed the garden or carried water" (100). Here we can see that
for some immigrants to the prairie west, and especially for those emigrating
from "more urban settings," outdoor work of any kind challenged their sense
of decency, and "some women were able to accommodate this work to their
construction of gender, while others continued to claim and preserve feminine
domestic privilege" (McManus 123).[20]

Changes in the boundaries of "women's work" were not simply a matter of historical progression, either; indeed, it would be erroneous to suggest
that those women who emigrated at the height of Victorian culture remained
firmly confined within the domestic sphere while women of later settlement
periods were increasingly liberated by changes in the wider world and consequently experienced freedom from domestic bonds. Rather, there is a real
disjunction between the ideal of separate spheres and the lived experience
of settlement life that allowed women across the historical spectrum represented by the memoirs in this study to make space, both within the cultural
moment of homesteading and within their narrative re-presentations of that
cultural moment, to challenge what Judy Schultz in *Mamie's Children: Three*

---

20   For more examples of attitudes towards milking and caring for cows as an appropri-
     ate chore for women, see also Anderson 72; Baldwin 220; Holmes 59; McClung
     334; Raber 48; Strange 44–48; and Thomson 46–47, 70–71.

Generations of Prairie Women (1997) labels "the myth of the good woman, a myth that began in Mamie's era and just won't go away" (108–9). When Katherine Magill announces in her memoir *Back o' Baffuf* her determination to "learn the necessary skills" of the farm wife, to adhere to "local standards, recognize the good old pecking order, evident in every rural district," and to "KEEP MY MOUTH SHUT about all and sundry experiences outside the sphere of this place" (14), she acknowledges a behavioural reality that exceeds the domestic "myth of the good woman," a reality that must be silenced in favour of seeming adherence to the boundaries of appropriate femininity. More importantly, Magill's ironic capitalization of the words "KEEP MY MOUTH SHUT" points to the function of the memoir as a temporally safe space in which the author is able to represent the reality of excessive, transgressive behaviour, so that our understanding of women's experiences of prairie life broadens in the act of reading.

While ideological constraints theoretically confined them to domestic duties, white, English-speaking, prairie women soon discovered that the practical necessities of prairie life often demanded their participation in work outside of conventional definitions of what constituted domestic space. Many prairie women also soon discovered that they actually desired to get beyond "the confining nature of women's work" (Sundberg 83), to enter more fully into the prairie landscape and experience physical labour beyond such traditional tasks as cooking, cleaning, and childcare. Willing or not, it is certain that "women's contributions to sustenance reached beyond the domestic sphere" (81). As Mary Kinnear discovered in her examination of women's responses to the question "Do you want your daughter to marry a farmer?", their answers "stress the interdependence of family members who, while accepting a rough sexual division of labour, were not immutably constrained by it" (149). Quite often, in fact, homesteading required both sexes to learn new skills and put aside, or hold in abeyance, traditional concepts of "'feminine' and 'masculine' behavior" (Bennett and Kohl 92). Women could, and did, participate beyond the confines of the household.[21] Nevertheless, although

---

21   Emily Ferguson notes the facility of rural isolation in allowing women some behavioural freedom when she notes of her penchant for "painting the vehicles" (which

the relative isolation of prairie life, especially in the early years of western settlement, "did permit greater variation from accepted behaviour and ideology," this "loosening of sex role definitions did not release women from their primary tasks" (Kohl, "The Making" 179), nor did it very often mean that they received help in accomplishing their domestic tasks; indeed, "while women were expected to adapt and take part in the 'male sphere' of farming activity whenever required, the opposite seldom held true" (Rollings-Magnusson 227).[22] It has become a critical axiom in Canadian women's historiography to repeat Veronica Strong-Boag's image of prairie women as not so much

---

she describes as her "master-passion"), "polishing the brass on the harness," and sometimes "bandag[ing] the horses' legs and giv[ing] them a special polish," that such activities result in social isolation within a village setting: "No! I may deceive the people several blocks away, but my neighbours are better posted. They can readily see that I am 'no lady,' and ought to be ashamed of myself. Now, in the country, without neighbours, I could sin against the law of the usual with impunity" (*Open* 116–17).

22　When men did engage in tasks traditionally seen as women's work, it was often regarded as a kind of joke. We see this in Jessie Raber's *Pioneering in Alberta* when she writes about the moment when she and her siblings arrive at the new family home built by their father and see "the man that had helped Daddy, cooking supper. It looked so funny to see a man doing the cooking that we started to laugh. Mother told us not to be so rude, that in a new country one would see many different things, so we felt rather ashamed then" (28). We can also see shock and surprise, and lurking danger, at the sight of a man undertaking "women's work" in Clara Middleton's *Green Fields Afar* when the author comments on attending the home of an Englishman bachelor with two other couples:

They looked on with surprise as Godfrey set the table, flipping white granite plates along the white oilcloth tablecover, and planting at proper intervals the granite cups and silver flatware. Their surprise was greater when he bore in a sirloin roast of beef, mashed potatoes and canned corn which he had prepared himself, and all cooked to perfection. Where he got the apple pies was his secret, but he whipped the cream for them and made the coffee. No woman was to be seen.

All through dinner he led with the stories and the laughter, and afterwards supervised the toss-ups which decided which men were to wash the dishes. The lot fell on my husband and Jack, the latter not practised in the art. Mary observed the operation with a kindling eye, and said as we drove home, "I didn't think he could do it; wait till I get him home – and I never ate so much in my life." (42–43)

"Pulling in Double Harness" as "Hauling a Double Load" in regards to the work of running a family farm operation.[23] While women rarely questioned their responsibility for domestic duties, they also accepted the need for their occasional participation outside the family home. "Occasional" is the keyword here, and certainly in much contemporary literature, women's farm labour was represented as a temporary measure – that is, it was not meant to "imply a permanent confusion of spheres" (Jeffrey 31) – that could be left behind

---

23   Commensurate with Strong-Boag's assertion that "for most women life continued to consist of hauling a double load, or, as today's feminists would have it, working a double shift" (418), Mitchell makes the following highly sarcastic comments regarding the notion of western equality and the unreality of men and women "Pulling in Double Harness":

> Canadian men in the West are usually very helpful, not at all "John Grumlies." … they are clever at housework, having mostly had some experience as bachelors. The Old-Country husband has a bad reputation on the prairie (among the men), as leaving too much to his wife. One man occasioned quite a scandal by allowing his wife to help him harvesting (he was not strong); another gave offence by making no attempt to give his wife, who had been a woman of leisure, any better dwelling than a wretched sod hut. But, in any case, the man has to go out to his work, and the wife has to look after the babies and cook the food and bake the bread and do the washing and keep the house decent, though she may leave any egg-collecting or milking to the man at bad times. There is no one to help; and so many a woman dies and many a baby dies, and some lose their health and their bloom, and many a wife is the cause of her husband's leaving the country and going to town. (48–49)

The sense of imbalance in Mitchell's list of the chores which, "in any case," "have" to be done by the husband and wife respectively already implicates the project of western settlement in a politics of inequality, then that critique is followed by the author's rather caustic suggestion that the woman who cannot cope with the reality of farm life is the "cause" of her well-intentioned husband's failure.

Similar to Mitchell, in *Crocus and Meadowlark* Thomson also suggests that concepts of women's work change depending upon the husband's geographic background: referring to the husband of Mrs. Hawk, who refused to milk cows, she states that "Mr. Hawk and the boys did all the outside chores, and we noticed that most American men did not consider these to be women's work. Farmers from Eastern Canada and from Britain, however, were for the most part less chivalrous and expected their women to rally round and do all sorts of jobs around the place" (100–101).

once economic security allowed her to adopt a more traditionally domestic role. In 1910, Marion Cran spoke to a prairie farmer who admitted his wife's unorthodox workload: "When she started here, I tell you, she often drove the hayrake with a pair of oxen, and I've known her pitch hay till sundown"; however, he assured his listener, "we're in better shape now and doing good; she doesn't do that any more" (132–33). As seen in the following fabulous gender distinction, complete deviation from strict domesticity resulted in condemnation: "With the family dog as companion ... the boys roamed the prairie or woodland and learned its lore. The house cat ... saw the little girls grow up into good housewives as they helped their mothers. Barn cats were not named" (Kamen-Kaye 8).

In the early years of settlement, when homes needed to be built and the land needed to be broken in order to fulfil cultivation obligations, and when no help beyond the family unit was available, prairie women often found themselves, as did Mary Hiemstra's mother, precariously perched on the edge of the domestic sphere while trying to lend a hand with those chores which, at least in Anglo culture, were traditionally deemed to be within a man's sphere of duty.[24] For example, as Mary Hiemstra describes in *Gully Farm*, during her family's first summer on the prairies, Mr. Pinder decided that ploughing the land and planting potatoes was necessary for survival in the coming winter, so he began the chore, unaware of the new geographic reality confronting him. In fact, in undertaking this crucial agricultural task, Mr. Pinder is constructed by the daughter-author as bordering on maniacal in terms of his adherence to the way things had been done in his country of origin:

> He looked the land over carefully and decided to plough a ten-acre patch not far from the tent. No trees or willows grew on it and he thought the work would be easy.

---

24   Some "men's jobs" that women had to perform in the early period of land settlement were housebuilding (Raber 44 and Holmes 100–102), digging wells (Campbell 98), haying (Holmes 84, 94) and clearing scrub (Johannson 182).

Furrows in England had always been straight, and Dad wanted the first furrow on the new farm to be perfect. He set up a line of stakes, sighting them carefully, and moving one or two that seemed a little out of line, then he hitched Darkie and Nelly, our two horses, to the plough.

Dad had often ploughed in England, but the earth there had been tilled for generations and turned easily. The new, unturned prairie sod resisted the ploughshare with root and stone. (126)

As the scene continues, Mr. Pinder discovers his inability to accomplish the work alone, and so he is forced by necessity to call on the aid, first, of his daughter, and second, his wife, who, as indicated in Chapter 3, has hitherto been painted as the prototype of the "reluctant emigrant":

Dad, however, didn't realize how tough the sod was, and thought Darkie and Nelly knew nothing about ploughing. He told me to get a stick and keep them going.

I did as I was told, and the horses made a little progress, but they didn't go straight as Dad thought they should. They wavered from side to side, and the furrow, instead of being straight, was a frightful zigzag. It went first east, then west, and in one spot it was almost a half-circle. "A fine farmer they'll think me," Dad fumed, and called to Mother to come and guide the team while he held the plough.

Mother had come to see the first furrow turned, but she knew nothing about ploughing, or even driving the team. She was, however, willing to help. (126–27)

There are several interesting things going on in this scene. First, the author seems to be toying with those futuristic cultural narratives that envisioned "an unbroken sea of wheat fields" (Hall 84), for in depicting her father's struggle with making even the first furrow on a landscape that now seems inimical to such an effort, she confronts both paternal ("he thought the work would be easy") and cultural authority/rhetoric on the purpose and process of western settlement. When the horses struggle with the reality of the task, they are disempowered ("Darkie and Nelly knew nothing about ploughing"), and when Mrs. Pinder is asked to lend a hand she is likewise disempowered of knowledge ("she knew nothing about ploughing"), and yet this scene clearly points to the father as being the truly disempowered one as he comes to realize that the idealistic narratives that lured him to the Canadian West, that veritable Garden of Eden, belied the truth of the prairie landscape. Mr. Pinder's frustration with his inability to perform the role of prairie farmer as idealized in the promotional literature is reflected in his concern for what some vague "they" will think of his skills.

Second, by depicting the massive difficulty ahead of the Pinder family if they are to succeed at farming, Hiemstra provides a context for understanding what a deviation this type of labour will be for her mother, who, very significantly, is here positioned as "willing to help." That willingness certainly challenges the boundaries of appropriate femininity as Mrs. Pinder has known them to this point in the memoir:

> Mother tried hard. Her round face got pink with sweat and excitement, and the hairpins came out of her neat bun of hair. She told me not to frighten the horses so, and shook the reins and waved her arms, but the horses still reeled from side to side.
>
> "Can't you even drive a team straight?" Dad snapped, and glared at her.
>
> "No, I can't." Mother's face was red by now, and she glared back at Dad. "And I never had to before I married you. If I'd only had sense and married Edmond Barstow – here, you drive if you think you're so smart, and I'll hold the plough. You always did take the easiest job if you could." She tossed the reins to Dad and took hold of the plough handles.
>
> Dad said she wasn't strong enough to hold the plough, but Mother said she was as strong as he was if not stronger, and for him to go ahead and drive if he thought it was so easy.
>
> "Well, have it your own way," Dad said, and took the reins. "Hold hard," he warned. "The plough jumps."

Mother told him to mind his own business and tend to his driving, she could plough as well as he could.

Dad looked doubtful, but he shook the reins and told the horses to get up.

The horses were tired by that time, and they jumped nervously. The plough jumped too, and since Mother wasn't holding firmly it tipped over, pulling her with it. (127–28)

Sally Pinder ends this effort by retreating in anger back to the family tent, but she is ultimately proven right in her assessment that she "could plough as well as [her husband] could," for as the scene continues on, and as Mr. Pinder gets more and more abusive towards the horses and his daughter ("Dad, also tired and excited, shouted at me and at the team" [128]), he is thrown off his own perch of self-righteousness:

Dad wasn't a bit pleased with the furrow, and shouted at me to go first right, then left. I tried hard, and so did the sweating team, but the plough wouldn't co-operate. At last, as if it, too, was tired of the struggle, its nose struck a stone and the handles flew high in the air, hitting Dad a smart blow on the jaw and, to use his expression, knocking him spinning into the middle of next week.

Throughout the course of this scene, Mr. and Mrs. Pinder are equalized; that is, the inability of Mrs. Pinder to successfully perform the work is never ascribed to her gender, as Mr. Pinder appears equally incapable of success. In fact, when discussing this event with her husband while dressing his wounds, Sally Pinder finds an alternative reason for their failure to accomplish this task, one that ultimately works to question the Anglo boundaries of appropriate femininity; to show those boundaries as being socially constructed rather than some natural state of being:

Mother was upset when she saw Dad's bruised and swollen jaw, but under her concern there was a noticeable trace of satisfaction. "I told you this prairie was never meant to be ploughed," she said as she put hot cloths on Dad's black-and-blue face. "Even the Indians had more sense than to try it."

"The Dukhobors ploughed it," Dad mumbled.

"The Dukhobors are a lot bigger than we are." Mother put water in the kettle and lit the fire. "This country was never meant for little people like us."

...

"If them Dukhobors can break this prairie so can I," Dad said. "Though I have heard tell the women do most of their ploughing." And miserable as he must have felt there was a chuckle in his thick voice, and a twinkle in his good eye. The other was swollen shut.

"Well, if you brought me to this god-forsaken place to plough for you, you can send me right back to England, then you can have one of your Dukhobors," Mother said, and, her pretty little figure stiff with indignation, she flounced into the tent. (128–29)

Again there is such complexity in this scene. In shifting the ground away from concerns of gender to concerns of cultural background, Hiemstra effectively confronts those cultural narratives which, at the time her family emigrated, were depicting the British as the ideal settlers to the Canadian West as a means to ensure imperial purity in the colonial project. While this passage appears to play into stereotypes of the Doukhobor people, and especially of Doukhobor women, as being less "civilized" than British people, that kind of image faces serious challenge at another point in the text (which I'll get to in a moment). Even here Hiemstra seems to be playing with Anglo notions of female "decency," as seen with that final image of Mrs. Pinder as a "pretty little figure stiff with indignation." That phrasing seems to me to encompass Anglo constructions – and simultaneously an implicit critique of those constructions – of appropriate femininity, especially as related to its unsuitability for the real conditions of prairie life.

A different image of femininity is recuperated earlier in Hiemstra's text, in a more dynamic image of Doukhobor women. When travelling around looking for a good homestead site, the Pinder family come upon a small Doukhobor settlement, and are greeted as follows:

The door of the nearest house opened, and four or five women
popped out and came towards us. They were not tall women, but
they were wide and strong looking, deep of bust and thick of thigh.
Their long, shapeless dark dresses hid their legs, but their bare feet
and ankles were as big as the feet and ankles of most men. If the
women had been horses they would have been *percherons*: large,
thick-chested animals, accustomed to hauling huge loads without
any fuss or bother. According to the stories we had heard these
women were also used to hard work. They toiled in the fields from
daylight to dark; hoeing potatoes, weeding, and cultivating gardens, ploughing the fields, and if a horse got sick they were said to
help pull the plough. Mother had always laughed at these stories,
and said the old-timers were having us on, but when she saw these
wide women, more like oaks than willows, I think she believed
part of the yarns, at least.

The faces of the women were brown and weathered, and they
had what in Yorkshire was known as a stolid look, but they were
not dull. Their small, light blue eyes, set deep in sun wrinkles,
were bright and intelligent, and their wide mouths were strong and
firm. They looked contented and capable, and oddly proud, as if
they enjoyed their lives and the work they did. Afterwards Mother
said: "You can't tell me anybody makes them women do anything.
If they plough it's because they like ploughing, not because some
man tells them to." (90–91)

Here we see Hiemstra at her usual clever work of balancing off cultural narratives ("According to the stories we had heard") with her own alternative
perspective. The overwhelming sense of the Doukhobor women in this scene
is positive, with an accumulation of generous words all meant to counterpoint
the image that has hitherto been drawn of Mrs. Pinder, both physically and
emotionally. The physical capability of these women is not condemnatory and
seems an interrogation of contemporary Anglo ideals of femininity. In *God
Bless our Home: Domestic Life in Nineteenth-Century Canada*, Una Abrahamson
provides an anonymous quote that identifies the prevailing concept of the ideal

female body in this period, a concept quite foreign to the descriptions provided by Hiemstra of the Doukhobor women: "Small feet and small ankles are very attractive, because they are in harmony with a perfect female form, and men admire perfection. Small feet and ankles indicate modesty and reserve, while large feet and ankles indicate coarseness, physical power, authority and pre-dominance" (6). Mrs. Pinder certainly encompasses this typology, for her "pe-titeness" is highlighted at several points throughout the text, and we are told at one point that she is "only a little woman with soft round arms and small hands, not the axe-swinging type at all" (156). We are also told that she "often said she wished she was a bigger and stronger woman" (162). There's also a difference in emotional capability, for Mrs. Pinder is most often depicted as being angry, partly at being in Canada, and partly at being unable to help her husband with the necessary work of farming. In contrast, the Doukhobor women are depicted as being "contented" and "proud." In fact, as Mrs. Pinder insists, these women seem to enjoy a greater degree of liberation than she was previously led to believe. This scene representing the Doukhobor women is thus important to our understanding of Sally Pinder's own desire to break free from domestic constraints at other points in Hiemstra's memoir, such as her "willingness" to try her hand at ploughing and, as already examined earlier in this chapter, her performance as "a Diana enjoying the chase" when in pursuit of a bear.[25]

---

25   Although Hiemstra provides a positive interpretation of Doukhobor women, con-temporary images of these women reinforce the idea that all female bodies were subjected to Anglo ideals of form and behaviour. For example, in his 1911 book titled *Canada's West and Farther West*, Frank Carrel, Journalist, includes an article (originally published in *Collier's Weekly*) written by Jean Blewett and titled "The Doukhobor Woman." Blewett focuses upon physical details, noting that "the Doukhobor woman is no Venus. A long while ago she acquired the habit of work-ing, and, theorists to the contrary, hard, incessant work does not tend toward beauty of face or form" (227). Blewett goes on to assert that "doing the whole year round a man's work, has given her the figure of a man. She has muscles instead of curves; there is no roundness or softness visible.... Her hands and arms are the hands and arms of a working man." Obviously, the concern here is that the female body and the labour it performs no longer acts as a physical marker of appropriate femininity; on the contrary, the bodies of the Doukhobor women are transparently "indecent" in their outright rejection of woman's traditionally domestic role. As Blewett con-cluded, supposedly in direct contrast to the ideal life of an Anglo woman settler,

While women helping with ploughing, as Mrs. Pinder wanted to do and the Doukhobor women contentedly do, demands that a woman's body exceed the domestic sphere at least to the extent of the family's homestead land, another common activity, wagon or buggy driving, provided women settlers with a sometimes more liberating vehicle of geographic and bodily transgression. Indeed, the act of driving allows a person to exist temporarily within a constantly moving, unsettling, and ambiguous space, one that defies the stasis of separate spheres. In Ferne Nelson's *Barefoot on the Prairie*, for example, the author remembers one particular woman who presented a stark contrast to her mother's domestic ideal of "settling down," which, "in Mama's world," means "to marry some decent man and assume the status and demeanour of a respectable married woman" (15). As Nelson writes about the "Rawleigh Company's representative,"

"there is no romance in the life of a Doukhobor woman" (Carrel 227). We can see similar judgments in Emily Ferguson's observation of a Doukhobor woman one year prior to Blewett's article:

> Our hostess does not bear the slightest resemblance to a Venus de Milo or Diana. She is deep-chested, iron-muscled, and thickset, like a man. Her legs are sunbrowned, her feet splayed like the saints in stained-glass windows, and her flat, stolid face bears the imprint of monotony.
>   It would appear as if the females of all races who are subject to undue physical exercise lose early their picturesqueness, comeliness, and contours. They tend to become asexual and to conform to the physical standard of the males. As this woman leaned over the swinging cradle and nursed her baby, even her breasts appeared shrunken and flaccid. (*Janey* 148)

Interestingly, while Ferguson seems to have felt it her duty to provide cultural criticisms through the image of Doukhobor women's bodies, she certainly did not appreciate being the object of a sort of reverse "illusion of transparency" (Lefebvre 28), which she experienced when visiting the "Doukhobor village of Vosnesenia": first she notes her "feeling that [she] was being examined with a directness that was disconcerting," then she admits her awareness that "they were taking us in, and it would doubtless have been a thorn in our pride if we knew what they thought of us" (40, 42).

> Any visitor was welcomed to our isolated farm, and Mrs. Krause
> was no exception. She came a couple of times a year, and in style,
> too, in a shiny black democrat buggy pulled by two lovely bays. I
> remember her as a sort of Queen Victoria, sitting regally on the
> front seat, holding the reins, and expertly controlling her spanking
> team. (27)

This early characterization of Mrs. Krause is interesting because by invoking
the image of Queen Victoria we have an ambiguous model of womanhood:
on the one hand, Queen Victoria was the inspiration for the rigid domestic
ideal of the nineteenth and early-twentieth centuries, but on the other hand,
as a figure of royalty, she was a woman with power that exceeded the purely
domestic realm. Mrs. Krause, too, is depicted as a woman who encompasses
two states of being, as seen in a physical description that at least appears to be
within the boundaries of appropriate femininity:

> Mrs. Krause was a sweet little woman. Did I say little? Well – she
> had tiny hands and feet. She was short, too, but very stout. She
> really was a lot like the famous old queen. Dumpy, I guess. Well-
> corseted, but no rigid stays could control the rolls of fat around her
> middle. Her hair was strawberry blonde, piled high, and always
> very neat. It was held in place with beautiful tortoise-shell combs.
> (27)

What a great figure of femininity here, as she hovers between containment
("Well-corseted") and excess ("the rolls of fat"). This woman is domestic, but
more than that, as she travels across the landscape, "sitting regally," "holding
the reins" and "expertly controlling her spanking team." She is a figure of
empowerment, but her perch is nonetheless precarious in relation to domestic
ideals. As we learn at the end of the chapter dedicated to Mrs. Krause, "She
had a husband and a houseful of kids at home. In our world, all the other

women stayed home, but she spent her days bumping over rutted roads, making a living. An early independent business woman" (29).[26]

In another instance, although it is not actually the settler woman driving, Nelson uses the space of her text to illustrate the power of geographic movement to confront traditional notions of female "decency" and "purity" in terms of a "dependence on males" (Carter, *Capturing* 8). In a chapter titled "Mama Makes Her Mark," Nelson writes about her mother's first time casting a political vote. On first reading, the events of this chapter appear to conform to a conservative image of the Prairie Woman, with Myrtle Alexander narratively positioned as the supposed butt of a clearly gendered joke that results from her supposed lack of political acuity; her absorption in the domestic sphere. In the days leading up to the election, Nelson's mother is constructed as struggling with what she feels is the impropriety of female enfranchisement. As seen in the following extended passage, behaviour is very clearly defined along the lines of gender:

> ... The men could talk of nothing else but the coming election. Mama was quite uninterested in this talk. She would sit quietly, darning a sock or crocheting a doily, offering no opinions and looking extremely bored. On the infrequent occasions when neighbour women visited, the talk was of cooking and sewing, babies and gardens. Mama seemed to feel that politics was somehow unladylike. She fidgeted uncomfortably when the men's voices were raised in heated debate.
>
> When Mrs. Wood sat in our front room and insisted on arguing with the men, Mama was quite disgusted. She was also unmoved

---

26   We can see Mrs. Krause's radical position in Ida Scharf Hopkins's memoir about homesteading life in the 1940s, *To the Peace River Country and On*, when the author assumes the masculine gender of company representatives throughout her narrative: for example, she says, "Watkins and Raliegh [sic] men were as much a part of the prairie as wheat. They were rival companies dealing in household products.... I don't think any farmer's wife had a preference for either companies' product. She bought from the one who came when she needed what he had to sell" (112–13). In *Prairie Dreams*, Adeline (Nan) Clark, too, talks about visits from "the Watkins man and the Raleigh man" (96–97).

when Papa kept reminding her that women now had the vote and that he expected her to go with him to the schoolhouse and make one more vote for "our man." She agreed to do that, but only to please him, not from any personal conviction. (93)

The scene is set and the result seems inevitable. In the buggy on the way to the schoolhouse, says Nelson, "Papa had questioned [his wife] again," had "coached her carefully," saying "'Remember, Myrtle, just put an X after the man's name. You know the one to vote for. Just one X, that's all.'" (93). The deliberateness of these words suggests to the reader that only a complete incompetent could possibly do wrong. Given that the author's mother has been consistently constructed as nothing less than "clever" and capable in her domestic role earlier in the text, we as readers feel assured when Nelson asserts the family's belief that Myrtle had certainly "voted right" (93). Nevertheless, the truth is revealed a few days later at Sunday dinner when the author's mother finally speaks for herself, seemingly ingenuously:

After election day, conversation went back to the topics of our workaday lives, but there was one comical incident on the Sunday that the Hansons came for dinner. At the table the talk turned again to the election. Papa said something about Mama's voting and joked that she had a lot to do with winning. Mama was all smiles.

"Easiest thing I ever did," she said, then added, "of course, the first X I made was for the wrong man. I was a little flustered, I suppose. But I stroked it out and finally got my X in the right place!" (95)

In an ironic reading of this seemingly nostalgic text, one encouraged by the author throughout the memoir, knowledge of Myrtle Alexander's spoiled ballot immediately changes the meaning of the chapter title, for, as I prefer to read it, in response to the "expectations" of her husband, "Mama [Very Deliberately] Makes Her Mark." In Nelson's translation of contemporary events, this eminently capable woman, who previously could only "fidget uncomfortably" while the men expressed their anger in "heated debate" and who only "*seemed* to feel that politics was … unladylike," first performs the political incompetence that has been attributed to her, then invokes the apparently unquestionable patriarchal language of "right" and "wrong" in order to render especially effective what I read as her geographic and bodily act of "confrontation" with conservative scripts. Just imagine what could happen were women themselves encouraged to drive a team of horses away from the family farm!

Beulah Baldwin makes space in *The Long Trail* to document the figure of a woman driving a wagon. Writing about her parents' journey to the Peace River region of Alberta in 1913, Baldwin notes that the Freelands come upon an unusual sight for the time period:

> Ahead, two outfits were travelling close together. A man handled the first rig while his wife drove the second one. Pulling over, the young man asked Dad for a cigarette, though he probably only wanted to break the monotony of the trail with a chat while resting the teams.
>
> My parents looked with admiration at the young woman driving her team with apparent ease. When Mother commented on her courage, she admitted that she had not planned it, but an extra rig was needed to bring their farm equipment and winter supplies. Looking mischievously at her husband, she said, "A lot of men's jobs aren't any more difficult than women's." (55–56)

Driving a wagon on the homestead trail was not a "planned" event, but necessity ensures the woman's participation in an activity beyond purely domestic definitions of women's work, and that participation results in the woman's knowledge that there is nothing very sacred about the spatial politics of labour along gender lines. Baldwin uses this moment to represent her mother's own developing and unspoken understanding that settler women often had to exceed behavioural boundaries:

> After they left, Mother could not help wondering how the young wife would manage the icy hills ahead, not realizing that the steep

river banks she had already encountered had been nearly as frightening. Pioneer women, Mother would learn, performed many
tasks they would have thought themselves incapable of, and she
would be no exception. (56)

In fact, much later in the text Baldwin documents Olive Freeland's own desire
to participate beyond the rather confined domestic space in a scene which
seems to repudiate notions of women's unwillingness to transgress cultural
norms, along with their supposed "frailty and delicacy," and to equalize male
and female abilities:

> Dad needed no instructions for clearing the land – just his strong
> back and good right arm. Sharpening his axe, he went to work.
> Except for a grove of spruce to the north, his quarter was sparsely
> wooded. But even so, unexpected help was welcome. After nursing
> and bathing Junior, Mother put him down for his morning nap,
> telling Carlton and me to look after him. Then she donned her sun
> bonnet, her old moosehide gloves, and pulled Dad's old overalls
> over her skirt, ready to help on the land.
>
> Crossing the meadow, she was deeply aware that the whole
> country was very quiet and open and free. This was why everyone
> they met was in such good spirits – like the country, their outlook
> had a fresh quality.
>
> Mother surprised Dad with the amount of clearing she accom-
> plished as she slowly and steadily hacked away at the underbrush
> and small trees with her sharp hatchet. She always preferred out-
> side chores to housework and was enjoying herself. The air was like
> wine, the skies blue, and the sunshine would be with them until
> ten o'clock at night. When her arms and back tired, she switched
> to piling brush. Her favourite job, as it had a bit of excitement to it,
> was taking the reins and urging the team on, while Dad pried out
> the stumps with his crowbar. It was not long before a small field
> emerged, giving them a great sense of accomplishment. (199–200)

Certainly part of the power of this scene stems from the fact that Mrs. Freeland taps into the ideal of Western exceptionalism, which figured the prairies as a space that was "open and free" and thus allowed for play with cultural norms. What I like about this scene, however, is the narrative movement from the idealization of the author's father as being physically well suited to the act of clearing the land to focus on the "unexpected help" of Olive Freeland, who is depicted as being equally well suited, physically and emotionally, to the work required for "a great sense of accomplishment." At the same time, the author's mother is depicted as a repudiation of binaries with her creative costume of sun bonnet and man's overalls, and her attendance to the domestic work of childcare as well as farming. This scene does not depict the victimized image of "hauling a double load," either, for Olive Freeland "crosses the meadow" of her own accord as a means to satisfy her labour preference.

For women settlers who had experienced extra-domestic, paid, war-time employment prior to their arrival in a prairie community, it quickly became apparent that "World War I had not had the broad effect on the reality of women's lives for which it has sometimes been given credit" (Vipond 5), at least not immediately. As a result, women settlers such as Kathleen Strange, who emigrated to Alberta in 1920, and who openly confesses in *With the West in Her Eyes* that "domestic life had never had any great attraction" for her (31), found it necessary to push the boundaries of "decency" and "purity" as related to the subject of women's work. Back home in England, Strange had worked in the "Ministry of Munitions," where, as she states it, "at a comparatively early age, I had learned to stand on my own feet and to fight my own battles. I had encountered men and competed with them on an equal footing, and had gained an experience of life that has undoubtedly stood me in good stead during the years that have passed" (5). As with her decision to keep her bobbed haircut and to continue wearing "breeches" while riding, Strange seizes more than one occasion to be disobedient to cultural norms of femininity, and once again we see an image of the prairie woman positioned on a "precarious perch." Feeling anxious about progress on the building of their new home, she offers one day to step outside of her domestic sphere:

Another time the work was held up because there was no one available to haul a load of lumber that had arrived at Fenn. "All right," I said, "*I* will go and haul it home for you!" They laughed at me but finally let me go.

At Fenn I enlisted the services of the elevator man and some other men who happened to be around to help me load the lumber onto my wagon. (54)

Once out upon the prairie landscape, Strange is quickly forced to acknowledge that she has perhaps exceeded her capabilities as a farm wife:

When it was all safely aboard I started for home. I managed nicely until I came to the hills. The first hill we went down, the horses, impelled by the loaded wagon behind them, started to gallop, and by the time we reached the bottom, I had practically lost control of them. I have always wondered why they do not put brakes on Canadian farm wagons, but I suppose it is for the good reason that an experienced driver knows how to "hold the horses in." At that time, however, I had neither the skill nor the strength to manage my team and I was very frightened indeed. (54–55)

The geography beyond the homestead continues to threaten her with defeat for, while the upward trend of the next hill slows down the uncontrolled progress of the horses, another challenge to her prowess soon occurs:

Now, however, another problem confronted me. We had been climbing for a few minutes when I noticed that I constantly had to allow the reins, or lines as they are called in the West, to slip through my fingers, until I seemed to be an extraordinarily long way from the horses. Looking downward I discovered that I was slowly but surely moving backward on the load of lumber! There was an increasingly widening space between the front end of the wagon and the ends of the boards up on which I was perched.

Suddenly I realized what was happening. Owing to the sharp incline upward, and to the fact that the boards had not been securely roped in, the entire load was slipping backwards. Presently, if we did not reach the top of the hill in time, it would slip right off on to the trail.

My hands were now nearing the ends of the lines, and there was nothing left for me to do but to jump down into the half-empty wagon box, lean over the front end, and concentrate all my attention on keeping the horses in hand. The boards, I decided, could take care of themselves.

Just before we reached the top of the hill, my load crashed off with a terrific clatter and was scattered all over the road. (55–56)

Unlike in the epigraph at the start of this chapter, when Sally Pinder determines to maintain both her perch and her sense of decency by letting the logs slip instead of herself, Strange rejects the helplessness of her situation and takes action. Although she does lose the load of lumber and becomes the subject of a "good laugh at [her] expense" (56) when she tells her family about her plight, the more important focus is that she does control the situation, she eventually makes it home safely, and the family home gets built. She also makes sure to advise her reader that the lost load of lumber did not happen as a result of any real incompetence on her part; rather, the precarious event happened because of the incompetence of the men who helped her at Fenn, for "the boards had not been securely roped in" (55).

At a later time, braced by the ultimate success gained in that first experience driving the wagon, Strange decides to once again exceed the normal course of events and strike out onto the landscape alone: noting that she had previously *"been driven by"* one of the men to Big Valley to get coal," the author writes that

One fall day, however, with a hint of winter in the air, I decided to take a wagon into Big Valley and bring back a load of coal for the farm myself. I had already driven a team several times. I had hauled lumber successfully from Fenn. So I felt confident that I could haul a load of coal. (92–93)

This time, Strange courts near disaster before she has even left town:

> On this particular occasion I drove safely onto the platform,
> climbed down and held my horses while my wagon was weighed;
> then proceeded to pull up underneath the chute. I remained on the
> seat while the wagon was being loaded and held on to the horses.
> Soon the box was full and I signalled to the man to close the trap.
> For some reason or other, the trap refused to close, and the coal
> kept pouring down. In the excitement of the moment I did not
> have the sense to pull ahead, but just sat there, watching the coal
> pour down on to my already over-full wagon. Suddenly an extra
> large lump of coal came down the chute, bounced off the wagon,
> and struck the rump of one of the horses. The horses jumped for-
> ward, broke the wagon pole, and almost threw me from my perch.
> There might have been a serious runaway had not several miners
> sprung forward and seized the horses' heads. (93–94)

Once again, however, Strange ultimately manages to complete her self-ap-
pointed task, even despite some activity that thrusts her beyond the pale of
female decency:

> It took considerable time to shovel off the excess coal from my
> wagon and clear away the heap that had piled up on the ground
> around me. I also had to get my wagon pole repaired and the har-
> ness fixed. I listened to some of the most expressive and colourful
> language I have ever heard in my life while all this was being done.
> (94)

In both of the above situations, Strange wilfully undertakes her geographic
and physical "confrontations" with domestic norms, and neither the threat of
falling from her "precarious perch," nor the less than supportive judgements

of men, deter her from inscribing her bodily resistance across the prairie landscape, across the memoir page.[27]

Many of the childhood memoirs indicate that the position of the farmer's
daughter is a case in point of the constantly shifting boundaries of "women's
work." Under the traditional rules of the "domestic and rural idyll," the need
for women to "know their place" was tantamount; indeed, "inculcation into
appropriate attitudes and behaviour started in early childhood" (Davidoff et
al. 165).[28] In *We Swept the Cornflakes Out the Door* (1980), Edith Hewson
documents the moment when she and a sister came to "know their place" as
being located in a different geographic and bodily space than that experienced by their older brother:

> Spring came and with it, change. Edith and Amy sensed it most in
> Buster. He treated them with greater condescension, left them the
> filling of the woodbox, and spent more time in the barn helping
> with the "chores."
>
> They yearned to assume his possessions, step into his shoes, and
> enjoy his privileges, a family promise that was constantly violated.
> His shoes were boy's shoes which they couldn't wear, his privileges
> widened because his preferred habitat was the barn, and his ac-
> quired possessions, its produce thereof. (109–10)

However, the less than idyllic situation of the Canadian prairies meant that
"the labor needs of the homestead placed great responsibility on children
and also made age and gender restrictions impractical. Where there were
sons, daughters worked in household production; where there were no sons,
daughters worked in the fields" (Bennett and Kohl 97).[29] As the example from

---

27 For more examples of women driving wagons, see also Roberts 163 and Thomson
    72.

28 For examples of such "inculcation," see Ebbers 49, 65; Hicks 10; Johannson 44–46;
    Nelson 14–16; Raber 30, 89, 118; and Schroeder 58.

29 Certainly the figure of the prairie daughter as farmhand is common enough in the
    literature of the period, as seen in Grove's *Settlers of the Marsh*: "Niels saw to his sur-
    prise the girl [Ellen Amundsen], clad like a man in sheep-skin and big overshoes,

Hewson's text illustrates, however, this is not to suggest that girls and young women were always reluctant to step outside the domestic sphere into the vast landscape of the prairies; on the contrary, many of the memoirists examined here use the temporally safe distance and space of the memoir to assert women's performance of men's work as a crucial part of their personal contribution to land settlement. For example, as Georgina Thomson and her sister Chaddy discover in *Crocus and Meadowlark Country* in the first decade of the twentieth century, farmer's daughters were often expected to assist "neighbors in times of crisis" (Bennett and Kohl 101):

> Father and Louis [Roy] worked together quite a bit, sharing machinery and labor, and sometimes Father shared us with Louis, sending us down to plant potatoes for him behind the plough and to pick them up in the fall. Louis always brought us out a lunch in midmorning or afternoon and paid us a little for our work. Very small change meant a lot to a homesteader's kids in those days. (41)

While it may not seem positive that the two sisters fit into the category of "machinery and labor" in their physical capacity as temporary farmhands, the work they perform does in some small measure become a space of liberation in the form of monetary reward, or public recognition, for one's efforts and

---

crossing the yard to the stable where she began to harness a team of horses. They were big, powerful brutes, young and unruly. But she handled them with calm assurance and unflinching courage as she led them out on the yard" (21–22). However, this situation is not presented as ideal, especially when the girl in question becomes questionable: for example, as Niels Lindstedt compares two female farmhands,

> whereas Ellen, when she donned her working clothes, had changed from a virgin, cool and distant, into a being that was almost sexless, Olga preserved her whole femininity. The nonchalance of her bearing also stood in strange contrast to the intense determination with which Ellen went after her work. About Olga's movements there was hesitation, an almost lazy deliberation very different from the competent lack of hurry in Ellen. Besides, Ellen ignored the men at their work; Olga stopped, looking on, and chatted with Nelson about his plans. (38)

contribution. At home, however, their contribution is unpaid and expected as a matter of course: "Not having any school to attend gave Chaddy and me a lot of time to fool around with our own interests and fun, but as time went on and the farm developed more, we were called on to do more around the place" (69). Some jobs were better than others, but then that qualification depended largely on the point of view of the women involved:

> Work we did not enjoy so well was picking stones. Father had by chance filed on a stony homestead, and before the land could be ploughed, as many stones as possible had to be removed. I was always a bit of a feminist and I had a strong feeling that picking stones was not a girl's work. Father had other ideas and so we all had to rally round, that is, all except Bee. She was a good cook and housekeeper and so was allowed to stay in and get the meals. Mother would rather be outside anyway. She always thought cooking was an awful waste of time, as you worked so hard only to have everything gobbled up in a hurry, and then you had to start all over again. (71)

Later in her text, when speaking critically of men's ideas of appropriate work for women, she repeats her father's phrasing and suggests that "farmers from Eastern Canada and from Britain, however, were for the most part less chivalrous and expected their women to *rally round* and do all sorts of jobs around the place" (100; emphasis added). Thomson has repeatedly pointed out her sister Bee's disdain for outside work, an attitude that is liberating for the author's mother, who obviously understood that a woman's domestic production was certainly crucial to the operation of the family farm, but that sometimes women wanted more of a return on their labour investment than mere consumption.

As the eldest daughter in her family, Nell Parsons takes pride and joy in the work that she performs on her father's homestead in the first decade of the twentieth century, as when the family is constructing their first prairie home: as she writes in *Upon a Sagebrush Harp*,

I helped Papa put on the sheathing. He called me "his boy," for Cecil was too young to be of any help. It was an exciting day when he allowed me to help with the roofing paper on that part of the roof which extended over the bedroom half of the building.

That was as far as the half roll of roofing paper brought from Iowa would reach. In Iowa all houses had been accomplished facts. Here I thrilled to the reality of learning how roofs and walls came into being. (18)

Importantly, the author's physical positioning in this task provides her with an awareness of the intimate structure of the domestic sphere as a human construction rather than an "accomplished fact" beyond transgression. As in Thomson's memoir, Parsons also notes that the performance of chores not traditionally delineated as women's work held the liberatory potential of monetary (and gustatory) rewards:

Later that summer I had a chance to earn more money. A farmer west of us had a mustard infested field of wheat. He hired Rena, myself, and Stella Mitchell to pull the yellow mustard. He paid us the princely sum of fifteen cents a day.

It took us six days, working from eight in the morning until five in the afternoon, to cover that thirty-acre field. There was time out for noon dinner at the farmer's bountiful table. We had canned tomatoes every day and several eggs. Each meal, dessert was a generous dish of fruit, with cake! (97)

Similar to Parsons, in *Prairie Dreams* Nan Clark's main character, Ruth, who, every summer morning, "escaped out the back door to join the wonderful farm activity" (50), takes pride in helping her father with farm chores: for example, writing about planting potatoes Clark notes that

Ruth rode the horse and guided it up and down the garden. Father held the small, one-furrowed plough which turned the soil and left a ditch for the seed potatoes. Ruth, aware of her importance, rode the big farm horse proudly, so high above Father, that even the fence seemed a long way down. She was relieved to be lifted down while the horse rested, and they set the potato pieces evenly in the moist black soil. Again, Ruth rode the horse, as the plough turned yet another furrow to cover the seed. It was triple companionship, as the three worked and rested together. (51–52)

After fall threshing, when the family had "settle[d] back to family routine," Ruth engaged in another farm chore that, as with Thomson and Parsons before her, had monetary rewards:

> Next day, beyond the cleared fields of golden stubble, Ruth searched for the "sets." The sets were hers to gather, clean and sell. These were the piles of wheat which, escaping the spout, were heaped on the ground, one by each straw stack. She carefully shovelled them into the sacks for Father to haul home. There, with help from Jim, she cleaned them in the fanning mill, so as to remove chaff and weeds. Gathering the sets was the final reward for a long season of faithful work. These plump sacks of grain were saleable merchandise, all hers. Ruth revelled in her sense of independence, of worth, and the respect she gained for work well done. (93)

When Sylvia Bannert's family emigrated to Canada in 1911 after the death of the author's father, much of the work on the Cooper family's farm near Truax, Saskatchewan, no matter what type, was necessarily performed by the then eleven-year-old author. As Bannert writes in *Rut Hog or Die*, her lack of formal schooling did not mean that she possessed no knowledge:

> I got work in Avonlea for a while. One lady asked why I didn't go to school. I said, "Where? There is no school in the hills."
> "Surely you could work for your board and go to school."
> "Yes, I have tried that. I worked for a lady for my board and school supplies. I got up at five in the morning, milked the cow, cleaned the barn, got breakfast for seven of us, did the dishes,

ran the six blocks to school, back at lunch, did the dishes, back
to school, hurried home, worked till ten at night. They also had
four children I had to help look after. What time did I have for
school? Then they did not want to buy my writing paper. I was so
far behind the other children, I felt ashamed. So I will just grow
up dumb."

"My dear child, I see what you mean!"

I thanked her for feeling sorry for me. Anyway, I could milk a
cow, hitch up a team of horses, clean a barn, wash clothes, make
bread, cook a meal, mind the babies and help take care of the sick.
I was not unhappy with what I knew. (74–75)

Unlike so many of the memoirists gathered for this study, Bannert's family
is definitely unable to pretend to middle-class notions of femininity; rather,
basic survival needs mean that the family is in a much more constantly precarious financial position and that the women of the family are required to
consistently "haul a double load." Indeed, the breadth of Bannert's knowledge
regarding the running of a farm, the fact that she "could do a boy's work as
well as a girl's" (78), meant that her family's well-being was largely dependent
upon her presence: "It was hard for Mother when I was away. She could not
hitch up a horse. There were so many things for which she depended on me"
(75). Here we see that, in some exceptional cases, the settler woman necessarily displayed a "dependence" on female labour rather than upon the protection
of men. Importantly, Bannert's extra-domestic work in childhood translates
into a wider behavioural definition of appropriate women's work when she
later marries a farmer. As Bannert remembers, domestic and farm work/space
often overlapped: "I did a man's work out in the field. The baby was good and
I would put him on a blanket while I stooked wheat" (121–22).

This overlapping of self-identification as both farmhand and domestic
worker also occurs in Myrtle E.J. Hicks's *The Bridges I Have Crossed* (1973),
a memoir of homesteading life in Manitoba in the first two decades of the
twentieth century. As Hicks remembers about her teen years, starting when
she was sixteen years old, "the fall of 1914 the grain was rusted badly, so I was
helping Dad to take off the crop. We had been taking turns. I would drive

the four horses on the binder and Dad would stook. Then we would change vice-versa" (11). As she goes on, we see that for young girls and women the expectation was that they could work quite fluidly, moving from working as a farmhand under certain conditions, then transitioning to more traditional domestic work in other conditions. Representing the exchange between these two roles in the memoir text often presents an opportunity for critique by close narrative comparison:

> I helped Dad with the harvest two years. As soon as the wheat was cut, if the other grain wasn't ready, we would stack the sheaves. With a team on a wagon with a rack on it, we would drive from one stook to the other. I would build the loads and Dad would throw on the sheaves. When a good big load was on, we would drive up beside where the stack was built. I would throw the sheaves onto the stack and Dad would build it. He always built oblong stacks and so high. Mother would bring us out lunch around 4 o'clock and we would work until eight or maybe longer if it looked like rain and we were finishing off a stack. When threshing started, I would go from one neighbour to the next helping to feed the men as soon as we at home had had our turn. We put in long hours but there was lots of fun too. The gangs would have their caboose for sleeping in but ate in the house. Any neighbours that were helping went home after supper and were not there for breakfast. There would be an average of ten to fourteen for breakfast. Of course you served potatoes, meat of some kind, porridge, three or four slices of toast, coffee and tea. At noon you would feed between twenty and twenty-five men. It would depend if they were hauling the grain to the elevator if more men were needed. Then lunch at 3:30 p.m. – pie, sandwich or hot biscuits or cake. Supper ranged from 7 p.m. to 9:30 p.m. It depended upon how the weather looked. If it looked like rain they would stay and finish what stacks were started. So you see us women didn't get finished very early. (12)

Hicks's ability to transgress spatial boundaries makes her especially valuable, as we see when she meets her future husband, the brother of a girlfriend, and her father, who is "dependent" upon her as a source of labour, becomes possessive: "My folks were interested in Lila but it was the last thing in Dad's mind that his girl would go out with Charley, or anyone else. He needed my help and that was that" (16).[30]

That, however, is not simply that, for in their representations of women's bodies chasing bears, fighting fires, running races, straddling horses, driving wagons and working in the fields, the memoirists examined here provide us with a narrative space in which to confront the domestic ideal that persisted throughout the different phases of western settlement. As we can see from the memoirs, lived experience of prairie life often resulted in the prairie woman needing and/or wanting to perform her disobedience to, her transgression of, the boundaries of appropriate femininity. Within the temporally safe space of the memoir, then, these authors demonstrate the precarious nature, the constantly shifting boundaries, of what it meant to be a "decent woman" in prairie society. For those early women settlers whose stories are written by daughters and grand-daughters, the pressure to conform to domestic ideals came largely from within, but that internal monitor of "decent" behaviour often had to be ignored when prairie isolation demanded the prairie woman's participation in activities beyond the pale of cultural norms. Extra-domestic activities thus became a necessity, and sometimes even a guilty pleasure. For those women writing about their own experiences, both as children and as adult women, the pressure to conform to domestic ideals came largely from without: indeed, even as late as the post-World War II period, Katherine Magill felt the necessity, "as in ancient Rome," to "conform with local standards and habits," to keep secret any transgressions of the farm wife role, to "bury" them, "deep. Not even relating them to the family" (14). In both cases, looking back across the gulf of time, the vast geography of the prairies and of the memoir text become narrative vehicles allowing for a more dynamic representation of the prairie woman's vital role in western settlement.

---

30   For more examples of girls and young women working as farmhands, see also Anderson 31–32; Hiemstra 287; Hopkins 87–88; Inglis 11, 40; Johannson 149–50; McClung 116; and Raber 108.

❈ 5 ❈

"The landscape behind it":
Re-Visioning Some "Other"
Subjects of Agriculture

But after reading a chapter or two a shadow seemed to lie across the page. It was a straight dark bar, a shadow shaped something like the letter "I." One began dodging this way and that to catch a glimpse of the landscape behind it. Whether that was indeed a tree or a woman walking I was not quite sure.

> – Virginia Woolf, *A Room of One's Own* (1929)

But the face of the red man is now no longer seen. All traces of his footsteps are fast being obliterated from his once favourite haunts, and those who would see the aborigines of this country in their original state, or seek to study their native manners and customs, must travel far through the pathless forest to find them.

> – Paul Kane, *Wanderings of an Artist among the Indians of North America* (1859)

I am I because my little dog knows me.

> – Gertrude Stein, *Everybody's Autobiography* (1937)

One of the most enduring cultural images of western land settlement is encompassed in a single tableau, one that recurs in prairie fiction, in television depictions of prairie life, and often in the memoirs studied here: that is, the image of the white (assumedly male) prairie farmer and the post-natural, agricultural landscape, usually devoid of any trace of either First Nations or non-human animal presence. It is an image that underscores the future-oriented, utopian, and large-scale cultural objectives of western settlement that have already been explored in Chapter Two. The final image in Douglas Durkin's *The Magpie* (1923), a relatively "obscure" novel that nonetheless is "importan[t] as a document of social history," represents the "adopt[ion]" of "one of the great themes of Canadian literature and intellectual thought, the agrarian myth" (Rider xii–xiii). As the main character Craig Forrester rejects city life and returns to the farm of his childhood, he witnesses the following picture: "a team of dark horses entered the field at the farther end and stood while their driver hitched them to a plough.... [Craig] watched them come down the full length of the field, leaving behind them a fresh new furrow through the stubble" (329). In this image, while the horses used to plough the land are mentioned, nevertheless it is the prairie farmer who controls them, and the reader's focus is ultimately turned towards the work accomplished. Also from Durkin's text, we see Craig Forrester walking alone across the prairie landscape in an image that optimistically suggests that the mere presence of the idealistic farmer ensures prosperity: "And in the sky before him as he walked steadily on, the shafts of gold shot to the zenith, flooding the earth with the faint glow of early dawn." The opening to the History Channel television series, *A Scattering of Seeds: The Creation of Canada*, similarly privileges the image of a lone human male seen literally and figuratively "scattering his seeds" in the cultivation of a nation. Although this series represents the family histories of people from across Canada's regions, and from a variety of cultural backgrounds, nevertheless it is this overriding image of "Man's" vertical relationship to the landscape as a symbol for the creation of a nation that has pertinence for a contextual understanding of land settlement issues.

The idealization of "Man" and agricultural production also often occurs within the prairie memoirs gathered for this study. In Marjorie Wilkins Campbell's *The Silent Song of Mary Eleanor* (1983), for example, the author describes her father as "a typically lone figure, the oxen's lines about his shoulders, his hands gripping the simple, single-share plough, [who] gloried in the prospect of mastering the virgin land" (28). In Campbell's suggestion of the "typically lone figure" of the prairie farmer, we see the simultaneous absence of any prior cultural presence, any dynamic form of the natural landscape (except as "virgin" in need of "mastering"), or any farm animals (except in the "lines about his shoulders"), a crucial part of the farm family's survival. This typical a"lone"ness is also evident in Sarah Ellen Roberts's *Of Us and the Oxen* (1968), in which the author describes her son, Lathrop, as saying that "when he first plows in the spring, he rests under a sort of illusion, for it seems that it is he and not the team ahead that is forcing the plowshares through the stubborn soil. The grasp of the plow seems to give him a sense of power" (99).

The inevitable result of such images is that, borrowing from Josephine Donovan's suggestion that "dominative modes pervade Western practice" ("Ecofeminist" 74), the mainstream narrative of western settlement privileges an agricultural discourse whereby such words as "cultivation," "domestication," and "improvement" refer to a geographic entity in which the naturally fertile landscape, different ways of being in that landscape, and non-human animals are absent. The "cultivated" landscape in Western Canada is a cultural construct, a human-made landscape, thereby eliding the natural state of the landscape that preceded the act of "domestication," the presence of other modes of relationship with the land, and the living beings whose bodies (alive and dead) sustained human efforts at "improving" that landscape. One of the engaging differences that I feel emerges from within the memoir texts included in this study is the representation – the re-visioning – of these absented realities of agriculture as viable and integral subjects of prairie life and experience. When I began reading these memoirs simultaneous with contemporary and historiographical constructions of prairie life, I could not help but notice that the authors tended to focus less on the specifics of, say, the number of acres ploughed, the kinds of crops harvested, the importance of fields laying fallow, the minutia of farm machinery, the cycle of weather patterns, the politics of tariffs, etc., than one who is familiar with the traditional settlement story might expect to find. Those kinds of concerns are there, certainly, in varying degrees, but there is comparatively more narrative space devoted to other, more personal, more tactile, subjects of the prairie story. In fact, I would suggest that, in the context of cultural constructions of the prairie settlement story, these memoirs extend the confrontational potential of the memoir genre by exhibiting an eco-consciousness that effectively re-visions the dominative and exploitive nature of large-scale agricultural practices.

It has been asserted that memoir writers encompass in their texts "a moral vision of the past" (Billson 261). Given that the writers examined here are providing us with the daily reality of lived experience of prairie settlement, the moral (and ecological) vision I see as an undercurrent at work in their narratives is a foregrounding of the immediate survival needs, both physical and psychological, of one's family unit as opposed to the profit-seeking imperative of large-scale agriculture. Given that most of the memoirs studied here were written long after World War II, when agriculture and its products had become politicized in the discourse of environmentalism, an eco-conscious reading of these texts seems particularly apt. Written both from within and, as I assert, over against agriculture and its images, however, it is important to remember that these memoirs exist as part of a heritage context in which Canada's agricultural past is lauded as the foundation of a nation, and to consider that such a context might well prevent an openly ecocritical purpose. Nevertheless, it is my desire as an eco-conscious reader to examine the tactics by which the authors of these prairie memoirs might implicitly confront agricultural narratives, thereby allowing other subjects of prairie life to erupt through a seemingly conventional surface.

In her "Introduction" to *The Ecocriticism Reader*, Cheryll Glotfelty states that "corresponding to the feminist interest in the lives of women authors, ecocritics have studied the environmental conditions of an author's life – the influence of place on the imagination – demonstrating that where an author grew up, traveled, and wrote is pertinent to an understanding of his or her work" (xxiii). Especially given that many of the memoirs studied here are written by women who spent their childhood years growing up on the prairies, Glotfelty's correspondence of "the environmental conditions of an author's life" to literary criticism provides me with a suitable starting point for consideration of these memoir narratives as eco-conscious texts. Although Glotfelty was referring specifically to the study of fiction and poetry, the prairie memoirs studied here also encompass the "fundamental premise that human culture is connected to the physical world, affecting it and affected by it" (xix), and so can reveal an alternative vision of that "interconnection" than traditional agricultural images of land settlement will allow. Interconnection is an integral part of memoir writing anyway. Going back to the suggestion from Chapter One that the memoir genre is a unique narrative choice for those authors who are less interested in an exclusive focus on the development of a unique selfhood (traditional autobiography) and more concerned with writing about a self in context, an essential component of memoir texts is that the author/narrator "always memorializes the other"; that is, "the narrator finds her own self-performance through the exploration of the biography of significant others who occupy the text as fully as she does" (Buss, *Repossessing* 37). What "significant others" are available to the memoir author when dealing with her experiences of life on an isolated, western Canadian, homestead in the late-nineteenth and early-twentieth centuries? Husbands, parents, grandparents, siblings, children, neighbours, certainly, but the texts gathered here suggest another "act of looking back" at selfhood in context. In most critical considerations of the "other," the "other" has always been the "same" on at least one level: that is, the "other" has always been human. However, for many settlers on the Canadian prairies, everyday life required a rather different, a rather more integrative, relationship with both the natural landscape and with non-human animals, as a means of physical and psychological survival. I would suggest that it is precisely by reading for the presence of these "other" relationships in memoir texts that we allow for the transformation of cultural images of western settlement.

The cultural image that I suggest has underscored mainstream representations of western settlement (the image of man's vertical relationship to the landscape as a symbol for the creation of a nation), as innocuous as it might seem on the surface, is a good example of what Riane Eisler calls "the *dominator* model" of social organization. In such a model, the main focus is on "*ranking*" as an organizing principle, whether of one gender over another, one culture over another, or even of humans over nature, and the privileging of such values as "aggression, dominance, and conquest" as a means to "maintain this system" ("The Dynamics" 161–62). The language used here by Eisler is certainly reminiscent of much of the language of agriculture that emerged as a product of the prairie settlement project. As noted in Chapter Two, prior to the mid-nineteenth century, the prairie region was considered to be nothing more than a veritable wasteland, an area "ill-suited for settlement and agriculture" (Owram, *Images* 1). From the 1850s/1860s, however, that negative assessment of the value of the region changed to the positive, and there was a corresponding transformation in cultural imagery that favoured the area as "an Agricultural and Commercial Hinterland" (74) that would help to achieve both national and imperial greatness. Speaking of "The Role of Illusion in North American Geography," J. Wreford Watson notes that "it is the mental picture a man has about a region that will qualify his use of it" and, further, that "actuality exists, of course, but people project what they hope can be done with it, thus seeing it as something different" (10).[1] The radically transformed "mental picture" of the prairie west had powerful implications; indeed, taking possession of that area would do no less than to rank Canada as a country, as well as British cultural norms, high in relation to other nations and cultures of the world. As enunciated in 1859 by Alexander Morris, taking control of the "new Eden" would help the new dominion to "advance steadily toward that high position among the nations which they may yet attain" (qtd. in Owram 90). And it was this desire for international advancement that would result in the language of domination becoming paramount in constructions of the prairie settlement project.

From the moment that western settlement was conceived as a dream of national/imperial expansion, the federal government undertook a deliberately engineered program of land use that marked the final phase in the "complex of challenge-conquest-domestication" (Osborne 6). "Domestication" is an exceptionally pleasant word (as are its agricultural synonyms, "cultivation," "colonization," and "improvement") that does much to obscure the cultural dedication to transform a land or region away from its natural state through use of force. All of these words imply inferiority, making something better/

---

1   Watson also makes the important point that "this often remains true even when the
     mental image is shown to be false, when it is in fact discovered to be an illusion"
     (10), which goes far to explain what I suggested in Chapter Two is a "next-year"
     dedication displayed by farm families that otherwise experience a dismal degree of
     economic failure at the project of homesteading.

more valuable, than it previously was; hence they again suggest a concern for ranking. As Stan Rowe asserts, "the land-use changes that began toward the end of the 19th century were no accident. They were the expression of European attitudes and perceptions of the prairies – occupied sparsely then by hunters-and-gatherers – as *nothing but* wilderness, waste, barren, desert and deserted until colonized and 'improved'" (13). The prairie region was rhetorically transformed from wilderness to hinterland, but it only ever held the *promise* of abundance – a promise that required intervention and control by human beings in order to reach its potential. One of the first tasks needed to be accomplished in order to make intervention and control possible was to impose a geometric system of land ownership upon a shapely world that often betrayed its reputation for extremes of expansive flatness.[2] Bringing to fruition agricultural dreams of economic prosperity necessitated the domination of nature's productions. In the land survey system adopted by the Canadian government as a means to prepare the vast untamed expanse for the advent of "civilization," we see a cultural narrative in which "the imposition of [a] mathematical model upon reality reflects a psychology of domination" that "requires that the anomalous other be forced into ordered forms" (Donovan, "Animal" 361–62, 367). On the one hand, the survey system used in Canada was a by-product of the need for the erection of empirical boundaries, as

---

2   The incongruity of the land survey system with the prairie land itself was poignantly articulated in Stan Rowe's 1987 essay "The First 100 Years: Land Use in the Prairies": "As we look out from the rectangular lots and fields that enclose us today in town and country – the legacy of the grid land surveys of the 1870s and 1880s – we find it difficult to imagine the curvilinear sights, sounds and smells of the primeval grasslands, now reduced to a few forlorn and untypical fragments" (13). Appreciation for the natural state of the prairie landscape can be seen in the memoirs gathered here. For example, in Clara Middleton's *Green Fields Afar: Memories of Alberta Days* (1947), the author makes the following note about the landscape just outside Carstairs, Alberta: "I noticed with delight that the prairie was not as dead-flat as in Saskatchewan or North Dakota" (4). Despite Middleton's assessment of Saskatchewan, however, Nell Wilson Parsons notes in *Upon a Sagebrush Harp* (1969) that in southern Saskatchewan "the land lay seemingly flat in all directions, save for the multiple, unseen folds of the coulees. Standing at any given flat point you could scarcely believe the coulees were there, unless you had seen them" (104). Similarly, in *Barefoot on the Prairie: Memories of Life on a Prairie Homestead* (1989), Ferne Nelson speaks of "the gentle curves of the prairie" in Alberta (42).

distinct from another nation: "The first essential was to give physical reality
to a boundary [Canada–U.S.] that so far had been drawn only by the pens
of cartographers" (Thompson, John Herd 45). On the other hand, that same
system was the condition necessary for control, or "settlement," of the natural landscape at the level of the individual farmer. In 1912, Emily Ferguson
recognized that the prairie landscape held "little practical value" before being
surveyed, and she highlighted the notion of cultural imposition when she
stated that "we may not write in the open volume of the land until the hardy
young men of the transit have ruled off the pages" (*Open* 52). The "open volume
of the land" merely awaited the "control" of individual farmers who would
"cultivate" at the micro-level the larger cultural desire for profit. Accordingly,
as indicated in Chapter One, for many settlers the important determination
of their arrival upon the Canadian prairies was either the recitation of one's
exact homestead location along the survey grid or the discovery of the survey
markers which set out the boundaries of the settler's land ownership, and
which in themselves symbolized the cultural and economic significance of
the settler's physical presence in that landscape.[3]

As suggested by Henry Kreisel, "to conquer a piece of the continent, to
put one's imprint upon virgin land, to say, 'Here I am, for that I came,' is as
much a way of defining oneself, of proving one's existence, as is Descartes'
Cogito, ergo sum" (48), thus establishing the importance of the land survey
system as a Cartesian, I-centric, plane. The individual, hence cultural, "imprint" was made first by placing those survey markers in the earth, then by
being present and beginning the process of "cultivation." The desire to "conquer," or to make an "imprint," is an ego-centred approach to the prairie

---

3   More than that, these markers suggest a "devotion to an unseen order which must
     be the object of faith rather than reason": referring to "a statue in the Alberta
     Provincial Museum" that depicts, "all in bronze," a "kneeling" man "holding the
     bridle of a horse which bears his wife and infant child," Dick Harrison asserts that
     "the grouping of man, woman, child, and patient beast suggests a nativity scene, but
     in this epiphany what the man kneels before with bared head is a squared mental
     [*sic*] survey stake with its cryptic notation of range, township, section, and quar-
     ter section" (79). For memoir examples illustrating the iconic status of the survey
     marker, see Campbell 23; Hiemstra 112–13; Holmes 74–75; McClung 48; Parsons
     5–6, 16; Roberts 17; Schultz 36.

landscape, which I believe is best figured by what Laurence Ricou identifies as Man's "dramatic vertical presence" in an otherwise "entirely horizontal world" (ix–xi). This presence gains expression in Wallace Stegner's oft-quoted prairie memoir *Wolf Willow* (1966), in which the author asserts that the landscape "is flat, empty, nearly abstract, and in its flatness you are a challenging upright thing" (8). The figure of the prairie farmer as "upright thing" is also commonly expressed in the works of the major western fiction writers, such as Robert J.C. Stead, Frederick Philip Grove, Martha Ostenso, Sinclair Ross, and W.O. Mitchell. In Martha Ostenso's *Wild Geese* (1925), for example, Caleb Gare is described as having "a towering appearance" (10), and his family farm becomes a psychological prison, a world of oppression, greed and violence, all stemming from the patriarch's desire to conquer and control everything and everyone around him. Caleb is often shown walking across "his" landscape, monitoring its productions: thus we see him standing upon "a ridge from which he could look east and west, north and south, upon the land that was his" and upon the land that he wished to have (17). He surveys his possessions, as his daughter Judith suggests, "to assure himself that his land [is] still there," that he still controls "the yield of the earth" and is thus "a successful owner and user of the soil" (89, 213). Similarly, in Frederick Philip Grove's *Fruits of the Earth* (1933), Abe Spalding is noted as being "extraordinarily tall, measuring six feet four" and "built in proportion to his height, broad-shouldered and deep-chested" (19). Most importantly, "temperamentally, [he] was impulsive, bearing down obstacles by sheer impetuosity" (19). The goal of Abe's homesteading project is made quite clear when we are told that "for a year he had mentally lived on that open, flat prairie, planning and adjusting himself. He needed room; he needed a country which would give scope to the powers he felt within him. Forbidding as it looked, this was that country" (22). Ultimately, we are told, "he would conquer this wilderness; he would change it; he would set his own seal upon it!"[4]

---

4   Judy Schultz represents this agricultural manifesto in *Mamie's Children: Three Generations of Prairie Women* (1997), wherein she states that "the frontier and everything on it had to be conquered. Sod had to be busted, horses had to be broken, dogs and women had to be tamed" (117).

Setting one's "own seal" ultimately meant the settler's commitment of his own piece of the geographic pie to the larger cultural project of "cultivation," or what Frieda Knobloch calls the "arts and sciences of improving nature" (75). It is:

> an act of transformation that takes "wild" territory – virgin land – and breaks it as one would break an animal or subjugate a slave, processes, incidentally, accompanying many agricultures sup- ported by states and empires. It is a process of domestication by which a plowman enforces his domination over cropland in such a way as to render the land permanently "improved."

As suggested here, "cultivation" often takes on an aggressive tone, thus sug- gesting a project of war-making, "an act of violence," as opposed to the more peaceful concept of land "settlement." In that cultivation project, the cultural/ personal agenda was clear: the prairie farmer "had to conquer.... And his weapon was the plough" (Kamen-Kaye 6).[5] Significantly, going back to Eisler's "*dominator* model" of social organization, she suggests that the overriding im- age for that model is the "blade," a symbol of "the ultimate power to establish

---

5   Despite the prominence of fictional representations of Man's dominating attitude towards the prairie landscape, some of these texts do contain alternative images of a human presence in the natural environment. For example, in *Wild Geese*, Ostenso presents a competing image when she depicts Judith Gare's psychological/physical escape from her father's self-engineered (farm) landscape to areas beyond Caleb's control – areas in which the "vertical man/horizontal world" image breaks down as we see the lone figure of Judith deliberately getting "horizontal" and embracing the earth for all it gives to her unforcedly. As Dick Harrison suggests, Judith's father "can be identified with the land only in the sense that 'land' is a human construct, property, a means to power" (111). Such a definition of "land" represents the dominant narrative of western settlement, in which "man's" chief motivation is to "capture the new space" by the processes of "surveying, fencing, building" (x) and the cultivation of cash crops. Meanwhile, says Harrison, the character of Judith Gare represents an alternative vision of the prairie landscape as "natural environ- ment" (110) – as beyond man's verbal or physical control – a vision all too often left unseen by settlers whose responses to that environment were "conditioned" to focus upon agricultural success. I would suggest that by reading prairie fiction for this alternative image of a human relationship with the landscape we can establish a necessary context for more eco-conscious readings of prairie memoirs.

and enforce domination" (*The Chalice* xvii).[6] This symbol thus connects to the technology of the plough as a central and romantic image in agriculture: as Knobloch notes,

> The plow is more than simply a piece a technology; it implies a system of domestication of animals and people, an emphasis on commodity rather than food production (and a division of labor by gender that removed women's expertise, though certainly not labor, from the field), an ideology of "improvement," a language of cultivation, culture, and work as opposed to wilderness, nature and idleness. An entire colonial technics is embodied in the plow. (Knobloch 49–50)

There are a number of rankings going on here, not the least of which is the ranking of "culture, and work" over "nature and idleness," which implies, amongst other things, that the environment is somehow static and thus justifiably prey to a plundering mentality. We can see this mentality at work in Nell Wilson Parsons's *Upon a Sagebrush Harp* (1969), in which the author quotes her father as saying, "We'll have that bumper crop one of these years! Why, one day all this land will be raising prime wheat, *not an idle acre anywhere.* Follow me, *and you'll wear diamonds yet!*" (134; emphasis added). The magnitude of Mr. Wilson's desire for a financial return on his cultural work is important to our understanding of the agricultural context of the memoirists gathered here, and of the more eco-conscious re-vision that I see happening in many of their texts.

It has been said that "one who looks on the world as simply a set of resources to be utilized is not thinking of it as an environment at all" (Evernden 99). This is certainly true in the transformation of the Canadian West from being feared as a wasteland to being subjected to "the concept of a vast agrarian empire, which emphasized the prosperity awaiting the farmer" (Owram, *Promise* 48). Moving quickly from one cultural construct to another, the natural

---

6   As seen in the title to her theorization of "Cultural Transformation," *The Chalice &
     the Blade: Our History, Our Future* (San Francisco: Harper & Row, 1987).

environment of the prairie region was effectively eradicated. The cultural focus of western settlement rested on "commodity rather than food production," as Knobloch notes, and the prairie farmer "was to be a man who bought and sold goods" (Owram, "The Promise" 24). Specifically, the focus was on the large-scale cultivation and production of a single crop, "King Wheat" (again we see a tendency to ranking as organizing principle in the adoption of that regal label), whether or not the soil conditions of the region were actually suited to that particular crop. As Owram explains, "from the time that the West had begun to be viewed as a potential agricultural region the greatest attention had been paid to the possibility of wheat cultivation. Its ability to produce wheat, more than any other single feature, would determine its worth to Canada" (112).[7] "King Wheat" and all that he represented, including personal land ownership, monetary success, a "new start" for the children of immigrants, etc., became the cultural icon that inspired millions of individuals to leave their homes with their families and emigrate to "the Promised Land." But this particular crop also had other implications, as "wheat, with beef, was the basic staple of the Anglo-Saxon and European world and as such had special qualities attributed to it": that is, besides being intended for the world's most highly "civilized" nations, wheat was also supposed to be productive of "the highest type of manhood" (Owram 112–13).

Despite the somewhat cozy ring to the word "domestication," then, western settlement had little to do with any personal or intimate kind of "interconnection" between humans and the land. On the contrary, the phrase "vast agrarian empire" suggests the large-scale and absolute domination of

---

7   As Ian MacPherson and John Herd Thompson note regarding this agricultural monopoly, "since the early years of the century, ideologists of mixed farming … had urged the western farmer to diversify into stock raising and end his precarious overdependence on wheat," but it was not until after World War II that "'King wheat' had been toppled as undisputed ruler of the western plains" (12, 15). See MacPherson and Thompson's "An Orderly Reconstruction: Prairie Agriculture in World War Two," in *Canadian Papers in Rural History*, ed. Donald H. Akenson, vol. IV (Gananoque, Ontario: Langdale Press, 1984), 11–32, for a discussion of the politics of agricultural diversification in the prairie west. For memoir examples of the power of wheat culture in the west, see Campbell 43; Hiemstra 180; and McClung 369.

nature and its productive capabilities. Inevitably, in order to create an empire big enough for the reign of King Wheat, in order to satisfy the desire to be "a lord of lands" (Ferguson, *Janey* 204), individual farmers were encouraged (and they desired) to turn more furrows, to get more acres under cultivation, even to purchase more land than the original "free" homestead quarter-section. The pursuit of "prosperity" at the individual level, a micro-version of the larger cultural imperative to create that "vast agrarian empire," was a rejection of any notion of self-sufficiency. From the beginning, prairie farming was conceived of as a business venture rather than a way of life, and the implications for the natural environment were clear: "The early insinuation into Prairie agriculture of the idea of farming as a *commercial enterprise*, as a business rather than as a provisioner of food for domestic consumption, lies at the root of the exploitive land uses that continue to plague the West today" (Rowe 14). Once again, we can see the accumulative approach to farming in contemporary prairie fiction. In Harold Bindloss's *Prescott of Saskatchewan* (1913), for example, the title hero/farmer enunciates the prevailing credo of land settlement as follows: "Here one goes on from task to task, each one bigger and more venturesome than the last; acre added to acre, a gasoline tractor to the horse-plow, another quarter-section broken. Mind and body taxed all day and often half the night. One can't sit down and mope" (33). Twenty years later, Grove's *Fruits* illustrated that the desire for dominance had not waned, for the main character of the novel, Abe Spalding, is "possessed by 'land hunger'" (17):

> He *must* have more land! He *must* get to a point where he farmed on a scale which would double his net income from a decreasing margin of profit. Nicoll's [his neighbour's] way was not his. He could not be satisfied with the fact that, if he killed a pig and a calf in the fall, there was meat in the house. To him, farming was an industry, not an occupation. (51)

When Abe's wife Ruth asks, "But why buy more and more machinery and land?," her sister-in-law Mary simply responds, "It's the way of the west" (53). In Abe's mind, the answer to that question is in the dream "of a mansion such as he had seen in Ontario, in the remnants of a colonial estate – a mansion dominating an extensive holding of land, imposed upon that holding as a sort of seigneurial sign-manual" (23). At about the same period, Ethel Chapman marked this frenzy about land ownership as an illness that sometimes threatened the farmer's completion of the other obligations of homesteading: regarding the hero of *The Homesteaders* (1936), Chapman wrote that "there was scarcely a day when [Peter Shoedecker's] axe could not be heard in the woods. Other work like building had to be done, but all the time an impatience to be at the business of making land possessed him – the 'clearing fever,' he called it" (191).[8]

Of course, it should be remembered that this seeming cultural mania for the establishment of a "vast agrarian empire" was inherently a future-oriented goal, and the reality for many settlers, as indeed for most of the memoirists studied here, was decidedly smaller in scale and focus. As Rodney C. Loehr suggests of the notion of "Self-Sufficiency on the Farm" in North America, it is "a nice dream of a golden age," and while it was "possible that on the frontier for the first year or two, when access to market was difficult and before the storekeeper made his appearance, living conditions approached self-sufficiency," nevertheless "when the storekeeper appeared and as transportation improved, self-sufficiency melted away" (41). But we are dealing with the power of rhetoric here, and how individual settlers both succumbed to and deferred from the stated cultural goals. In that regard, even without the inculcated quest for ever-increasing land-holdings, the original homesteading laws already represent the antithesis of self-sufficiency, as seen in the physical size of the homestead sites: "By orders-in-council in the spring of 1871, entries were to be accepted on 'homesteads' for 160 acres (a quarter-section) in exchange for a fee of ten dollars" (Friesen, *The Canadian* 183). The Canadian homestead system was based upon the American one (Spry 3), and as Knobloch says of the latter,

---

8   For memoir examples of this "land hunger," see Campbell 133; Ebbers 7–9; Hewson
     159; Hiemstra 180, 274; McClung 225; and Parsons 40–42.

[T]he size of the homestead indicates at least two things: the determination on the part of the federal government to recode a "wild" landscape as quickly as possible by creating vast domesticated fields and the commercial nature of western farming. When producing food, a household can live on the grains and food plants cultivated on about one to five acres, depending on the quality of the soil and the skill of the farmer....

The agriculture that came west with European settlement was ... a great devourer of farmland. Each 160-acre homestead on good land could have provided food for thirty households or more if every acre were under cultivation. If only a quarter of that acreage produced food, a homestead might still support eight households. Truly, the homestead plowman had become his own lord and tenant, the breadwinner, taking the produce of land that could otherwise have been divided exclusively for himself and his family. (54–55)

As Knobloch continues, "of course, any smaller scale of land division was unthinkable ... because it took 160 acres at least, and often more than that, to support only one family in a society and an agriculture based on the exchange of commodities for cash." The real importance of Knobloch's calculations is that they convey a sense of the mindset promoted by the homestead policy itself, one avidly adopted by so many immigrants to the west. We can see this "mindset" in Nellie L. McClung's *Clearing in the West: My Own Story* (1935), wherein the author notes that her brother Will's enthusiasm for the prospect of emigrating westward in the 1870s was based on comparisons with eastern farming standards: for example, he says, "Out West they do things in a big way.... Fifty acres is the size of a field not a farm" (31).

The dominative and exploitive obsession with establishing a "vast agrarian empire" and producing "commodities for cash" seems to preclude the existence in the prairie west of Riane Eisler's second model of social organization, the *"partnership* model," in which "social relations are primarily based on the principle of *linking* rather than ranking" and "difference is not necessarily equated with inferiority or superiority" (*The Chalice* xvii). In contrast to the dominator model, the values associated with the *"partnership* model" are "caring, compassion, empathy and non-violence" ("From Domination" 77). This second model, in addition to equalizing relationships between genders, cultures, and nations, would also inherently bring balance between humans and the natural environment. In fact, Eisler's focus on the concept of "linking" is reminiscent of the principal of "ecology,"[9] which is also about interconnection and balance as opposed to the hierarchical notions of domination and exploitation. We can see something similar happening in what Joseph W. Meeker refers to as a "climax community," or

> extremely diverse and complicated groupings of living things which exist in a relatively balanced state with one another and with their nonliving environment. A climax ecosystem is much more complicated than any human social organization, if only because it integrates the diverse needs and activities of a very large number of *different* species. (162)

In a phrasing that is eerily reflective of my discussion of land settlement in the Canadian West, Meeker goes on to assert that

> no human has ever known what it means to live in a climax ecosystem, at least not since the emergence of consciousness which has made us human. We have generally acted the role of the pioneer species, dedicating ourselves to survival through the destruction of all our competitors and to achieving effective dominance over other forms of life. Civilization, at least in the West, has developed as a tragedy does, through the actions of pioneering leaders who break new ground and surmount huge obstacles. (162–63)

While the ideology behind cultural narratives of western settlement promoted the *"dominator"* type of relationship with the prairie landscape, nevertheless it

---

9   The word "ecology" was "coined in 1866 by Ernst Haeckel" as "a descriptive study of relations between organisms and their environments" (O'Brien, Susie 26).

would be my suggestion that in the gap between ideology and actual attainment of the future-oriented goals of that ideology, the daily reality of survival for many settlers demanded a greater degree of eco-consciousness than the agricultural vision appeared to allow, and that an "other," more "partnership"-oriented consciousness is avidly represented in the memoirs gathered here. I am not speaking of some politically charged and explicitly environmental agenda to defer from mainstream cultural thinking. Rather, I am reading these memoirs for the ways in which the authors document a consciousness, an ongoing awareness, that there was another way of being in the prairie landscape; a different imperative for survival that focused on the immediate needs (physical and psychological) of the farm family unit, but that also respected other presences in the surrounding environment. I believe that this eco-conscious perspective is particularly prominent in the memoirs written by women as a result of their largely domestic role, one which necessitated (as already alluded to in Chapter Two) a "*subsistence perspective*," a "necessary precondition for survival" (Mies and Shiva 297–98), as opposed to a commercial perspective. The work that women performed outside the home so often had to do with survival, with the need "to provide staple foods apart from grains" (Knobloch 53), as a means of filling the considerable gap between the ideal and the real.

Women "engaged in home food production as a direct contribution to the uncertain family economy" (Armitage 468), and one of the most common outdoor activities for prairie women was maintenance of a family vegetable garden, from which the family unit (as opposed to the world's hungry masses) could be sustained throughout the year. A garden, then, acted as a small-scale literalization of one of the prevailing metaphors of the prairie west as a "Garden of Eden" or a "garden of abundance." Much attention has been paid by historiographers to the importance of vegetable gardens. For example, Frieda Knobloch suggests that "gardening in the West was never seen as more than a supplement to the income gained from the fields, even if it provided the means of subsistence for a family improving a homestead" (72). She then quantifies the subsistence potential of the family garden by saying that, "in the West, gardens produced between 50 and 70 percent of a farm family's food." As Mary Kinnear discovered in her study of women's "domestic economy," "rural women did have one advantage over town dwellers: their large vegetable gardens. Many could preserve a considerable amount of their food for their families. This would reduce their expenses, but added to their work load" (*A Female* 73). Contemporary writer Marion Dudley Cran provides an illustration of a prairie woman's concern for the productivity of the garden plot when she remarks on her experience of a

> kitchen garden, where we gather some squaw corn for breakfast, and I have time to admire the pitch of cultivation to which it has been brought, – onions, beets, celery, potatoes, carrots, cabbages, turnips, peas, beans, all growing luxuriously in the rich black loam. "I love the garden," she says; "I do most of it myself." (131)

The diversity and the subsistence potential of this garden seems especially confrontational with the more metaphorical goals of wheat growing, as seen in the borrowed agricultural language which suggests that this prairie woman has "brought" her garden plot to the "pitch of cultivation."

Given the reality of their primarily domestic responsibilities, it was often difficult for prairie women to find the time to explore the natural environment beyond the immediate boundaries of the homestead, so that a relationship with the physical landscape was often confined to vegetable and/or flower gardening. The obvious first question here is to what extent can the activity of gardening, in which the human participant first changes the nature of the land being used, then to a large extent controls what that land will produce, be considered as anything different from the agricultural pursuits of their husbands? As Leonore Davidoff et al. suggest, historically gardens have been a space "where nature could be enjoyed but was also tamed and controlled" (160). Similarly, as Andrea Pinto Lebowitz asserts about a specific genre of nature writing called "garden writing," "it can be quite diametrically opposed to nature writing in its attempt to control and transform wilderness into human landscape rather than to appreciate the natural world in and for itself" (5).[10] However, one obvious difference between the activity of gardening and

---

10   As Lebowitz continues, however, "yet the desire – and need – to garden is often
     part of a nature writer's life and the gardening events that happen spontaneously

large-scale agriculture is the size of the undertaking: that is, while the cultural project of prairie settlement sought to "transcend nature" (Mies and Shiva 8), to effectively obliterate any traces of "the non-humanized landscape" (Rowe 82), home gardens are decidedly small-scale and thus relatively non-interruptive to the continuing presence of that landscape. In addition, while the agricultural privileging of wheat farming reflects an exploitive motivation in the primary goal of "capital accumulation" (Mies and Shiva 2), vegetable gardening reflects "nature's subsistence potential" and a motivation that stays within the "realm of necessity" (Mies and Shiva 8). And that "necessity" could be physical (vegetable gardening) or spiritual (flower gardening). In contrast to the rhetorical reign of "King Wheat," the prairie memoirs make clear that subsistence gardening is about diversity and that prairie women often adapted their cultural expectations about what should be grown to the production capabilities of the prairie soil.

One of the things that needed to be learned in order to maximize the subsistence potential of a prairie garden was how the climate of any given part of the prairie region would affect different plants. In Donnie M. Ebbers's *Land across the Border* (1978), a memoir of homesteading life "in the Shellbrook area" (21) of Saskatchewan in the late-nineteenth/early-twentieth centuries, the author writes about her family's intimate awareness of seasonal growth patterns, both domestic and natural:

> Everything grew rapidly in the new, rich soil and the long summer days. Vegetables grew extra large and tender and flower gardens were beautiful from June to September. A profusion of wild flowers covered the country-side, from May to September. The crocus in early May, fragrant pink roses in June and July, the red tiger, or prairie lilies in August (now named Saskatchewan's Provincial flower) and the purple fire-weed and golden-rod and Indian Pinks in September. There was also white babybreath and daisies and

---

and with an unplanned felicity often bring garden writing into the sphere of nature writing" (5).

Brown-eyed Susans in summer and fall, and yellow buttercups in
the spring. (40–41)

The equation of "vegetables," "flower gardens" and "wild flowers" in this catalogue of "everything" that grows on the Saskatchewan prairies suggests a more
balanced perspective of the human presence on the landscape than does the
notion of a "vast agrarian empire." I would even suggest that by devoting more
narrative attention to natural productions than cultivated ones, Ebbers manages to reject the notion of the prairie landscape as "idle" and show it, rather, as
being "more than object; it is presence" (Mann 49–50). As Ebbers's narrative
continues, she illustrates that awareness of seasonal growth patterns translates
to knowledge about successful vegetable gardening:

> The ground which was frozen one to four feet deep all winter, was
> not warm enough to plant garden till the middle of May, even
> then a late spring frost might nip off the bean sprouts, requiring a
> second planting of bean seed. Tomato plants (grown from seed in
> boxes in the house during the winter) might freeze if planted out
> in the garden before the first of June, but by August the vines were
> covered with large green tomatoes. When the men came in from
> doing chores saying, "Afraid we are going to get a frost tonight!"
> the women would run to the garden and cover tomato plants with
> old sheets, thin blankets, etc. to keep them from freezing so they
> could keep on growing and hopefully some would ripen in the
> warm days to follow. They seldom ripened on the vines but had
> to be gathered green. Those not used for pickles and relish were
> individually wrapped in newspaper and put in a warm dry place.
> They ripened beautifully in a month or two.
>
> Because of the short summer season cucumbers, cantaloupe,
> pumpkin and watermelon were never grown; but the best beets,
> carrots, and potatoes in the world grow in Saskatchewan. The po-
> tatoes grew very large and yet were mealy and good flavored. (41)

Very often, the memoirs studied here represent women's gardening labours in narrative "juxtaposition" to the large-scale agricultural activities of the family farm. "Juxtaposition," or the "ironic arrangement" in written literature of, for example, "titles, epigraphs, the placements of stanzas, voices, or paragraphs," is often used by women writers as a "coding strategy," a means of "covert expression" of dissonance with the "dominant culture" (Radner and Lanser 13–14). We see this strategy at work in Jessie Browne Raber's *Pioneering in Alberta* (1951), a memoir of homesteading near Lacombe, Alberta, in the late-nineteenth/early-twentieth centuries. Raber's mother's gardening and preserving achievements often occupy more narrative space in juxtaposition with her father's less-than-successful farming activities. For example, Raber begins a paragraph speaking about the increase of her father's cultivated acreage, but very quickly and unexpectedly makes a narrative switch to a discussion of the "abundance" of her mother's and nature's gardens:

> More land was being cleared. Dad hired Nels Neirgaard, to cut brush and plow for him. We had a lovely garden of potatoes, cabbage, turnips, rutabagas, carrots, parsnips and radishes, which Mother planted along with the turnips. They couldn't be found so readily, so we children couldn't eat them all up. The lettuce did well. We grew turnips and rutabagas in big patches because the cows liked them in winter. We also picked whatever berries grew wild. Raspberries were the best and grew abundantly during some years. Wherever brush had been left, after being cut down and piled, there lovely raspberries would be growing the next summer. Saskatoons were easy to pick and Mother dried a lot of them for winter use. Blueberries were our favorites, we went many times after them. (125)

It is imperative here that we read Raber's unannounced narrative slip from agriculture to home gardening and berry-picking within the context of the rest of the memoir in which the author clearly shows displeasure at her father's seemingly endless quest for more and better land. Indeed, Raber's rather cursory mention of land clearing versus her concentration on her mother's subsistence practices suggests that narrative juxtaposition, or the relative amount of space devoted to these two acts, becomes a tool of confrontation with cultural expectations about appropriate subjects for the prairie memoir.

Both an intimate knowledge of the natural environment and an ability to provide subsistence for her family through her gardening labours are a part of Mamie Harris's experience of life in "the grasslands of southern Saskatchewan" (11), as seen in Judy Schultz's memoir *Mamie's Children: Three Generations of Prairie Women* (1997). For example, in a chapter titled "In Mamie's Gardens," the author works to establish both Mamie's, and hence her own, eco-conscious vision of the prairies:

> Mamie had two gardens, and she loved them equally. One was the grassland itself, the whole blooming prairie, rolling out its scented carpet of flowers and shrubs from early spring until fall, and in any year with enough rain it was, and still is, a wonderful sight to behold. The other was the spot she worked so hard to tame, her private garden where she planted carefully hoarded seeds, coaxing an abundance of food and flower from the reluctant earth. (82)

Despite the implied ownership of the natural prairie here, what I find delightful is the fact that the author indicates the equal valuation of the "grassland itself" and Mamie's "private garden," a balancing act that confronts cultural notions that rank non-humanized land as *less than* "improved" land. In fact, Schultz goes on to indicate how the produce of the grasslands was quite valuable to prairie health, especially dandelions, those culturally denigrated "weeds":

> Next would come the dandelion, despised by city folk, but one of Mamie's useful plants because of its bitter, vitamin-rich leaves, which nobody especially liked, but lots of people ate anyway, as they were such a tonic after a long winter. Cook them like beet greens, with a small onion, a discreet blob of bacon fat and a dribble of vinegar at the last minute; so says the Cash Book. (83)

Even in the previous description of Mamie's "private garden" we can see some confrontational tactics at work, specifically in some interesting juxtaposition of vocabulary. While it is clear that her grandmother cultivates, or "tames," the spot of earth that makes up her garden, nevertheless the use of the word "coaxes" rather than the cultural attitude of "conquering" suggests a different sort of human-landscape relationship, one that allows for her family's subsistence:

> Her big garden was more than a pleasure. It was essential to her main job: feeding her family year round. Setting a good table was only possible if she grew an abundant garden, and while the planting and growing seasons were busy, the harvesting was an even bigger job because everything had to be readied for storage. *Putting things up for winter*, she called it. *Putting things by.*
>
> Mamie grew every root vegetable that her well-thumbed seed catalogue offered. Uncle Ken remembers it as being from Stokes, or Burpees, but a woman in Rockglen thinks Mamie got her seeds from the Eaton's catalogue, like everybody else. She was right – among the pages of the Cash Book I find an Eaton's mail order form for farm and garden supplies. She grew cabbage and cauliflower and eventually kohlrabi my uncle thinks, but she never attempted a broccoli plant. Although there were green onions in spring and big paper-skinned granex for storage and even an experimental shallot given to her by a neighbor, she never attempted nor wanted garlic in her garden, associating it with the mysteriously aromatic cooking of the eastern Europeans she referred to as Galicians. Still, she learned to use it sparingly, one clove at a time, in her dill pickles.
>
> She did grow tomatoes, cucumbers and dillweed. In these ways she was a sensualist: the smell of the tomato plant when she pinched out the sucker leaves – that intensely green, faintly dusty and totally tomato smell – was one she loved and pointed out to me on hot July mornings in my mother's small vegetable patch, long after she had left her own massive garden behind. Sometimes

she'd pick dillweed and crush it between her fingers. "Sniff," she'd say, sticking a crumpled dill frond under my nose. "Good? That's why the pickles taste the way they do." (89–90)[11]

For Schultz, to explore her grandmother's gardens is to understand Mamie herself. For example, she writes of the "wild tiger lily," "an independent flower" that speaks to the emigrant woman's experience of place: "Mamie taught me not to pick them because the shock of being yanked from their chosen spot is too much to bear and they would wilt before we could get them home and into a fruit jar of water" (84). Speaking of her grandmother's "private garden," Schultz says, "like Mamie, this garden is a survivor" (85). Mamie's companionate relationship to both the natural landscape and her private garden has transformative power, for her physical aspect begins to mirror the natural elements:

> Her skin dried up in the heat, wrinkled early, turned leathery, the color of a walnut. The photo album shows Mamie at forty-two with white hair, weathered face, looking like she was sixty. The relentless sun and wind turned her hair brittle and dry as straw. Lips and fingers cracked, eyes were gritty and sore because the wind was her constant companion in those early years. (87)

In this description of Mamie Harris, we start our return to the beginning of this study, to the original impetus to my consideration of these women's memoirs, for in this description we see the image of a prairie woman who, like my own grandmother, presents a physical rejection, and hence transformation, of predominant cultural images, such as the unweathered purity of Caroline Ingalls.

While prairie farmers were out in the fields attempting to harvest "the [metaphoric] fruits of the earth" as "commodities for cash," prairie women

---

11   For more examples of the importance of the settler woman's garden to family subsistence, see also Baldwin 207; Campbell 101; Johannson 16–17, 119–21; Magill 11; Nash 245–47; Parsons 3; and Strange 224.

were often attending to the more immediate nutritional needs of their family by going beyond the boundaries of the family farm to partake of the naturally occurring fruits of the prairie landscape. Indeed, many of the memoirists in this study represent the activity of berry-picking as traditionally within the female domain and as far more memorable than agricultural pursuits in terms of culinary bounty. In *Barefoot on the Prairie: Memories of Life on a Prairie Homestead* (1989), a memoir of life in Alberta's grasslands in the second and third decades of the twentieth century, Ferne Nelson illustrates "A Berry Bonanza" that would offset a winter season in which nutritional variety decreased considerably; indeed, the joy of knowing that there would be colour added to the family table during the white and grey expanse of winter went a long way to make up for the sometimes frustrating conditions of the task of berry-picking. As Nelson writes,

> Some of the neighbours reported that the berry crop was very good this year, and when Mama heard that, she decided we would all go and stock up for the winter.
> Mama was an ardent berry-picker. My earliest memories contain glimpses of her surrounded by tall grass and mosquitoes, patiently filling a dishpan with the biggest, juiciest wild strawberries I have ever seen. Since the sort of weather that produces an excellent strawberry crop also produces a hearty insect population, the bites had to be endured. Nothing could keep our mother from the berry patch. She would build a smudge in an old pail and pick on. (64)

Later on in the same chapter, the author provides an alluringly abundant description of the products gained from this natural harvest:

> On the third day, it was time to start home. Every pot and pan was filled with berries, and yet all over the place, the bushes were loaded as though none had been picked.
> Mama was ecstatic. There were gallons of saskatoons, ripe brown gooseberries, pincherries, chokecherries, wild cranberries,

raspberries – full of delicious promise of jams and jellies, preserves,
and juicy pies. We had picked quarts and quarts of summer's
bounty, to be spooned from Mama's mason jars when the winter
winds blew and summer was only a memory.

...

Some busy days followed, with the preserving kettle bubbling
away on the hot stove and rows and rows of jelly jars shining like
clear red *jewels* as they cooled on the kitchen table. (66–67)

The Canadian West had been billed, amongst other things, as "The Promised
Land," but for many settlers the promise of a "vast agrarian empire" never
materialized. In Nelson's text we see the tactic of literalization used, for she
borrows the propagandist language of western settlement when she refers to
the berries as being "full of delicious promise," then moves towards fruition
of that promise when she ends this passage with the abundantly rewarding
valuation of "rows and rows of jelly jars shining like clear red *jewels*."

When reading Nelson's text, I cannot help but wonder whether Myrtle
Alexander's "ardency" about picking berries comes more from pride about her
contribution to the family's subsistence purse or in response to the release from
domestic routine. In Adeline (Nan) Clark's *Prairie Dreams* (1991), a memoir of
homesteading near Oxbow, Saskatchewan, in about the same time period as
Nelson's family was in Alberta, "Berry Picking," because it often necessitated
organized travel away from the homestead site, provided a rare occasion for
female companionship:

In the late summer, berries ripened in the ravines along the Souris
River. Then Mother joined the neighbours for a joyous excursion
to the treed valley.

Early morning sun greeted our expedition. Horses stepped
lively and wheels spun noisily along the deeply rutted prairie roads.
All of us exchanged places in each other's rigs, so that we could
visit together, happy with this break in daily routine and long
missed companionship.

The valley was at the bottom of a precariously steep hill, down which we walked the horses. The dramatic feat accomplished without spills or runaways, we clopped across the timbered wooden bridge above the Souris River. Not daring to stop, we glanced sideways at the river far below. An easy trail led to the ravines where saskatoon and chokecherry bushes crowded. In the Indian summer sunshine, clusters of berries hung, sweet smelling and richly purple. (76)

This movement of women away from the domestic space is interestingly labelled: it is an "excursion," which is "a short journey or ramble for pleasure" (*OEED*), thus making the task of berry-picking as much about self-gratification as domestic production, but it is also described as an "expedition," which is "a journey or voyage for a particular purpose, esp. exploration, scientific research, or war," which puts the significance of the undertaking the women are engaged in on a par with traditionally masculinist pursuits. This activity is a big deal, both personally and publicly. The non-agricultural landscape that the women move into, the "ravines," become a physical as well as a psychological space of liberation from prairie isolation, a space in which adult women and nature become one intermingled identity:

With jam pails tied around our waists, we excitedly started our task. Mother moved with business-like quickness from bush to bush, as she gathered the dark purple fruit, while we shouted, played, and sometimes picked berries. Periodically our mothers called out orders.

"Remember to keep the saskatoons and chokecherries separate."

Our mouths stained purple, we wandered idly from bush to bush, speculating on the contents of the picnic baskets everyone had brought.

But our mothers, like birds who had taken wing, revelled in the fall sunshine, the gossiping, the unaccustomed freedom from routine. Bright red-winged black birds gathered too, settling in long lines on the fences, twittering, calling, gorging on the juicy berries. Restless with migratory fever, they would soon leave us with only a few winter bird-friends. (76–77)

When representing the morning hours of berry-picking, Clark's language is filled with expectancy and excitement, such as "joyous," "lively," "revelled," "twittering"; however, we are told that as the day progresses and a return to normal routine is closer, the mood of the group changes considerably:

But after lunch, berry picking became more serious. Our mothers urged us on to the task of serious picking. The great milk pails must be filled before the afternoon was over.

Early shadows began to fall as we quietly hitched the horses and began the slow, steep climb back to the town and along the main street, homeward. As each buggy left the caravan, everyone waved good-bye.

Once at home, there would be eggs to gather, chickens and turkeys to feed. Mother would light the kitchen range in order to prepare tea. Ruth would plod through the maples, gathering the next days kindling. Mother would plan her preserves for the winter ahead. (77)[12]

As seen in Clark's text, berry-picking often necessitated women's physical transgression of the confines of the family farm in favour of rambling along the many prairie trails that existed, some of which still left their imprint upon the landscape from the days when Native, Métis and fur trade people led a migratory life, and some created by cattle and wagons. Although the (invisible) land survey system could not literally be escaped, nonetheless much of the prairie landscape remained without actual physical boundaries far into the twentieth century, so that women could, and did, find a certain measure of freedom from domestic routine in the simple act of taking a walk. In

---

12   For more examples of women's berry-picking, see also Baldwin 207; Holmes 153; Nash 244–45, 272–73; Schroeder 82–83; Strange 72–74; and Thomson 155.

particular, women found freedom by taking to the trails which criss-crossed the prairies and which unsettled – or denied physical reality to – the straight lines imposed by agriculture. As Bill Waiser asserts regarding the ego-centric approach that had been taken in surveying the prairie landscape, "the system, based on astronomical observation, completely ignored the natural contours of the land in favour of an artificial, standard checkerboard ordering" (156). Many contemporary writers mocked the straitjacket approach to the environment that the land survey system presented and also remarked upon the liberatory facility of a trail: for example, in 1915 Elizabeth Mitchell wrote that *In Western Canada* "a *Trail* is a natural track made by traffic, following the lie of the land and running where people wish to go. As the country is settled and enclosed, these are superseded by a gridiron of wide made *Roads*, running perfectly straight north and south and east and west" (16). Similarly, three years earlier, Emily Ferguson, in her aptly titled *Open Trails*, wrote, "every day I explore a new trail, for the country is seamed with them. In the North, they are vastly appreciative of the straight line ... but the blessed trails are an exception; they wander free as the air" (150). Some forty years later, Wallace Stegner, in his seminal work *Wolf Willow* (1955), would also assert his preference for prairie trails, and yet his tone is crucially different from that of Mitchell and Ferguson:

> And that was why I so loved the trails and paths we made. They were ceremonial, an insistence not only that we had a right to be in sight on the prairie but that we owned and controlled a piece of it. In a country practically without landmarks, as that part of Saskatchewan was, it might have been assumed that any road would comfort the soul. But I don't recall feeling anything special about the graded road that led us more than half of the way from town to homestead.... It was our own trail, lightly worn, its ruts a slightly fresher green where old cured grass had been rubbed away, that lifted my heart. It took off across the prairie like an extension of myself. (271)

In such words and phrases as "insistence," "we had a right," "owned and controlled" and "an extension of myself," we again see the "*dominator* mode" in
action. We see the cultural need to impose oneself on the landscape as a means
to confirm the identity of the conquering hero: says Stegner, "here is the pioneer root-cause of the American cult of Progress, the satisfaction that *Homo
fabricans* feels in altering to his own purposes the virgin earth" (272). Stegner's
reminiscence is perversely aggressive, as when he suggests that "wearing any
such path in the earth's rind is an intimate act, an act like love" (273). It is no
wonder that Stegner's text has become a popular and academic icon of prairie
reminiscences in North American culture for, as suggested by Glen A. Love,
"critical interpretation, taken as a whole, tends to regard ego-consciousness as
the supreme evidence of literary and critical achievement" (230). In contrast
with Stegner's I-scape vision, I would suggest that for many of the memoirists
included in this study, the paths and trails along which they wander represent
the development of an "eco-consciousness," an increasing groundedness in the
prairie landscape as "other" presence; they allow for a transformation of our
understanding of human survival on the prairies by revealing that "there's no
such thing as a self-enclosed, private piece of property, neither a deer nor a
person nor a text nor a piece of land" (Campbell, SueEllen 133).

Returning to Adeline Clark's *Prairie Dreams*, we see the author's alignment of the women's communal berry-picking expedition, an activity that
forms a crucial part in the subsistence economy of women's work, with the
brief "settling in" of the birds represented as "gorging in" on the natural fruits.
The birds are then overcome by a "migratory fever," one in which the women
themselves cannot participate, having instead to return to the isolation –
one might even say, "unnatural" isolation, given that the homestead system
is culturally designed – of living a settled and agricultural life. Subsistence
and migration, an "other" way of living within the prairie landscape, is thus
discernible when prairie women move beyond the homestead and head out
upon the prairie trails; when they leave what Edith Hewson in *We Swept the
Cornflakes Out the Door* (1980), a memoir of prairie life "on a Saskatchewan
farm during the first thirty years of the century" (n.p.), calls the "world of flat
dry fields" and enter the "magic land" accessible only by prairie trails (127).

For example, in Hewson's text an "expedition" to go berry-picking becomes a lesson, passed on from mother to daughter, in subsistence culture:

> Indian summer came and everything sang with colour. At night the moon, big as a ripe pumpkin, rose and hung cloudy red-orange on the dark horizon. In the morning, blue skeins of mist trailed across the hills and frost touched the woods with yellow fire. The sun in the afternoon was a dull copper from the forest fires which burned in the mountains to the west. Down in the valley a patch of chokecherries hung in great purple clusters, ready for picking. "I just love chokecherries. Do you think the Indians liked choke-cherries too, Mama?" Mary asked. She was helping get the children ready to go berry-picking.
>
> "Yes, it was important for their health. They killed the buffalo and then hung the meat to dry and when it was dried they pounded in the chokecherry juice like Dad puts salt on the winter meat. The berries gave the meat a good taste and kept them healthy in the winter." (66–67)

Beyond re-visioning the natural landscape in this scene, Hewson also manages to re-vision another way of life on the prairie landscape than the agricultural one. She starts this passage, ironically, by using an idiom ("Indian summer") that, similar to the western settlement project itself, effectively erases the real presence of First Nations people, but then by representing her mother's simple, non-romantic and non-judgmental awareness of "Indian" culture the author manages to repudiate the "*dominator* mode" of ranking, the tendency to assert superiority, by suggesting the similarities between that culture and her own. Further, in fact, I would suggest that by recuperating the "Indian" way of doing things as a "healthy" approach to life on the prairies, Hewson implicitly re-values the berry-picking activity about to be undertaken. And re-valuation is clearly needed for, as we are told later on in the berry-picking scene, denigration of the activity sometimes comes from an intimate source: the author notes the presence of her brother, Willie, in this instance, and shows him complaining, "I don't like chokecherries! This here's a girl's job. I just like horses!"

Like Hewson, many of the memoirists gathered here do make a genuine (if sometimes amorphous and sometimes naïve) attempt to pay tribute to the First Nations presence on the prairie landscape prior to the imposition of agriculture. In *Porridge and Old Clothes* (1982), a memoir of homesteading life in Manitoba in the late-nineteenth/early-twentieth centuries, Eileen M. Scott has a chapter titled "Red is Beautiful," for which she provides the following epigraph from a "Dakota Indian Prayer (author unknown)": "Grandfather, Great Spirit, fill us with the light. Teach us to walk the soft earth as relatives to all that live" (51). After this very deliberate invocation of an ecological principle oft-repeated in a variety of First Nations stories, Scott goes on to begin her chapter in the following openly confrontational way:

> I wonder what jackass, and I'm not referring to the four-legged variety, first claimed that the Indian people were savages? Frankly, I have never been able to understand how people can call themselves Christians and, at the same time, steal land from the Indian people, eliminate their source of food, and deny them their culture and religion. After all, they did believe in a spiritual god as we do. The only difference was that they called Him by another name. They believe in eternal life, as we do, the only difference being that they had a different name for Heaven. I seriously question who the real savages are.
>
> The Indian people claim that they will, eventually, have their land returned to them. I don't know why they would want it after the unholy mess the white man has made of it but, if that is what they want, I hope they get it. They are, apparently, able to laugh at the horrible situation in which they find themselves. It takes a nation of indomitable people to laugh at themselves in the face of adversity. Maybe it's the only thing that keeps them sane in the white man's idiotic world.
>
> No story of Manitoba, especially in the early days, would be complete without mention being made of the "red-man," an intelligent, sensitive people whom the white man wantonly murdered or starved out of existence if they dared to protest the rape of their

land. It was once a beautiful and fertile country. Now, through incorrect farming methods and the use of artificial fertilizers and pesticides, the white man has succeeded in reducing this land to a mere shadow of its former self. Prairie wheat now produces only sixty-six percent of its original nutrition. Some of the land could be reclaimed and brought back to its former fertility by the use of natural fertilizers, but a great deal of it is now beyond help. In the not too distant future, the prairies will be another Sahara Desert. (51)

Writing in 1982, there is an astute awareness (and acceptance) of native political agenda here, especially in the use of such keywords as "claim" and "nation," as well as in the assertion that "No story of Manitoba … would be complete" without restoration of First Nations people. If Cole Harris is correct in asserting of First Nations people that, in the context of westward expansion, "their erasure was textual" rather than actual (408), then their restoration, or re-vision, can be textual as well, as it often is in memoirs such as Scott's. The other striking element of the above passage is how Scott recuperates the idea of the natural environment as subject rather than object, as seen when she asserts that unconscionable farming practices have "reduce[ed] this land to a mere shadow of its former self." The author goes on to enunciate the subsistence relationship that "Indian people" had with the natural landscape, and as she does so her narrative eventually slips into illustrating how her own grandparents, Agnes (Agabella) Rutherford Thomson and Robert Thomson, were similarly inclined:

The Indian people must have eaten well before the arrival of the white man. To augment their diet of bison meat, they had prairie chickens, ducks, rabbits, fish, and countless other species. They also had hazel nuts, wild berries, pigweed, rose hips, et cetera. The fruit of the chokecherry was pounded into a mush before being added to bison meat to make pemmican. Pigweed was the first edible green to appear in the spring and the homesteaders gathered it for food until their gardens began to produce. Rose hips, high in vitamin

C and bioflavinoids, were also eaten. The children who went to the Tarbolton school in the early days picked hazel nuts on their way to school. Grandpa Thomson made wine from chokecherries, dandelions, and rhubarb. Grandma gathered wild strawberries, Saskatoon berries, pincherries, cranberries, and gooseberries. They had a wonderful taste that no cultivated berry could match, and they made excellent jellies, jams, pies, and some of them were good eaten raw. It was truly a land of milk and honey. (51–52)

The final line of this delectable treatise on the landscape's natural productions – "It was truly a land of milk and honey" – represents a narrative appropriation, and subversion, I would suggest, of a key phrase in settlement propaganda, one that was meant to entice prospective emigrants to Canada with images of the wealth and abundance that would (supposedly) be easily achieved through agricultural efforts to "improve" the natural landscape.

Writing *Barefoot on the Prairie* from the temporal distance of 1989, Ferne Nelson is obviously aware of current debates regarding land ownership and use, an awareness that allows her to revise western settlement myths which figured the prairies as an "open volume" (Ferguson, *Open Trails* 52) awaiting "civilization's" imprint. Indeed, she seems acutely aware that the prairies were anything but "open," which implies "empty," or as *tabula rasa*, as when she provides the following glimpse into the Alberta grasslands, which were

crisscrossed with buffalo trails, [which] stretched all around my parents' farm. Here and there bare bones of these magnificent animals bleached on the short, woolly prairie grass. The terrain was gently rolling, dotted with poplar bluffs, willow, and the occasional small, scrubby birch. There were frequent sloughs, some ringed with a white alkali deposit in dry weather. There were no roads, only trails, and very few fences. In travelling, one took the shortest route, hampered only by nature's boundaries. (1)

In Nelson's description we see the difference between a tourist and a resident of a landscape, for it is only the latter that "sees a landscape not only as a collection of physical forms, but as the evidence of what has occurred there" (Evernden 99). When she turns to representing the human presence on the prairie landscape prior to "contact," Nelson, wittingly or not, taps into some familiar stereotypes, including the image of the "Noble Savage" and the concept of the "Vanishing Indian."[13] Nevertheless, I find it difficult to condemn any of the writers examined here for using the only language they had available to them (in most cases, the language of popular culture as opposed to academia) in making an honest attempt to acknowledge their own/their family's/their culture's role in radically altering the lives of another group of people. However unpalatable the language might sometimes be, I have found nothing openly racist, and the very fact that these women made space in their narratives to acknowledge native presence, and even to acknowledge the politics of land ownership, seems worthy of recognition. Most often, the representation of native peoples is an attempt to critique the rhetoric that transformed the prairie landscape into a mythical rather than a real agricultural paradise. For example, Nelson writes the following about her father's participation in the land grab of the early twentieth century:

> My father had stood in line all night in Edmonton to file claim on this worthless homestead on the Alberta prairie. Its alkali soil begrudged every bit of nourishment it gave to the crops. They were planted so hopefully every spring and watched so optimistically through rain and sun, but were usually ruined by an early frost or a steady rain of hail that dashed my father's hopes for another year.

---

13   The concept of the "Noble Savage," which posited the belief that native people are less corrupt and more admirable than "civilized" people, has generally been attributed to eighteenth-century philosopher and novelist Jean-Jacques Rousseau. In Canada (although it also occurred in other colonial settings), the idea of the "Vanishing Indian" arose in the second half of the nineteenth century and was a widespread (and erroneous) belief that "the Natives were disappearing from the face of the earth, victims of disease, starvation, alcohol and the remorseless ebb and flow of civilizations" (Francis, Daniel 23). In short, it was an idea well suited to allow white people to ignore the presence of living native people, both those living on reserves and those who had adapted to Anglo culture.

Looking at the flattened fields, deep in ice pellets, he knew in his
heart that he would never make it on this poor farm. (42)

At the level of vocabulary choice, Nelson is providing us with a juxtaposition
here between the "hope" and "optimism" which, as I indicate in Chapters Two
and Three, was inculcated in settlers by the promotional materials for western
settlement, and the reality of prairie farming for so many settlers, as contained
in words such as "worthless," "begrudged," "ruined," "dashed" and "flattened."
Having given the lie to Anglo-centred constructs of the settlement project,
Nelson goes on to re-vision concepts of land ownership and appropriate usage:

> In those days, our part of the prairie still bore evidence of the noble
> tribes who had called that land home. Bare buffalo bones bleached
> beside the rutted trails, worn by the animals' hoofs as they sought
> the brown waters of the sloughs or the salt lick or the huge rock
> that was worn smooth as they rubbed off their heavy winter coats.
> This land had been Indian land, but we children were only faintly
> aware of it. In those days we were totally unconcerned that the
> rightful owners of this miserable terrain had been pushed back
> from their lands, lands so much better suited to their existence
> than the pitiful farming that Papa attempted. He had nothing else.
> Farther north, maybe thirty miles away, lived a few sad remnants
> of a band that had once chased the buffalo over the trails, picked
> the wild strawberries and saskatoons, killed the prairie chickens
> and rabbits. They had probably enjoyed a much better life than my
> poor parents, who struggled to somehow wrest a living from this
> unproductive tract. (43)

I think that all Nelson is guilty of here is overstatement – of the "much better
life" experienced by the "noble tribes" prior to white western settlement and
of her parents' victimization in comparison. But again I find myself wanting
to give her the benefit of the doubt; I want to recognize her confession of
childhood "unconcern" for the rights of native peoples and also her memoir attempt to redress that unconcern by providing "evidence," "faint" as it might be,

that First Nations people had existed, that they had done so differently, albeit legitimately, and that they had been dispossessed. When Nelson appears to devalue the prairie landscape itself, in phrases such as "this miserable terrain" and "this unproductive tract," I do not believe that she is actually adopting an agricultural vision that determines the value of the natural environment based on an ability to control its productions; rather, in the context of the rest of the passage, I read these phrases as an appropriation of such a vision as a means to criticize the western settlement project itself. She is reflecting her anger at the mythologizing and homogenizing of the prairie region that obscured differences in soil conditions, climate, etc., and that "lured" (Preface n.p.) people like her parents to take up the agricultural dream in an effort to "wrest a living."

For some of the memoirists, a movement into the natural environment did not reveal the presence of other people, but rather allowed for the development of an awareness of "what the prairie actually is" (Drake 127) and also sometimes of a strong consciousness of selfhood. Nature as presence, as vital subject as opposed to passive object, often becomes a vehicle of empowerment. In Marjorie Grace Johannson's memoir about prairie life near Elfros, Saskatchewan, in the second decade of the twentieth century, the author remembers evenings walking barefoot along the "little cow paths [that] criss-crossed the open land" (79). As she writes in *The Pink House on the Hill* (1986), she and her siblings "knew all these little paths and every foot of the area," and this familiarity allowed them to appreciate the natural rhythms of the prairie landscape:

> I liked running along these little trails. The evening was always so alive, frogs croaking as you passed the sloughs and swampy areas, prairie chicken and partridges scuttling away through the long grass and brush, ducks quacking on the sloughs as they dive for bugs and insects. Woodpeckers with their rhythmic tapping, an occasional hooting of an owl and a chorus of birds singing, whistling and chirping. A little squirrel flicking his bushy tail, twittering excitedly, dashes up a tree and a little grey rabbit scoots quietly across our trail into the bushes. (79–80)

What an exciting passage, with Johannson moving from animal to animal, from backdrop to foreground, building an exciting crescendo of vibrancy that brings the prairie landscape "alive" for the reader. In *Upon a Sagebrush Harp*, a memoir of homesteading life in southern Saskatchewan in the early-twentieth century, Nell Parsons juxtaposes the constraints of cultural authority versus the liberatory potential to be found in a relationship with the natural environment. Speaking of a time when the population was increasing and when the old "wagon trail" had become "a well-travelled road," Parsons notes the entrance in her community of certain institutional figureheads, including schoolteachers and a "scarlet-coated Mountie" (100). She also notes that

> Twice that summer an "itinerant preacher" stopped. Once he paused for the noon meal, stayed long enough to conduct a brief prayer meeting afterward.
>
> Kneeling beside my chair, at Mama's bidding, I felt stiff and strange. Bedside prayers were one thing, but this kind of public confession was quite another. I preferred running against the wind outside. Strong wind and noon were synonymous on the prairie. Often it was almost a physical effort to stand against the wind.

Parsons's brief but nonetheless compelling scene invites the reader to invert cultural assumptions that "nature is static and culture is dynamic" (Alaimo 4–5), for it is the preacher, the physical embodiment of religious culture and authority, whose presence threatens the young girl with stasis, with loss of personal identity ("bedside prayers") by submission to social convention ("public confession"), while it is the "strong wind," a vital and reliable physical element of the prairie landscape, which allows for self-definition in the act of "running against," even "stand[ing] against," the noon gale. In using the word "against" here, Parsons is not alluding to domination and control but rather is expressing a sense of invigoration, of life-giving, in the presence of this natural element, one which is so often stereotyped as the soul-draining symbol of prairie isolation and despair. As this scene from Parsons's text illustrates, "once we engage in the extension of the boundary of the self into the 'environment,' then of course we imbue it with life and can quite properly regard it as animate – it is animate because we are a part of it" (Evernden 101).

Jessie Raber, who often exhibits feelings of personal inadequacy in her memoir, also represents a childhood experience on the prairies that provides for a moment of self-definition, self-re(e)valuation: as she describes in *Pioneering in Alberta*,

> One day Sis and I were scrubbed and cleaned up to go over to the neighbors, the Zuelhke's, to get some eggs as our chickens were not laying. The place wasn't many miles away, but the timber was very thick with spruce and tamarack and willows. There were no roads, just cow trails. But we were old enough to go. We got there all right. Their place was a regular farm, everything very plentiful. It looked queer to us to see the mother and children, all barefoot, working in their garden, which was a wonderful one. They were very kind to us, gave us bread, butter and milk to eat and drink, then filled a bag with some vegetables for us to take home. They also sent an invitation to the family to come over and visit.
>
> The shadows were getting quite long, so Margaret and I thought we had better start for home. We started all right, but there were so many cow trails, and they all looked alike through the timber. So we kept on walking and walking.
>
> I knew we were not getting on in the right direction but didn't dare tell Sis. We were lost. Nothing to see but trees and cow trails. When happily we came to the big old muskeg. I knew it was the only one that size up around there. Now all we had to do was walk around the edge. Yes, but which edge? I thought, now which way is the sun. Oh, then I recognized an old tamarack tree, nearly by our path to the house. I gave a little sigh of relief, was I glad, but now we had all that brush to walk through. Sis was whimpering and saying, "I'll tell Mother when I get home, you took me through all these old sticks and brush." I thought, "All right, little Sis, but I'm not positive whether we'll ever get home or not. No telling what we have to go through." It was a long rough road around that

old muskeg but finally there was the path to our house. I was so
thankful, I nearly cried, but not in front of Margaret. I never will
forget that feeling of being uncertain of ever getting home. I didn't
tell any one for years. (69–70)

Initially in this scene, the natural environment is depicted as concealing; it
is threatening in its ability to appear as an alien environment. However, as
Raber soon realizes, she is "at home" in nature, for her knowledge of successive
landmarks – "the big old muskeg," "the sun," "an old tamarack tree," and "our
path to the house" – allows her to navigate safely the "long rough road" to
home. The experience is so unsettling that she kept it secret for years, but the
retrospective space of the prairie memoir empowers her to publicly represent
the experience of self-in-environment, to confess her empowered part in the
happy ending.[14]

   In delineating how the memoirists gathered here provide an alternative
"partnership" mode or "subsistence" perspective of human survival on the prairie landscape, some "other" subjects of western settlement keep appearing:
that is, intermingled in discussions of gardening, berry-picking and prairie
trails, mosquitoes, horses, birds, chickens, turkeys, frogs, partridges, squirrels, buffalo, ducks, rabbits, fish, and cows are an insistent presence. In fact,
I would suggest that the non-human animal presence within women's eco-
conscious texts allows for a particularly effective re-visioning of agricultural
myths and images. As suggested at the beginning of this chapter, the dominant image of prairie settlement seems to favour homogenous "Man's" vertical
relationship to the landscape, his role as sole protagonist in the fight to "settle"
the natural environment. The image is an heroic one, and in putting humans
at the apex of agricultural efforts, it effectively obscures the very real presence
of "other" participants in the project. In prairie memoirs, however, we begin
to find a narrative redress of that absence. In these texts, we are provided
with more individualized, more down-to-earth, portraits of the homogenized

---

14   For more examples of women's experiences of prairie trails of all types, see also
     Baldwin 142–44; Hewson 111; Hopkins 64–65; Johannson 41–42; and Thomson
     16, 125, 261.

heroes who have traditionally been the subjects of regional history and national heritage-seeking, and these portraits allow the authors to use "personal
history to inquire into mythic construction" (Buss, "Memoir" 23) in a variety
of ways. One way to provide such an "inquiry" is to "use" non-human animals
as "bellwethers for judging people's character" (Preece xxii), thereby allowing
for the possibility of confrontation with the supposed moral/cultural superiority of heroic figures. We see this, for example, in *Land across the Border*, when
Donnie Ebbers indicates the importance to women of being able to discern
male character in this way: as her father says to her regarding his approval
of her future husband, "that fellow of yours must be a good *farmer*. He sure
knows how to handle his horses. When his team were nearly stuck with that
load, he never used a whip. He just spoke quietly to urge them along and they
got right down and pulled that load out for him" (103). In 1915, Elizabeth
Mitchell asserted that *In Western Canada*, "it is noticeable how more than
merciful the prairie man generally is to his beasts.... I heard of one man with
a reputation for cruelty, and it stood as a mark against him for miles around"
(43). Without supporting Mitchell's general contention of "merciful" treatment by "prairie man," I do agree that in the memoirs gathered here violence
and aggression towards non-human beings is made a disreputable and public
matter, while caring and empathy become valued qualities that allow for the
re-visioning of animals as partners in the story of western settlement.

In childhood memoirs, fathers are often represented in terms of their
treatment of animals. True to her dedication of *Upon a Sagebrush Harp* to
"Papa," Nell Parsons often represents her father as heroic in his endeavours
to succeed at homesteading on the Canadian prairies, indicating through his
kindness towards animals that he possesses all the qualities desired in a settler,
including the ability to meet the needs of any situation, a courageous response
to danger, and innovativeness. On a family trip to the watering hole, for example, Mr. Wilson's commitment to the family horses is apparent:

We had reached the knoll where we had our picnic over a faint,
grassy track from the main trail. A shorter way back to the trail
led across one of the sun-baked mud flats, an expanse of bare earth
probably sixty feet wide.

When we were ready to leave, Kit and Major moved into their collars and stepped confidently out on the cracked surface of the flat. Papa looked backward a moment, checking to see that the barrels rode well, that each of us was on the wagon.

In that instant something went wrong. Kit and Major were lunging, terrified, fighting to pull their feet from slimy, sucking mud which lay beneath that deceptive surface. That sun-baked surface hid a sea of treacherous alkali slime. (47)

Although Major manages to get loose, Kit sinks and lays "still as death in the dangerous ooze" (48), so that Mr. Wilson is forced to chain her neck and hook her to Major to pull her free, a sickening sight for the young author:

Startled, blind Major leaped. The tugs jerked taut. Kit's thin neck stretched. I turned my back, but even when I did not look my stomach churned. Papa yelled again, a desperate yell that echoed from the coulee rim.

I turned to see Major straining, his belly almost flat to the ground. But Kit was not moving.

Papa dropped the reins, fighting to keep his feet from sinking too deeply, and stooped to put his arms under Kit as if he would lift her bodily. Perhaps his touch roused the worn nag to make a final effort. More likely it was his urgent voice as he coaxed, 'Come Kit, come on, old girl,' that spurred her to effort.

She lifted her head. Major's tugs tightened again. Papa gave a mighty heave. With him supporting her mud-covered frame, Kit fought to safety. (48)

The language used here is unequivocally not about domination and exploitation, and not about self-interest, as is sometimes seen when animal bodies are constructed as commodities to be lost and gained; rather, in words such as "desperate," "stooped," "urgent," "coaxed" and "supporting" we see emotional connection to the non-human animal who shares in prairie life. This connection is confirmed afterwards in conversation about the event:

"I don't know how you saved her, Amos," Mama said.

"Why, I had to save her." He looked at Mama in surprise. "I think I would have carried her out, if she hadn't made it."

I stood pressed against him, behind the seat, leaning against his shoulders, wanting to feel his power and his strength. (49)

Again, the "power" and "strength" here are not violence or aggression related; rather, they bespeak a moral capacity that encompasses caring for one of the most significant "others" in the western settlement story. And it is not only familiarity with Kit that allows for Mr. Wilson's kindness, either; indeed, when in a later scene the horse is gored by a cow who has escaped from another farm, the author's father does not react with revenge against the "other" animal, but instead shows consideration of a being in need: "He had milked the cow to relieve the strain on her overfull bag, and then he had turned her loose" (72) to find her way home.

Not all fathers are depicted as favourably as Parsons's, however, as seen in Judy Schultz's *Mamie's Children*. In 1996 the author made a visit to the home of her Aunt Violet and there she sees a photograph that sparks the following public confession:

Another photo: the old corral I remember from my childhood visits. The roundup, calves bawling, pink tongues lolling, big calf eyes rolled back in terror, the smell of burning hair and burning flesh, the almost bloodless castration that I wasn't supposed to see, my dad telling me the branding didn't hurt the calf, he was just bawling for his mother; wanting to believe my dad, knowing it was a lie. (124)

Again we have an author who uses juxtaposition to critical advantage, as the words "bawling," "lolling," "terror," and "burning," and the accompanying images to those words, together pull more narrative weight than her father's assertion that "branding didn't hurt the calf," and thereby cause not only the young author but also the reader to give the "lie" to this particular use/abuse of an animal body.

Georgina H. Thomson's *Crocus and Meadowlark Country: A Story of an Alberta Family* (1963), a memoir of homesteading near Nanton, Alberta, in the early decades of the twentieth century, also questions paternal authority about the subject of animals and their place on a family farm. After Thomson's brother Jim is sent away to medical school, her father takes on a series of hired men, whom the author recalls positively or negatively depending upon their treatment of animals: for example, as she says of Harry Wakeman, "we girls always remembered him for his kindness to the horses" (247). Harry is immediately contrasted with another hired man:

> Another man we had, Roy Butler, a cousin of John Wilson's, was quite rough with the horses and careless about their grooming. His interest lay with the cows, and of his own accord he got up early and did the milking. This was a break for us "women-folk," but we still didn't like his treatment of the horses. One night he rode Dixie to see some girl friend and rode him very hard. He was a heavy man and not a particularly good rider, and we hated to see our little saddle horse ridden so hard. Mother said something to him about it, which annoyed him, and he went into his room, packed his trunk and hauled it out to the road without accepting help. Father said he was a good worker and he hated to lose him, but he thought he must have wanted an excuse to quit and used Mother's few words of reproof as a pretext. (248–49)

Although Thomson certainly does not represent her father as unkind to the animals who work on his farm, nevertheless she uses this discussion of the hired men as a subtle means of paternal criticism; that is, while it is Mrs. Thomson who claims authority here on the issue of the use of animals' bodies and who responds to evidence of cruelty with verbal confrontation, her father's initial response to the situation is to show concern for the loss of a human labouring body as opposed to caring for a non-human one. Sometimes, in the farm economy, good work appears to have been privileged over the humane treatment of the very animals without whom that work could not be accomplished. Mrs. Thomson has previously been shown to side with the non-human animals in her family, as seen with the family's first horse team:

> Buck and Queen were not a very well matched team. Buck, or Billy Buckskin as we used to call him, was buckskin in colour, tall and rangy with a gentle head. When occasion demanded he could be taken out of harness and used as a saddle-horse, and had an easy, rocking gait. Queenie was a dark bay mare, shorter and heavier in build than Buck, with narrow suspicious eyes and a Roman nose. Both horses had reason to be disillusioned, as they had been overworked on a railway construction project before father bought them. Father was good to his horses, and while he got a good day's work out of them, he fed them well and was never rough with them. Jim was inclined to be impatient and when he held the lines, some current seemed to run along them to Queen, making her become difficult and sometimes even to balk. She had also a habit of jerking her head up when he went to put the bridle on her, and hitting him a crack with that hard Roman nose. This was probably due to some mistreatment by a previous owner, but it did not endear her to Jim. I remember one time when father was away and Jim was working the horses in the field. In the middle of the afternoon Queenie balked, and Jim got so angry he put some pieces of wire on the end of the whip to try to make her move. Mother went out to see what was the matter, and when she saw the wire on Jim's whip, she said, "Unhitch the team and put them in the stable." When mother spoke like this, no one questioned her authority. Jim's quick temper had already cooled anyway, and he felt a little sheepish, so he meekly did as he was told. In later years mother always said she was glad that by the time Jim became a doctor, automobiles had replaced the horse and buggy. (16–17)[15]

---

15   For more examples of this "bellwether" judgment of male character, see also Anderson 79–82; Clark 46–47; Inglis 46–51; Johannson 140–41, 175; McClung 112–13, 163; Roberts 191; Schroeder 32, 36–37, 53–54, 94–95; Schultz 48–49; and

As with Mrs. Thomson, many of the women memoirists studied here claim authority to speak on behalf of the labouring bodies of non-human animals by dedicating entire chapters to the representation of those beings who shared in the human struggle of western settlement. Indeed, in their considerable narrative attention to "other" animals, the authors indicate a desire to root the experience of western settlement in something other than agricultural success or failure; to value the production of human-animal relationships over and above "commodities for cash." An ongoing concern in the debate on representations of animals, however, is the human tendency to anthropomorphize them. The double-bind is clear: as Onno Oerlemans states, "not representing animals at all robs them of their subjectivity and the influence they actually have on our lives. At the other extreme, casting them as fully developed and seemingly human characters robs them of their difference from us and among one another" (181). One of the greatest difficulties for people interested in animal representation, then, is finding some middle ground; but unfortunately, in the fear of committing the latter sin, too many people end up "not representing animals at all." Most recently, however, the critical tide has begun to turn across the disciplinary spectrum and, as Oerlemans notes specifically regarding the world of science, it is now believed that "the interdiction against anthropomorphism is inherently speciesist, since it assumes that all qualities of mind we appear to perceive in animals are merely projections rather than similarities shared to differing degrees" (183). It is my belief that the memoirists studied here tend not to be naively or overly anthropomorphic; rather, they exhibit an honest desire to express a subject-subject paradigm of human-animal relationships. Sentimentality is normally eschewed in favour of respect.[16] As Heather Gilead states in *The Maple Leaf for Quite a While* (1967), a memoir of homesteading life near Red Deer, Alberta, in the second quarter of the twentieth century, "in my day we were far too dependent upon our animals to feel superior

---

Scott 14, 37.

16   Which is not to suggest that these women alternatively conform to a rationalist "bias" regarding the "ethic[s]" of animal treatment"; on the contrary, they often display a deep "sense of emotional bonding" (Donovan, "Animal" 351) with those non-human beings who become the subjects of the memorializing function of their texts.

to them or to sentimentalize them" (96). In some cases, the assumption of shared subjectivity occurs as a result of naming one's animal companions, of conferring upon them a marker of individuality; nevertheless, it is not always necessary for animals to be named in order to make their presence felt, to recognize their "qualities of mind," their capacity for individual character and their possession of a vibrant emotional life.

Barbara (Hunter) Anderson's *Two White Oxen: A Perspective of Early Saskatoon 1874–1905* (1972) is dominated by the presence of non-human animals of all kinds, but especially by the titular "two white oxen," who "were to be bought because they could live on the prairies and horse [*sic*] could not, so the circulars issued by the promoters of the Temperance Colonization Society said" (13). The two oxen chosen for the homesteading project are described simply at first as "a nice pair of cattle, well matched in color and disposition, 'for they were twins, identical twins.'" It soon becomes obvious to Thomson that the patient and hard-working animals, together with the family's "two cows," are "the nucleus of a living for ourselves" (34). The family project is temporarily decentred, however, when the two white oxen are "lost" in mysterious circumstances: "In the summer of 1886 Father was making another trip to Moose Jaw for supplies. He had our two white oxen, 'Brisk and Lively' and camped for the night about 30 miles north of Moose Jaw. When he wakened in the morning, the oxen were gone.... We never saw or heard of them again" (76). After this experience, Thomson enunciates the difference between viewing animals as interchangeable objects versus knowing them as individual characters in one's life:

The loss of our TWO WHITE OXEN "Brisk & Lively," as we always called them, was a much greater loss then we at first realized, as we had felt if they did not turn up again we could easily replace them. We never again were able to get oxen with the intelligence, endurance and good dispositions as "Brisk and Lively," our TWO WHITE OXEN, which on so many occasions had proved so reliable and trustworthy, and assisted us so greatly in establishing our new home in the Saskatchewan Valley. Although we never again heard of them, we often spoke of them in later years with fond memories and grateful hearts.

Sometimes animal images are used to confront ideals of technological "progress" in the search for agricultural success. For example, at about the same time period as Anderson's family in Saskatchewan were appreciating the help of two oxen in the establishment of a family farm, in Manitoba, Nellie L. McClung's family were anticipating "a great event," the arrival of a new binder (126). As the author remembers in a chapter of *Clearing in the West: My Own Story* (1935) titled "Men, and Machines," the new binder makes manifest "the excitement of the coming harvest" and brings "seeming security" to agricultural production on a vast scale; however, the "state of reverent expectation" is profaned slightly when one member of the horse team meant to pull the machine becomes ill, "so the first day of the cutting was robbed of part of its glory," and the binder itself begins to break down (126–28). As a result, the Mooneys find it necessary to rely upon their one remaining horse, Kate, who is forced by necessity to do double duty:

> Kate was hitched beside the oxen and although she gave every evidence of hating her work-mates, the binder was put into action; the wheels turned, the knives bit greedily into the yellow stalks, the canvas carried them aloft; they fell into the bundles and were tied by the binding twine and dropped on the stubble. Will drove the binder and the sheaves were set into stooks by Jack and Father. George was working for a neighbor.
>
> The first round was accomplished with difficulty for Kate could not accustom her pace to the slow steps of the oxen, and could not refrain from nipping them. But this was remedied by checking her head up, so she could not reach them. The second round was better, but the third round the knotter broke – a casting was faulty and snapped off – and each sheaf was thrown down loose, and a piece of idle twine with it....
>
> Father wanted to go on, he would bind the sheaves the old way, anything was better than to let the grain stand, for it was dead ripe and every minute was precious, but Will thought it would be

better to go to Millford and get a new knotter. The agent said there would be "parts" kept there and it would save time in the end.

In Millford, he found there were no knotters, so he had to push on to Brandon, thirty miles away, and could not get back until the next morning. So the first day was lost.

Kate made the trip to Brandon, gallant Kate, with her ears back and her head up. She was a quick traveller and evidently never tired. With a couple of hours rest, after coming back from Brandon she went on the binder again, leaning over to take a bite at the ox nearest to her, to let him know that, though she might be a little tired with the long hours, she still had her pride. I do not know how many times Kate was driven to Brandon through the night that harvest, but I do know that she showed no sign of weariness at any time. (128)

After documenting her obvious "reverence" for the non-human contribution of Kate in contrast with the new and "faulty" machine, it is no wonder that McClung chooses to end this chapter with narrative attention directed to this more than productive animal labourer: "Before I leave this part of my story, I want to pay my tribute to Kate, the horse who worked beside the two red oxen with such contempt for her humble helpers. Her bones lie deep in the soil of the farm she helped to make in the Souris valley, but her memory will endure as long as any of our family are in the land of remembering" (133). And, one might add, as long as there are sympathetic readers of McClung's text.

For Jessie Raber, whose frame of reference when *Pioneering in Alberta* is "Grandfather's [diversified] farm" back Home in England (43), the presence of animals rather than agricultural production becomes a measure of the growth of a "real" homestead. In preparation for emigration to Canada, we are told, the author's father "read every book he could get, pertaining to Canada. They all told of the beautiful country where the head of the home could take up a farm of one hundred and sixty acres, and raise cattle, horses and hogs, all sorts of grain and vegetables" (10). Keeping this idealistic image in mind, Raber periodically provides for her readers a tally of her own family's progress: for example, fairly early on in the homesteading project she tells us,

"Our farm" hadn't anything on it yet. But one day Dad and my
two oldest brothers went over to Mr. Zuelhke to see his farm. He
told them they could buy a few hens if they wished. They came
home to see what Mother thought, as we didn't have a henhouse.
Mother said he could buy three if he wished and we could manage
somehow. Early next morning the three of them went over to buy
the hens. We were pleased; now our farm would be starting. The
ones that stayed home kept a watch for Dad and the boys to be
coming home. Soon we saw three black specks away over by the
hills. Yes, the specks were moving so it must be Dad and the boys.
Soon we could tell it was them and they were carrying something.
Oh, now we would be farmers. We raced down the hill to the creek
where they would have to cross. (No bridge yet.) With grinning
faces, they said they had a surprise for us.

Up we ran to tell Mother – oh, oh, three hens and Mrs. Zuelhke
had given them a rooster. We were thrilled. When he was taken
out of the sack, the poor bewildered bird looked around, as much
as to say, "Some farm," but walked a little way from us, flapped
his wings, stretched his neck out and crowed. It certainly sounded
grand, our first rooster. The hens didn't seem very well pleased,
either. We fed them some scraps which they ate.

Daddy fixed a little lean-to for them to roost in. That night, all
was quiet until around daylight, when Mr. Rooster began to crow,
but it sounded grand. (36–37)

Despite the fact that western society exhibits a "culturally conditioned indifference toward, and prejudice against, creatures whose lives appear too slav-
ishly, too boringly, too stupidly female" (Davis, Karen 196), chickens being
one of the most despised groups of animals, prior to these animals' arrival
Raber can only conceive of the family homestead in theoretical terms – hence
the phrase "our farm" couched in quotation marks. Immediately upon their
arrival at the "farm," an event attended with great anticipation, the hens are
rather humourously acknowledged by Raber as being vital characters in the

family undertaking. Later on that same page, after noting that "Daddy went to town one day and brought home a little kitten," Raber considers the family's progress, saying, "so there we were with three hens, one rooster and one kitten. Gradually growing" (37). The tally continues apace, and she is eventually able to note that "we had two cows, one heifer, three horses, a pony and colt, also a few chickens and the cat. So 'our farm' was growing" (65). It is interesting to note Raber's continued use of quotation marks when speaking of "our farm," a usage that suggests deferral of official farm status until the requisite level of participant animals was reached.

Raber's assumption of the subjectivity of non-human animals is evident in an anecdote about one particular creature who does not belong to her own family circle. As seen in Chapter Two, one of the values most esteemed in prairie society is hospitality, "the friendly and generous reception and enter-tainment of guests or strangers" (*OEED*), which often manifests itself as a willingness to lend a hand in times of crisis. While respect for hospitable val-ues occurs on a daily basis, it becomes doubly important in the case of a prairie blizzard. One of the most unforgettable opening scenes in Canadian prairie fiction is to be found in Frederick Philip Grove's *Settlers of the Marsh* (1925), in which Lars Nelson and Niels Lindstedt are fighting their way through the Manitoba bush in a snowstorm and are turned away from the home of another settler, an inhospitable act that becomes an immediate gauge for the reader of that character's personality. In *Pioneering*, Raber provides a very similar scene, which, however, ends with a very different result:

One night was terribly stormy with snow and wind and cold. We finished the chores early and were playing games when suddenly we heard a scratching at the door. Dad said, "Quiet," quite sharply, so we knew something was wrong. There it was again, so he opened it a tiny bit. A big blast of cold air came in and he couldn't see a thing. He was just going to close the door, thinking it must be the wind, when down at his feet a large white thing crawled inside. We were all agape, it was so dark outside we couldn't distinguish whether it was a man on all fours, or a wild animal, as it was cov-ered with ice and snow. It could barely move. Dad took hold of it and found out it was a large collie dog, almost giving its last breath. The people east of us had two beautiful collies. Evidently this one had started to follow someone or started to our place in the storm. It was almost four miles from home. We rubbed and picked ice off him as fast as it melted a little. His feet were nearly frozen. Mother warmed a little milk as Dad said not to give him too much to start with. The poor thing was nearly gone. When he was stronger, he would roll his big, brown eyes at each of us, as much as to say how grateful he was.

He slept all night on some old blankets. We kept him until the storm was over. Then Mr. Perkins, the young man, came looking for him. When Dad told him how we had found him and taken the poor dog in, the tears ran down his face and he could hardly talk. He said he had expected to run across him out on the trail, frozen to death. Mr. Perkins said the poor dog must have seen our light or heard our laughing and followed the noise, as I don't think it could see at all, the way the ice covered its face. Many poor animals were caught the same way and never reached a home. (58–59)

In this scene, there is not even a moment of doubt as to helping "the poor thing," a homesteading neighbour of the four-legged kind, especially given an established prairie etiquette in which such a crisis demands attention (for the Rabers at least) whether it involves man or "beast." In her discussion of how human beings can "restore power to the animal victim" in western culture, Marian Scholtmeijer examines the work of Philip P. Hallie on *Cruelty*,[17] and especially his suggestion, as Scholtmeijer summarizes it, that "hospitality gives the necessary recognition of the victim's identity, and replaces the 'I-it' power relation with 'I-you' equality" (*Animal* 66). Hallie's proposal for human-animal relationships, says Scholtmeijer, is "a highly civilized one," which is "what makes it so difficult to apply to animals. By convention, social graces like hospitality have been developed in opposition to animality" (67).

---

17   See Philip P. Hallie, *Cruelty* (Middletown, CT: Wesleyan University Press, 1969; rpt. 1982).

More importantly, "hospitality coming from humankind to other species would likely imply to most people treating all animals as pets," which would be "its own kind of trespass against [them]." In Raber's scene, however, we are already looking at a "pet," a domesticated animal, so in extending hospitality to the collie dog the Raber family are not guilty of trespass. Rather, Raber's scene with the collie dog, in its direct invocation of a social convention created in response to the specific conditions of a specific environment – a convention that is then extended to an animal who is part of that environment, without question, and without any sign of the condescension assumed by some to be inherent to owner/pet relationships – puts Hallie's hospitable "I-you" theorization into practice.

There is one animal in particular whom I would suggest provides an especially effective narrative pivot upon which to mount an alternative representation of prairie life as being about more than agricultural success: the gopher, the supposed bane to every farmer's productive existence. For example, in a chapter of Ferne Nelson's *Barefoot on the Prairie* titled "Papa Vanquishes a Bogeyman," the author begins with the following seemingly complicit scene:

> We were out to poison gophers. After harrowing the north field, Papa had been very alarmed at the number of gophers running about and had decided to take some action to get rid of the little pests. So he had sent us out, on this breezy day, in an effort to cut down the population before the field was planted. Papa had furnished each of us with an old pail filled with a sloppy wet mash, which was laced with some sort of poison. Along with our bucket went a piece of shingle – Mama couldn't spare any old spoons – and all we had to do was put one scoop of the mixture in every gopher hole we could find.
>
> We hated the gophers because everyone told us we should. Papa said they were a nuisance. The government took an even stronger attitude and paid us – in cash – two cents apiece for gopher tails. We had to agree with wiser heads, but in our secret childish hearts, I think we really liked the lively little brown animals.

For one thing, gophers were always one of the first signs of spring, and we longed for spring after the long cruel winter. When the days grew warm and the crocuses bloomed on Tidy's Hill, they would appear, as sure as the early buttercups. All over the prairie, the cheeky little animals would stand erect at the entrance to their burrows, their shrill whistles piercing the air on all sides. They scurried back and forth, beady eyes bright and watchful, sometimes disappearing into the safety of their underground homes just a whisker ahead of Rover.

But the holes riddled the knolls and fields. Old Buck stepped in them frequently, causing my poor old roan to stumble. In the grain fields, the pesky little rodents did a lot of damage. So we pursued the gophers in a sort of love-hate relationship, drowning them out of their burrows and always eager to add to our frowsy collection of tails.

Papa said it was war, and we were to put out poison. So today, here we were in the north field with our deadly meal for the brown creatures that even now were running all over the place. (52–53)[18]

Nelson's delineation of the children's task, a sort of "love-hate relationship," remains nicely ambiguous as the author vacillates between calling the gophers "little pests," "lively little brown animals," "cheeky little animals," "pesky little

---

18   It is amazing to what extent the language here used by Nelson about gophers duplicates Western culture's obsession with "weeds": as Knobloch writes of the latter menace,

> Weeds become objectionable not because they are inherently ugly or useless, or because their growth is rapid and unchecked, but because they take territory and profit away from agriculture in some way. This may seem obvious – certainly every society must deal with weeds that interfere with food production – but the *form* of food production that developed in the West guaranteed a short list of useful plants and a growing list of weeds and determined how losses to weeds would be described and controlled. (114)

The connection between weeds and gophers can also be seen in one of the prairie memoirs: see Johannson 129–30.

rodents," and "brown creatures." She enunciates the ways that gophers pose a problem for agricultural interests, albeit fairly vaguely ("a lot of damage"), but she also questions cultural authority on the matter of gophers, as when she notes that "we hated the gophers because everyone told us we should," "everyone" being "Papa" and "the government." This cultural construction of the gopher as "bogeyman" to the land settlement project is encapsulated in Papa's hyperbolic declaration of "war" against them. Thus does the reflective adult-author use the innocence of childhood to oppose the official version of the gopher menace with a more harmonious view of the animals as being a vital part of the natural environment; as being harbingers of spring and living symbols of a new cycle of growth and sustenance on the prairies.[19]

Like Nelson, Georgina Thomson and her sister were supposed to attend to the unpleasant task of murdering gophers: as the author remembers in *Crocus and Meadowlark Country,*

> With the sprouting of our first crop Chaddy and I acquired a new job. The gophers much preferred the tender green shoots of grain to the tough prairie grass, and they soon began to make inroads on the crop. Instructions were published by the Agriculture Department at Regina on how to deal with them. Strychnine had to be mixed with soaked grain and a spoonful of this put at the mouth of each gopher hole. Chaddy and I had to go back and forth, systematically covering the ground, each of us with an old spoon and a lard pail of the dangerous mixture. We were told to put the stuff far down in the holes so none of our pets or stock or wild birds could get at it, and we certainly took no chance. Unfortunately a cat was likely to get a poisoned gopher, and then there was grief and tears. At first we had only one cat, Laddie, and he and Buckles would be closely guarded at poisoning time. This gopher poisoning was not

---

19 In *Upon a Sagebrush Harp*, Nell Parsons provides a similar springtime image of the prairie gopher, this time using language that reflects domestic homesteading life: as she describes, "gophers came out of their winter lairs to stand straight as *eight-inch wooden pegs* beside their holes whistling gaily at each other like neighbors exchanging happy greetings after a snowbound winter" (17–18).

a job Chaddy and I liked, but our opinion wasn't asked. At this time there were quite a few striped gophers left, though later they entirely disappeared, driven out, it was said, by their bigger grey cousins. One day after a poisoning job I sat down and wrote a story about one of these little striped gophers who ran away from home. I called it "Stripes the Prodigal" and told about all the adventures he had and how glad he was to get home again. This was the story I have already mentioned in a previous chapter, which I sent to the Prairie Chicken Club in the Winnipeg Telegram. (132–33)

Once again we see an author use the reflective space of the memoir text to juxtapose official opinion on the de-valuation of gophers' lives in the pursuit of agricultural success with her own sympathetic identification with these intriguing little characters, whom she feels are worthy of considerable narrative space. In the production and publication of Thomson's fictional story we see the young girl's rebellion against dominant discourse – a behavioural precursor, I would suggest, of the act of writing a memoir text of western settlement – through the construction of a narrative that values an"other" side of the gopher tale.[20]

Both Nelson's and Thomson's narrative appreciations of gophers bring to light another issue that receives notable attention in women's memoir texts: animalcide, the deliberate putting to death of an"other" living being, one of the more gruesome realities of human survival on the prairie landscape. The two forms of animalcide, the hunting of wild animals and the slaughter of domestic animals, were traditionally within the masculine domain, as John Mack Faragher suggests: "work which nonetheless played an important role in male thinking, was hunting. For the early pioneers game provided most of the protein in the family diet.... The hunting legacy had one practical consequence for male work loads: men had primary responsibility for slaughtering and

20 Sympathetic identification with non-human animals in women's memoir texts occurs so often that it is impossible to note every instance here, however the following examples are particularly interesting: Clark 22–25, 36–42, 50–51; Ebbers 73–74; Holmes 94; Johannson 140–50, 158; Keyes 12–14, 19–20; McClung *passim*; Nash 301–15; Schroeder 57; and Scott 50, 85, 88–90.

butchering large farm animals" (50). While I do believe that the memoirists considered here accept the necessity of animalcide as a part of the subsistence perspective of settlement life[21] – indeed, I do not intend to interrogate this acceptance by foisting an animal rights/vegetarian agenda upon their written reminiscences – nevertheless I do want to suggest that the considerable amount of textual space devoted to the re-presentation of the animal behind the act of killing provides modern-day readers with an opportunity to re-vision an agricultural myth that pervades much public knowledge, especially childhood knowledge, about farming life: specifically, the myth of Old MacDonald's Farm, which poses a static vision of rural life, devoid of any reality regarding one of the primary ways that animals contribute to human survival. As Carol J. Adams suggests, "Western culture" is characterized by "patriarchal texts of meat," in which the animal source from which meat derives is made absent through the use of "gastronomic language": "Animals in name and body are made absent *as animals* for meat to exist. Animals' lives precede and enable the existence of meat" (14, 40). The very term "meat" – like all other terms of concealment related to meat-eating, such as "pork chops, hamburger, sirloins, and so on" (67) – is a linguistic "mystification" that works to "rename dead [and previously whole] bodies before consumers participate in eating them," so that "we do not conjure dead, butchered animals" but, rather, focus upon "cuisine" (40). However, it is obvious from even a brief examination of women's prairie memoirs that settlement culture was very different from what is now an urban-centric world in which children's closest relationship to animals is with "frozen meat wrapped in plastic" (Sanders 193).[22] The authors of these texts undoubt-

---

21   For examples of how animalcide functions in the subsistence economy of the family farm, see Hooks 55; Hopkins 50; Inglis 3, 51, 76; Magill 15–16, 43–44; Moorhouse 33; Nash 32–33, 248–51; Parsons 64–65, 131–32; Schroeder 7; Scott 65; and Thomson 225–26.

22   As Upton Sinclair's groundbreaking 1906 novel *The Jungle* made clear, and as Adams re-asserts, "patriarchal culture surrounds actual butchering with silence. Geographically, slaughterhouses are cloistered. We do not see or hear what transpires there" (49). She goes on to suggest that "the institution of butchering is unique to human beings. All carnivorous animals kill and consume their prey themselves. They see and hear their victims before they eat them. There is no absent referent, only a dead one" (50).

edly accept the "expectation that people should eat animals and that meat is good for you" (Adams, Carol J. 14), but their fairly frequent representations of such activities as hunting, butchering, and slaughtering in the context of the family farm allow readers to "re-member" animal bodies and, hence, to "make animals present" (40) in the story of western settlement.

Hunting wild animals for food was a generally accepted practice on the prairies, and for the memoirists studied here it was clearly a matter of subsistence necessity. However, for Donnie Ebbers, the masculinist culture behind the act of hunting provides a narrative moment in which to privilege the animal as living being prior to the act of killing. As she remembers in *Land Across the Border*, hunting was a measure of manhood for her brothers, as evidenced in a scene in which her little brother Joe, jealous of his older brother's hunting skills, tries to measure up:

> Donnie had three experiences with wild animals which were still vivid pictures in her memory: One morning a big moose came close enough to the house to see him plainly. It was early autumn, and a light snow had fallen the night before, spreading a white blanket of sparkling diamonds on the hillside in the morning sunshine. Joe had gone to the wood-pile for an armful of wood for the kitchen stove. He came running back exclaiming, "Look out the North window! See that big moose! On the hill, across the valley, over there!" She, Gertie and Mama had run to the window.

In *The Maple Leaf*, Gilead illustrates the social change from present to absent referent when she contrasts her own childhood with that of the nieces and nephews she visits on a return trip to her mother's prairie home in the 1960s: as she states,

> I suppose that mine was almost the last generation, in our civilization at least, for whom the ancient symbiotic relationship of man with animal kept its meaning intact; the last generation for which, during childhood, the animals worked their immemorial magic of mediation between child and the earth. Henceforth, however, animals may be chemical processes producing protein, mere pets, performers of tricks, curios and exhibits, tourist attractions, or emblems of conspicuous consumption, but they cannot conceivably mediate between anything and anything. (95)

There, silhouetted against the sparkling white hillside, was the biggest animal they had ever seen, and his big flat forked horns were really frightening.

That morning Papa, Jackson, and Ottie had gone to haul hay. Ottie was the one who hunted (and got) the deer and moose. Joe had only hunted prairie-chickens, partridge, and rabbits with a twenty-two rifle. But Joe declared, "I'm going to try to get that moose, myself, with the big rifle."

He was only thirteen years old and not sturdy or large for his age, but he hurriedly loaded the heavy rifle and ran out with it, as Mama called a warning after him, "Don't get too close to that huge animal! If you should just wound him, he might charge at you. Be careful!"

Joe didn't have time to listen to warnings. He was gone! She, Gertie and Mama had kept anxious watch at the window as Joe ran quickly, but silently in his moccasin clad feet, towards the moose. The window framed a life-sized picture, still vividly etched on her memory, of that beautiful moose. He was as quiet as a statue, his big head with the huge horns, held high, standing majesticly [*sic*] there as if he knew he was king of the Canadian woods. (34)

Rather than go on immediately to describe the end result of Joe's exertions – a miserable failure, by the way, as the moose's own olfactory hunting skills, his ability to pay attention to "others" in his environment, helps him to effect an escape – Ebbers interrupts the hunting narrative of chase and conquest with the above "majestic" tableau, an ironic inversion of the prevalent belief in Anglo culture that "Meat is King" (Adams, Carol J. 32). In addition to this word image, Ebbers provides her reader with a picture of the whole animal, a "Canadian Moose," to offset the intentions of her brother. Later in her memoir, in a chapter titled "Butchering and Fall Work," Ebbers writes about subsistence necessity on a family farm and implicitly questions the notion of "meat" being "raised and butchered" – it is, after all, the animal who is raised and butchered – by providing a lengthy and painstakingly detailed description of the task of turning every last part of the dead animal into usable products for the consumption needs of a family:

> There were no butcher stores or even grocery stores near enough to buy meat, so the homesteaders raised and butchered their own meat.
>
> For the summer's supply of pork, a pig was usually butchered in the spring or early summer. Butchering was a day's job for men and women. It was a job Donnie hated, but it had to be done to have meat for the family, and hard-working men needed meat.
>
> The killing of the pig and cutting up of the meat all seemed so gruesome, and all the greasy smells in the kitchen when Mama was working with the lard, head-cheese, etc. made her feel ill.
>
> On butchering day, early in the morning the copper boiler was filled with well-water and put on the kitchen stove to heat. The big iron boiler was also filled with water and set on four smooth rocks over an outside fire. After the pig was killed, all this boiling water was poured into a big wooden barrel and the dead pig was plunged into the scalding water to loosen the bristles (hair) on its skin. Then the pig was laid on a make-shift table of boards outside, where Papa and the boys scraped all the bristles off with dull knives until the rind (skin) was white and clean. Then they cut off the head and hung the carcass up by the front feet and removed the heart, liver and intestines. Then Mama's disagreeable work began! (45)

The description of "Mama's disagreeable work" and all the products created from the body of one dead pig goes on for another page, but already we can see Ebbers re-presenting the animal behind the "meat," first by the seemingly simple suggestion that in order to obtain "the summer's supply of pork, a pig was usually butchered," then by making reference to the "dead pig," and also by using words denoting carcass details followed by live animal explanations in brackets (e.g., "bristles" followed by "hair," "rind" followed by "skin"). That the reader can infer some level of critique of "patriarchal texts of meat" is also evident in the paragraph that immediately follows this scene, wherein Ebbers juxtaposes the less gruesome harvest of garden produce:

> Autumn was also a busy time on Saskatchewan farms. As soon as threshing was over the vegetables had to be taken from the garden before a heavy frost, or the cold fall rains, or an early snow. A quiet team of horses was hitched to a walking plow and the long rows of potatoes were plowed out of the ground. Then everyone of the family who was able to carry a pail and stoop over, got busy picking up potatoes out of the loose dirt. In the new soil potatoes grew big and mealy, some were as wide as a man's hand and long enough to lay across a large dinner-plate. They kept well all winter in a big bin in the cellar under the house and were one of the main articles of food served daily all year. Mama cooked them many different ways for variety. Fried and eaten with cabbage cold-slaw and onions they were *as satisfying as a steak dinner*. Scalloped with milk and butter in casserole or boiled and mashed with cream and butter, or even baked in their jackets and served with butter or thick sour cream they were always good. She had disliked potato-digging time; picking them out of the dirt made her hands rough and chapped. But she had to admit no potatoes bought in a store ever had the good satisfying taste of those she had helped pick up in Saskatchewan. (46; emphasis added)

The farm animal is generally assumed to be available in one way or another to satisfy domestic consumption/production needs; however, in the context of the family farm, is there any truth to the assertion that the difference between a pet and a farm animal is that the latter "is dispatched and dismantled with as little feeling as that which attends a car to the scrap heap" (Scholtmeijer, *Animal* 81)? In *The Pink House on the Hill*, Marjorie Johannson writes fairly unemotionally about her father's hunting activities, but when it comes to the killing of farm animals she is willing to court family disapproval rather than participate:

The time I hated most of all was in the fall, when twenty or thirty roasters and turkeys had to be killed, plucked and dressed. Butchering time always made me ill and I could not touch meat for days. I didn't get much sympathy nor did they have time to think about my gentle and humane feelings, but were very cross with me because I was nowhere to be found when they needed some help. (115)

What Johannson indicates here – being unable to "touch meat for days" after becoming aware of the animals behind the food produced from their bodies – is not an unusual reaction for children who realize where meat comes from, and neither is the lack of sympathy for that reaction unusual, especially in a subsistence economy that requires a realistic focus on survival needs. In *Crocus and Meadowlark Country*, Georgina Thomson also appears to dispute the distinction between pets and farm animals:

Most of our meat was our home-cured pork which kept well. Once we began to raise pigs we always had plenty of this. They were butchered in the fall, and it was a sad day for Chaddy and me. We would go to the farthest corner of the house and plug our ears so we would not hear their despairing shrieks. Father would never stick a pig nor even kill a chicken. He always had a neighbor come to kill the pigs, and Mother used to wring the necks of chickens. She didn't like doing it any better than he did, but she was realistic and if we were going to eat, someone had to do the deed. She did it as she did many of the unpleasant things that had to be done. I can't remember Father doing anything he didn't want to do. (225)

There seems to be a bit of a split agenda here. On the one hand, Thomson notes the difficulty with which she, her sister, and her father endured the act of killing animals and she makes clear her belief in animal sentience when she uses the phrase "despairing shrieks." On the other hand, she is also using this moment to clarify the subsistence necessity of such an act ("if we were going to eat"), which allows her to represent her mother as the more "realistic" participant in prairie life. Thomson is not going to allow her reader to ignore the "unpleasant things" that happened in farm culture. While Thomson is open about the ugly realities of prairie life, she nevertheless does draw some clear emotional boundaries across the subject of meat-eating:

> But when one of the calves we had raised was slaughtered, it was different. When Father brought home a big roast from the carcase of "Ben Hur" it was too much for Chaddy and me. We would have felt like cannibals if we had eaten any. Probably farmers who do not name their animals, or otherwise show interest and affection, save themselves a lot of grief, for farming is a business, though a sad business at times. (226)

Thomson's invocation here of the image of "cannibalism," "the ultimate savage act" (Adams, Carol J. 31), is important because it implies something more than mere "interest and affection" in Ben Hur's existence; rather, it implies a recognition of independent subjecthood normally reserved for other humans. This assumption of animal subjectivity is what stimulates the sense of a personal boundary or taboo regarding meat-eating, and it is Thomson's evident "grief," her "activation of conscience," that helps the reader to re-member Ben Hur's presence in the "patriarchal texts of meat." But do animals first need to be named and individualized, be made subjects rather than objects, before they can be re-membered in this way? Is it unequivocally true that "farm animals are so profoundly entrenched in society as economic units that the attempt to find moral significance in their situation seems foolish" (Scholtmeijer, *Animals* 81)? Not for Nellie McClung, who, no stranger to making the personal political, includes in *Clearing in the West* the following (rather lengthy) lament for the fate of her family's pigs on a farm in Ontario: writing of "a mellow evening in early autumn," she notes,

> I was being taken down to the lower meadow by Lizzie, the good angel of my childhood, for this was the evening when the pigs were being killed, and my heart was ready to break. Not that I had a pet pig or cared about the pigs as individuals. I was a little afraid

of pigs, and thought they were greedy, ill-mannered brutes, but
even so, I felt they had a right to live, or at least to die without pain.
All day I knew what was coming! The pigs were being starved for
the killing, and they squealed in their pens and quarrelled among
themselves. The hole was dug for the barrel, which would be filled
with boiling water from the boiler set on stones with wood laid
under. The gruesome scaffold had been erected, and the whole
farmyard had been changed from a friendly playground, to a place
of evil.

We walked over the hill behind the house just as the sun was
dipping into the mist of evening, and a queer green light came into
the upper and eastern sky. Lizzie's hand was very comforting in
mine now that my world had gone wrong, and the sorrows of life
were overflowing. She told me she had a new pattern for a dress
for me, with a little scalloped collar, which would be edged with
turkey-red, and the tie-backs would have scalloped ends, and the
dress would have red pearl buttons, with one on each pocket.

We sat beside the little stream just before it lost itself in the
meadow, and she found stovepipe grass for me to piece together
into a chain.

She thought that by taking me over the hill the sounds would
not come through, but just as I had almost forgotten why we had
come, in my delight and surprise at the honey sandwiches which
she had produced from under her coat – the terrible cry came drill-
ing through the hill, and tore through us like a thousand poisoned
arrows. I knew then, that life was a place of horror, in spite of
flowers and trees, and streams, and I flung myself down on the
grass and cried my heart out in an agony of helplessness. I remember how she put her two kind hands over my ears, but that piercing
cry came in at every pore of my body.

Lizzie told me God made pigs for meat for people. They were of
no other use and if they were all let live there would be pigs everywhere, and how would I like that? But I asked her why they had
to suffer like this; why didn't God make them like trees or grain?

They didn't squeal when they were cut down. God could have done that, if He wanted to. He made everything. Lizzie admitted she did not know why there had to be such pain in the world; she said she often wondered, but it wasn't right to criticize God, His ways were always right. But I was rebellious. I didn't think much of the world, and I was through with being a Christian. (22–24)

For the reader concerned for animal rights, McClung's inclusion of this gut-wrenching episode in her memoir illustrates the political power of "describing exactly how an animal dies, kicking, screaming, and is fragmented" (Adams, Carol J. 51–52). However hard her sister tries to prevent young Nellie's awareness of the brutal nature of the slaughterhouse, for McClung this experience is a painfully transformative lesson in cultural realities: specifically, she learns about the non-recognition of the "rights" of "others," as well as the power of religion to justify human cruelty.[23]

In some cases, the memoir authors included in this study find power in self-identification with non-human animals, a suggestion that may seem to be contradicted by the historical truth that "the ideological justification for women's alleged inferiority has been made by appropriating them to animals" (Donovan and Adams 1). Without in any way desiring to contradict this awareness of the alignment of sexism and speciesism, I would still like to suggest, borrowing from Marian Scholtmeijer's readings of twentieth-century women's fiction, that non-human animals often provide a means of "defiance" for female authors; indeed, that these "other" figures provide "a double source of power: recognition of the degree to which women are victimized by andro-centric culture, and realization of solidarity in defiance of cultural author-ity" ("The Power" 232–33). I would suggest that prairie women's "defiance of cultural authority" is located in the politics of personal experience as repre-sented in their memoir texts and that, by simultaneously aligning themselves with the oppressed image of the domesticated farm animal and appropriat-ing the strengths of any given species, these women manage, however subtly,

---

23   For more examples of the absent (animal) referent made present, see Hewson 101–2; Hicks 17; Holmes 116–17; and Magill 15–16.

to contradict those cultural constructions of prairie settlement which deny the free range of women's sometimes less than positive experiences of prairie life. For example, fairly quickly upon her arrival on an Alberta homestead, Sarah Roberts begins to align herself with the family's team of oxen, Tom and Bruce, who, says the author of *Of Us and the Oxen*, "are faithful, patient, long-suffering animals" (11). This is possibly the best description we could be provided of Roberts herself in relation to the decision to homestead. She is certainly "faithful" to what she describes as her husband's air of "dauntless optimism" (37) about western Canada's prospects and his belief in the "glowing accounts" provided by others (2). Indeed, throughout the text, whenever the family faces some crisis of faith in the homesteading project, Roberts is there to ensure that "no one admit[s] discouragement" (124) and to reaffirm their unwritten agreement to maintain a deliberately optimistic spirit in the face of adversity. She is certainly also "patient," especially when work on the family home is repeatedly and (necessarily) delayed in favour of farming operations and she must endure living in a "style to which [she is] not accustomed" (7). As she writes,

> we lived in terrible confusion for five or six weeks, and until some of these things were done I couldn't bring order out of chaos, while the dust and dirt were simply terrible. I thought at times that I would just go crazy, but I've tried to be as patient as possible, for I knew that Papa and the boys were bringing things to pass as fast as they could. (52–53)

Finally, she is definitely "long-suffering" for, especially during the long winters, she finds herself "constantly confined" (65) within her modest house, very often alone as the men usually work together. In the extremity of her experience of isolation, Roberts searches for emotional support, and at one point she finds it in an appreciation of the presence of some non-human animals who provide a poetic image of something "other" than the circumstances in which she finds herself: as she remarks, "there were times when the loneliness was so oppressive that to see even a herd of cattle moving toward a little meadow

where the grass looked greener gave me a distinct sense of relief and companionship" (31).

Despite her surface appearance of "faithful, patient, long-suffering"
conformity to the settlement project, however, Roberts also provides herself
with a space for active rebellion. Going back to her characterization of the
oxen, Roberts tells us that although they "*seemed* very gentle and thoroughly
broken," "however, in certain circumstances, this *appearance* of gentleness was
deceptive" (9; emphasis added), and she goes on to tell the following story:

> The boys, Jack Gatliff, and Papa were standing near the oxen one
> day when Jack remarked that he had touched Tom in the ribs and
> Tom had kicked at him. Lathrop, strong in his faith in Tom said,
> "Aw, Tom won't kick," and accompanied the words by putting his
> toe up and touching Tom in the ribs. With a quickness almost
> unbelievable in a creature usually so slow, Tom brought his hoof
> forward and landed it with force on Lathrop's shin. (9)

If we accept the alignment of the author with the nature of the oxen, then
clearly Roberts is a more complicated person than her surface narrative suggests. Although she seems to characterize the family's move to Alberta as a
mutually desirable "adventure" (2), Roberts provides another animal image
that I would suggest encapsulates her true feelings about having to participate
in the undertaking. Juxtaposed with the image of the subtly rebellious oxen,
those figures of physical and psychological endurance, is another of the farm
animals:

> About this time, Papa bought a cow with a young calf. She was
> a good milk cow, but had one serious fault: she did not like to
> be milked and usually protested by kicking vigorously. However,
> Papa managed to milk her by tying a rope around her body in front
> of her udder and drawing it so tight that she was not able to use,
> with any ease, the muscles required for kicking. It was because of
> this amiable trait that she was promptly dubbed "Crabby," a name
> that she still bears even though she has, to a considerable degree,

reformed. However, she still resents having anyone milk her but Papa. (11)

Like Roberts, Crabby has an "unlovely disposition" in terms of total psychological commitment to the settlement project, yet even she is appreciated for her "perseverance and skill," and for being the "old standby" (143–44).

Beulah Baldwin, whose memoir *The Long Trail: The Story of a Pioneer Family* (1992) depicts her family's homesteading experience in the Peace River region in the second and third decades of the twentieth century, sometimes represents her mother's feelings about participating in her husband's "adventure" in northern Alberta through animal images. For example, when representing her family's preparation to leave their hotel business and home in Edmonton to seek their fortunes further north, Baldwin provides a comic deflection of the pain of departure onto the family dogs:

> "Look," said Sam, pointing to the window above. Brownie, my parents' beautiful red setter stood on her hind legs with such a mournful expression at being left behind, that tears were quickly forgotten as everyone burst into laughter. Dad had bought Brownie when she was only a few weeks old, hoping she would become a watchdog, but his real intention had been to take Mother's mind off her homesickness. Brownie was leaving with Sam the next day. Their other dog, Trixie, was also sad at being left behind. Trixie, a fox terrier so tiny that when Dad brought him home as a puppy he fit into the bib pocket of Dad's overalls, would not be joining them for several months. Sam helped Beulah out of the sleigh, saying, "Let's you and I go upstairs and cheer up the dogs." (4)

After Olive Freeland has made the trip north, and has even begun to feel a bit of the adventurous spirit possessed by her husband in spades, Baldwin provides another image of Brownie, this time parodying the stereotyped cultural image of the courageous settler woman arriving in the Promised Land: "An hour later they heard the jingle of harnesses and, looking back, saw Sam's rig approaching at a brisk pace. Mother and Dad laughed at Brownie proudly perched on the seat beside Sam, 'Looking,' according to Mother, 'for all the world like a princess being driven through the streets of her capital by her coachman'" (17). Baldwin's mother also experiences a psychological closeness with the family's other dog, Trixie: as the author explains,

> Sam had brought Trixie to Grouard on his last trip from Edmonton. "Never again," he told my parents. "That little dog thinks he's a Doberman. He stood his ground against an Indian's husky. The big brute lunged at him and would have torn him to pieces if the animal's chain had been a few inches longer." Glaring at Mother, Dad said, "I told you, Ollie; we should have left him with the Henderson's. Now, he could be killed by one of the big brutes that roams the streets." She refused to be intimidated. Her answer was, "And so could I be killed by one of the drunken brutes that roam the streets. Trixie helped me through my homesickness, Wilbur, and I won't abandon him now." (140)

Olive Freeland's alignment of herself and Trixie in terms of potential victimization, as well as her alignment of the "drunken brutes" and the "big brutes" "roaming the streets" of Grouard, calls into question her husband's essentially selfish decision to seek after adventure in the "wilds" of northern Alberta when he should have been, according to his promises at the beginning of the book, "settling" down to life with his wife and children. However, it is equally important to note that Baldwin's mother equates herself with the little dog who, despite her disadvantageous situation, possesses a fighting and courageous spirit that demands admiration. In the parallel movement from identification with Brownie's sadness at departure to her regal entrance at a northern stopping-house, from identification with Trixie's physical vulnerability to her psychological strength, we see Baldwin's use of human-animal relationships to represent the transformative potential of her mother's settlement experience.

Non-human animals were also a vital part of identity-making for prairie children who often had little access to playmates beyond their own family circle. In their study of written reminiscences of pioneer life in the United States and Canada, John W. Bennett and Seena B. Kohl assert that siblings were the primary playmates, which led to many nostalgic comments in the local history books about the closeness of family members. A more complex record is presented in the longer auto-biographies that contain descriptions of differences among siblings and among parents, leading toward a recognition that close inter-action among family members can both reinforce family ties and also exacerbate conflict. (101)

This is certainly the case in Georgina Thomson's *Crocus*, wherein the author uses animal images to delineate a sense of personal discontinuity with the family circle in general and an outright antagonistic relationship with her older brother in particular. It all begins with her family's acquisition of one of the most common – and certainly most crucial in terms of subsistence poten-tial – farm animals:

"There were two [cows] we liked," said Father, "but we couldn't decide which to take so we came home to ask the rest of you. One was a big roan muley, rather shaggy-looking but quiet, and the other was red and white."

"What's a roan and what's a muley?" Chaddy asked.

"A muley hasn't any horns," explained Jim rather importantly, "and a roan has a mixture of red and white hairs all over."

"Let's get the roan, Father," I said. "Plain red and white cows are so common."

The rest of the family agreed, so next day the two men made another trip to Nanton to fetch the cow. Late in the afternoon they came home again without her.

"The roan opened the gate of her pasture and is now wandering on the prairie," Father explained, "we should have been warned."

"So many trips for one old cow," grumbled Jim.

"Another day of canned milk," complained Chaddy.

But the day passed quickly as days did then, and toward even-ing the wagon drove into the yard with a big cow trailing behind, and a little roan calf, the image of his mother, in the back of the wagon.

"His name is Samson," said Jim, "because he's the strongest calf I ever saw. I've had a dickens of a time holding him in all the way from Nanton."

"What's the cow's name?" I asked.

"I guess we'll have to call her Roany," said Father.

"Oh not Roany!" I objected. "That's so obvious."

"I think it's quite good enough for her," sniffed Chaddy. She had been walking around our new possession taking a good look. "She's as ugly and stupid looking as can be."

"Well we might call her Roany for everyday," I compromised, "but her real name will be 'Annie Rooney.' If anyone asks, we'll tell them that." (27)

It is significant to the rest of her memoir that Thomson herself leads the decision-making process here and shows a special concern for the animal, who is named to give her an identity beyond the "obvious," and who immediately proves to have a less than complacent nature.

Thomson's relationship with the cow deepens when she and her sister Chaddy are given the task of taking Annie Rooney to the watering hole, where they promptly attempt to ride the animal, who is described as having an "ungainly figure," an activity that affords the author narrative space for self-reflection:

One day as we moved slowly along the trail in gloomy silence, we saw a small bunch of range cattle in a little hollow near the spring. "What would you do if they chased us?" Chaddy asked hopefully.

"I'd jump on Annie Rooney and ride away," I bragged.

This made her hoot with laughter, for I was short and fat, and to picture me climbing on the cow at all, and then ambling over the prairie on her back, needed quite a bit of imagination.

I was a bit nettled at being laughed at. "It isn't as if I couldn't do it," I said, and catching Roany by the shoulder, I tried to spring on, but couldn't make it. Chaddy stopped laughing and came to help me, but she was too small and slight to boost me up. Then we tried leading the cow to a buffalo wallow, and I would stand on the higher ground and jump, but in vain. At last, quite red in the face and annoyed by Chaddy's giggles, I caught hold of her.

"See if you can do it," I said and gave her a powerful hoist. She was quite active, and easily scrambled astride Roany's shoulders. I picked up the rope and away we went.

"It's grand up here," Chaddy called from her perch.

"You look like those people in India who ride elephants and have their pictures in the geography," I said, a bit enviously, as I plodded along on the ground. I felt that Chaddy always succeeded where I failed. She was slim and pretty with big blue eyes and white skin. I was fat and freckled, and red hair wasn't fashionable in those days. Everyone liked her better than they liked me, I thought morbidly. (33)[24]

The author's negative self-image is evident in the balancing of terms to describe herself and her sister, as we move from "short and fat" to "small and slight," from "easily scrambled" to "plodded," and from "slim and pretty" to "fat and freckled." Thomson's freckled features and red hair recuperate a sense of sisterhood, however, although with Annie Rooney rather than her human sister.

Both girl and cow certainly share the experience of being relative outsiders to the family unit, as evidenced, for example, in Thomson's recounting of her family's treatment of another animal she loved:

There was a happy reunion at Mrs. White's front door. Mine was marred by Jim's answer to my immediate inquiry if "Muff" had

---

24 Interestingly, despite the belief that our cultural obsession with weight is a product of contemporary society, more than one of the women memoirists in this study shows a concern with being fat: for example, Parsons says at one point, "I was, frankly, plump" (96) and Nelson admits to being called "Fatty" by another member of her family (51).

arrived. She had been my pet cat in Galt, a pretty tortoise-shell, but not popular with the rest of the family for a number of reasons. She liked to lie on the most comfortable chair and left her hairs there. She was always having kittens, on one of the beds if she could arrange it, and the kittens had to be given away or drowned. One of her favorite foods was a plain boiled potato which she did not leave on her dish but dragged on to the floor, leaving bits to be stepped on. She howled a lot, and over and above all this, was not completely housebroken, making the odd "mistake."

Once she was taken by father away out into the country and left at a farm. I was not told this and hunted the place for her. However, I need not have worried. Two nights later I heard her cry at my bedroom window and calling joyfully, "Muff's home," I let her in. Then my eldest sister, Winnie, bought poison for her, but just hadn't the heart to give it to her. At that time there were no veterinarians in our town such as now put animals "to sleep" swiftly and painlessly. (14–15)

Despite the attitude against Thomson's cat, the family decides to take the animal on their journey west, although, after having been "probably terrified by the noise and strangeness of her new surroundings," Muff escapes from the train car full of "'settlers' effects'" and leaves behind "her current family of kittens," who are then given "'to a kind-faced woman' in Gravenhurst" (15). Upon hearing the story from her brother Jim, Thomson expresses her discontinuity with the family's "happy reunion": "I turned my face to the wall and had a little weep, and for years was to be haunted by the idea of Muff, the pampered household pet, trying to survive in the wilds of Muskoka."

Thomson also shares another anecdote which makes clear her sense of incongruity with her family unit, an anecdote about having a family picture taken, an extraordinary "event" in those early days. She explains the fury of preparation on the farm:

Then the whole farm went into a state of action, for in those old-time photographs every person and every animal on the place had to be seen. We had to bring the cows in so that they would be in the picture. Winnie and Ethel, our two sisters back in Galt, Aunt Mary and all the other relatives there simply had to see what Annie Rooney looked like. Buck and Queen were turned loose inside the yard and given oats on the ground to keep them quiet. Jim saddled and mounted Dixie and posed in the foreground complete with sombrero and rope. The rest of the family grouped themselves in front of the house according to directions from the professor as he emerged from time to time from under the dark cloth of his camera on its tall tripod.

"My, but the folks will think Dod [the author] has certainly got fat when they see the picture," called Jim.

Being fat was a sore point with me and Jim knew it. I immediately flew into a temper.

"You eat so much you get thin carrying it around," I shouted back angrily, and then ran weeping into the house. Mother coaxed me out again but my red swollen eyes and rumpled hair didn't improve my looks. (66–67)

Up to this point in the text, Thomson's relationship with her brother Jim has been less than harmonious; indeed, when she says of her brother's effect upon one of the family horses that when "he held the lines, some current seemed to run along them to Queen, making her become difficult and sometimes even to balk," she is reflecting what happens in her own narrative at any point that she mentions her brother. It is interesting to note that with her "swollen eyes and rumpled hair" Thomson almost mirrors the "rough and shaggy" Annie Rooney, who becomes the subject of the author's further sense of isolation in terms of the finished portrait:

A few days later the professor brought over the finished photograph and we all gathered eagerly around to have a look at it.

There was the house looking plain and unadorned, the stable, and the other little building which was sure to appear in all the pictures we took. There was Buckles with his back to the camera,

Dixie with arched neck and Jim proudly in the saddle, while Bee reclined gracefully on the front doorstep. Father posed as the landed proprietor, with Mother nearby. Chaddy stood rather belligerently in the foreground, and while I looked as broad as I was long, no one would have noticed that my eyes were swollen.

The grind-stone and the wood-pile were near the house and the manure-pile near the stable, but suddenly I realized there was something missing.

"Annie Rooney isn't there! Oh the mean old professor to leave old Roany out!"

Sure enough, Buck and Queen were where they should be, Fanny Fern and Lassie were eating at the haystack. We could make out the pigs and the odd hen, but not a sign of Roany was to be seen. At the last moment she had taken it into her stubborn head to go behind the stack, so Winnie and Ethel would have to wait till they came west to see what she looked like after all. (67–68)

Thomson details the photograph of the family farm and its members so precisely that there is an overwhelming sense of artistic unity and coherence, an aesthetic nevertheless undermined for the reader who is aware of the earlier emotional state of the memoir's author.

Annie Rooney's "stubborn" nature becomes figured as a tendency towards rebellion against authority, as when she displays a penchant for escape from the confines of the family farm: speaking of the gate positioned "at the entrance to the barnyard" (125), Thomson notes:

It was a very annoying kind of gate to open or shut, especially if you were a girl and were short and had short arms. It was often stiff to manipulate and one's sleeve would catch on the barbed wire. But it was a point of honour and still is never to leave a man's gate open. Annie Rooney, unfortunately, soon became very adept at opening of this type of gate. She would work patiently at the top loop, which was of plain wire with no barbs, till she got it free, and the other cows came to know that she could do this and would line up

behind her at the gate waiting to be let through. Of course she was
much too sly to do it when we were around, but if the cows were
shut in the barnyard or pasture overnight, we would often find
them gone in the morning. It taxed all Jim's and Father's ingenuity to invent a fastener she could not open. One common device
instead of a loop was to have a sharpened stick on the end of a piece
of wire attached to the side post. This would be brought around
the top of the gate end and stuck into a small loop of wire, but it
was child's play for the old roan cow to open this. They eventually
figured out something that fooled her, but she was never really
resigned to defeat and kept on trying. (126)

In this context of animal-identification, then, it might not seem unimportant
to note that Thomson's "favorite Shakespeare plays" were "'The Taming of
the Shrew' and 'King Lear,' not exactly children's fare, but good stories" (53),
and both tales which feature daughters who are not exactly calmly obedient
to patriarchal authority. As Thomson's narrative moves forward in time, her
connection to the rebellious cow becomes further entrenched. For example,
one day Georgina goes Saskatoon-picking with her sisters and some neighbours and, although she is given charge of one of the younger boys present,
she nevertheless decides to go home early as she is suffering from headache
and heat exhaustion (151–52). When she arrives home, however, she finds
maternal sympathy for her condition to be less than forthcoming:

> The mile and a half seemed much longer than it did on the way
> down, and when at last I got home to the cool haven of our sitting-
> room, I found the minister (I forget which one) there.
>
> I went out to the kitchen to tell Mother my troubles but she was
> getting supper for the minister and had no time to listen.
>
> "I'm sorry your head's aching," she said "but we have no sugar
> for tea, and I wonder if you could go to Ellison's or Louis Roy's
> and borrow some."

Thomson does as she is told, but the situation gets worse while she's away from
the homestead and, once again, she positions herself as emotional outcast in
need of retreat from the family unit:

> Meantime Bee and Chaddy had arrived home in an indignant
> frame of mind, because not only had I deserted them, but in my
> haste I had left my saskatoons in the shade, so they had to carry
> them as well as their own. Actually Mrs. Lowther had given them
> a lift as far as Ellison's corner so they hadn't so far to carry them,
> but Mrs. Lowther was annoyed because I had cuffed Leslie and
> they had to bear the brunt of it.
>
> When I got back they couldn't say much because the minister
> was there but they gave me black looks. They had washed them-
> selves and put on clean dresses, while I looked and felt in disgrace
> with my rumpled dress and hot sweaty face. I wouldn't come in to
> supper but went off to the garden to eat green peas and indulge in
> bitter thoughts.
>
> "Even if I did leave them to carry the berries, they should
> have let me know where they were. It wasn't any fun looking after
> Leslie," I thought. I could hear the cheerful supper sounds of
> laughing voices and clinking dishes and felt very sorry for myself.
> (153)

Thomson's language here is precise – she speaks of cleanliness and dirtiness,
of disgrace, personal indulgence and non-charitable thoughts – and sharply
discontinuous with the presence of the minister within the family home.

After reading Thomson's evocation of the cozy domestic atmosphere in-
doors, the reader almost expects the young girl to feel chastened of her stub-
bornness and to make a move towards reunion with this scene of cultural
authority; however, the rebellious Thomson ultimately moves in a completely
different direction, towards the barnyard:

> Then weeping with frustration I went over to old Roany, set my
> stool down beside her, and burying my head against her shaggy

side, began to milk her rather roughly, but the big cow never stirred. After a time the soft churn-churn of the milk in the pail began to have a soothing effect on me. I wiped my tears and stopped scowling. Roany went on peacefully chewing her cud and gazing with dreamy eyes at the sunset above the Rockies.

"Roany doesn't care a bit if I'm freckled and fat and bad-tempered," I thought.

I began to feel rather ashamed and confessed as much to Roany there in the barnyard in the quiet of the twilight. Father came and carried my pail of frothing milk to the house. I told him I would take the cows down to the pasture. (154)

Thomson's barnyard "confession" effectively undermines cultural authority, as she herself humorously realizes when she returns from the pasture:

Buckles and I raced happily home and I ran into the house just as the minister was leaving.

"Good-bye Georgina," he said to me, shaking hands in a friendly way. He probably wondered at the improvement in my expression, and if he had known that a shaggy old cow had anything to do with it, he would have wondered more. (155)[25]

Most of the memoirs examined here document emigration to Canada, or movement from eastern Canada to the prairies, as a means to provide a more independent living than could be achieved "back home," economic security for children, and sometimes even health benefits; but these positives were gained, at least initially, at the expense of extended family and community. Sylvia Bannert's *Rut Hog or Die* (1974), however, tells the story of a lower-class family already experiencing dislocation and breakup after a father's death. Hers is a

---

25   Thomson's humorously irreverent tone regarding this figure of organized religion also occurs in her remark that "the Lintons [neighbours] had two cats, Quaker and Booker T. Washington who used to come to the [church] services and one Sunday Quaker came in and rubbed endearingly around the minister's legs, which added to Chaddy's and my interest in the service" (136).

family for whom the move to Canada from the United States in 1911 represents, in addition to supposed economic renewal, a chance to gather together the family unit. It is no wonder then that they easily fall prey to propaganda claims:

> They had got hold of some papers from Canada advertising for settlers. Homesteads of one hundred and sixty acres of land were going for ten dollars. There were special rates on the train and you could bring anything in the box car except gold. Aunt Bea and Uncle Frank were planning to move out there and they wanted Mama and O.W. to come also. Mama could get her own homestead and we could all be together again. Mama decided we would go, but said it would be a while before we could get enough money for the trip. By the end of their visit we had all made big plans for Canada. (19–20)

As Bannert suggests, "Canada was our hope for the future," "we would get rich [there] and then go back to Iowa" (22, 26). Nevertheless, the very title of Bannert's text provides us with a clue as to the results of that early optimism. This title is a fortunate misrepresentation of the well-known cultural phrase, "root hog or die," which appropriates the resourcefulness of the pig species and is generally interpreted as "the necessity of labour or exertion to maintain life or prosperity" (*OEED*). In addition, in the context of a prairie settlement text, the word "root" provides a sense of establishing one's roots, of achieving a stability and endurance of the family unit. If Bannert had chosen this "correct" phrasing, her text would be fronted by the optimistic "promised land" (24) image of prairie settlement. However, her slippage into the phrase "rut hog or die," and her decision to make it the title image of her text, conveys a less positive lived reality of prairie life. Indeed, the word "rut" itself is highly negative, as to be "in a rut" means to experience a "fixed (esp. tedious or dreary) pattern of behaviour that is difficult to change" (*OEED*), which certainly picks up on the reality of the farm animal's life. The Bannert family, like most immigrants to the Canadian west, discovered upon their arrival to the prairies that life was not going to be as easy as suggested in the settlement pamphlets. In fact, life continues in much the same "rut" for the Bannerts as it had in the United States, with all members of the family again finding it necessary to disperse and go out to various places to work – far from the expected ideal of the whole family gathered together and working towards the agricultural fruits of the homesteading project.[26]

Indeed, Bannert's story of her life on the Canadian prairies is the complete antithesis of most settlement memoirs, which usually begin with a nuclear family's decision to emigrate, the parting from friends and extended family, arrival in the new land, initial feelings of isolation and deprivation, with the gradual re-establishment of community and varying degrees of economic success. In contrast, Bannert's family experiences a far more chaotic version of the typical settlement pattern, for, at the time of her family's arrival in Canada, the author was only ten years old, her father was dead, and, despite the fact that an older brother and an uncle are both already established on homesteads, her mother and older sister had to go out to work in order to save the money required for the purchase of their own land and the building of a house. When the older women are gone, the young author is variously housed with her Uncle Frank or whatever other family needs cheap labour. While Bannert never openly criticizes the state of affairs in which she finds herself, nonetheless through all the episodes represented in the text (some of which are frankly abusive),[27] the author's title begins to take on another meaning as

---

26   That ideal image is provided by Bannert, briefly, in her presentation of a small family, significantly named "the Farmers," also originally from Iowa, who live next to her older brother's homestead (35).

27   For example, when staying one time at her Uncle Frank's place, a particularly hostile environment, Bannert indicates through animal images her depression over her family situation as well as a sense of familial neglect. On this occasion, Bannert has had to take some of her family's animals with her to her Uncle's farm, including a favourite horse named Sue: as Bannert unemotionally remembers, "Uncle Frank told me I had better go see how Sue had fared during the night. I went out and saw that she had 'fared' very badly. She was dead, in fact. She had twisted herself in her rope and committed suicide. Don't know as I blamed her much" (63). The probability of a horse committing suicide is slim; however Bannert's decision to read the event in this way has repercussions for our understanding of her own state of mind at the time. Indeed, she goes on to suggest her feeling of being merely an extra mouth to feed, an appendage to her family's settlement project, when she notes that her Uncle

the words "root" and "rut" slip into the word "runt," which the author repeatedly uses to describe both her position in the family unit and her seeming
physical unfitness for the hard work of prairie life. We are told that Bannert
was considered by her parents as the "runt" of the family litter (25, 29), which
immediately implies a certain neglect in how she is treated. Indeed, as her
father once explained to her, "a mama pig has twenty-one dinner baskets; the
last two are small ones and the runts feed on them" (29). By appropriating
this image of maternal lack, Bannert implicitly criticizes the lack of nurturance and support that she experiences in her own family. Here we see that it
is not so much the cultural ideology of prairie settlement itself with which the
author finds fault, but rather her own family's, and especially her mother's,
inability to materialize their expectations and achieve the desired ideal of the
nuclear family farm.

Once she is in Canada, Bannert continually notes people's reaction to
her as being "runty" for her age, which does not bode well for her success as
a "pioneer," given that, as she is told by a neighbour named Mr. Daniels, "it
was a hard country and you had to be strong to take it" (28). Before filing on
a homestead, the women have to find work to make money:

> Later, when Mrs. Daniels was talking to Mama, she said, "Your
> son must be a good boy. It will be hard for him to look after you
> and the girls, him being only eighteen."
> "Merlie and I will have to find work," Mama answered. "But
> what to do with Sylvia? She is so little, she can't do very much."
> (29)

The designation of "runt" is thus a condemnatory evaluation of the author's
worth, her market value in the settlement project, and this valuation is reflected in her physical weight. Indeed, while she is working for the Mac family
we find out that Bannert is incredibly small:

"said the chickens, the cats and I were only a bill of expense and that it was a good
thing old Sue had died. At least that saved the expense of feeding her."

The town was called Patterson and it had one general store and
post office. At the store [Mrs. Mac] bought candy for the children
and for me, too. She told the storekeeper all about me and my
family and how we were going to have our house built by fall.
"You must be about six years old," said the storekeeper.
"Oh, no! I will be eleven in August!"
"I'll bet you don't weigh forty pounds," he said.
He put me on the scales. I weighed only thirty-five pounds. (41)

It is thus significant that, not even one year later, after having proven her
emotional strength, she has almost doubled her weight:

One day Brother said he was going by the Davies and I could come
along. They took one look at me and said, "My, you have grown!
Let's see how much you weigh."
They put me on the scale. What a surprise! I now weighed
sixty-five pounds. "Well," they said, "the little Yank will soon be
a big Yank." (53)

This dramatic change in Bannert's weight documents a change in her status
within the family unit as she appropriates the feisty fighter status of the "runty"
underdog and begins to take action against her oppressive circumstances.
Although Bannert appears on the surface to be fairly philosophical about the
failure of her widowed mother's dream to keep her family together and provide
a stable home by emigrating to a homestead in Canada, nevertheless there are
moments when Mrs. Cooper is clearly held accountable by the reminiscent
author for not taking charge. Almost as soon as they arrive in Canada, the
Cooper family begins to disperse in search of work. Sylvia's older brother,
who has filed for his own homestead, initially stays on his mother's land in
order to build a home for the family, and the young author, who has been living at an Uncle's home temporarily, eventually goes to help him in that task.
Indeed, she becomes instrumental, despite her small size, in completing the
family dwelling, although anticipation of the moment of reunion is effectively
quashed for the young author:

When I finally cleaned up the floor, the place had begun to look like a home.

The next day dawned cold and snowy. It was November eleventh, nineteen hundred and eleven, and we were to be united at last in our new home. We were expecting Mother and Merlie and they arrived about noon. I was so proud of our little home, but Mother took one look and said, "How will we live in this little place?"

However, she unlocked the trunks, got out the bedding, and she and Merlie made up the beds. After we had eaten supper, Mother and Merlie went to bed and bawled like babies.

"Oh, this awful country!" Mother wailed. "Our money nearly gone and no coal or wood!"

After all the work Brother had done to get the place ready, he felt really bad about their reaction, but he never let on. (52–53)

Bannert's decision to describe the elder women of her family as "bawling like babies" clearly indicates her sense of their (and especially her mother's) abdication of domestic responsibilities, but it is interesting to note her deflection of disappointment upon the figure of her brother who, like herself, worked very hard and "felt really bad about their [ungrateful] reaction."

After this inauspicious beginning, Bannert is forced to go out to work to contribute to the family purse (57, 59–60), as is her mother, a situation that indicates there is no real home for the young girl to return to, so that she ends up moving to her uncle's place, then a neighbour's place, then eventually home again with her mother. Years of unsettlement now ensue for the Cooper family, until finally Sylvia attains a permanent home through marriage to a young farmer, Frank Bannert. Despite her mother's reluctance to let her daughter marry at the age of sixteen, as Sylvia's older brother (and the authority figure of the family) assures Mrs. Cooper, "I know Frank. He is a good man. Sylvia will be better off looking after her own home than working for all kinds of people" (110). By taking over the maternal role of provider, both before and after her marriage, she breaks free from the family "rut" and "roots"

out an existence for everyone, thus defying her "runty" position. In fact, it
is after her first act of independence helping her brother to build the family
home that Bannert experiences personal growth, both physical and emotional.
She effectively summarizes her own story by representing an experience with
another of her mother's employers:

> Before she left the farm, I went out in the pasture and found a
> heifer with a calf that was so little it would not suck the mother.
> I picked it up and carried it home over my shoulder. The mother
> followed me. I put the calf in the barn and the mother went in, too.
> Just then Mr. Sandy came along and saw it. "What a little calf!" he
> said. It's no bigger than a jack rabbit. I might just as well knock it
> in the head. It will never survive."
>
> "Oh, no, Mr. Sandy! It's a girl calf. Can't I milk the cow and
> feed it?"
>
> He told me to go ahead, so I got a little bowl, milked the cow
> into it and the little calf drank the milk. By the next day, I had that
> calf feeding from its mother.
>
> "Well, you saved the calf's life," said Mr. Sandy as he turned
> the cow and calf out to pasture. "I never thought that calf would
> make it."
>
> "He wouldn't have, if it hadn't been for that girl," his mother
> said. (61)

Bannert's immediate personal identification with the abandoned and frail calf
reinforces the ambiguity of her memoir's title, and the anecdote assures the
reader that the calf, like the author herself, survives against all the odds of human devaluation and transforms to become a productive part of prairie life.[28]
    For Bannert and many other of the memoirists whose texts are the sub-
ject of this study, agricultural myths failed to live up to settlers' dreams, thus

---

28   For more examples of self-identification with non-human animals, see also Hiemstra
      63–64, 79–81, 96, 102, 138, 194–95; Keyes 7–14; Moorhouse 7; Parsons 70, 79, 87;
      Raber 63–64, 71–76, 92–94, 107; Schultz 117; and Strange 186–205.

making it inevitable that a narrative consideration of self in environmental context would find expression in some things "other" than a "vast agrarian empire." For many settlers, prairie life necessitated a rejection of notions of dominance and exploitation and the adoption of a "subsistence perspective" that regarded the natural environment as an active and productive partner in the work of survival. Whether in prairie gardens or in partaking of the literal "fruits of the earth," the natural environment had presence, and recognition and knowledge of that presence allowed for both physical and psychological survival. Sometimes in the act of recuperation of a subsistence perspective there is recognition that an Anglo-centred belief in the need to "conquer" and "control" the productive capabilities of the prairie landscape, as well as the goal of transforming that landscape into an agricultural Eden, were not the only visions available to participants in western settlement. There had been "other" ways of relating to the natural environment, as evidenced by the (sometimes painfully generalized) lifestyles of the "Indian people," and practising such ways would prove to be more valuable to prairie families in the gap between ideals of agricultural success and the reality of settlement life. It has long been recognized that the "*dominator* mode" of relationship between humans and nature leaves people "spiritually alienated" (Harrison 101) from the landscape, and many of the memoirists examined here prefer to represent an intimate relationship to nature as presence, as dynamic force inspiring self-reflection as well as cultural critique. But perhaps one of the most surprising elements of these women's texts has to do with the amount of narrative space they devote to re-membering the animals who shared in the realities of prairie life. While settlement narratives have tended to privilege the lone human, memoir writers have re-visioned our focus onto the labouring and sacrificial bodies of those animals without whom the work of prairie life could never have been accomplished. In the restoration of some "other" subjects of western settlement, then, the writers examined here provide us with a more fully fleshed, more eco-conscious, re-vision of an agricultural story.

Sadie Victoria Landry Matthews,
Regina, Saskatchewan, circa 1995.

❊ 6 ❊

Conclusions:
"The Ragged Garment of Memory"

Such is the ragged garment of memory – the trivial remembered,
the unforgettable forgotten.
                    – Annora Brown, *Sketches from Life* (1981)

Some time in the fall of 2000, when I was writing the first full draft of this
study, my father came to me with several pictures of my grandmother (and
other members of my extended paternal family) and asked if there was anything
in the collection that I would like to copy. Most of the pictures were black and
white images of the past, including a picture of Sadie Matthews as a young
woman standing in front of the family home on a farm in Saskatchewan. This
image interested me at once, mainly because it represents my grandmother
somewhere in her late twenties, and it is the first time I have seen her without
the deeply entrenched facial lines and slightly curved back that became hers
with old age. She looks to me to be a proud, capable, even fashionable, young
woman, who, with a slight smile on her face, stands patiently waiting to have
her place in history documented on film. Knowing that single images have
an untrustworthy relationship to "truth" and that I needed recourse to the
cumulative evidence provided by the memoirs that form the basis to this study,

nevertheless this picture provided me with the spectre of the individual prairie woman set against a background that is primarily domestic, while also exceeding that background, standing out from it and looking beyond to a larger picture of the Prairie Woman's reality.

Then my father turned over another picture on the pile, and my grandmother's black and white image became alive to me immediately. This second picture, taken when my grandmother was about eighty years old, shows her seated on a Yamaha motorcycle belonging to my Uncle (her youngest son), with whom she stayed while on a visit "home" to Saskatchewan. Although my earliest memories of my grandmother certainly include a woman who had a great sense of humour, was capable of a loving warmth, and tickled childhood imaginations with "daring" language (one of my greatest joys was when she would say, "You little shit," and pretend to swat at me when I did or said something to make her laugh), later memories suggest a woman who was reserved, resigned, possibly even a little bit scared of the constantly changing world around her; a woman who seemed out of place, incongruous, compared to the sturdier image in the black and white photograph. In the colour photograph, however, the dynamic grandmother of my childhood re-emerged, and, in its new position hanging directly above my desk at home, the picture provided a sort of spiritual inspiration to the production of this study of those women who, like her, called the prairies "home." Although this photograph is contrived (my grandmother, after all, never really rode the motorcycle, but merely posed seated upon it), it, too, like the first photograph, is nevertheless evocative in helping to destabilize a general cultural reliance upon "either/or"isms in representations of prairie women's lives.

Indeed, for me, this picture encapsulates the overarching purpose of this study; it forms a sort of visual "confrontation" between sanitized cultural images of what a Prairie Woman is/does and the lived experience – the experienced difference – of real life, white, English-speaking women who lived on the prairies across a broad spectrum of time. Cultural narratives of western settlement – those of the contemporary moment, of early historiography, and of the heritage discourse in the second half of the twentieth century – privilege a linear representation of prairie life; that is, they begin with the raw material of an "empty" landscape which is then pieced together through the

heroic, the "unforgettable," efforts of pioneering individuals, the end result
being a precisely tailored narrative of nation- and empire-building, a sort of
golden age that obscures anything that deviates from the standard pattern.
However, as I have attempted to illustrate in preceding chapters, at the level of
individual experience is the more "ragged garment of memory," which, when
it is remembered in the act of looking back in the memoir text, figures daily
detail and daily survival as the foundation of an accretive, non-linear, reality of
prairie life. While cultural narratives follow the traditional autobiographical
model of beginnings and endings, and favour projected images of success, the
memoir text rejects expectations of some culminative or climactic moment
in favour of attention to the thread and weave of life that happens along the
way. In this way do the authors considered here provide us with an alternative
heritage based in the politics of individual experience and survival. In this way
do they "weave narratives like cloth, creating multipatterned garments that we
inhabit as memory" (Cavanaugh and Warne, Introduction 3).

In the shadow of cultural narratives and images that predominate in the
public imagination, this alternative heritage is often neglected until it is too
late. My grandmother Sadie died in the spring of 1999, at the age of eighty-
four, and later in the summer of that year her bodily remains were laid to
rest beside those of her husband in a small community graveyard in Lestock,
Saskatchewan. Although I did not participate in that event, my father told me
that the funeral that had been intended for family members only was attended
by some forty to fifty people from the local community, people who had, at
one time or another, known my grandmother or my grandmother's family
and who clearly remembered her with fondness and respect, despite the fact
that it had been more than twenty years since she had left the farm and just
over a decade since she had moved away from the prairies entirely. This communal outpouring for my grandmother was apparently not an unusual event
in rural prairie culture; it was not unusual that a prairie dweller's life would
be remembered by the settlement community to which they once belonged,
for, as the choice of memoir form for the "act of looking back" tells us, prairie
people possess an intense sense of personal experience as communal experience. The authors of the memoirs gathered here are motivated by the desire
to represent themselves, their mothers, their grandmothers, as belonging to a

very specific cultural moment. Their memoir texts are a legacy, to their families, to their communities, and to their readers, of personal participation in a defining, if problematic, event of Canadian nation-building. Nevertheless, despite the desire to assert identification with a much-lauded heritage moment, it is important to discern that the memoirists examined here do not adhere unconditionally to popular and idealistic cultural images of prairie settlement; on the contrary, what I have attempted to illustrate in this study is that the authors of these texts make abundant space in which to negotiate between representing acts of complicity with cultural norms and also constructing personal experiences that "confront" those norms; between a "surface" conformity to readerly expectations of a western settlement text and those "undercurrents" of difference that allow for the (sometimes subtle) re-visioning of history.

In the middle of the nineteenth century a major transformation took place in cultural constructions of the prairie region, a transformation from barren and unproductive "wasteland" to agricultural paradise. Given that this transformation was ideological rather than real, a vast and concerted promotional campaign was necessary to draw prospective settlers to the region as a means to effect that transformation in more than simply cultural images. But the gap between ideal and real remained when those settlers arrived. In the promotion of western settlement as an imperial and "civilized" undertaking, then, it was necessary to elide the sometimes rudimentary conditions of prairie life and maintain a cultural focus upon the apparently inevitable "future plenty and success" that was to accrue to those individuals who answered the call of immigration. In women's memoirs, however, we see that remembrance of prairie life most often centres upon what Annora Brown in the epigraph above calls the "trivial," the everyday details and needs of a world in which a "Home"stead is immediately constituted through the human senses rather than by ideology and images. Thus do we find the majority of narrative attention paid to the physical and psychological needs of today rather than the imagined riches of "next year country"; to issues of space and privacy in the construction of a prairie home; to the familial/cultural connectedness provided by "sacred objects" used in the creation of a Home place; and to the many creative productions that transform that Home into a vital economic centre.

When the futuristic focus of western settlement was secured in the contemporary cultural imagination, consideration had to be given to precisely what
type of individuals would be best suited to the "civilizing" project. Perhaps
first and foremost amongst those qualities desired in immigrants to the prairies was a spirit of "dauntless optimism," a psychological fortitude that would
stand the farm family in good stead when conditions proved to be tougher
than what had been promised in propaganda literature. Thus were white,
English-speaking prairie women expected to follow the typological Traill of
Canada's "pioneer" past, on pain of being judged as failures in a westward-
looking culture. Although these women certainly represent an awareness of a
Ruthian script of female adaptive behaviour, nevertheless they also indicate in
various ways that lived experience complicated the Traill to cultural esteem;
that lived experience "moodified" the prescription of "cheerful conformity"
to circumstances which often ended up being a less than personally or economically fulfilling reality. The authors of these memoirs deviate from the
established path and "jolt" their readers into an understanding that settlement
success was a relative and all-too-often unromantic story, one in which prairie
women participated on a "deep" emotional level, as seen through their tears,
their homesickness, and their occasional psychological "incoherences."

One of the ways that a reader is able to discern textual confrontations
with prevailing cultural images and the rhetoric of western expansion is to
begin to re-map the spatial politics of gender that dominated contemporary
narratives of settlement. Constructed as a space in which women would assist
in the creation of "a dream of the future," the prairies inherited the ideological boundaries that had dictated female behaviour in Anglo-culture more
generally; indeed, as prairie society cohered and gained stability, behavioural
dictates lagged behind changes in gender norms in more cosmopolitan places.
The cultural quest for a geographic space where moral and civic perfection
would be attained, where the norms and values of the British Empire could be
re-invigorated, necessitated that female bodies become a site of "transparency,"
a readable space that could be judged for the "decency" of its reproductive
performances. As seen in the memoirs written by prairie women, and the
daughters and granddaughters of prairie women, cultural expectations often
resulted in individual adherence, but room was certainly made for excessive

behaviours, for bodily transgressions of geographic boundaries, both in the moment of lived experience of prairie life and in the representation/recreation of that lived experience within the memoir text. Using the space of the memoir as a tool for cultural change, these authors reflect upon issues of female fashion and constructions of "women's work" as a means to reveal the "precarious perch" of the "decent woman."

To speak of the space of the prairies is to speak of a very specific cultural context in which the human relationship with the landscape has historically featured domination and exploitation as an inevitable consequence of large-scale agricultural designs. Indeed, cultural images of western settlement have privileged the prairie farmer as an heroic individual and "vertical" presence engaged in the act of "cultivation," the control and production of "commodities for cash," with little reference to the daily reality of an economy of "subsistence-survival" based on a subject-subject engagement between humans and nature, including both the natural environment and non-human animals. Into that crucial gap between filing a claim to a homestead site and attainment of the "vast agrarian empire" conceived in the wheat dreams of a dominative culture, prairie women poured their energies into the small intimate spaces of the family garden, they wandered down a prairie trail in search of the literal "fruits of the earth," they recognized the traces of an"other" way of being in the prairie landscape, and they acknowledged the labour and companionship potential of those non-human "others" who contributed to the settlement project. By taking a re-visionary approach to the memoirs gathered here, we are thus able to glimpse "the landscape behind" agriculture; that is, we are able to re-present those subjects of prairie life that have otherwise been made absent in cultural narratives of western settlement.

In this study, the overriding purpose has been to "reveal a woman writer's unstable and ambiguous positioning between cultural affirmation and cultural critique" (Georgi-Findlay xii). It has been to illustrate that, while the act of publishing a memoir of prairie life may well mark the woman writer as complicit with the late-twentieth century drive to document a shared and usually homogenous vision of the past, it is nevertheless important to recognize that women's retrospective narratives also provide us with a very different heritage of settlement experience than the either/or-isms of cultural images tend to allow. In the extra-ordinary act of letting their voices, their experiences, be heard, be reconciled to the public record of western settlement, these women's memoirs allow readers to confront simplistic visions of prairie life and to bring renewed life to otherwise static images. In changing our focus away from dominant cultural narratives, these women's memoirs bring lived experience to bear upon traditional versions of the past and, in the act of looking back, become a sort of narrative redress that allows us to re-vision our collective understanding of what it means to have been a "Prairie Woman."

Bibliography

THE MEMOIRS

Anderson, Barbara (Hunter). *Two White Oxen: A Perspective of Early Saskatoon 1874–1905.* Eds. George W. Anderson and Robert N. Anderson. Saskatoon, SK: G.W. Anderson, 1972.

Baldwin, Beulah. *The Long Trail: The Story of a Pioneer Family.* Edmonton: NeWest Press, 1992.

Bannert, Sylvia. *Rut Hog or Die.* n.p.: Orris Press, 1974.

Campbell, Marjorie Wilkins. *The Silent Song of Mary Eleanor.* Saskatoon, SK: Western Producer Prairie Books, 1983.

Clark, Adeline (Nan). *Prairie Dreams.* Port Alberni, BC: Blue Nun Press, 1991.

Ebbers, D[onnie] M. *Land Across the Border.* Sonora, CA: Mother Lode Press, 1978.

Gilead, Heather. *The Maple Leaf for Quite a While.* London: J.M. Dent & Sons, 1967.

Hewson, Edith. *We Swept the Cornflakes Out the Door.* Langbank, SK: Edith Hewson; Saskatoon, SK: Modern Press, 1980.

Hicks, Myrtle E.J. *The Bridges I Have Crossed.* Brandon, MB: Myrtle E.J. Hicks, 1973.

Hiemstra, Mary. *Gully Farm: A Story of Homesteading on the Canadian Prairies.* 1955. Calgary: Fifth House, 1997.

Holmes, Peggy. *It Could Have Been Worse: The Autobiography of a Pioneer.* Toronto: Collins, 1980.

Hopkins, Ida Scharf. *To The Peace River Country and On.* Richmond, BC: Crestwood Press, 1973.

Hutton, Winnie E. *No "Coppers" in Saskatchewan!* Regina, SK: Banting, 1973.

Inglis, Velma. *Summer Storm.......A Manitoba Tragedy.* Virden, MB: V. Inglis, 1985.

Johannson, Marjorie Grace. *The Pink House on the Hill.* N.p.: Marjorie Grace Johannson, 1986.

Keyes, Annie. *Down Memory Trails With Jip.* Regina, SK: Banting, 1972.

McClung, Nellie L. *Clearing in the West: My Own Story.* 1935. Toronto: Thomas Allen, 1964.

Magill, Katherine. *Back o' Baffuf.* Cobalt, ON: Highway Book Shop, 1977.

Middleton, Clara, and J.E. Middleton. *Green Fields Afar: Memories of Alberta Days.* Toronto: Ryerson Press, 1947.

Moorhouse, Myrtle G. *Buffalo Horn Valley.* Regina, SK: Banting, 1973.

Nash, Kathreen A. *The Maypo Lea Forever: Stories of a Canadian Childhood.* Victoria: Trafford, 2002.

Nelson, Ferne. *Barefoot on the Prairie: Memories of Life on a Prairie Homestead.* Saskatoon, SK: Western Producer Prairie Books, 1989.

Parsons, Nell Wilson. *Upon a Sagebrush Harp.* Saskatoon, SK: Prairie Books, 1969.

Raber, Jessie Browne. *Pioneering in Alberta.* New York: Exposition Press, 1951.

Roberts, Sarah Ellen. *Of Us and the Oxen.* Saskatoon, SK: Modern Press, 1968.

Schroeder, Anna. *Changes: Anecdotal Tales of Changes in the Life of Anna Born 1888–1992.* Winnipeg, MB: Bindery Publishing House, 1995.

Schultz, Judy. *Mamie's Children: Three Generations of Prairie Women.* Red Deer, AB: Red Deer College Press, 1997.

Scott, Eileen M. *Porridge and Old Clothes.* Victoria, BC: Plume Publications, 1982.

Strange, Kathleen. *With the West in Her Eyes: The Story of a Modern Pioneer.* Toronto: Macmillan, 1945.

Thomson, Georgina H. *Crocus and Meadowlark Country: A Story of an Alberta Family.* Edmonton: Institute of Applied Art, 1963.

PRIMARY AND SECONDARY SOURCES

Aberdeen, The Countess of. *Through Canada With a Kodak.* 1893. Toronto: University of Toronto Press, 1994.

Abrahamson, Una. *God Bless our Home: Domestic Life in Nineteenth-Century Canada.* N.p. Burns & MacEachern, 1966.

Adams, Carol J. *The Sexual Politics of Meat: A Feminist-Vegetarian Critical Theory.* New York: Continuum, 1990.

Adams, Kate. Review of *Tales of the Lavender Menace* by Karla Jay and *A Fragile Union* by Joan Nestle. *Women's Review of Books* 16, no. 12 (September 1999): 8–10.

Alaimo, Stacy. *Undomesticated Ground: Recasting Nature as Feminist Space.* Ithaca, NY: Cornell University Press, 2000.

Allen, Ralph. "Clifford Sifton's Medicine Show." *Canadian Content.* Eds. Nell Waldman and Sarah Norton. 3rd ed. Toronto: Harcourt Brace, 1996. 260–66.

Anderson, Ann Leger. "Canadian Prairie Women's History: An Uncertain Enterprise." *Journal of the West* 37, no. 1 (January 1998): 47–59.

———. "Saskatchewan Women, 1880–1920: A Field for Study." *The New Provinces: Alberta and Saskatchewan, 1905–1980.* Eds. Howard Palmer and Donald Smith. Vancouver: Tantalus Research, 1980. 65–90.

Armitage, Susan H. *Women in the West: A Guide to Manuscript Sources.* New York: Garland, 1991.

———. "Household Work and Childrearing on the Frontier: The Oral History Record." *Sociology and Social Research* 63, no. 3 (April 1979): 467–74.

———, and Elizabeth Jameson, eds. *The Women's West.* Norman: University of Oklahoma Press, 1987.

Balay, Anne G. "'Hands Full of Living': Birth Control, Nostalgia, and Kathleen Norris." *American Literary History* 8, no. 3 (Fall 1986): 471–95.

Baring, Anne, and Jules Cashford. *The Myth of the Goddess: Evolution of an Image.* London; New York: Arkana, 1993.

Barnes, Ruth, and Joanne B. Eicher. Introduction. *Dress and Gender: Making and Meaning in Cultural Contexts.* Eds. Ruth Barnes and Joanne B. Eicher. New York: Berg, 1992. 1–7.

Bennett, John W., and Seena B. Kohl. *Settling the Canadian-American West, 1890–1915: Pioneer Adaptation and Community Building: An Anthropological History.* Lincoln: University of Nebraska Press, 1995.

Bennett, Paul W., et al. *Emerging Identities: Selected Problems and Interpretations in Canadian History.* Scarborough, ON: Prentice-Hall Canada, 1986.

Berger, John. *Ways of Seeing.* London: Penguin, 1972.

Billson, Marcus. "The Memoir: New Perspectives on a Forgotten Genre." *Genre* 10, no. 2 (Summer 1977): 259–82.

Bindloss, Harold. *Prairie Gold.* New York: Grosset & Dunlap, 1925.

———. *Prescott of Saskatchewan.* New York: Grosset & Dunlap, 1913.

Binnie-Clark, Georgina. *Wheat and Woman.* 1914. Toronto: University of Toronto Press, 1979.

Bliss, Jacqueline. "Seamless Lives: Pioneer Women of Saskatoon, 1883–1903." *Saskatchewan History* 43, no. 3 (Autumn 1991): 84–100.

Blunt, Alison, and Gillian Rose. Introduction. *Writing Women and Space: Colonial and Postcolonial Geographies.* Eds. Alison Blunt and Gillian Rose. New York: Guilford Press, 1994. 1–25.

Bowering, George. *Caprice.* Markham, ON: Penguin Canada, 1987.

Brandt, Di. *Wild Mother Dancing: Maternal Narrative in Canadian Literature.* Winnipeg: University of Manitoba Press, 1993.

Broadfoot, Barry. *Next-Year Country: Voices of Prairie People.* Toronto: McClelland & Stewart, 1988.

———. *The Pioneer Years 1895–1914: Memories of Settlers Who Opened the West.* Don Mills, ON: PaperJacks, 1978.

Brown, Annora. *Sketches from Life.* Edmonton: Hurtig, 1981.

Bruce, Jean. *The Last Best West.* Toronto: Fitzhenry & Whiteside, 1976.

Buck, Claire, ed. *Bloomsbury Guide to Women's Literature.* London: Bloomsbury, 1992.

Burman, Barbara. Introduction. *The Culture of Sewing: Gender, Consumption and Home Dressmaking.* Ed. Barbara Burman. Oxford: Berg, 1999. 1–18.

———. "Made at Home by Clever Fingers: Home Dressmaking in Edwardian England." *The Culture of Sewing: Gender, Consumption and Home Dressmaking.* Ed. Barbara Burman. Oxford: Berg, 1999. 33–53.

Buss, Helen M. *Repossessing the World: Reading Memoirs by Contemporary Women*. Waterloo, ON: Wilfrid Laurier University Press, 2002.

———. "Settling the Score with Myths of Settlement: Two Women Who Roughed It and Wrote It." *Great Dames*. Eds. Elspeth Cameron and Janice Dickin. Toronto: University of Toronto Press, 1997. 167–83.

———. "Memoir with an Attitude: One Reader Reads *The Woman Warrior: Memoirs of a Girlhood among Ghosts*." *a/b: Auto/Biography Studies* 12, no. 2 (Fall 1997): 203–24.

———. "Listening to the 'Ground Noise' of Canadian Women Settlers' Memoirs: A Maternal Intercourse of Discourses." *Essays on Canadian Writing* 60 (Winter 1996): 199–214.

———. *Mapping Our Selves: Canadian Women's Autobiography*. Montreal & Kingston: McGill-Queen's University Press, 1993.

Cairns, Kathleen V., and Eliane Leslau Silverman. *Treasures: The Stories Women Tell about the Things They Keep*. Calgary: University of Calgary Press, 2004.

Cameron, Agnes Dean. *The New North: An Account of a Woman's 1908 Journey through Canada to the Arctic*. 1909. Ed. David Richeson. Lincoln: University of Nebraska Press, 1986.

Campbell, SueEllen. "The Land and Language of Desire: Where Deep Ecology and Post-Structuralism Meet." *The Ecocriticism Reader: Landmarks in Literary Ecology*. Eds. Cheryll Glotfelty and Harold Fromm. Athens: University of Georgia Press, 1996. 124–36.

Carpenter, Carole Henderson. *Many Voices: A Study of Folklore Activities in Canada and Their Role in Canadian Culture*. Canadian Centre for Folk Culture Studies. Paper No. 26. Ottawa: National Museums of Canada, 1979.

Carrel, Frank. *Canada's West and Farther West*. Toronto: Musson, 1911.

Carter, Kathryn. "A Contingency of Words: Diaries in English by Women in Canada 1830–1915." Diss. University of Alberta, 1997.

Carter, Sarah. "Categories and Terrains of Exclusion: Constructing the 'Indian Woman' in the Early Settlement Era in Western Canada." *Telling Tales: Essays in Western Women's History*. Eds. Catherine A. Cavanaugh and Randi R. Warne. Vancouver: UBC Press, 2000. 60–81.

———. *Capturing Women: The Manipulation of Cultural Imagery in Canada's Prairie West*. Montreal: McGill-Queen's University Press, 1997.

————, Lesley Erickson, and Patricia Roome. Introduction. *Unsettled Pasts: Reconceiving the West through Women's History*. Eds. Sarah Carter et al. Calgary: University of Calgary Press, 2005. 1–13.

Cavanaugh, Catherine A. "Irene Marryat Parlby: An 'Imperial Daughter' in the Canadian West, 1896–1934." *Telling Tales: Essays in Western Women's History*. Eds. Catherine A. Cavanaugh and Randi R. Warne. Vancouver: UBC Press, 2000. 100–122.

————. "'No Place for a Woman': Engendering Western Canadian Settlement." *Western Historical Quarterly* 28, no. 4 (Winter 1997): 493–518.

————, and Randi R. Warne. Introduction. *Telling Tales: Essays in Western Women's History*. Eds. Catherine A. Cavanaugh and Randi R. Warne. Vancouver: UBC Press, 2000. 2–31.

————, eds. *Standing on New Ground: Women in Alberta*. Edmonton: University of Alberta Press, 1993.

Chapman, Ethel. *The Homesteaders*. Toronto: Ryerson Press, 1936.

Coe, Richard N. *When the Grass Was Taller: Autobiography and the Experience of Childhood*. New Haven, CT: Yale University Press, 1984.

Connor, Ralph [Charles William Gordon]. *The Foreigner: A Tale of Saskatchewan*. New York: George H. Doran, 1909.

————. *Gwen, an Idyll of the Canyon*. Toronto: Fleming H. Revell, 1899.

Conway, J.F. *The West: The History of a Region in Confederation*. 2nd ed. Toronto: James Lorimer, 1994.

Copping, Arthur E. *The Golden Land: The True Story of British Settlers in Canada*. London: Hodder and Stoughton, 1911.

Cran, Mrs. George [Marion Dudley]. *A Woman In Canada*. London: John Milne, 1910.

Davidoff, Leonore, Jean L'Esperance, and Howard Newby. "Landscape with Figures: Home and Community in English Society." *The Rights and Wrongs of Women*. Eds. Juliet Mitchell and Ann Oakley. New York: Penguin, 1976. 139–75.

Davin, Nicholas Flood. *Homes for millions: The great Canadian North-West, its resources fully described*. Ottawa: B. Chamberlin, Queen's Printer, 1891. (Peel #1946).

Davis, Angela E. "'Country Homemakers': The Daily Lives of Prairie Women as Seen through the Woman's Page of the Grain Growers' Guide 1908–1928." *Canadian Papers in Rural History*. Ed. Donald H. Akenson. Vol. VIII. Gananoque, ON: Langdale Press, 1992. 163–74.

————. "'Valiant Servants': Women and Technology on the Canadian Prairies 1910–1940." *Manitoba History* 25 (Spring 1993): 33–42.

Davis, Karen. "Thinking Like a Chicken: Farm Animals and the Feminine Connection." *Animals and Women: Feminist Theoretical Explorations.* Eds. Carol J. Adams and Josephine Donovan. Durham, NC: Duke University Press, 1995. 192–212.

Dawson, C.A., and Eva R. Younge. *Pioneering in the Prairie Provinces: The Social Side of the Settlement Process.* Eds. W.A. Mackintosh and W.L.G. Joerg. 9 vols. Canadian Frontiers of Settlement. Vol. VIII. Toronto: MacMillan Canada, at St. Martin's House, 1940.

Dean, Misao. *Practising Femininity: Domestic Realism and the Performance of Gender in Early Canadian Fiction.* Toronto: University of Toronto Press, 1998.

De Brou, David, and Aileen C. Moffatt. "Introduction: 'Other' Voices and the Challenge from Within." *'Other' Voices: Historical Essays on Saskatchewan Women.* Eds. David De Brou and Aileen Moffatt. Regina, SK: Canadian Plains Research Center, University of Regina, 1995.

Doane, Janice, and Devon Hodges. *Nostalgia and Sexual Difference: The Resistance to Contemporary Feminism.* New York: Methuen, 1987.

Dodds, George Livingstone. *The last West: The latest gift of the lady bountiful: The granary of the greater British Empire.* Winnipeg: Winnipeg Printing & Engraving, 1906. (Peel #2945).

Donovan, Josephine. "Ecofeminist Literary Criticism: Reading the Orange." *Ecofeminist Literary Criticism: Theory, Interpretation, Pedagogy.* Eds. Greta Gaard and Patrick D. Murphy. Urbana and Chicago: University of Illinois Press, 1998. 74–96.

————. "Animal Rights and Feminist Theory." *Signs* 15, no. 2 (Winter 1990): 350–75.

————, and Carol J. Adams. Introduction. *Animals and Women: Feminist Theoretical Explorations.* Eds. Carol J. Adams and Josephine Donovan. Durham: Duke University Press, 1995. 1–8.

Drake, Diane. "Women and the Metaphor of the Prairie." *North Dakota Quarterly* 63, no. 4 (1996): 124–36.

Duck Lake Agricultural Society. *In the Saskatchewan country: Facts about the wheat growing, cattle raising and mixed farming of the great fertile belt: The Duck Lake district of Saskatchewan, Northwest Territories of Canada.* Winnipeg: Printed by Acton Burrows, at the Western World Office, 1893. (Peel #2079).

DuPlessis, Rachel Blau. *Writing Beyond the Ending: Narrative Strategies of Twentieth-Century Women Writers*. Bloomington: Indiana University Press, 1985.

———. "For the Etruscans." *The New Feminist Criticism: Essays on Women, Literature and Theory*. Ed. Elaine Showalter. New York: Pantheon, 1985. 271–91.

Durkin, Douglas. *The Magpie*. 1923. Toronto: University of Toronto Press, 1974.

Eggleston, Wilfrid. "The Old Homestead: Romance and Reality." *The Prairie West: Historical Readings*. Eds. R. Douglas Francis and Howard Palmer. 2nd ed. Edmonton: Pica Pica Press, 1992. 339–51.

Eisler, Riane. "From Domination to Partnership: Meeting the UN Millenium Goals." *Convergence* 38, no. 3 (2005): 75–94.

———. "The Dynamics of Cultural and Technological Evolution: Domination Versus Partnership." *World Futures: The Journal of General Evolution* 58, nos. 2/3 (2002): 159–74.

———. *The Chalice and the Blade: Our History, Our Future*. San Francisco: Harper & Row, 1987.

Eliot, Elinor Marsden. *My Canada*. London; New York; Toronto: Hodder and Stoughton, 1915.

Evernden, Neil. "Beyond Ecology: Self, Place, and the Pathetic Fallacy." *The Ecocriticism Reader: Landmarks in Literary Ecology*. Eds. Cheryll Glotfelty and Harold Fromm. Athens: University of Georgia Press, 1996. 92–104.

Fairbanks, Carol. *Prairie Women: Images in American and Canadian Fiction*. New Haven, CT: Yale University Press, 1986.

———, and Sara Brooks Sundberg. *Farm Women on the Prairie Frontier: A Sourcebook for Canada and the United States*. Metuchen, NJ: Scarecrow Press, 1983.

Faragher, John Mack. *Women and Men on the Overland Trail*. New Haven, CT: Yale University Press, 1979.

Ferguson, Emily. [Janey Canuck]. *Open Trails*. London: Cassell, 1912.

———. *Janey Canuck in the West*. London and Toronto: J.M. Dent & Sons, 1910.

Floyd, Janet. *Writing the Pioneer Woman*. Columbia: University of Missouri Press, 2002.

Foster, Franklin. Foreword. *Gully Farm*. By Mary Hiemstra. 1955. Calgary: Fifth House, 1997. vii–x.

Fowler, Marian. *The Embroidered Tent: Five Gentlewomen in Early Canada*. Toronto: Anansi, 1982.

Francis, Daniel. *The Imaginary Indian: The Image of the Indian in Canadian Culture.* Vancouver: Arsenal Pulp Press, 1992.

Francis, R. Douglas. Introduction. *The Prairie West as Promised Land.* Eds. R. Douglas Francis and Chris Kitzan. Calgary: University of Calgary Press, 2007.

———. *Images of the West: Changing Perceptions of the Prairies, 1690–1960.* Saskatoon, SK: Western Producer Prairie Books, 1989.

Free homes in Manitoba and the Canadian North West. Winnipeg, s.n., 1886. (Peel #1566).

Friesen, Gerald. "Historical Writing on the Prairie West." *The Prairie West: Historical Readings.* Eds. R. Douglas Francis and Howard Palmer. 2nd ed. Edmonton: Pica Pica Press, 1992. 5–26.

———. *The Canadian Prairies: A History.* Toronto: University of Toronto Press, 1987.

Frye, Marilyn. *The Politics of Reality: Essays in Feminist Theory.* Trumansburg, NY: Crossing Press, 1983.

Georgi-Findlay, Brigitte. "Women in the Canadian-American West." *Zeitschrift für Kanada-Studien* 22, nos. 1–2 (2002): 26–42.

———. *The Frontiers of Women's Writing: Women's Narratives and the Rhetoric of Westward Expansion.* Tucson: University of Arizona Press, 1996.

Glotfelty, Cheryll. "Introduction: Literary Studies in an Age of Environmental Crisis." *The Ecocriticism Reader: Landmarks in Literary Ecology.* Eds. Cheryll Glotfelty and Harold Fromm. Athens: University of Georgia Press, 1996. xv–xxxvii.

Goldie, Terry. *Fear and Temptation: The Image of the Indigene in Canadian, Australian, and New Zealand Literatures.* Montreal & Kingston: McGill-Queen's University Press, 1989.

Goldman, Anne. "'I Yam What I Yam': Cooking, Culture, and Colonialism." *De/Colonizing the Subject: The Politics of Gender in Women's Autobiography.* Eds. Sidonie Smith and Julia Watson. Minneapolis: Minnesota University Press, 1992. 169–95.

The granary of the British Empire: The western provinces of Canada: Manitoba, Saskatchewan, Alberta, British Columbia. Calgary: Canadian Pacific Railway, Department of Natural Resources, 1914. (Peel #3998).

Grant, George M. *Ocean to ocean: Sandford Fleming's expedition through Canada in 1872: Being a diary kept during a journey from the Atlantic to the Pacific with the expedition of the engineer-in-chief of the Canadian Pacific and Intercolonial Railways.* Toronto: John Campbell & Son, 1873. (Peel #642).

Gray, Charlotte. *Sisters in the Wilderness: The Lives of Susanna Moodie and Catharine Parr Traill.* Toronto: Viking, 1999.

Grayson, Ethel Kirk. *Unbind the Sheaves: A Prairie Memoir.* Saskatoon, SK: Modern Press, 1964.

Grove, Frederick Philip. *Fruits of the Earth.* 1933. Toronto: McClelland & Stewart, 1965.

———. *Settlers of the Marsh.* 1925. Toronto: McClelland & Stewart, 1965.

Gusdorf, Georges. "Conditions and Limits of Autobiography." *Autobiography: Essays Theoretical and Critical.* Ed. James Olney. Princeton, NJ: Princeton University Press, 1980. 28–48.

Hall, David. "Clifford Sifton's Vision of the Prairie West." *The Prairie West as Promised Land.* Eds. R. Douglas Francis and Chris Kitzan. Calgary: University of Calgary Press, 2007. 77–100.

Hallie, Philip P. *Cruelty.* Middletown, CT: Wesleyan University Press, 1969.

Harris, Cole. *The Reluctant Land: Society, Space, and Environment in Canada before Confederation.* Vancouver: UBC Press, 2008.

Harrison, Dick. *Unnamed Country: The Struggle for a Canadian Prairie Fiction.* Edmonton: University of Alberta Press, 1977.

Harrison, Marjorie. *Go West – Go Wise! A Canadian Revelation.* New York & Toronto: Longmans, Green; London: Edward Arnold, 1930.

Hart, Francis Russell. "History Talking to Itself: Public Personality in Recent Memoir." *New Literary History* 11, no. 1 (Autumn 1979): 193–210.

Heilbrun, Carolyn G. *Writing a Woman's Life.* New York: Ballantine, 1988.

Higonnet, Margaret R. "New Cartographies, an Introduction." *Reconfigured Spheres: Feminist Explorations of Literary Space.* Eds. Margaret R. Higonnet and Joan Templeton. Amherst: University of Massachusetts Press, 1994. 1–19.

Hill, Douglas. *The Opening of the Canadian West: Where Strong Men Gathered.* New York: John Day, 1967.

Huffer, Lynne. *Maternal Pasts, Feminist Futures: Nostalgia, Ethics, and the Question of Difference.* Stanford, CA: Stanford University Press, 1998.

Hutchinson, Bruce. Introduction. *Prairie Dreams.* By Adeline (Nan) Clark. Port Alberni, BC: Blue Nun Press, 1991. x–xi.

Jackel, Susan. *Canadian Prairie Women's History: A Bibliographic Survey.* The CRIAW Papers 14. Ottawa: CRIAW, 1987. 1–22.

———. Introduction. *Wheat and Woman*. By Georgina Binnie-Clark. Toronto: University of Toronto Press, 1979. v–xxxvii.

Jacques, Edna. *Uphill All the Way: An Autobiography*. Saskatoon, SK: Western Producer Prairie Books, 1977.

Jameson, Anna. *Winter Studies and Summer Rambles in Canada*. 1838. Toronto: McClelland & Stewart, 1990.

Jeffrey, Julie Roy. *Frontier Women: "Civilizing" the West? 1840–1880*. Revised edition. New York: Hill and Wang, 1998.

Kamen-Kaye, Dorothy. "The Composite Pioneer." *Saskatchewan History* 8, no. 1 (Winter 1955): 6–10.

Kane, Paul. *Wanderings of an Artist Among the Indians of North America: From Canada to Vancouver's Island and Oregon Through the Hudson's Bay Company's Territory and Back Again*. 1859. Edmonton: Hurtig, 1968.

Kates, Judith A., and Gail Twersky Reimer. Introduction. *Reading Ruth: Contemporary Women Reclaim a Sacred Story*. Eds. Judith A. Kates and Gail Twersky Reimer. New York: Ballantine, 1994. xvii–xxv.

Kennedy, Howard Angus. *The Book of the West*. Toronto: Ryerson Press, 1925.

Kerber, Linda K. "Separate Spheres, Female World, Woman's Place: The Rhetoric of Women's History." *Journal of American History* 75 (June 1988): 9–39.

Kimball, Gayle. "Women's Culture: Themes and Images." *Women's Culture: The Women's Renaissance of the Seventies*. Ed. Gayle Kimball. Metuchen, NJ: Scarecrow Press, 1981. 2–29.

Kinnear, Mary. *A Female Economy: Women's Work in a Prairie Province, 1870–1970*. Montreal: McGill-Queen's University Press, 1998.

———. "'Do you want your daughter to marry a farmer?': Women's Work on the Farm, 1922." *Canadian Papers in Rural History*. Ed. Donald H. Akenson. Vol. VI. Gananoque, ON: Langdale Press, 1988. 137–53.

———, ed. *First Days, Fighting Days: Women in Manitoba History*. Regina, SK: Canadian Plains Research Center, University of Regina, 1987.

Knobloch, Frieda. *The Culture of Wilderness: Agriculture as Colonization in the American West*. Chapel Hill: University of North Carolina Press, 1996.

Kohl, Seena B. "The Making of a Community: The Role of Women in an Agricultural Setting." *Kin and Communities: Families in America*. Eds. Allan J. Lichtman and Joan R. Challinor. Washington: Smithsonian Institution Press, 1979. 175–86.

————. "Women's Participation in the North American Family Farm." *Women's Studies International Quarterly* 1 (1977): 47–54.

Kolodny, Annette. *The Lay of the Land: Metaphor as Experience and History in American Life and Letters.* Chapel Hill: University of North Carolina Press, 1975.

Kreisel, Henry. "The Prairie: A State of Mind." 1968. *Essays on Saskatchewan Writing.* Ed. E.F. Dyck. Regina, SK: Saskatchewan Writers Guild, 1986. 41–54.

Langford, Nanci. "Childbirth on the Canadian Prairies, 1880–1930." *Telling Tales: Essays in Western Women's History.* Eds. Catherine A. Cavanaugh and Randi R. Warne. Vancouver: UBC Press, 2000. 147–73.

————. "First Generation and Lasting Impressions: The Gendered Identities of Prairie Homestead Women." Diss. University of Alberta, 1994.

Langton, Anne. *A Gentlewoman in Upper Canada: The Journals of Anne Langton.* Ed. H.H. Langton. Toronto: Irwin, 1950.

Lassiter, Collette, and Jill Oakes. "Ranchwomen, Rodeo Queens, and Nightclub Cowgirls: The Evolution of Cowgirl Dress." *Standing on New Ground: Women in Alberta.* Eds. Catherine A. Cavanaugh and Randi R. Warne. Edmonton: University of Alberta Press, 1993. 55–69.

Lebowitz, Andrea Pinto. Introduction. *Living in Harmony: Nature Writing by Women in Canada.* Ed. Andrea Pinto Lebowitz. Victoria, BC: Orca, 1996. 1–7.

Lefebvre, Henri. *The Production of Space.* Trans. Donald Nicholson-Smith. Oxford: Basil Blackwell, 1991.

Lewis, Norah L. Introduction. *Dear Editor and Friends: Letters from Rural Women of the North-West, 1900–1920.* Ed. Norah L. Lewis. Waterloo, ON: Wilfrid Laurier University Press, 1998. 1–17.

Lewthwaite, Elizabeth. "Women's Work in Western Canada." *The Fortnightly Review* 70 n.s. (1901): 709–719.

Lindgren, Elaine. *Land in Her Own Name: Women as Homesteaders in North Dakota.* Fargo: North Dakota Institute for Regional Studies, 1991.

Loehr, Rodney C. "Self-Sufficiency on the Farm." *Agricultural History* 26 (1952): 37–41.

Love, Glen A. "Revaluing Nature: Toward an Ecological Criticism." *The Ecocriticism Reader: Landmarks in Literary Ecology.* Eds. Cheryll Glotfelty and Harold Fromm. Athens: University of Georgia Press, 1996. 225–40.

Loveridge, Anna. *Your Loving Anna; Letters from the Ontario Frontier.* Ed. Louis Tivy. Toronto: University of Toronto Press, 1972.

Lucas, Alec. "The Function of the Sketches in Susanna Moodie's *Roughing It in the Bush.*" *Re(Dis)covering Our Foremothers: Nineteenth-Century Canadian Women Writers.* Ed. Lorraine McMullen. Ottawa: University of Ottawa Press, 1990. 146–54.

McCarthy, Dermot. "Ego in a Green Prison: Confession and Repression in *Roughing It in the Bush.*" *Wascana Review* 14, no. 2 (Fall 1979): 3–16.

McClintock, Anne. *Imperial Leather: Race, Gender and Sexuality in the Colonial Contest.* New York: Routledge, 1995.

McClung, Nellie L. *The Stream Runs Fast: My Own Story.* 1945. Toronto: Thomas Allen & Son, 1965.

———. *In Times Like These.* 1915. Toronto: University of Toronto Press, 1972.

———. *The Second Chance.* Toronto: Ryerson Press, 1910.

———. *Sowing Seeds in Danny.* 1908. Toronto: Ryerson Press, 1922.

McManus, Sheila. "Gender(ed) Tensions in the Work and Politics of Alberta Farm Women, 1905–29." *Telling Tales: Essays in Western Women's History.* Eds. Catherine A. Cavanaugh and Randi R. Warne. Vancouver: UBC Press, 2000. 123–46.

McMullen, Lorraine, ed. Introduction. *Re(Dis)covering Our Foremothers: Nineteenth-Century Canadian Women Writers.* Ottawa: University of Ottawa Press, 1990. 1–4.

MacLulich, T.D. "Crusoe in the Backwoods: A Canadian Fable?" *Mosaic: A Journal for the Comparative Study of Literature and Ideas* 9, no. 2 (1976): 115–26.

MacPherson, Ian, and John Herd Thompson. "An Orderly Reconstruction: Prairie Agriculture in World War Two." *Canadian Papers in Rural History.* Ed. Donald H. Akenson. Vol. IV. Gananoque, ON: Langdale Press, 1984. 11–32.

Mair, Charles. "The New Canada." *The Search for English-Canadian Literature: An Anthology of Critical Articles from the Nineteenth and Early Twentieth Centuries.* Ed. Carl Ballstadt. Toronto: Toronto University Press, 1975. 151–54.

Mann, Susan Garland. "Gardening as 'Women's Culture' in Mary E. Wilkins Freeman's Short Fiction." *New England Quarterly* 72, no. 1 (March 1998): 33–53.

Martin, Chester. *"Dominion Lands" Policy.* Eds. W.A. Mackintosh and W.L.G. Joerg. 9 vols. Canadian Frontiers of Settlement. Vol. II. Toronto: MacMillan Canada, at St. Martin's House, 1938.

Maynard, Fredelle Bruser. *Raisins and Almonds.* Don Mills, ON: PaperJacks, 1964.

Meeker, Joseph W. "The Comic Mode." *The Ecocriticism Reader: Landmarks in Literary Ecology.* Eds. Cheryll Glotfelty and Harold Fromm. Athens: University of Georgia Press, 1996. 155–69.

Mies, Maria, and Vandana Shiva. "Introduction: Why We Wrote this Book Together." *Ecofeminism.* By Maria Mies and Vandana Shiva. Halifax, NS: Fernwood; London: Zed Books, 1993. 1–21.

Mitchell, Elizabeth B. *In Western Canada Before the War: Impressions of Early Twentieth Century Prairie Communities.* 1915. Saskatoon, SK: Western Producer Prairie Books, 1981.

Moffatt, Aileen C. "Great Women, Separate Spheres, and Diversity: Comments on Saskatchewan Women's Historiography." *"Other" Voices: Historical Essays on Saskatchewan Women.* Eds. David De Brou and Aileen Moffatt. Regina, SK: Canadian Plains Research Center, University of Regina. 1995. 10–26.

Moodie, Susanna. *Life in the Clearings versus the Bush.* 1853. Toronto: McClelland & Stewart, 1989.

———. *Roughing It in the Bush; or, Life in Canada.* 1852. Toronto: McClelland & Stewart, 1989.

Morris, Audrey Y. *Gentle Pioneers: Five Nineteenth-Century Canadians.* Toronto: Hodder and Stoughton, 1966.

Morris, Elizabeth Keith. *An Englishwoman in the Canadian West.* Bristol: J.W. Arrowsmith; London: Simpkin Marshall, 1913.

Moyles, R.G. Introduction. *'Improved by Cultivation': An Anthology of English-Canadian Prose to 1914.* Ed. R.G. Moyles. Peterborough, ON: Broadview Press, 1994. 7–11.

———, and Doug Owram. *Imperial Dreams and Colonial Realities: British Views of Canada, 1880–1914.* Toronto: University of Toronto Press, 1988.

Myres, Sandra L. *Westering Women and the Frontier Experience 1800–1915.* Albuquerque: University of New Mexico Press, 1982.

New homes, free farms in Alberta and Saskatchewan, Western Canada. Winnipeg: Osler, Hammond & Nanton, 1893. (Peel #2100).

The new settlements in Canada: homes for millions. Canada: Government of Canada, 1898. (Peel #10537).

New, W.H. *Land Sliding: Imagining Space, Presence, and Power in Canadian Writing.* Toronto: University of Toronto Press, 1997.

Norcross, E. Blanche. *Pioneers Every One: Canadian Women of Achievement*. N.p.: Burns & MacEachern, 1979.

O'Brien, Mary. *The Journals of Mary O'Brien, 1828–1838*. Ed. Audrey Saunders Miller. Toronto: Macmillan, 1968.

O'Brien, Susie. "Nature's Nation, National Natures? Reading Ecocriticism in a Canadian Context." *Canadian Poetry* 42 (Spring–Summer 1998): 17–41.

Oerlemans, Onno. "A Defense of Anthropomorphism: Comparing Coetzee and Gowdy." *The Animal: Part II*. Spec. issue of *Mosaic: A Journal for the Interdisciplinary Study of Literature*. 40, no. 1 (March 2007): 181–96.

Osborne, Brian S. "From Space to Place: Images of Nationhood." *Reflections from the Prairies: Geographical Essays*. Eds. H. John Selwood and John C. Lehr. Winnipeg: University of Winnipeg, 1992. 1–13.

Ostenso, Martha. *Wild Geese*. 1925. Toronto: McClelland & Stewart, 1961.

Owram, Doug. "The Promise of the West as Settlement Frontier." *The Prairie West as Promised Land*. Eds. R. Douglas Francis and Chris Kitzan. Calgary: University of Calgary Press, 2007. 3–28.

———. *Promise of Eden: The Canadian Expansionist Movement and the Idea of the West 1856–1900*. Toronto: University of Toronto Press, 1980.

Palmer, Howard. "Strangers and Stereotypes: The Rise of Nativism, 1880–1920." *The Prairie West: Historical Readings*. Eds. R. Douglas Francis and Howard Palmer. 2nd ed. Edmonton: Pica Pica Press, 1992.

Parsons, Nell Wilson. *The Curlew Cried: A Love Story of the Canadian Prairie*. Seattle: Frank McCaffrey, 1947.

Perkin, Joan. *Women and Marriage in Nineteenth-Century England*. Chicago: Lyceum Books, 1989.

Pickering, Jean, and Suzanne Kehde. Introduction. *Narratives of Nostalgia, Gender, and Nationalism*. Eds. Jean Pickering and Suzanne Kehde. New York: New York University Press, 1997. 1–8.

Preece, Rod. *Animals and Nature: Cultural Myths, Cultural Realities*. Vancouver: UBC Press, 1999.

Prentice, Alison, et al. *Canadian Women: A History*. Toronto: Harcourt Brace Jovanovich, 1988.

Quinby, Lee. "The Subject of Memoirs: *The Woman Warrior's* Technology of Ideographic Selfhood." *De/Colonizing the Subject: The Politics of Gender in Women's*

Autobiography. Eds. Sidonie Smith and Julia Watson. Minneapolis: Minnesota University Press, 1992. 297–320.

Radke, Andrea G. "Refining Rural Spaces: Women and Vernacular Gentility in the Great Plains, 1880–1920." *Great Plains Quarterly* 24, no. 4 (Fall 2004): 227–48.

Radner, Joan Newlon, and Susan S. Lanser. "Strategies of Coding in Women's Cultures." *Feminist Messages: Coding in Women's Folk Culture*. Ed. Joan Newlon Radner. Urbana and Chicago: University of Illinois Press, 1993. 1–29.

Rasmussen, Linda, et al. *A Harvest Yet to Reap: A History of Prairie Women*. Toronto: Women's Press, 1976.

Rees, Ronald. *New and Naked Land: Making the Prairies Home*. Saskatoon, SK: Western Producer Prairie Books, 1988.

Ribeiro, Aileen. *Dress and Morality*. London: B.T. Batsford, 1986.

Rich, Adrienne. *On Lies, Secrets and Silence*. New York: W.W. Norton, 1979.

Ricou, Laurence. *Vertical Man/Horizontal World: Man and Landscape in Canadian Prairie Fiction*. Vancouver: University of British Columbia Press, 1973.

Rider, Peter E. Introduction. *The Magpie*. By Douglas Durkin. 1923. Toronto: University of Toronto Press, 1974. vi–xxi.

Riley, Glenda. *The Female Frontier: A Comparative View of Women on the Prairie and the Plains*. Lawrence: University Press of Kansas, 1988.

Ritchie, J. Ewing. *To Canada with Emigrants: A Record of Actual Experiences*. London: T. Fisher Unwin, 1885.

Rollings-Magnusson, Sandra. "Canada's Most Wanted: Pioneer Women on the Western Prairies." *Canadian Review of Sociology and Anthropology* 37, no. 2 (May 2000): 223–38.

Roome, Patricia. "Remembering Together: Reclaiming Alberta Women's Past." *Standing on New Ground: Women in Alberta*. Eds. Catherine A. Cavanaugh and Randi R. Warne. Edmonton: University of Alberta Press, 1993. 171–202.

Ross, Sinclair. *As For Me and My House*. 1941. Toronto: McClelland & Stewart, 1957.

———. *The Lamp at Noon, and Other Stories*. Toronto: McClelland & Stewart, 1968.

Rowe, Stan. *Home Place: Essays on Ecology*. 1990. Edmonton: NeWest Press, 2002.

Rukszto, Katarzyna. "Representing Canada: Heritage, History and the Politics of Belonging." Nationalism, Citizenship and National Identity Conference. Mount Allison University, Sackville, New Brunswick, November 11–13, 1999.

Ryden, Kent C. *Mapping the Invisible Landscape: Folklore, Writing, and the Sense of Place.* Iowa City: University of Iowa Press, 1993.

Sanders, Scott Russell. "Speaking a Word for Nature." *The Ecocriticism Reader: Landmarks in Literary Ecology.* Eds. Cheryll Glotfelty and Harold Fromm. Athens: University of Georgia Press, 1996. 182–95.

Schlissel, Lillian. *Women's Diaries of the Westward Journey.* New York: Schocken Books, 1982.

Scholtmeijer, Marian. "The Power of Otherness: Animals in Women's Fiction." *Animals & Women: Feminist Theoretical Explorations.* Eds. Carol J. Adams and Josephine Donovan. Durham, NC: Duke University Press, 1995. 231–62.

———. *Animal Victims in Modern Fiction: From Sanctity to Sacrifice.* Toronto: University of Toronto Press, 1993.

Showalter, Elaine. "Piecing and Writing." *The Poetics of Gender.* Ed. Nancy K. Miller. New York: Columbia University Press, 1986. 222–47.

Siddall, Gillian. "Pioneer memoirs." *The Oxford Companion to Canadian Literature.* Eds. Eugene Benson and William Toye. 2nd ed. Toronto: Oxford University Press, 1997. 921–24.

Silverman, Eliane Leslau. "Foreword" to Mary Eleanor Campbell's *The Silent Song of Mary Eleanor.* Unpublished, 1999.

———. "Women's Perceptions of Marriage on the Alberta Frontier." *Building Beyond the Homestead.* Eds. David C. Jones and Ian MacPherson. Calgary: University of Calgary Press, 1988. 49–64.

———. *The Last Best West: Women on the Alberta Frontier, 1880–1930.* Montreal: Eden Press, 1984.

———. "Women and the Victorian Work Ethic on the Alberta Frontier: Prescription and Description." *The New Provinces: Alberta and Saskatchewan, 1905–1980.* Eds. Howard Palmer and Donald Smith. Vancouver: Tantalus Research, 1980. 91–99.

Simcoe, Elizabeth. *Mrs. Simcoe's Diary.* Ed. Mary Quayle Innis. Toronto: Macmillan, 1965.

Sinclair, Upton. *The Jungle.* 1906. Ed. Clare Virginia Eby. New York: W.W. Norton, 2003.

Spry, Irene M., and Bennett McCardle. *The Records of the Department of the Interior and Research Concerning Canada's Western Frontier of Settlement*. Regina, SK: Canadian Plains Research Center, University of Regina, 1993.

Stadler, Eva Maria. "Addressing Social Boundaries: Dressing the Female Body in Early Realist Fiction." *Reconfigured Spheres: Feminist Explorations of Literary Space*. Eds. Margaret R. Higonnet and Joan Templeton. Amherst: University of Massachusetts Press, 1994. 20–36.

Stegner, Wallace. *Wolf Willow: A History, a Story, and a Memory of the Last Plains Frontier*. 1955. Toronto: Macmillan, 1967.

Stein, Gertrude. *Everybody's Autobiography*. New York: Random House, 1937.

Stoeltje, Beverly J. "'A Helpmate for Man Indeed': The Image of the Frontier Woman." *Journal of American Folklore* 88 (January–March 1975): 25–41.

Stoler, Ann L. "Making Empire Respectable: The Politics of Race and Sexual Morality in 20th-Century Colonial Cultures." *American Ethnologist* 16, no. 4 (November 1989): 634–60.

Storrie, Kathleen. "Introduction: The Ecology of Gender." *Women: Isolation and Bonding: The Ecology of Gender*. Ed. Kathleen Storrie. Toronto: Methuen, 1987. 1–11.

Stringer, Arthur. *The Mud Lark*. Indianapolis: Bobbs-Merrill, 1931.

———. *The Prairie Wife*. New York: A.L. Burt, 1915.

Strong-Boag, Veronica. "Pulling in Double Harness or Hauling a Double Load: Women, Work and Feminism on the Canadian Prairie." *The Prairie West: Historical Readings*. Eds. R. Douglas Francis and Howard Palmer. Edmonton: Pica Pica Press, 1992. 401–23.

Sundberg, Sara Brooks. "Farm Women on the Canadian Prairie Frontier: The Helpmate Image." *Farm Women on the Prairie Frontier: A Sourcebook for Canada and the United States*. Carol Fairbanks and Sara Brooks Sundberg. Metuchen, NJ: Scarecrow Press, 1983. 71–90.

Thompson, Elizabeth. *The Pioneer Woman: A Canadian Character Type*. Montreal: McGill-Queen's University Press, 1991.

Thompson, John Herd. *Forging the Prairie West*. Toronto: Oxford University Press, 1998.

Traill, Catharine Parr. *The Canadian Settler's Guide*. 1855. Toronto: McClelland & Stewart, 1969.

———. *The Backwoods of Canada: Being Letters from the Wife of an Emigrant Officer, Illustrative of the Domestic Economy of British America*. 1836. Toronto: McClelland & Stewart, 1989.

Tuan, Yi-Fu. *Space and Place: The Perspective of Experience*. Minneapolis: University of Minnesota Press, 1977.

———. "Place: An Experiential Perspective." *Geographical Review* 65 (1975): 151–65.

Vipond, Mary. "The Image of Women in Canadian Mass Circulation Magazines in the 1920s." *Modernist Studies* 1, no. 3 (1974–75): 5–13.

Voisey, Paul. "Rural Local History and the Prairie West." *The Prairie West: Historical Readings*. Eds. R. Douglas Francis and Howard Palmer. Edmonton: Pica Pica Press, 1992. 497–509.

Wagner-Martin, Linda. *The Age of Innocence: A Novel of Ironic Nostalgia*. New York: Twayne; London: Prentice Hall International, 1996.

Waiser, Bill. "'Land I Can Own': Settling in the Promised Land." *The Prairie West as Promised Land*. Eds. R. Douglas Francis and Chris Kitzan. Calgary: University of Calgary Press, 2007. 155–74.

Watson, J. Wreford. "The Role of Illusion in North American Geography: A Note on the Geography of North American Settlement." *Canadian Geographer* 13, no. 1 (1969): 10–27.

Weir, Allison. *Sacrificial Logics: Feminist Theory and the Critique of Identity*. New York: Routledge, 1996.

Wekerle, Gerda R., Rebecca Peterson, and David Morley. Introduction. *New Space for Women*. Eds. Gerda R. Wekerle, Rebecca Peterson, and David Morley. Boulder, CO: Westview Press, 1980. 1–34.

Welter, Barbara. "The Cult of True Womanhood: 1820–1860." *American Quarterly* 18 (1966): 151–74.

Williams, Robert Chadwell. *Horace Greeley: Champion of American Freedom*. New York: New York University Press, 2006.

Woolf, Virginia. *A Room of One's Own*. 1929. London: Grafton Books, 1977.

Index